THE ROAD TO THE EUROPEAN UNION

VOLUME 1

MANCHESTER
UNIVERSITY PRESS

EUROPE IN CHANGE

SERIES EDITORS *Thomas Christiansen and Emil Kirchner*

already published

Committee governance in the European Union
THOMAS CHRISTIANSEN AND EMIL KIRCHNER (EDS)

Theory and reform in the European Union, 2nd edition
DIMITRIS N. CHRYSSOCHOOU, MICHAEL J. TSINISIZELIS, KOSTAS IFANTIS AND STELIOS STAVRIDIS

German policy-making and eastern enlargement of the EU during the Kohl era
Managing the agenda?
STEPHEN D. COLLINS

The European Union and the Cyprus conflict
Modern conflict, postmodern union
THOMAS DIEZ

The time of European governance
MAGNUS EKENGREN

Greece in a changing Europe
Between European integration and Balkan disintegration?
KEVIN FEATHERSTONE AND KOSTAS IFANTIS (EDS)

An introduction to post-Communist Bulgaria
Political, economic and social transformation
EMIL GIATZIDIS

The new Germany and migration in Europe
BARBARA MARSHALL

Turkey's relations with a changing Europe
MELTEM MÜFTÜLER-BAC

The road to the European Union, volume 2
Estonia, Latvia and Lithuania
VELLO PETTAI AND JAN ZIELONKA

Righting wrongs in Eastern Europe
ISTVAN POGANY

Two tiers or two speeds?
The European security order and the enlargement of the European Union and NATO
JAMES SPERLING (ED.)

Recasting the European order
Security architectures and economic cooperation
JAMES SPERLING AND EMIL KIRCHNER

The emerging Euro-Mediterranean system
DIMITRIS K. XENAKIS AND DIMITRIS N. CHRYSSOCHOOU

Jacques Rupnik and Jan Zielonka
EDITORS

THE ROAD TO THE EUROPEAN UNION
VOLUME 1

THE CZECH AND SLOVAK REPUBLICS

MANCHESTER UNIVERSITY PRESS
Manchester and New York

distributed exclusively in the USA by Palgrave

Published by Manchester University Press
Oxford Road, Manchester M13 9NR, UK
and Room 400, 175 Fifth Avenue, New York, NY 10010, USA
www.manchesteruniversitypress.co.uk

Distributed exclusively in the USA by
Palgrave, 175 Fifth Avenue, New York,
NY 10010, USA

Distributed exclusively in Canada by
UBC Press, University of British Columbia, 2029 West Mall,
Vancouver, BC, Canada V6T 1Z2

British Library Cataloguing-in-Publication Data
A catalogue record for this book is available from the British Library

Library of Congress Cataloging-in-Publication Data applied for

ISBN 0 7190 6596 8 *hardback*
0 7190 6597 6 *paperback*

First published 2003

11 10 09 08 07 06 05 04 03 10 9 8 7 6 5 4 3 2 1

Typeset in Minion with Lithos
by Northern Phototypesetting Co Ltd, Bolton
Printed in Great Britain
by Biddles Ltd, Guildford and King's Lynn

Contents

	List of tables	*page* vii
	List of contributors	viii
	Acknowledgements	ix
	Introduction: enlargement and the study of European integration *Jan Zielonka*	1
1	Joining Europe together or separately? The implications of the Czecho-Slovak divorce for EU enlargement *Jacques Rupnik*	16
2	Slovakia's democratic awakening *Martin Bútora, Zora Bútorová* and *Grigorij Mesežnikov*	51
3	The Czech road towards a consolidated democracy *Steven Saxonberg*	69
4	The Czech Republic as an EU candidate: strengths and weaknesses *Michael Leigh*	87
5	The European Union's policies towards Slovakia: carrots and sticks of political conditionality *Darina Malová* and *Marek Rybář*	98
6	The economic criteria for EU accession: lessons from the Czech and Slovak Republics *Susan Senior-Nello*	113
7	Who is in, who is out? Citizenship, nationhood, democracy and European integration in the Czech Republic and Slovakia *Tibor Papp*	138
8	Return to Europe? Patterns of Euroscepticism among the Czech and Slovak political parties *Petr Kopecky* and *Peter Učeň*	164
9	Czech perceptions of EU membership: Havel vs. Klaus *Peter Bugge*	180
10	Local political elites' perceptions of the EU *Catherine Perron*	199
11	Germany and the enlargement of the European Union to the Czech Republic *Anne Bazin*	220
12	Cross-border co-operation between Germany and the Czech Republic *Emil J. Kirchner*	250

Chronologies 271

Select bibliography 275

Index 289

Tables

3.1 The 1990 election results *page* 71
3.2 The 1992 election results for the Czech National Council 72
3.3 The 1996 election results 74
3.4 The 1998 election results 76
6.1 Main macroeconomic indicators for the Czech and Slovak Republics 117
6.2 Increase in the EU share of the total trade of the Czech Republic and Slovakia over the 1989–97 period 125
6.3 The structure of foreign trade 126
6.4 Foreign direct investment 128
6.5 The fiscal criteria in the Czech Republic and Slovakia 130
6.6 Inflation and long-term interest rates in the Czech Republic and Slovakia 131
6.7 Exchange rates in the Czech Republic and Slovakia 132
7.1 Varieties of citizenship 145

Contributors

Anne Bazin is a PhD of the Institut d'Etudes Politiques in Paris

Peter Bugge is Associate Professor at the Slavisk Institut at the University of Aarhus

Martin Bútora is the Slovak Ambassador to the United States

Zora Bútorová is an external scholar at the Institute for Public Affairs

Emil J. Kirchner is Professor of European Studies and Honorary Jean Monnet Professor in European Integration at the Centre for European Studies at the University of Essex

Petr Kopecky is Lecturer of Political Science at the University of Sheffield

Michael Leigh is Director at the European Commission

Darina Malová is Associate Professor of Political Science at Comenius University in Bratislava

Grigorij Mesežnikov is President of the Institute for Public Affairs in Bratislava

Tibor Papp is Advisor to the Chairman of the National Council of the Slovak Republic

Catherine Perron is a PhD of the Institut d'Etudes Politiques in Paris

Jacques Rupnik is Director of Research at the Centre d'Etudes et de Recherches Internationales (CERI), Foundation Nationale des Sciences Politiques Paris and Professor at the College of Europe in Bruges

Marek Rybář is Assistant Professor of Political Science at Comenius University, Bratislava

Steven Saxonberg is Associate Professor of Political Science at Dalarna University in Sweden

Susan Senior-Nello is Associate Professor in the Faculty of Economics at the University of Siena

Peter Učeň is Programme Assistant at the International Republican Institute and the Regional Office for Central and Eastern Europe in Bratislava

Jan Zielonka is Professor of Political Science at the European University Institute in Florence

Acknowledgements

This is the first of two volumes that look at the EU's accession process in individual post-communist countries. This volume focuses on the Czech Republic and Slovakia, while the subsequent volume focuses on Estonia, Latvia and Lithuania. The objective is to reveal the Eastern European part of the enlargement story, and to show how enlargement is being played out in the domestic politics of the candidate countries.

Both volumes result from a large-scale research project on the EU's eastward enlargement conducted by the Robert Schuman Centre for Advanced Study at the European University Institute in Florence. With the help of the Austrian Ministry for Science and Transport, the project was initiated in 1998, focusing on the Czech Republic and Slovakia. The Academy of Finland backed the second component of the project focusing on the Baltic Republics. The editors are grateful to both sponsors for their initial encouragement and excellent cooperation throughout the implementation phase.

Special thanks go to Professor Joseph Marko from the University of Graz for co-chairing with Jan Zielonka a special Steering Committee on this project. The exceptional commitment and expertise of individual members of this Steering Committee should also be praised. They included Alfred Ableitinger (University of Graz), Judy Batt (University of Birmingham), Maarten Brands (University of Amsterdam), Mahulena Hoškovà (Max Planck Institute, Heidelberg), Emil Kirchner (University of Essex), Krzysztof Michalski (Institute for Human Sciences, Vienna), Milan Sojka (Charles University, Prague), Sona Szomolànyi (Comenius University, Bratislava), Klaus Von Beyme (University of Heidelberg), Roeland in't Veld (University of Utrecht) and Friedl Weiss (University of Amsterdam).

We are particularly grateful to Tony Mason from Manchester University Press and to the series editor, Emil Kirchner, for their continuous support in preparing this publication. Several anonymous reviewers have helped us to improve the successive drafts of this book. Angelika Lanfranchi and Francesca Parenti provided excellent secretarial assistance.

Jacques Rupnik and Jan Zielonka

Jan Zielonka

Introduction

Enlargement and the study of European integration

The process of the EU's eastward enlargement is usually analysed in a broad regional perspective. Both the EU and the candidate countries tend to be viewed as unitary actors. The enlargement strategy is also seen as uniform and designed to suit all the different candidate countries. The analysis is technical if not schematic, leaving little space for political nuances. At the centre of attention are numerous conditions laid down by the Union that the candidate countries are expected to meet, and their progress (or lack of it) in achieving these. The implications of enlargement for the functioning of the European institutions are also a frequent topic of debates. In such studies in particular, the analysis is largely West-centred.

This book looks at the eastward enlargement from a different angle. It analyses the enlargement process from the perspective of two applicant countries. The analysis is political rather than merely technical. We see how enlargement has become one of the most important variables in the political life of both countries. Enlargement as seen from this perspective is more about party politics, state-formation and identity building than about complying with the 100,000 pages of *acquis communautaire.* Obviously, the analysis is also East rather than West-centred. The book is concerned much more with the implications of enlargement for these two applicant countries than for the current EU Member States and the European Union as such.

The purpose of this exercise is not only to reveal the 'other' (Eastern) part of the enlargement story, but also to help us understand how an enlarged EU would look and behave in practice. The applicant countries, when admitted, will have an impact on the functioning of the enlarged Union. It is therefore important to comprehend their vision of Europe, their perceptions of the enlargement process and expectations concerning their future membership.

The two cases scrutinised here are very special. In the early 1990s Czechoslovakia was seen as the most likely candidate for EU membership. However, the country soon split, and the only positive thing the EU could say about this split was that it was 'velvet'. Since 1993 both the new Czech and Slovak republics experienced difficult relations with the EU. Slovakia under Prime Minister Mečiar was considered to be in breach of the EU's basic set of conditions for membership, especially democratic ones. The Czech Republic under Prime Minister Klaus was seen as a champion of Euroscepticism, even though the country was making good progress in meeting the EU's conditions for membership. As this book goes into print both countries are in the group of 'official' front-runners to the EU, but some problems persist nevertheless. Vladimir Mečiar still has a lot of followers in Slovakia and no amount of his recently manifested Euro-friendly rhetoric will give much comfort to West European decision-makers. The Czech Republic, on the other hand, is embroiled in a political 'war of words' with its neighbour, Austria, about the use of a Soviet-type nuclear plant, and emigration issues. These factors make it hard to predict whether the Czech Republic and Slovakia will join the Union as united and committed integrationists at ease with their neighbours. What we do know is that this accession will in the end be a painful process of mutual learning, compromise and adaptation. Above all, each country would need to follow its own path of accession because of its different historical, cultural, economic and political background and subsequent trajectory of development. In short, each country represents a special case; a fact often neglected in the study of European integration with its tendency to regional generalisations and neglect of historical and cultural nuances.

However, the aim of this book is not only to provide a different approach to enlargement but to provide some basic, and largely unavailable, information about two important European countries. The post-1993 developments in the Czech Republic and Slovakia are still very much under-researched, and this book hopes to be of use for those interested in the politics and government of Eastern Europe and not merely for those interested in European integration.[1]

This introductory chapter will try to draw some lessons from the accession process of the Czech Republic and Slovakia for the study of European integration in general, and the enlargement process in particular. Three issues will receive special attention. First, we will show that it is difficult to comprehend the dynamics of accession without looking at the state-building process in the candidate countries. Second, we will argue that the study of the enlargement process should go hand-in-hand with the study of politics and economics in the countries concerned. Third, we will show the importance of regional co-operation and bilateral state-to-state relations in the study of enlargement. The accession to the Union is negotiated between the EU and individual applicants, and this is why most studies focus on this largely bilateral process.[2] However, this book demands a broadening of our perspective in the study of enlargement. Enlargement is a complex process with many different actors pursuing different, if not conflicting, policy objectives. This book tries to shed some light on this enormous complexity and to help us design a more adequate research agenda.

Enlargement and state-building

Joining the Union may well be about diluting the notion of a territorial state.[3] However, this book clearly shows that a country cannot be expected to give up certain basic state prerogatives without acquiring them first. Sovereignty needs to be regained before it can be shared. Turning national civil servants into European ones implies, first of all, creating one's own national civil service. It is difficult to negotiate an alignment of national laws with European laws if the former are in the early stage of development. A 'national' economy needs also to regain a minimum of vitality and competitiveness before joining the single European market.[4] Above all, a weak and divided state can hardly meet all the EU's difficult conditions for accession. Several post-communist candidates to the EU are new states, while some others have borders that are being questioned. The creation of a strong, legitimate and coherent territorial state seems indispensable for the enlargement to be a success. However, the two cases discussed in this book show that the state-building process might also have a negative impact on the enlargement process. In other words, the two projects are not always complementary and they may even be in conflict. In any case, the interplay between them is very complex. As Jacques Rupnik put it in his chapter:

> Czechoslovakia was created on the basis of the principle of self-determination of nations as part of a new European order shaped by Western powers in 1918. Seventy-five years later it disintegrated in the name of the same principle of self-determination, reclaimed by the Czechs and Slovaks, as part of the post-Cold War recasting of the European order. For both Czechs and Slovaks, the 'velvet revolution' of November 1989 heralded the exit from communism and a 'return to Europe' that became identified with the prospect of joining the European Union.'

Protagonists of the split had hoped that their policy would smooth the accession process to the Union. Those in the Czech Republic wanted to get rid of the Slovak 'burden', while those in Slovakia wanted to deal with Brussels directly from Bratislava, and not via Prague. Yet both countries soon discovered that building a new independent state does not always help in joining the Union. This is partly because state building absorbs energies that are needed for making a country ready for EU membership. Moreover, and more relevant to the cases discussed in this book, divorce and subsequent state building tend to bring about separatist, if not nationalist policies that are at odds with the spirit of integration. New state entities are being built in opposition to the 'other' and based on the principle of self-determination and exclusive sovereignty.

This brings us to another important issue. State building is often coupled with nation building and the latter is usually a matter of symbolic politics rather than *realpolitik*. Not surprisingly therefore, mutual relations between the Czechs and Slovaks have not only been driven by interests, but also by sentiments and the superiority–inferiority complex. At stake were not only effective self-rule, but also national pride and self-esteem. Czechoslovakia that had existed only since

1918 was unable to produce a viable Czechoslovak nation, and this could not but influence the process of state building. Moreover, the Slovaks, unlike the Czechs could not draw on a very successful history of either state or nation building.

After the fall of communism the Slovaks found it difficult to influence, let alone control policies made in the Bohemian capital of Czechoslovakia, Prague, and this only reinforced their feeling of inferiority. The Czechs felt hostage to the Slovak 'obstructionist' policy, which reaffirmed their feeling of 'exceptionalism'. Slovak insistence on a federal, if not confederal, state structure was seen by many Czechs as a recipe for institutional paralysis and psychological deadlock. The Czech insistence on a more integrated, if not unitary, state structure was seen by many Slovaks as an effort to (re)impose Czech hegemony. In the end, separation rather than integration was chosen by both protagonists as a preferred way of coping with the problem of self-rule and self-esteem.

However, European integration is likely to bring problems of self-rule and self-esteem back onto the agenda of both countries. Have Slovaks gained enough confidence to join a Union of countries with even more glorious national histories than those of Czechs? Some statements of Slovak politicians quoted in this book suggest that this might not be the case. Will Czechs accept from the Union what Slovaks were unable to accept from Czechoslovakia? Will they believe that decisions made in Brussels are as good as those made in Prague? Some statements of Czech politicians quoted in this book suggest that this might not be the case either. Of course, in the final analysis the answer to these questions will depend on the depth of centralising tendencies in the enlarged EU and the progress (or lack of it) of actual integration, especially in the field of culture. It will also depend on the evolving nature of the Czech and Slovak states. Will they be guided by the principle of closure or openness; of sovereignty that is absolute or shared? But it is clear that the historical legacies of Czech and Slovak state and nation building will have a considerable impact on these countries' relations with the EU after their accession.

The most intractable problems are likely to emerge concerning the movement of people, land and real estate purchases and the treatment of ethnic minorities. (After all, state building is largely about borders, citizenship, and property.) The creation of the Slovak state left the Hungarian minority in Slovakia without their Bohemian protection. Although the EU requires Slovakia to install a broad catalogue of minority rights prior to accession, the EU itself has not developed a collective mechanism for minority rights protection within its own Member States.[5] In the future, this can obviously create problems. The Czechs have also been under EU pressure to improve treatment of their Roma population. At the same time, however, several EU Member States have tried to curb any kind of Roma immigration into its own territory in quite a discriminatory manner. When the Czech Republic joins the Union the issue of Roma is likely to re-emerge.

Foreign acquisition of land and real estate property might also remain a difficult issue. This is not only because new states are particularly sensitive about possible 'loss' of 'their' land to foreigners (one may add, with superior purchasing power), but also because the issue of property restitution is at the centre of controversy between the Czech government and the governments of two EU Member States, Germany and Austria. (I refer here to the so-called Benes decrees discussed in several chapters of this book.)

A differentiated schedule of accession between Slovakia and the Czech Republic would also create border problems. If Slovakia were to join the Union at a later date than the Czech Republic, controls on the movement of people as well as goods and services would be much stricter than is the case now. This cannot fail to have serious humanitarian, economic, and political implications. The full adoption of the so-called Schengen *acquis* by the Czech Republic, for instance, would make it more difficult for Slovaks to enter the former Czechoslovak space where mixed families and businesses abound.

In summary, nation-state building and European integration processes are clearly inter-linked in both our cases, and they should be studied in conjunction. New states are not only less self-confident and secure; they are also confronted with a set of specific problems that are less prominent in well-established states. This makes them awkward negotiating partners for the EU, although the extent of difficulty also depends on their individual patterns of domestic competition. This leads us to the next main finding of the book: the fundamental importance of domestic political competition in the process of enlargement.

Enlargement and domestic competition

Some leading politicians in the candidate countries might be desperate to join the European Union, but they cannot do so at a prohibitive price. They need to listen to their respective domestic electorates and not only to EU officials. They also need to see the enlargement process as a means of making their country more secure and prosperous. However, evaluation of various pros and cons of enlargement is anything but a simple, straightforward, let alone objective, exercise. Different actors view enlargement from different angles and they also try to utilise enlargement for their specific political purposes. In other words, domestic political competition in the candidate countries shapes their perceptions of and policies towards the enlargement process and often independently of the EU's policies as such. In this sense, Eastern Europe looks very much like Western Europe, although political cleavages and issues of contention are not always the same.[6]

Two hypotheses can be drawn from this observation, one for political and the other for academic uses. The political hypothesis would say that the EU can hardly meet its own objectives in Eastern Europe unless it is able to 'play' within the candidate states' political and economic arenas. The academic hypothesis would say that the understanding of the enlargement process requires careful study of domestic competition, both in the Member States and in the candidate states. This book chiefly focuses on the latter issue.

The relatively low level of public support for joining the EU shows that EU membership is not always seen as a means of advancing economic and political fortunes in the Czech Republic and Slovakia.[7] Several chapters in this book indicate a number of specific reasons behind this Euroscepticism. These reasons vary depending on the ideological position of individual actors. Liberals are afraid, in particular, of 'smuggling socialism' back to their country and subjecting it to a uniform and centrally governed regulatory frame. Former, but largely unreformed communists fear that the Union is an agent of multi-national capital taking over profitable firms, and squeezing out non-competitive local firms with important social functions. Nationalists would add that the foreign capital arriving with enlargement is not so much multi-national, as German, and that its ultimate function is political rather than economic. In extreme cases, the EU is even seen as a tool of German imperialism. Conservatives fear that accession to the Union will expose their country to 'decadent' universal materialism leaving little space for local tradition and spiritual values.

There is also variation among countries and political parties in the origins and manifestations of Euroscepticism. The Czechs have a greater fear than the Slovaks that EU membership will imply German domination – a fear that is constantly being reinforced by the assertive behaviour of the Sudeten Germans.[8] The Slovaks, unlike the Czechs, often fear that EU membership will prevent them from acting as a bridge between the West and the East – the latter exemplified by Russia in particular. Different parties also have different policies concerning Europe, and these often fluctuate depending on the political environment of the day. As Petr Kopecky and Peter Učeň put it in their chapter, Euroscepticism can be seen as largely a 'matter of electoral politics and appeals, or the dynamic of government–opposition divide, rather than of party identity.'[9]

It would be wrong, of course, to focus only on the most extreme manifestations of Euroscepticism. Moreover, Eurosceptic arguments ought to be balanced by Euro-enthusiastic ones. That said, students of enlargement tend to assume that post-communist countries are very eager to join the Union, and the only challenge is to prepare them for such a membership through a comprehensive system of conditionality. However, this book shows that one of the greatest challenges is to make these countries see enlargement not as a necessary evil or even a threat, but as an opportunity. Assertive conditionality may only reinforce fears grounded in the striking discrepancy of power and *de facto* limited sovereignty. And this is not only a matter of symbolic politics. As Susan Senior-Nello's chapter shows, for instance, there is some tension between the economic accession criteria and the prerequisites for rapid economic growth of the candidate countries. Moreover, some of the accession criteria are vague and imprecise leaving a large degree of discretion to EU officials. These officials, according to Eurosceptics, tend to abuse their positions of power in order to enhance partisan, if not parochial, interests. In sum, it would be difficult to foster the European integration project without addressing these kinds of concerns.

The phenomenon of Euroscepticism shows how the enlargement issue is being used and misused in the domestic political competition. However, it is not only anti-Western and anti-European politicians that are trying to enhance their political fortunes by exploiting the enlargement issue. The popularity of enlargement is also being exploited. Like their Western counterparts, national leaders in the Czech Republic and Slovakia often quote the EU as a reason for undertaking painful and unpopular reforms. They also try to discredit their political opponents by capitalising on their difficult relationship with Brussels. For instance, the argument that the continuation of the Mečiar regime would prevent Slovakia from joining the EU clearly contributed to the 1998 electoral victory of the alliance of four opposition parties led by Mikuláš Dzurinda. Four years later some students fear that the disillusionment with the EU's policies may cause a fall of the Dzurinda government in the forthcoming national elections, and the subsequent return to power of Vladimír Mečiar.

All this does not mean that the EU should give up its policy of conditionality *vis-à-vis* the candidate states. When candidate states cite public opposition as a reason for failing to introduce genuine minority rights protection or insist on protectionist trade practices, this does not have to be accepted by the EU. But the Union could take greater account of domestic sensitivities in the candidate countries. Above all, it should realise that its policies towards these countries can be effective only if they are properly adjusted to the complex and usually quite specific pattern of national political competition. What is needed is a greater recognition of different political actors in the candidate states and application of a diversified set of political measures towards them (both positive and negative). This has been well illustrated by the chapter of Darina Malova and Marek Rybár. They found that the impact of EU conditionally increases if it does not treat enlargement as a bilateral issue involving the EU and Slovakia, but as a trilateral issue between the EU, the Slovak government and the Slovak opposition.[10] According to Malova and Rybář, 'the EU political conditionality does not work formally, i.e. stability of institutions cannot be achieved only by establishing legal changes of political system, it also requires a corresponding set of political actors, who comply with democratic rules and procedures'.

In conclusion, the key to a successful enlargement process lies not only in the recognition of differences among individual candidate states, but also in the opening of the political 'black box' within each of these states and tailoring EU policies accordingly. By the same token, it is difficult to comprehend the enlargement process by looking merely at bilateral relations between officials from the EU and candidate states.

Europe, regions and states

The candidate countries are not simple unitary actors, but neither is the EU. Enlargement is chiefly about managing complex mutual interdependencies between the eastern and the western parts of the continent. Interactions take place at different local, national and pan-national levels. Moreover, a variety of public and private actors are engaged in these interactions depending on the particular functional field. As Emil Kirchner puts it in his chapter: 'A more holistic approach is in order which links meso level issues with macro-concerns of European integration and which is concerned with the interaction dynamic of the local/regional, national and European Union level.'

This book, of course, is unable to do justice to all the different actors, and levels and types of interaction. However, most of the chapters look at the enlargement process in terms that go beyond a simple bilateral relationship between the EU and the candidate states. Two different types of interaction receive special attention: regional co-operation, and bilateral relations between two nation-states, Germany and the Czech Republic.

So far, regional co-operation has not been a great success story despite EU efforts to promote it. Candidates for the EU are not very eager to work more closely with each other, not even within a relatively homogenous group such as the Visegrád one, including Poland, Hungary, the Czech Republic and Slovakia. The pattern of co-operation is very much along a 'centre–periphery' line that runs between Brussels and individual capital cities in Eastern Europe.

Regional co-operation across the current borders of the EU is not a great success either. Euro-regions that were set up with the help of either PHARE or INTERREG cross-border co-operation programs are largely unknown, under-funded and faced with mounting bureaucratic and political constraints. This is regrettable because integration cannot only be a matter of central governments engaged in inter-state negotiations. It should also be a matter of various grass-root voluntary and local government initiatives functioning across the existing borders in a largely spontaneous manner. After all, it is primarily ordinary citizens and non-governmental actors rather than national or European officials that are able to forge shared norms, and values.[11] A genuine sense of European identity and solidarity can not be achieved merely through wider (and hopefully stricter) adoption of the *acquis communautaire*. A study of the reasons behind the relative failure of regional co-operation within the East European context is therefore crucial for understanding the course of European integration, and several chapters in this book are of some help in this respect.

One of the reasons explored in more detail is the persistent salience of bilateral state-to-state relations in European politics. Several chapters focus on relations between Germany and the Czech Republic, and these are indeed extremely illustrative and important. The border between the two countries is currently the external border of the Union. Germany is said to be the greatest beneficiary and supporter of the enlargement process. The Czech Republic is said to be a leader in the run-up to EU accession. Both countries have flourishing economic ties and tourist exchanges. And yet, as this book clearly shows, both countries find it difficult to cope with their complex historic legacies, psychological prejudices and power asymmetries. Officials from both countries regularly exchange angry remarks if not insults, and even more heated controversy takes place at an unofficial level. All this has implications for our discussion because the EU often finds itself at the centre of the ongoing argument. We see in particular how national politics mixes with European politics in the enlargement process. First of all, the European and German policies in the region are closely inter-linked, if not fused altogether. This is not only because the policies of Commissioner Verheugen (who is German) look very German but also because Germany is clearly the most important European actor when it comes to enlargement, and it frames its own national policies in European terms. In fact, it is difficult to distinguish clearly between German foreign policy conducted through traditional bilateral channels and through the European ones. It is difficult to say whether the European policy towards the region is being shaped by German concerns or the other way around. It is also difficult to assess who benefits more (and how exactly) from the adopted enlargement line. What is certain, is that one policy would not be able to be equally efficient and legitimate without the other. What is also certain, is that this fusion of German and European policies presents the candidate states with fundamental dilemmas. As Anne Bazin put it in her chapter: 'Germany as a "vehicle of integration" the CEEC count on, is also the one which can set conditions to enlargement . . . In the last decades, "Europe" has been the key word of (West-) German foreign policy. German support for enlargement can be seen within this framework. Nevertheless it seems legitimate to question the convergence of German 'national interest', and the interests of the rest of Europe as well as Central Europe.'

There is no doubt that small and relatively poor Eastern European countries are better off when dealing with their German neighbour within the European framework. However, there is a danger that European politics will became hostage of parochial German concerns. As Jacques Rupnik pointed out in his chapter, at least three largely German (and Austrian) concerns have been 'Europeanised' in the process of enlargement: the free movement of labour, the safety of nuclear plants, and the Sudeten German demands concerning the Benes decrees of 1945.

The last case is especially interesting for students of European integration because it shows how a relatively small, but vocal and well-organised pressure group can utilise the enlargement process for its own and rather partisan ends.

In summary, enlargement is a multi-level game. It is being played out not only between the candidate states and the EU as a whole: individual EU Member States try to secure their own national interests vis-à-vis the candidate states by using EU machinery and the leverage of EU accession. Non-state actors at regional and local level also play their part in this game, turning an understanding of the enlargement process into a truly formidable challenge.

Structure of the book

This book has twelve chapters that can be grouped under five different headings: historical legacy, domestic politics of EU accession, EU policy of conditionality, discourse and perceptions, and finally, the transnational dimension.

The first chapter provides a broad historical background of the Czech and Slovak road to the Union. It looks at how Czech and Slovak perceptions of and policies towards Europe have evolved since the creation of the Czechoslovak state in 1918 through the fall of communism in 1989, the split of the Czechoslovak federation in 1992 and up until the final stages of accession negotiations in 2002. The chapter identifies and scrutinises four major legacies of the Czechoslovak partition in the context of enlargement: the cultural, economic, constitutional and international legacies. It also shows the evolution of the two countries' relations with their neighbours under the title: the end of Czech 'exceptionalism' and of the Slovak exception. In its conclusions, the chapter argues that in the end enlargement induced the Czech and Slovak republics to interact more closely with their Central European partners such as Poland. Enlargement also encouraged the two republics to work closer with each other, even though in the aftermath of the collapse of the communist regime they chose to go to Europe separately.

The next two chapters analyse the interplay of European integration and domestic developments in the two republics. Chapter 2 analyses the turbulent political scene in Slovakia after the split of Czechoslovakia, and its implications for Slovak accession to the European Union. The chapter shows how the two 'velvet revolutions' resulted in two different types of development in the Czech Republic and Slovakia. The years under the autocratic government of Prime Minister Mečiar are examined and followed by an analysis of the regime change in 1998 and the installation of a pro-European government under Prime Minister Dzurinda. The chapter argues that the tension between the principles of liberal democracy and the Slovak national question is still present in Slovak politics, shaping the Slovak attitude towards membership of the EU.

Chapter 3 analyses the paradoxes of Czech politics after the 'velvet' breakdown of Czechoslovakia. The Czech Republic seemed to be the most EU-compatible Eastern European country in terms of economy and political system but the political rhetoric of its prime minister, Václav Klaus, made it an ambivalent if not reluctant aspirant to EU membership. The new government coalition led by Prime Minister Milos Zeman seemed to be more eager to endorse the EU's regulatory schemes and conditions, but it began to look increasingly less EU-compatible in structural terms. The chapter analyses the consolidation of the party system, the government formation processes and the politics of reform in the Czech Republic, and shows their implications for EU membership.

Chapters 4, 5, 6 and 7 examine the European Union's enlargement policies and the Czech and Slovak responses to these policies. Two chapters focus separately on each of the two countries, and two other chapters focus on two specific fields across both countries: economics and constitutional politics. Chapter 4 examines how the Czech Republic has responded to the EU accession criteria. Rather than reproducing or summarising the Commission's Regular Reports on the Czech progress in meeting these criteria, the chapter looks at the factors influencing the Czech efforts to complete economic and democratic transition and to prepare for EU membership. Special attention is paid to the Union's ability to promote 'institution-building' in the Czech Republic, not only to stimulate general systemic transformation, but also to address some specific issues such as the marginalisation of the Roma community. The chapter shows which problems of meeting the EU's accession criteria have gradually been overcome, and which are still outstanding. The chapter concludes that the EU's *acquis* has become a model for the Czech reform effort in line with not only the Czech Republic's European aspiration, but also with the requirements of economic inter-dependence.

Chapter 5 analyses the character of the European Union's political conditionality and illustrates the role it has played in political developments in Slovakia. The chapter shows, in particular, how EU political conditionality towards Slovakia has facilitated political co-operation between non-nationalist political parties and shaped the nature of party competition. This political process resulted in fundamental reforms that made Slovakia more suited for EU membership. However, the chapter argues that EU conditionality can hardly work if it is applied only through formal laws and institutions. It also requires a corresponding set of political actors, who comply with democratic rules and procedures.

Chapter 6 monitors the economic progress of the Czech and Slovak Republics in preparing for EU accession. The 1993 Copenhagen criteria set out the conditions for accession, but there was room for considerable discretion in deciding whether these have been met. Distortions in the privatisation process, and the slow transformation of the financial sector have proved to be major stumbling blocks in both countries. The chapter argues that although the Czech and Slovak Republics should prepare for eventual full membership of the Economic and Monetary Union, they should be wary of premature attempts to meet the Maastricht criteria.

Chapter 7 analyses the ways in which the Union applies the political criteria of accession to the Czech Republic and Slovakia. It finds some of these criteria vague and insufficient. The criteria are hardly geared to the specific circumstances of individual applicant states, and they ignore crucial aspects of the democratic transition. In particular, the issue of citizenship is found to be largely neglected by the Union even though it seems crucial in making post-communist countries ready for EU membership. The chapter shows that the politics of citizenship is crucial for integration because of the explicit theoretical link to the understanding of nationhood on the one hand, and to the degree of democracy on the other. The presented comparison of EU integration policies in the Czech Republic and Slovakia enables us to evaluate the candidate states progress in meeting the political criteria for accession in a systematic and objective manner, the chapter argues. And in this respect Slovakia seems more ready for the EU accession than the Czech Republic.

The following three chapters analyse the political discourse on and public perceptions of the process of EU accession. While unqualified support for European enlargement was typical for all Eastern European countries in 1989, more varied practice and stances on European integration have been a corollary of intensified talks on enlargement towards the end of the 1990s. Chapter 8 provides an overview of stances on European integration among Czech and Slovak political parties. It explores and explains the patterns of party positions and, in addition, speculates about their future developments. In particular, the chapter is interested in what has been termed Euroscepticism, that is, a relatively broad diversity of positions encompassing contingent, qualified, or outright opposition to the process of European integration. The exploration of these strands of Euroscepticism is confined to the elite level, and namely to the level of political parties, as the authors detected them through the study of party programmes and documents, political speeches and various journal and newspaper articles.

Chapter 9 offers a detailed analysis of the discourses on Europe and the EU by two leading Czech politicians: Václav Havel and Václav Klaus. The chapter shows that the long Czech march since 1989 towards the EU has not only been a question of specific policies. Czech politicians have also striven to develop a discourse that could explain and justify these steps by presenting 'Europe' as a proper 'home' for the Czech nation, and the EU as a reasonable incarnation of the 'European idea'. Undoubtedly, the two key actors in this process have been Václav Havel and Václav Klaus, and the chapter analyses their various public statements. The chapter argues that their divergent views on European integration stem from their sharp disagreement on the role of the nation-state. For Klaus the nation-state is the cornerstone of sovereignty, identity, and political and economic decision-making. For Havel, by contrast, the nation-state is not a value in itself. He dissociates identity from sovereignty and seeks to present Europe, and increasingly even the existing EU, as the natural 'home' for the Czechs.

Chapter 10 examines the attitudes of Czech local politicians towards European integration. In what has been until now an elite driven process, it seems important to pay attention to the role and function of the people who hold intermediary positions between central elites and local populations. Not much attention has been devoted to their vision, even though on the one hand, some of them are bound to become tomorrow's national elites, and on the other hand, they play a major role in the diffusion of knowledge about the EU. The chapter therefore examines the importance of the issue of integration to local political elites, their feeling of belonging to Europe, and their attitudes towards the EU. The chapter is based on the author's interviews with the most influential local politicians on the city councils of three Czech cities: Plzen, Olomouc and Kladno.

Although enlargement negotiations are conducted between the Union and individual applicant states, other actors are crucial players too. Chapter 11 focuses on Germany's role in shaping the accession process of the Czech Republic, while chapter 12 considers the regional dimension of enlargement. Chapter 11 starts with a report on the state of co-operation between the Czech Republic and Germany within the context of the EU. It then examines how the Czech Republic envisages its relations with Germany at the European level and analyses the nature of German support in the process of enlargement. The chapter concludes on the link between the 'German question' and the future configuration of Central Europe and of Europe as a whole.

Chapter 12 shows that cross-border co-operation between (national) border regions has represented a significant dimension in the EU integration process, contributing to feelings of trust and a sense of community. Although there is a general understanding that cross-border co-operation makes a positive contribution to EU integration, its role as a link between formal and informal integration is not sufficiently understood, especially in the context of EU eastern enlargement. The chapter therefore attempts to examine this link in the context of cross-border co-operation between Germany and the Czech Republic. The research employs both the transactionalist approach of Karl Deutsch, and the constructivist approach of Wendt, Katzenstein, and Risse in its analysis of various efforts to foster cross-border co-operation.

Conclusions

The enlargement process is not confined to negotiations and diplomacy; it is about politics in the broad sense of this word. It involves state building at both national and European levels that will determine what kind of polities evolve on the continent. Enlargement also touches on various aspects of domestic politics. In fact, it increasingly structures domestic competition and produces cleavages along which domestic political wars are fought. Enlargement is also about new-style international relations where different national, regional, and local agendas are mixed, if not fused. Despite the enormous asymmetry in power between the Union and the candidate states, enlargement is anything but a 'one-way street'. Not only is it highly questionable whether imposed policies could ever work; to be effective the Union must be able to play within the domestic political arena of individual candidate states. Needless to say, a truly successful enlargement policy must also take account of domestic politics in the current Member States.

Students of European integration cannot confine their analysis to EU institutions and their objectives. They must look at the enlargement issue in a wider European context. To paraphrase Helen Wallace's expression, enlargement is matter of Europeanisation, not only EU-isation. This has enormous implications for the research agenda on European integration because it asks us to multiply the variables that potentially shape the process of integration. It also urges us to apply a broader variety of methods and theories that have been elaborated by various schools of International Relations and Comparative Politics. By the same token, European integration can no longer be treated as a unique phenomenon that requires a 'special' let alone 'single' theory of integration. European integration is about a complex multi-level game that can only be comprehended with the use of a broad range of social science instruments, paradigms and theories. This book has tried to show that such an approach is not only possible, but also indispensable. The challenge ahead for future publications on this topic is to bring the kind of research proposed in this book a step further in both theoretical and empirical terms.

Notes

I would like to thank Grzegorz Ekiert, Ania Krok-Paszkowska and Helen Wallace for their helpful critiques in the process of preparing this chapter.

1 So far, there is no single book on the market that has looked at these two cases of accession. In fact, there are hardly any books currently available that focus on the post-communist politics of these two countries. There are numerous splendid but short articles analysing the post-1989 transition and describing the nascent pillars of democracy and market in both countries. But as far as academic literature in English is concerned, this book fills an important gap in the market. One notable exception here is: A. Innes, *Czechoslovakia: The Short Goodbye* (New Haven: Yale University Press, 2001).

2 Accession negotiations take place in the form of an intergovernmental conference (IGC) between member states (as a collective) and the individual applicant state. In practice, negotiations are bilateral because they take place between the Commission (which negotiates on the basis of a common position unanimously agreed upon by member states) and an individual candidate. See G. Avery and F. Cameron, *The Enlargement of the European Union* (Sheffield: Sheffield Academic Press), pp. 28–29.

3 For an opposite view see A. Milward, *The European Rescue of the Nation-State* (London: Routledge, 1992) or A. Moravcsik, *The Choice for Europe: Social Purpose and State Power from Messina to Maastricht* (Ithaca: Cornell University ress, 1998).

4 Of course, as H. Wallace pointed out, 'old' states not only from Eastern, but also Western Europe also have problems in adjusting to integration. However, the two cases discussed in this book show that there is a qualitative difference in the situation of new and old states joining the Union, because the former are less self-confident and mature. See H. Wallace, 'Enlarging the European Union: Reflections on the Challenge of Analysis', *Journal of European Public Policy*, Vol. 9 (2002), pp. 658–665.

5 See B. de Witte, 'Politics versus law in the EU's Approach to Ethnic Minorities', in J. Zielonka, ed., *Europe Unbound* (London: Routledge, 2002), pp. 137–160.

6 In other words, a 'two-level game' identified by Robert Putnam can also be applied to the candidate states. Sometimes the Union is being used as a scapegoat for implementing unpopular, but necessary measures. At other times, public opposition is quoted as an excuse for failing to meet EU demands. See R. Putnam, 'Diplomacy and Domestic Politics: the Logic of Two-level Games', *International Organization* Vol. 42 (1988), pp. 427–460.

7 In the Czech Republic the 2001 rates of support for EU membership were as low as 46 per cent, while in Slovakia it was 58 per cent. See *Applicant Countries Euro-barometer* (Brussels: European Commission, 2001), p. 5.

8 As this book goes to print, questions are again being raised about what the (Sudeten) Germans see as 'a Czech unwillingness to distance itself from the injustice of ethnic cleansing'. It has been suggested that the so-called Benes decrees should have been made into an issue under the Copenhagen political criteria on respect for human rights and protection of minorities. See B. Kohler, 'Question of Relevance' on Opinion page of *Frankfurter Algemeine Zeitung*, 13 March 2002. English translation on www.faz.com (14 March 2002).

9 Although the authors also insist that Euroscepticism in the countries cocerned is also in tune with declared ideological principles of the parties involved. This is in line with

P. Taggart's observation concerning the pattern of Euroscepticism in Western European parties. See P. Taggart, 'A Touchstone of Dissent: Euroscepticism in Contemporary Western European Party Systems', *European Journal of Political Research*, Vol. 33 (1998), pp. 363–388.

10 See also G. Pridham, 'Rethinking Regime Change Theory and the International Dimension of Democratisation: Ten Years after in East-Central Europe', in G. Pridham and A. Ágh (eds), *Prospects for Democratic Consolidation in East-Central Europe* (Manchester and New York: Manchester University Press, 2002), pp. 72–73, and K. E. Smith, 'The Use of Political Conditionality in the EU's Relations with Third Countries: How Effective?', *European Foreign Affairs Review* Vol. 3 (1998), pp. 253–274.

11 For a more comprehensive argument about the integrationist function of grassroot cross-border interactions see K. Deutsch *et al. Political Community and the North Atlantic Area* (New York: Greenwood Press, 1957), pp. 117–161. Also T. Christiansen and K. E. Jørgensen, 'Transnational Governance "Above" and "Below" the State: The Changing Nature of Borders in the New Europe', *Regional and Federative Studies* Vol. 10 (2000), p. 66.

Jacques Rupnik

1

Joining Europe together or separately?

The implications of the Czecho-Slovak divorce for EU enlargement

Czechoslovakia was created on the basis of the principle of the self-determination of nations as part of a new European order shaped by Western powers in 1918. Seventy-five years later it disintegrated in the name of the same principle of self-determination, reclaimed by Czechs and Slovaks as part of the post-Cold War recasting of the European order. For both Czechs and Slovaks, the 'velvet revolution' of November 1989 heralded the exit from communism and a 'return to Europe' that became identified with the prospect of joining the European Union. Less than ten years and a 'velvet divorce' later, the Czech Republic was included in the first circle for the enlargement of the Union (along with Poland, Hungary, Slovenia and Estonia) while Slovakia was not.[1] Hence the first question: was this 'verdict' concerning enlargement a consequence of the partition? Without the partition, would Czechs and Slovaks be 'in'? Or – and this is a hypothesis that cannot be excluded – without partition would both of them be 'out'? The first implies the role of Prague as a kind of guarantor of Slovakia's democratic and Western orientation. The second (and more generally the evolution of Slovakia under Mečiar between 1993 and 1998) was implicitly used by the Czech media and the then Prague government as a vindication of the Czecho-Slovak divorce. Since the departure from power in 1998 of both main protagonists of the Czecho-Slovak divorce (V. Klaus and V. Mečiar) the two successor states embarked on a rapprochement particularly with regard to issues related to their accession to the European Union. Joining the EU together or separately was (and in some ways remains) part of the Czech and Slovak enlargement dilemma.

'Alone into Europe or together to the Balkans' ran the headline in the Prague weekly *Respekt* in the Autumn of 1992. More generally, the assumption that the integration into Western institutions could be speeded up without Slovakia as a political and economic 'burden' was part of the prevailing thinking among Czech political and media elites at the time. A parallel argument about joining Europe as an independent state had been voiced by Slovak prime minister Jan Čarnogurský in 1991 and, more forcefully, by his successor Vladimír Mečiar in 1992. This raises the question: to what extent was the partition part of a European integration strategy? The argument implicit in the question is not altogether convincing as neither of the main protagonists of the split, Václav Klaus and the Civic Democratic Party (ODS) on the Czech side, and Vladimír Mečiar and his Movement for a Democratic Slovakia (HZDS), had entry into the European Union as a priority. Klaus, an outspoken critic of the EU, focused on economic transformation and integration with 'the West' in general terms. Mečiar's priority was the consolidation of his power through nation-state building rather than merging with Europe: recognition rather than integration was what he expected from Europe. His ambition of giving Slovakia a 'visibility', distinct from the Czechs, took precedence over any EU agenda. And, in his own way, he has succeeded.

However, the demise in 1998 of Václav Klaus and Vladimír Mečiar, the two main protagonists of the Czecho-Slovak split who had so clearly dominated the political scene in their respective countries and represented a problematic relationship with the EU, opened a new phase in relations between the two nations. It also prompted a shift in their policies and their prospects of regional and wider European integration.

The Czecho-Slovak split raises issues of broader significance concerning the relationship between patterns of democratic transition, nation-state building and European integration. It will be examined here through three main questions:

1 To what extent does the Czecho-Slovak partition point to two models of post-communist transition with two different prospects for European integration?
2 What are the contrasting Czech and Slovak perceptions and policies towards the European Union?
3 How does the policy convergence of the Czech lands after Klaus and Slovakia after Mečiar impact on Central European co-operation and the EU enlargement process?

The 'velvet divorce': two modes of transition and integration?

The fact that the end of the Czechoslovak federation was, like the end of communism in Czechoslovakia, speedy and non-violent, sometimes gave the somewhat deceptive impression that it was of little consequence for the respective developments of both successor countries or for the broader situation in Central Europe. In fact the Czechs and Slovaks pursued markedly different courses after their split at the end of 1992. The Czech Republic, like Poland and Hungary, moved from 'transition' to 'consolidation of democracy', that is, a situation where the constitutional and institutional framework is accepted by all political actors.[2] In contrast, Slovakia under Vladimír Mečiar had moved away from the

'Central European model' of transition towards an increasingly authoritarian and unpredictable system where the very nature of the regime was the major stake in the political game. Between 1993 and 1998 Slovakia drifted closer to a second group of authoritarian post-communist countries (or 'electoral democracies', as Larry Diamond called them) including, among others, Croatia or Bielarus. The systematic disrespect for the rule of law is also what led Fareed Zakaria to include Mečiar's Slovakia among 'illiberal democracies'.[3] The political wisdom of the 1997 EU decision separating candidates for enlargement into two groups (and ruling out Slovakia on the grounds of its 'democratic deficit') was debatable; but its actual diagnosis about the state of Slovakia's democratic transition at the time was accurate.

The connection between the two patterns of transition to democracy on one hand and two prospects for European integration should be understood as related to some of its underlying causes. It is not just as a side effect or an unintended consequence of the partition of the country. Four main relevant aspects that should be examined, at least briefly, are: (1) political culture and legacies of the past; (2) the dynamics of modernisation and the conversion to a market economy; (3) the crisis of federalism, constitutional nationalism and the role of post-communist political elites; and (4) the regional/international environment.

Political culture and legacies of the past

After the return of democracy, one of the difficulties faced by Czechs and Slovaks in redefining their common state institutions was related to their contrasting perceptions of their relatively brief shared history. For a thousand years the two nations had lived side by side but separately. The Czechs had a tradition of statehood (the kingdom of Bohemia) while the Slovaks did not. Under the Habsburgs, Bohemia became the industrial heartland of the empire while Slovakia was a rural part of Hungary. The relative ease with which Czechoslovakia was established in 1918 was deceptive: linguistically the two nations were close but hardly knew each other. Most importantly, the new state was established on the ambiguous concept of a 'Czechoslovak nation' which referred to the civic concept of the nation as formulated by the first President, T. G. Masaryk, but also had a legitimising function (lumping together Czechs and Slovaks who made up two-thirds of the population) *vis-à-vis* important German and Hungarian minorities.

Neither the ambiguous definition of the nation nor the state survived the Munich agreement in 1938, and the Czecho-Slovak relationship since then has been a story of mutual disappointments with somewhat different chronologies. Seen from Bratislava, the Czech elites did not fulfil Slovak expectations for autonomy after 1918, or again after 1945, keeping a centralised, Jacobine concept of the state. Seen from Prague, the Slovaks twice gave priority to their separate, national interest over that of Czechoslovak democracy: after Munich in 1938, and again after the Soviet-led invasion of 1968 when the Slovak political leadership gave precedent to federalisation of the state (even under Soviet auspices) over the defence of its democratisation.

The external weakness of the Czechoslovak state revealed tensions in the relationship between the two nations and tended to reinforce Czech centralism, thus frustrating Slovak aspirations of autonomy. Carol Skalnik Leff noted that the Slovaks 'compensated for an unequal balance of power within the state by alignments with foreign allies [. . .] Slovak nationalism has thus appeared to the Czech opinion, successively, as the cat's paw of Magyar irredentism, German imperialism and Soviet hegemony: the perception of Slovak opportunism in such cases has put additional stress on the Czecho-Slovak relations'.[4] The point here, of course, is not to evaluate the accuracy of such a reading of history but to take into account the importance of differing perceptions and misperceptions of history. A 1992 poll asked people which period in their history they considered as most positive: the Czech respondents put top of the list the reign of Charles IV (who in the fourteenth century made Prague the capital of the Holy Empire) and Masaryk's First Republic (1918–38). Slovak respondents put first the period 1948–89 and second the period of the Slovak state (1939–45).[5] When asked about favoured historical figures there was again no overlap between Czechs and Slovaks. The striking thing here is the absence of shared political and state symbols. That at the very moment when the future of the Czechoslovak state was being decided, two totalitarian experiences (fascist and communist) that were rejected by Czechs were considered positive by Slovaks, has implications for the understanding of their 'divorce' and the difficult emergence of a shared democratic culture.

It is not easy to conceive of a common future with such opposing perceptions of the common past, especially if these perceptions tend to overlap with different political cultures. Professor Miroslav Kusy from the Comenius University in Bratislava summed up the alleged Slovak characteristics with the following formula: 'Slovaks are, in comparison with Czechs or other Central Europeans, more separatist, more nationalistic, more Christian-, Left and Eastward oriented'.[6] Like many stereotypes, this characterisation contains an element of truth. And it would be tempting indeed to find a correlation between the two attitudes towards the legacies of the past or common statehood, and the two political cultures related to their two modes of post-communist transition. Yet such an explanation might just prove to be too convenient and misread the dynamics of change which, as the developments since Autumn 1998 suggest, challenge established patterns or dominant political cultures. On the Czech side Klaus's neo-conservative, free market liberalism represents a sharp break with the pre-war tradition of Masaryk's 'democratic humanism with a social conscience', and it simply has no antecedents in Czech political culture. Similarly, in Slovakia, with its strong tradition of political Catholicism, one would have anticipated an important role for Christian-Democracy, which, under Carnogursky's leadership, has barely won over 10 per cent of the electorate. However, as electoral studies have shown, Mečiar's electoral base matches almost perfectly that of the pre-war People's party; Mečiar's national-populism on the left in the footsteps of Hlinka's national-populism on the right?

Modernisation and socio-economic differences

A fairly widespread thesis about the Czecho-Slovak split runs like this: for the Slovak post-communist elites, the split represented a political gain and an economic loss. For their Czech counterparts it was the other way around: the political loss related to the demise of Czechoslovakia was to be compensated for by anticipated economic gains, as they expected that the road to Europe or to the West would be faster without the Slovak burden. The quest for identity, recognition and nationalist ideology prevailed over economic rationality on the Slovak side. For the Czech governing elite, narrowly defined economic interests (or selfishness) allegedly prevailed over nationalist passions. It could be argued that Czech 'economic nationalists' in disguise thus joined a familiar club made up of Balts or Slovenes who were eager to leave their respective federations in the post-communist East. Or, perhaps in a different context, they resemble those in Western Europe (such as Italy's Northern League and Belgium's Flemish nationalists) undermining the cohesion of their respective states. However, this thesis sticks too closely to the then prevailing discourse of Václav Klaus's party to be entirely convincing.

The uneven level of development has, of course, been an important factor in the shaping of an asymetric Czecho-Slovak relationship since 1918. The difference was important not just in economic development but also in urbanisation, education (merely 1.4 per cent university students in Hungary at the turn of the century were Slovaks) and secularisation (much more advanced in Bohemia where the harshness of the counter-reformation in the seventeenth century and rapid industrialisation in the nineteenth century eroded religious practice, while Slovak society remained marked by traditional Catholicism). However, due to inter-war development, and particularly due to the investment policies of the post-war communist regime, Slovakia was catching-up.[7] Paradoxically, the Czecho-Slovak separation took place at the very moment when the economic catching-up (as measured by GNP per capita) was almost completed. Rather than uneven development, it became the two societies' different attitudes towards the market and civil society, attitudes rooted in their different experiences of modernisation, which mattered.

The modernisation of Bohemia took place in the context of a market economy and a civil society going back to late nineteenth-century Austria and the inter-war First Republic. By contrast, the modernisation of Slovakia was mainly carried out in the context of post-war Soviet-style socialism; that is, with the complete liquidation of the market and of civil society by the state. These contrasting experiences of modernisation account, at least partly, for the different attitudes, within Czech and Slovak societies, to the legacies of the old regime and the introduction of radical market reforms. For the Czechs, the communist period with its emphasis on heavy industry has been one of relative 'de-modernisation (dropping from the seventh rank in per capita GNP after the Second World War, to the fortieth). For Slovakia, it has represented a delayed, accelerated modernisation, with all the accompanying pathologies which Slovak sociologists have described as follows:

> enforced state-paternalist orientation, learned helplessness and social infantilism . . . Extensive modernisation, in the absence of a civil society, has helped to introduce strong statist and anti-liberal values and codes of behaviour in the population. Nevertheless, this period was not seen by the inhabitants of Slovakia in purely negative terms.[8]

Thus while the introduction of market reforms was perceived by Czech society as a reconnection with Western modernity, it was experienced in Slovakia as another modernisation, imposed from above and outside, this time under the banner of economic liberalism.[9] Combined with the fact that the social impact of the market reforms was much worse in Slovakia than in the Czech lands, this explains why political elites on both sides were able to exploit economic resentment. In Slovakia they could play on the fear of becoming the 'losers' of yet another modernisation imposed from Prague. In the Czech lands they recycled the complaint about 'ungrateful, subsidised laggards' slowing down the Czech's bid for rapid integration with the West.

There was no economic fatality in the Czecho-Slovak separation. It was when the divide between the two nations overlapped with the divide between the two societies and the two diverging political orientations that the split became a possibility. To the extent that joining the EU entails accepting the constraints of a 'single market' and the interpenetrating of civil societies, these sociological differences, rooted in their different experiences of modernisation, continue to have important implications for the way both societies approach the prospect of European integration.

Federalism, constitutional nationalism and post-communist elites

The third legacy of the Czecho-Slovak partition with implications for European integration concerns nation-state building and the failure of federalism. Federalisation of the state was the only reform of 1968 that was implemented under the Soviet-imposed 'normalisation' that followed. It was therefore emptied of its democratic promise and was seen by most Czechs as a Soviet attempt to play the 'Slovak card' against the Prague Spring heresy. The Slovaks saw it as merely a revamped version of Prague-centralism. Havel appropriately spoke of 'federalised totalitarianism'. As a result the word 'federalism' came to represent something as discredited as 'socialism' by the communist experience.

Could federalism have been rescued by the return of democracy? There was indeed an opportunity to use the collapse of communism and the consensus it generated as a defining moment for a new federal constitution. For more than two years this constitutional issue dominated the political agenda, with over twenty Czecho-Slovak 'summits' held in the vain search for a viable compromise.[10] Indeed, the use and abuse of constitutional nationalism on both sides eventually helped to bring about the partition. The Czech position could be summed up as 'federalism from above': both nations first pledge their commitment to a common state and then proceed to devolve powers to their constituent republics. The Slovak position (as expressed by the Čarnogurský government, and later merely radicalised by Mečiar) could be described as 'confederalism from below': two distinct political entities adopt a 'contract' or a 'treaty' concerning matters such as defence or the currency.

Although Mečiar's party (unlike its ally, the Slovak National Party) never overtly advocated separatism, the substance of his political message came very close to it. In fact, as Michael Kraus pointed out, it was Čarnogurský's approach which had 'blurred the line between his party's goals and that of the Slovak separatists, for the only difference between the governing Christian Democratic movement, the separatist opposition and the confederalists led by Mečiar now appeared to be one of tempo'.[11] This became the dominant perception on the Czech side, once Mečiar (the Slovak National Council) opposed all the successive constitutional compromises worked out between Prague and Bratislava (in September 1991 he rejected such an agreement because Slovakia had 'an inalienable right to adopt its own constitution', and again in February 1992 as a launch to his electoral campaign). Mečiar's party electoral programme for the June 1992 election proved decisive for the fate of the federation. It clearly proposed: (1) a Slovak declaration of sovereignty (which was voted for by the Slovak parliament in July 1992); (2) a Slovak constitution (adopted in August 1992 precisely by those who had refused to compromise on a federal constitution); (3) the election of a Slovak President, a farewell to Havel as the symbol of the common state; (4) Slovakia was to become a 'subject of international law' with its own diplomatic representation, its own seat in the UN (and its 'own star on the European flag'). For all practical purposes this amounted to an independent state within a common state.

At their first meeting after their victory in the election, the new Czech prime minister, Václav Klaus, asked Vladimír Mečiar, his Slovak counterpart, whether he stood by all of his electoral programme (suggesting Mečiar would not have been the first in history to fail to fulfil all of his electoral promises). When Mečiar gave a positive answer, Klaus indicated he would not prevent its implementation. However, he also insisted on the necessity to accept the full consequences of this agenda. That is, a speedy and peaceful separation. But by the same token, Klaus had taken away from Mečiar one of the main ingredients of his use and abuse of constitutional nationalism.[12]

Mečiar's entire political strategy played on what could be described as the 'insatiability of the junior partner', and this could work only as long as the well tested assumption on which it rested – that is, the much stronger identification by Czechs with the common state. The problem of asymmetrical loyalties *vis-à-vis* the common state (in this respect, the Slovaks found themselves in a similar situation to that of the Vlams in Belgium or the French-speaking Quebecois in Canada) was, in principle, meant to be corrected by federalism. Yet federalism with only two components tends to be confrontational and in the long run unviable since any political conflict is seen as a zero-sum game: every 'gain' made by one side is seen as being made at the expense of the other. In this context the role of political elites acquired a particular importance. Both Mečiar's Slovak populist left led by and Klaus's Czech liberal right used this situation for purposes of polarisation, political mobilisation and (after the split) legitimisation. Both, albeit with very different styles, benefited from the shift of the political centre of gravity from the federal level to the constituent republics, maximising their own power and that of the emergent political elites.[13]

Could the federation have been saved by a 'European' solution? A 'Czecho-Slovak Maastricht'? This idea was initially floated by Slovak Prime Minister Čarnogurský and was then revived in the Autumn of 1992, when Mečiar hinted at the possibility of preserving a common currency and a common defence strategy. Klaus politely declined the offer: how could you have one currency and two divergent economic policies? How could you have one defence strategy and two foreign policies? To accept Mečiar's offer would, he argued, be to provide a Czech insurance policy for Slovak irresponsibility.

The days of the Czechoslovak federation are over and it will not be put back together again. Its failure, however, need not imply that there is a fundamental incompatibility between the two protagonists that will be problematic within the broader programme of European integration, which itself involves creating a single currency and a common security policy. In this respect, one should distinguish between what Francis Delpérée has called '*federalism by dissociation*' and '*federalism by association*'. Federalism by dissociation, as found in the Belgian, Canadian and Czechoslovak cases, increasingly leads the state to 'divest itself from a part of its activities and delegate a part of its responsibility, and thus of its political choices, to new entities',[14] so that eventually the federal state is left as just an empty shell. By contrast, '*federalism by association*' involves different subjects jointly establishing the terms and the degree of their co-operation. Moving from the former to the latter is what the Czech and Slovak states are trying to do.

The international dimension

The simultaneous break-up of Czechoslovakia, Yugoslavia and the Soviet Union has often been presented as part of a broader process of dissolution of federal states inherited from communism. The somewhat simplified thesis was: post-communist fragmentation in the East vs. enhanced integration in the West. The protagonists of the 'velvet divorce' did little to dispel it. Even Mečiar's predecessor, Slovak Prime Minister Čarnogurský, stated in July 1991 that 'the events in Yugoslavia and in the Soviet Union will find their echoes here, too. The Slovaks have a sense of national solidarity. But the Czechoslovak federation is not a priority for them, on the contrary'.[15]

The comparison with Yugoslavia was particularly tempting since both states were created simultaneously in 1918 as part of the Versailles system, both were dismantled by the Nazis during the Second World War, federalised under communism and dissolved in the first phase of the post-communist transition. There were also parallels between the dominant position of the Czechs and the Serbs in their respective states and between the positions of the Slovaks and

Croats, the 'junior partners' who identified closely with traditional Catholicism and nationalism, and who had experienced short-lived independent statehood under Nazi protection. There are also striking similarities between the populist nationalism of Mečiar and that of Tudjman, the founding fathers of their new states. And in many respects Mečiar's assessment of the European situation was shared by his Croat counterpart: the idea that the post-Cold War realignments in Europe opened a 'window of opportunity' which must (despite certain risks) be seized by the new nations in quest of their own statehoods, because such situations occur so rarely. Mečiar was fairly clear about that in September 1991:

> Considering the international situation and the efforts of many nations of Central and Eastern Europe to emancipate themselves, the time has come for the Slovak Republic to demand the right of self-determination and achieve sovereignty. Postponing this matter is a grave political mistake that will leave Slovakia outside an integrated Europe.[16]

However, the simultaneity and parallels between the break-up of Czechoslovakia and Yugoslavia should not obscure essential differences. Unlike Yugoslavia, those who pressed for independence in Czechoslovakia were neither the most economically prosperous, the most Western oriented nor the most advanced in their transition to democracy. Slovakia was no Slovenia and Havel was no Milosevic – a major factor in the peacefulness of the divorce. Two other elements also proved to be crucial. First, there was no dispute between Czechs and Slovaks over borders or ethnic minorities. The border is a thousand-year-old dividing line between the Crown of Saint Stephen and the Kingdom of Bohemia, rather than a communist fabrication. And there were almost 300,000 Slovaks living in the Czech Republic who chose to stay there and acquire Czech citizenship after the partition, rather than an 'ethnic minority' seeking separation and attachment to the 'mother-nation'. If anything, the Yugoslav break-up was not an 'inspiration' but a warning that cautioned even the separatists and engendered resignation in everyone else.

Since its inception in 1918, all the great turning points in Czechoslovak history coincided with, or were determined by, international influences. The foundation of the state in 1918 was associated with Western democracies. In 1938 its demise was the work of Hitler's *Drang nach Osten*, assisted by Britain and France. The 1948 communist takeover marked the country's insertion in the Soviet bloc and the beginning of the Cold War. The crushing of the 1968 Prague Spring marked the failure to overcome the partition of Europe. And even the velvet revolution of 1989 was part of a chain reaction that swept across the whole Soviet empire in East-Central Europe.

In contrast to this pattern, the peaceful Czecho-Slovak divorce in 1992 was carried out without significant external influence and without foreign policy differences playing a major role. There was a new regional and international environment that loosened the external constraint and allowed local actors a greater margin of manoeuvrability. Russia was retreating from Central Europe,

Germany was self-absorbed in the reunification process, and while Poland and Hungary hoped their Czech and Slovak neighbours would stay together, they were not in a position to do much about it. The European Union did point out that 'integration rather than disintegration'[17] should be the aim of future candidates but, on the eve of Maastricht, it too had other priorities on its mind. Some analysts called on the EU to make the prospect of integration with Europe explicitly conditional on the preservation of the federation, but these cries were largely ignored.[18] This time, external circumstances cannot be blamed for what Istvan Bibo called 'the misery of the small East European states'. It was instead the joint making and the prime responsibility of democratically elected Czech and Slovak political elites. In the Czechoslovak case, just as in former Yugoslavia, the federation now tends to be seen as a transition phase between multinational empires and homogenizing nation-states.

Czech and Slovak perceptions of and policies towards Europe

The prime motives of the Czech and Slovak Republics for European Union membership – not unlike those of other Central European pretenders – can be summed up as follows: the identification with European culture and values, the joining of the Western democratic club as a means to make the democratic transition irreversible, the EU as means of access to and sharing in Western modernity and prosperity, and finally, for reasons (though not always clearly formulated as such) of security and geopolitics.[19]

These motives also structure the major themes of Czech and Slovak attitudes and debates on the prospect of the enlargement of the European Union: (1) national and European identity; (2) democracy and sovereignty; (3) security concerns.

National and European identities

In their 1989 hope of 'returning to Europe', neither Czechs nor Slovaks had the slightest hint of apprehension that there could be a tension or a difficulty in articulating the relationship between their national and European identities. Their separation in 1993 brought to the surface a striking reversal, as two types of anti-EU discourse emerged, emphasising threats to national identity. One was a Czech version of 'Thatcherite', liberal anti-Europeanism. The other was a nationalist/populist Slovak version.

A dominant theme of debates amongst the Czech cultural milieu of the 1980s was the congruence between Czech and European identities, and this was widely reflected in the opinions of ordinary people. The writings of the philosopher Jan Patocka on this subject were an important reference for the dissident community. In line with T. G. Masaryk (at least on this point), he identified the Czech national project with European humanism and universal democratic values.[20] Václav Havel, too, has frequently written about the connection between the partition of the continent, the development of totalitarianism and the crisis of European culture. In 1983, Czech writer Milan Kundera published an essay entitled 'The kidnapped West: the tragedy of Central Europe', which became a catalyst for a wider Central European debate. Europe was not just a 'Common Market', it was a civilisation, a culture, a set of values that were most forcefully defended precisely where they were most directly threatened by Soviet/Eastern totalitarianism. The Czech predicament, and the Central European predicament more generally, was to be 'culturally part of the West, politically part of the East, and geographically in the centre'.[21] In other words: the boundaries of civilisations cannot be drawn by tanks. The idea of 'Europe' is stronger at its periphery than at the centre; indeed the periphery *was* the centre!

After the collapse of the Soviet empire there was a shift in the Czech discourse on Europe. At first the theme of the 'return' to (Western) Europe eclipsed the 1980s identification with Central Europe (as an alternative to the Soviet bloc). By the early 1990s joining 'the West' became increasingly substituted for talk of joining 'Europe'. In a shift from the cultural anti-politics of the dissident era to the resurgence of democratic politics, the debate on 'Europe' from then on concerned the relationship with the 'European Union'. In that new context the discourse of the 1980s on Central Europe as a cultural identity, as a 'kidnapped West', became quaintly antiquated. When the then Czech ambassador to Britain entitled his contribution to a volume on Europe: 'The Czech Republic is an integral part of European civilisation',[22] the assertion sounded dated and, in a way, self-denying. If the statement were obvious, there would be no need to assert it.

More interestingly, the prospects of European integration raised concerns not only about its desirability, but also about the place of small nations and respect for diversity. It was raised by several writers such as Ludvik Vaculik and Václav Havel. Milan Kundera summed up the question as follows: 'Is Europe capable or not of protecting itself against the rampant uniformisation of the planet and to create a common home where diversity would be respected as a supreme value? This bet will never be won or lost, since Europe *is* this wager'.[23]

In the 1990s, especially under the influence of Prime Minister Václav Klaus, the idea of 'Europe' became increasingly identified with the EU no longer perceived just as an economic organisation, but also as a process of integration, which could allegedly threaten the national identity of small nations. Klaus's favourite rhetorical metaphor is: 'Shall we let our identity and sovereignty dissolve in Europe like a lump of sugar in a cup of coffee?'[24] Since he left the government and became the speaker of the lower house of parliament at the end of 1997, government policy has become more favourable towards the EU, but his party's nationalistic and anti-Europe themes became more explicit. Describing himself as a Czech and a 'patriot', he criticised President Havel's pro-European stance. He denounced the dangers of European unification, referring to a book by John Laughland entitled *The Undemocratic Origins of the European Idea* that, according to Klaus, contains evidence that the prime goal of Nazi ideologists was a united Europe. 'If I were to quote them, you could attribute them to speeches by any of today's proponents of the EU. It makes fascinating reading', he has said.[25] The building of a nation-state and the defence of the national interest are presented as distinct from, or even in contradiction with, the European project. Klaus adds: 'One of the greatest tragedies of this continent is today's empty Europeanness on which a political organisation is built. I consider this to be a fatal mistake. .., but at the same time know that this process is already so advanced that I do not know what can be done about it'.[26] With the failure of their economic promises, Václav Klaus and his party have clearly moved from 'free-market' rhetoric to 'defence of the nation', shifting their emphasis from classical liberalism to identity politics and their source of inspiration from Milton Friedman to pre-war conservative nationalist leader Václav Kramar.

The Slovak variations on the national and/or European identity theme reveal certain differences from the Czechs. Czech intellectual discourse traditionally stressed the 'centrality' of the Czech position in Europe (from Jan Hus, the forerunner of the Protestant reformation, to the Prague Spring of 1968, the great impulses of Czech history were part of the mainstream of European history. Each of the famous 'eights' of twentieth-century Czech history were turning points for the continent: 1918, 1938, 1948 and 1968). The Slovak self-definition is, on the whole, more unassuming and ambiguous. A leading Slovak historian, Lubomir Luptak, formulated the thesis of Slovakia as *a frontier rather than a crossroad*:

> our territory almost regularly found itself at the edge of the influence of great empires, civilisations, 'worlds' (the Roman border, the Avars, Greater Moravia, the Mongol invasions, the Ottoman empire, the industrial civilisation with its heart in Western Europe, the socialist camp). The territory of Slovakia, however, has not been the target of the main drive, of the most important clashes, the waves of events pass usually to the North or to the South of us. We are on the border, not at a crossroads.[27]

The second contrast is that of cultural, religious and even political orientation. Luptak suggests that 'Slovakia is the most Western country of Eastern Europe, the Czech lands are the most Eastern country of Western Europe'.[28] The proposition has a historical and religious background going back to Cyril and Methodeus' apostolic mission (863–907) and the rivalry between Byzantine and Latin influences. In the 1990s, the leader of the Slovak Christian Democrats, Jan Čarnogurský, liked to stress the importance of the Eastern Churches for Slovak religious identity. If the Czech self-image identified with the idea of a 'kidnapped West', many Slovak Catholics felt closer to the Pope's vision of a united Christian Europe.

The third difference concerns the implications of the Czecho-Slovak separation. For the Czechs, the split was undoubtedly perceived as a failure. The anticipated acceleration of the Czech entry into 'Europe' was seen as compensation, a balm for a bruised national ego. For the Slovaks, the belated completion of a nation-state building process was meant to provide access to a 'Europeanness' which would no longer be mediated by Hungarians or Czechs. 'Visibility' and recognition is primarily what Slovaks wanted from Europe. And Mečiar has played skilfully on this ambivalence *vis-à-vis* Europe.

The EU, democracy and sovereignty

The issue of the compatibility of national and European identities in the process of EU enlargement could always be answered by stating the obvious: the EU is not Europe. A similar cop-out, however, is not very plausible on the question of democracy and the rule of law. The EU norm setting in this respect is more difficult to dismiss by would-be candidates, and this is also where the aims of the democratic transition and European integration seem most clearly to overlap.[29]

Democracy is the first *acquis communautaire*. It is naturally the first condition for membership, as established in June 1993 by the Copenhagen summit of the EU. The 'Copenhagen criteria' are: (1) democracy and human rights; (2) economic readiness for the single market; and (3) the capacity to implement EU legislation. The degree to which the candidates met these conditions was assessed by the EU Commission in the '*avis*' ('opinions') published as part of Agenda 2000 in July 1997. The Czech Republic was among the five countries recommended for opening negotiations for accession (along with two of Slovakia's other neighbours, namely Poland and Hungary), while Slovakia was the only country explicitly excluded on political grounds. It failed to meet basic democratic criteria. A major foreign policy setback for Slovakia was essentially a domestic one:

> A democracy cannot be considered stable [said the Commission statement on Slovakia] if respective rights and obligations of institutions such as the presidency, the constitutional court, or the central referendum commission can be put into question by the government itself and if the legitimate role of the opposition in parliamentary committees is not accepted.[30]

Therefore, the meeting of democratic criteria was the clearest contrast between the Czech Republic and Slovakia in this respect. The Czech Republic is in a phase of democratic consolidation, to the extent that basic freedoms are guaranteed, that none of its political actors question the binding nature of the constitutional framework and what is at stake in elections is the future government not the nature of the political regime. In Slovakia, the underlying leitmotif of political life until autumn 1998, was precisely the debate over constitutional rules. And, in elections in both 1994 and 1998, it was the nature of the Slovak regime (not just the political colour of the government) that was at stake.

The two main problems emphasised in the European Union's assessment of democracy in Slovakia were the rule of law and the treatment of minorities. The violation of the constitutional order by the Mečiar government was a major case in point, and particularly the fact that Slovakia passed the highest proportion of laws in the region that did not conform to the constitution. More generally, the instability of the political system, the regular calls by Mečiar for the resignation of the president and the fact that the opposition was not treated as a legitimate political actor (and was thus barred from adequate representation, even in parliamentary committees), distinguished Slovakia not just from the Czech Republic but from the rest of Central Europe.

A second point of comparison was provided by the EU's concern about citizenship and minority language laws. In the Czech Republic, this referred to 'the Roma question'; in Slovakia it implicated mainly the situation of the Hungarian minority. The two are not quite comparable, if only because the Roma issue (unlike that of the Hungarian minority) does not affect relations with neighbouring states. The Czech citizenship law has been criticised by the EU for not being inclusive enough, and it was therefore amended in 1996 and 1997 in order to prevent a Roma from being denied citizenship on the grounds of a criminal record or Slovak origins. The majority of the Roma in the Czech Republic came from Slovakia either in the aftermath of the Second World War, when they were encouraged to settle in the Sudetenland (from where the German population had been expelled), or more recently, at the time of the Czecho-Slovak split when many assumed they would be better off on the Czech side of the divide.

However, the main difference between the situation of the Roma in the Czech lands and in Slovakia concerns neither their numbers,[31] nor the xenophobic attitudes of some sections of the population. Rather, it lies in the fact that the latter have been forcefully condemned by the Czech president and the government, and that a special commission was established in early 1998 to deal with the problem. By contrast, the then Slovak prime minister (Mečiar) openly encouraged xenophobes with statements such as: 'If we don't deal with them, they will deal with us'.[32] Quite apart from its internal importance, it remains notable that for both the Czech Republic and Slovakia, the Roma issue became a point of contention with certain EU members, particularly Britain and Finland. Faced with Roma immigration from both countries, these members threatened to impose previously abolished visa obligations on the Czech Republic and Slovakia.[33] This brought home the message about the EU's sensitivity to Central European xenophobia.[34] However, in July 2001, under pressure from London, the British and Czech governments made an agreement allowing British imigration officers to check passengers for London (presented as a British attempt to reduce the number of potential asylum seekers and the only alternative to the re-introduction of visas). It was widely seen by Czech public opinion as an illustration of EU double standards, a discriminatory measure with racial overtones imposed on Prague by an EU member state.[35] It remains to be seen if such measures are helpful in attempting to overcome xenophobia, or whether they might actually make things worse by turning part of the population against the Roma (and against the EU).

For both the Czech and Slovak societies, the Roma issue is as revealing of a social problem as it is an indicator of xenophobia. However, in terms of its relevance to issues of identity, democracy and relations with a neighbouring state, it cannot be compared with the importance of the question of the Hungarian minority in Slovakia. In a country of 5.5 million the confrontational attitude adopted by the Mečiar government *vis-à-vis* the 650,000-strong Hungarian minority was seen by Budapest and the EU as a major weakness in Slovakia's democratic credentials. The passing of a language law in 1996 increased the tensions, with Slovakia ignoring several recommendations of the EU and of the constitutional court to amend the legislation. And this only seemed to confirm that the minority issue was an essential part of Mečiar's strategy of nationalist mobilisation. His statement, in the face of the Hungarian prime minister, that if the Hungarians in Slovakia were dissatisfied they were free to go (to Hungary), was a clear signal to the Hungarian minority that no compromise would be possible with that government.[36] What distinguished Mečiar from Tudjman or Milosevic was not his objection to 'ethnic cleansing' but the context (a war) and the political 'feasibility' (including the degree of acceptance by the rest of Slovak society).

Independently of these main differences concerning the degree of consolidation of democracy, the rule of law and the question of national minorities, parallels can be drawn between Klaus's and Mečiar's stances on sovereignty, as well as between the way the Czech and the Slovak oppositions played the European card. Both contributed in the late 1990s to turning the 'European question' into one of domestic politics.

In Slovakia, the opposition and representatives of the Hungarian minority increasingly used EU criticisms of Mečiar's policies in an attempt to internationalise the democracy issue. Conversely, Mečiar denounced the opposition as damaging Slovakia's image abroad and serving foreign interests. Mečiar's government dismissed the demarches of the EU concerning the violations of democracy (one a year) and resolutions of the European Parliament directly referring to the possibility of exclusion from the enlargement process as misinformed. And it likened them to outside interference in the past (that is, 'about us without us' in 1938, 1939 or 1968).[37] The comparison between the EU's democracy warnings and Hitler's imperialism was revealing of two things: the assumed illegitimacy of such interference in the affairs of a sovereign state, and the siege mentality of those who proclaimed themselves the upholders of sovereignty as a means of insulating their authoritarian power.

Václav Klaus's defence of sovereignty had a different base. He has never missed an occasion to stress how much he owed to Mrs Thatcher in his views on politics in general and on Europe in particular. There he found a convergence between the critique of the Brussels Commission and an ardent defence of national sovereignty. 'We have not escaped from the controls of Moscow's bureaucracy only to replace it by a more civilised version from Brussels' was the substance of his message while he was prime minister. When discussing the IGC institutional reform proposals in 1996, Klaus clearly stated his opposition to the introduction of qualified majority voting since it would amount to 'a loss of national sovereignty'.[38]

This defence of the sovereignty of a nation-state under the double threat of supra-national Europe and regionalism has become an even more prominent part of the ODS 'ideological' and political platform since it left the government in 1998. At the May 1999 ODS ideological conference the Shadow Minister of Defence, Petr Necas, emphasised that:

> we do not want a Europe of regions, we do not want a European super-state without nation-states, we do not want a supranational structure built from above by a distant federal bureaucracy. The nation-state is and will remain for us a basic building block of Europe. We want a Europe of nation-states, a Europe of fatherlands.[39]

In a similar vein the ODS shadow foreign minister, Jan Zahradil, released in April 2001 a *Manifesto of Czech Eurorealism.* Interestingly, overtly Eurosceptic or even europhobic positions tend, in the Czech Republic, to be presented as 'eurorealist'. The manifesto clearly states the defence of the sovereignty of the nation-state and of national interests as the basis of its approach to the EU. Rejecting any 'federalist' developments in the EU, including the extention of the powers of the Commission, of qualified majority voting or of EMU which, as the authors (correctly) guess, is likely to lead to the harmonisation of economic, fiscal or social policies.[40] The manifesto rejects anything but a liberal approach to Europe. That rejection includes not just fascist or marxist attempts at forced unification but also social-democratic and christian-democratic approaches. The authors seem to forget that half a century of European integration was carried out primarily by the combined efforts of Christian and Social democrats and that it has produced a largely liberal order.

The polarisation of the European debate on the issue of sovereignty became all the more explicit as the two most articulate protagonists (Havel and Klaus) became increasingly outspoken. In a speech before a joint session of the French Parliament in March 1999, Václav Havel called for the 'parliamentarisation and a *federalisation*' of an enlarged European Union, and the drafting of a *European Constitution* 'not very long, intelligible to all, provided with a preamble describing the meaning and the idea of the Union before defining its institutions, their mutual relations and their competencies'.[41] Havel also advocated a bicameral system for the European Parliament, 'like in classical federations'. Havel's 'federalist paper' was the first significant statement by a leader of a candidate country actually reflecting upon the purpose of, and making concrete suggestions for, the future constitution of an enlarged Union. It preceded German Foreign Minister Joschka Fischer's call in May 1999 for a European constitution and clearly fits in the debate launched within the EU's convention.

Havel's call for a European constitution provoked, however, a convergent rebuff at home from the parliamentary speaker, V. Klaus ('I am categorically opposed to the United States of Europe'), but also from then prime minister Milos Zeman. Klaus's defence of sovereignty became his favorite leitmotif: 'Europe now experiences a moment of fundamental challenging of the nation-states, i.e. their sovereignty', he argued, adding that the way the EU handled Austria (after Haider's party joined the government), the intervention in Yugoslavia the year before and the treatment of Central and East European candidates by the EU are all 'from the same barrel', three illustrations of the EU syphoning off the sovereignty of the nation-states.[42]

When in opposition, the Social-Democrats had professed support for the EU as a way of opposing Klaus's eurosceptic posture. Once in government (with Klaus's support), their position became balanced by concerns over excessive interference by the EU which was resented less on ideological grounds than as a challenge to some of the government's practices and ability to carry out necessary reforms. This sometimes showed in over-reactions to the EU Commission's annual reports, but the legitimacy of the process was not questioned. The most overtly pro-European figures among the social democrats were Jan Kavan Foreign minister (1998–2002) and the head of the parliamentary committee on European affairs Zaoralek who, in July 2002, became the Speaker of the Czech National Assembly. Kavan came closest to giving a clear rebuff to the sovreignists by arguing that 'Today we are subjected to the EU constraint, we are subjected to most of the duties, but have no rights to influence the decisions. It is easier to accept EU decisions concerning us if there is a shared responsibility'.[43]

NATO's intervention in Kosovo led President Havel to broaden his arguments about the re-definition of sovereignty within the context of European integration and of an international community built around the notions of human rights and an international civil society at the expense of traditionally defined sovereignty of nation-states.[44] It also revealed a 'sovereignist' component in Czech politics, where both main parties (the ODS and the Social Democrats) converged in a reluctant posture towards Western intervention in the 'internal affairs' of a sovereign state.[45] In contrast to the Czech Republic's reticence, merely a week after it had become a member of NATO in March 1999, the Dzurinda government in Slovakia was more forthcoming in its support for an intervention which, though unpopular at home, was seen as a long-term investment in the country's bid to join Western institutions. This is also where the issue of sovereignty overlaps with that of security.

Security: between Europe and the transatlantic dimension

The third dimension of the contrasting Czech and Slovak attitudes towards the European Union concerns the issue of security. In the immediate aftermath of the collapse of Soviet hegemony in 1989, there was a brief period when President Havel and the then Czechoslovak foreign minister, Jiri Dienstbier, envisaged a Europe re-united through a parallel withering away of the two Cold War military pacts with the CSCE as a possible base for a new European security architecture. By the time the last Russian troops had left the country in 1991, the Atlantic Alliance was clearly identified with democratic security in Central Europe. With the Czecho-Slovak split, two quite different approaches to the EU and security appeared. The Czech policy considered joining NATO as a priority over joining the EU. The priorities of Slovak policy were the other way around.

After 1992, Czech foreign policy tried to make a virtue out of necessity and claimed that the separation changed the geoplitical situation of the new state since it no longer had borders with the former Soviet Union (Zielenec) and thus had an allegedly better chance of joining Western institutions, particularly NATO. That orientation prevailed during most of the 1990s, until the country's actual inclusion in the Alliance in March 1999. The Prague authorities, on the whole, showed little sympathy with those West Europeans who had problems with the primacy of American power in the post-Cold War era and pressed for a European Defence Identity (EDI: either within WEU or as part of a European pillar of NATO). In the debate about the prospects of a Common Foreign and Security Policy (CFSP) the Czechs (much like the Poles and Hungarians) have been rather 'conservative'. This was partly because, as the war in Bosnia had shown, there was not yet much to speak of in terms of a European CFSP. And it was also partly because, in the discussions concerning NATO's new strategic concept, the Czech position remained sceptical about the 'new NATO' with EDI and preferred the 'old NATO' whose purpose was 'to keep the Russians out, the Americans in and the Germans down'.

Seen from Prague, the United States' primacy remained necessary to protect Europe against its own demons. After the First World War, the United States had left Europe with disastrous consequences for the continent. After the Second World War it stayed, thus helping to preserve peace and democracy for at least the Western half of Europe. The attraction of NATO for the Czechs (as for the Poles or the Hungarians) was related precisely to the fact that it was a US-led institution. In the words of Otto Pick, then Director of the Czech Institute of International Affairs (and deputy Foreign Minister between 1998 and 2002):

> It is the only organisation that links the United States with Europe. The EU is important to the Czechs, but in the EU the most influential country is Germany. In NATO, it is the United States. So to many people, NATO seems to be a political counterbalance to membership of the EU which many people see as being dominated by Germany.[46]

Hence the suggestion of turning the Czech Republic into a special ally of the United States.[47] Contributing to peace-keeping missions in Bosnia or Kosovo provided a convenient compromise between a European effort carried out under American leadership. However, the idea that new Central European NATO members and candidates for EU membership are primarily seeking to enhance the US role in Europe (as advocated, particularly for Poland, by Z. Brzezinski) has not always contributed to the strengthening of their 'European' credentials.

The problem with Slovakia's 'European' credentials in this respect was quite different. Although the Mečiar government never explicitly rejected the goal of joining the EU and NATO between 1994 and 1998, it demonstrated itself to be unwilling, in practice, to meet the basic prerequisites at the intersection of domestic and foreign policy. Three factors played a part in the process: the anti-Western stance of the HDZ coalition partners, the Russian option, and the sabotage of the referendum on NATO for domestic political reasons.

Mečiar had maintained European integration at least as part of a declaratory government policy. But he also toyed with the idea of a Slovakia open to its Eastern neighbours – a bridge between East and West. His coalition partners, the ultra-nationalist Slovak National Party and a small crypto-communist Workers' Party were both, for different reasons (nationalism in one case, antipathy to capitalism in the other) hostile to a clearly Western orientation for Slovakia.

As Western criticism of the domestic political conditions became explicit in the mid-1990s, Slovakia looked increasingly to Russia as a partner in both economic and security affairs. The Slovak military-industrial complex had suffered from the Prague-inspired ban on arms sales to former clients from the Warsaw Pact days (Syria, Iraq, Libya, etc.). New ties with Moscow led eventually to the signing in Bratislava of a five-year agreement on military-technical co-operation in April 1997.[48] The Soviet Ambassador to Bratislava, S. Zotov, clearly indicated that this co-operation 'would become problematic in case of Slovakia's entry in NATO'.[49] The Slovak–Russian rapprochement became explicit when, in Bratislava, Prime Minister Chernomyrdin, promised support for Slovakia's neutrality (in answer to Slovak concerns about Russian guarantees for Slovak neutrality).[50] The Chair of the Russian Duma visiting Bratislava went as far as suggesting to his counterpart that Slovakia should join the Confederation of Independent States. However, he admitted, the problem was that 'Slovakia does not have, for the time being, common borders with us'.[51] For the time being? In other words, if the Ukrainian situation evolved in a direction favourable to Russia, Slovak 'neutrality' could acquire a new meaning.[52]

Mečiar´s confrontational approach to domestic politics as well as his efforts to keep certain foreign policy options open fitted his reservations on the European integration project. After comparing the EU criticism of Slovak democracy to war-time German hegemony, the decision to hold a referendum in May 1997 on the country's possible accession to NATO was problematic on two grounds: to the general question on membership another two, rather loaded ones, were added concerning the stationing of foreign troops and of nuclear weapons in Slovakia. Most importantly, the referendum was also to include a domestic constitutional question concerning the direct election of the president. Eventually, amidst great confusion as to whether this was a domestic- or foreign-policy referendum, less than 10 per cent of voters turned out. The exercise was thus considered null and void. Two months later, in July 1997, Slovakia was ruled out of the first wave of enlargement by NATO and the EU on grounds of democratic conditionality. But the point of the matter was rather Slovakia's then deliberate self-exclusion from the double enlargement process. It is also a measure of the domestic and foreign policy changes introduced by the Dzurinda government since 1998 to note that in May 2001 Bratislava was able to host a meeting of ten prime ministers of East-Central European countries in a common bid to join NATO. The main speaker at the meeting and the most forceful advocate of the second wave of NATO enlargement, particularly to Slovakia, was no other than Czech president Václav Havel.

Returning to Europe via Central Europe?

A balance sheet drawn five years after the Czecho-Slovak separation would have given a clear, yet somewhat deceptive, picture: two distinct itineraries, two modes of transition (a consolidated democracy in the Czech case, an 'illiberal' democracy in Slovakia) leading to contrasting prospects of European integration with the Czechs 'in' the first wave of enlargement of both the EU and NATO and the Slovaks in both cases 'out'.

The contrast, however, was too neat to be true and the almost simultaneous demise of Klaus in Prague and of Mečiar in Bratislava opened a new phase in the two countries European policy which invites somewhat different scenarios for the future. Both leaders left the centre stage with poor economic situations and empty state coffers, and both left to their successors the task of picking up the pieces while coping with the legacy of years of official anti-European rhetoric. Both countries found themselves somewhat at a loss: the Czechs after the exhaustion of Klaus's free market utopia and the Slovaks after the exhaustion of Mečiar's nationalist illusion.

The end of Czech 'exceptionalism' and of the Slovak exception

A largely self-serving argument of the Czech political elite in the aftermath of the split with Slovakia, was based on the notion of Czech exceptionalism that implied a separate EU and NATO integration strategy from its Central European neighbours. In the words of a Czech observer, this prevailing argument was based on the following premise: 'the prospect that a post-communist country could join the EU in the foreseeable future was so dim that only a solo effort, rather than a joint, co-ordinated campaign with Budapest and Warsaw, would give any chance of "ducking under the gates"'.[53]

There were indeed specific features of the transition in the Czech lands. For the first time in its history, the country became a homogeneous nation-state. The transition during most of the 1990s was carried out by right-wing liberals while, elsewhere, ex-communist left-wing parties were already returning to the fore. No less importantly, Czech Social Democrats (the main opposition force till 1998) were not the heirs of the old communist party. After the separation from Slovakia, the Czech Republic no longer had a border with the former Soviet Union and instead shared its longest borders with two EU members – Germany and Austria. All of these specific features were meant to substantiate a would-be 'doctrine' of Czech exceptionalism.

This, of course, was making virtue out of necessity and provided a soothing rhetoric to cover the sense of loss. Never has a state been born in a more prosaic atmosphere. In contrast to Masaryk's view of the foundation of Czechoslovakia in 1918 as part of a universal democratic movement, the Czech Republic was born in 1993 out of pragmatic reasons or even by default ('a Czech state founded by the Slovaks', Havel quipped ironically). It tried to compensate for the feeling of failure by cultivating a self-satisfied image of a small, but stable and prosperous, country with little interest in its neighbours. At the beginning of the century the Czechs had made an (admittedly modest) contribution to the dismantling of Austria. At the end of the century they seemed to aspire to nothing more than becoming another Austria.

Not only did this parochial vision of the newly created state not help to shape a 'European' ambition, it combined with an ideologically motivated bout of premature Euroscepticism which managed to alienate not only neighbours but also potential allies within the EU. Klaus's approach could be described as Marxism of the Groucho tendency ('I wouldn't join a club that would have me as a member!'). His clash at the 1996 World Economic Forum in Davos with the European Commissioner in charge of enlargement as to whether it was the candidates or the EU who had to do more reforming, prompted Hans van den Broek to conclude the exchange by reminding the Czech prime minister that 'it is not the EU who wants to join the Czech Republic but the other way around'.

The Czech exceptionalism of the Klaus era faltered on two grounds:[54] it misread the geopolitical implications of enlargement (strategically, it is Poland that matters most to West Europeans), and it did not have the economic results to match its rhetoric. Voucher-privatisation turned out to be a brilliant political move but produced mediocre economic results: the vouchers were bought-up by investment funds backed by five still state-controlled banks which postponed the restructuring and modernisation of Czech industry. While Poland has had an average growth rate of between 5 and 7 per cent between 1993 and 2000, Klaus presided over a slow decline that had reached zero growth by the time he left power. The combination of liberal rhetoric and social-democratic practice left the Czech Republic with the lowest rates of unemployment in Europe (only matched by Liechtenstein and Luxembourg), brought some dividends in domestic politics, but left the country ill-prepared for the challenges of the European single market and lagging behind other Central European candidates.[55]

From the point of view of future European integration, a related weakness of the Czech transition during most of the 1990s was the underestimation of the rule of law and of a proper legal and institutional framework for the emerging market economy. This eventually backfired in terms of both irregular practices and disaffection by investors, and it was also singled out by the European Union's Agenda 2000 (as well as successive progress reports between 1998 and 2000) as a major weakness in the Czech Republic's preparation for joining the EU. Klaus's emphasis on economic liberalism (the primacy of a rapid conversion to the market) at the expense of political liberalism (the rule of law, decentralisation and civil society) turned out to be counter-productive, especially from the point of view of European integration.

Czech 'exceptionalism' was based on an economic strategy that did not succeed. The Slovak exception was essentially political. Between 1993 and 1998 Slovakia departed from the Central European pattern of democratic consolidation towards a nationalist brand of authoritarianism which thrived on an adversarial concept of politics focussing on alleged external enemies (Czech,

Hungarian) or internal ones (the opposition). Slovakia's 'regression' as, Stefan Hrib has suggested, was related to the fact that – unlike its Central European neighbours – it placed nation-state building at the 'pinnacle of national life', subordinating economic and geopolitical advantages to that goal.[56] This Slovak exception was eventually sanctioned by the EU 1997 enlargement decision to leave Slovakia out of the Central European enlargement process.

Both Czech 'exceptionalism' and the 'Slovak exception' came to a close with the simultaneous departure from the government of the two main protagonists of the Czecho-Slovak divorce and the need to come to terms with the failure of the respective visions and priorities that they had represented. The change in leadership was also a necessary pre-requisite for envisaging a re-launch of Central European co-operation, and for making up for the 'European deficits' (of an admittedly different kind) left behind by Klaus and Mečiar.

CZECHS AND GERMANS

One of the ironical legacies of the Czecho-Slovak separation is that, in its aftermath, both protagonists rediscovered that they were not really each others'constitutive other, central to the definition of their identity and their European prospects. For the Czechs it is not the relationship with Slovakia, but with Germany. that matters in this respect. For the Slovaks it is the relations with the Hungarians. In other words, the end of Czechoslovakia meant the return of the German question for the Czechs and the return of the Hungarian question for the Slovaks. In the nineteenth century, the leading political figure and historian, Frantisek Palacky, wrote that the 'meaning of Czech history' was to be found in its 'contact and conflict' with the Germans. What then is supposed to be 'the meaning' of Czech history now that its constitutive 'other' is gone? Similarly, since the nineteenth century, 'Slovaks have built their history, national consciousness and national identity not only out of the Hungarian tradition but also in opposition to that tradition'.[57] Much the same could be said of the Czech–German relationship. There is, of course, a difference between the two relationships in that the German question is now an external problem for the Czechs while the Hungarian issue remains also an internal one for Slovakia. The Czech Republic has become a homogeneous nation-state: no more Germans, no more Jews and now freshly separated from the Slovaks. Alone at last!

However, the German question has gradualy returned to the fore, albeit in a new, European context. The Czech political elite seemed to be in two minds in the 1990s: at first the dominant view saw Germany as the main vector of Central Europe's integration into the European Union and it seemed plausible to play the 'German card' to enhance Czech EU prospects. The argument was reinforced by the assumption that EU membership was also the best way to balance German influence in Central Europe: the EU as a functional equivalent of the Hapsburg empire.

Yet, to the extent that integration into the EU became in some respects identified, in the eyes of a part of public opinion, with the spread of German influence ('in Europe's name', to use the title of a study of German Ostpolitik[58]) the enlargement prospects started to provoke certain apprehensions. In the early 1990s such apprehensions were politically confined to the communists and the extreme right's anti-German rhetoric. They have since become part of the mainstream, in direct relation to the uses and abuses of the Sudeten German question in the European accession process. This is apparent according to a March 2002 CVVM poll indicating that only a quarter of Czechs consider relations to be good with Austria and only half with Germany (a drop of 35 per cent for the former and of 21 per cent for the latter in two years). Simultaneously, there was an erosion of support for EU enlargement and, perhaps more importantly, a rise in the number of opponents to EU entry (about a third of the population).

Joining the EU was meant to defuse concerns about the imbalance in the Czech–German relationship (Czecho-Slovakia is separated, Germany is reunited); it gradually became a means to highlight it. The endorsement by the Bavarian CSU and later by the CDU as well in their joint electoral platform of calls by the Sudentendeutsche Landsmanschaft for the Czech authorities to satisfy their demands for a 'right to a homeland' and the abolition of the so-called 'Beneš decrees' of 1945 as an implicit condition for joining the EU, did not help to defuse Czech apprehensions. This linkage became first apparent when an April 1999 resolution of the European Parliament, initiated by German CSU MEPs (namely B. Poselt, chairman of the Sudetendeutsche Landsmannschaft), adopted the argument.[59] The European Parliament's resolution has promptly been used used as a legitimising precedent by the political forces that endorsed demands of the Sudeten German expellees.[60] In May 1999 the Austrian Parliament adopted a resolution about the incompatibility of the Beneš decrees with European law. In June 2000 the CSU and the CDU jointly presented to the Bundestag (without success) a similar resolution refering to the one adopted by the European Parliament. The choice of Edmund Stoiber, the Bavarian leader, as the German CDU/CSU opposition's candidate for the post of chancellor in the 2002 general elections, only reinforced Czech concerns that conservative and populist forces in Germany (and Austria) may be tempted to instrumentalise the process of the Eastern enlargement of the EU for settling bilateral scores of the past.[61]

The political developments in Bavaria and Austria have been described as part of 'Alpine populism'[62] (a trend also including Christoph Blocher's movement in German-speaking Switzerland or Umberto Bossi's Norhern League in Italy) which combines economic prosperity, regionalism, harsh criticism of 'Brussels' buraucracy', hostility to imigration and, last but not least, to EU enlargement to poorer Eastern neighbours. The least enthusiastic neighbour concerning the enlargement of the EU to include the Czech Republic and Slovakia is Austria. Since the coming to power in 1999 of a Schüssel–Haider coalition the reluctance has been formulated in terms of conditionality for EU accession on two main issues: the safety of nuclear plants and the abrogation of the Beneš decrees of 1945. Austria demanded first the closure of nuclear plant in Slovakia (Mochovce) and later focussed on the Czech Republic (Temelin).[63] Despite an agreement between the Czech Republic and Austria brokered in November 2001 by the EU (recognising the neighbouring country's 'specific interst in a high level of security', but also the 'sovereign right to chose its energy policy' for each country),[64] Haider's party, a member of the government coalition, has launched a petition explicitly linking linking the abandoning of Temelin and the blocking by Austria of EU entry for the Czech Republic.[65] Where all the parties seem to converge is in expressing the fear that the enlargement would mean the arrival of cheap labour from the neighbouring countries.[66] An EU-wide opinion poll by Eurostat revealed that only 6 per cent of Austrians and 3 per cent of Germans were in favour of the free movement of the labour force from the Eastern neighbour candidate countries.[67] These are not just the voters of Haider, but also those of Schröder. In the two neighbouring EU countries on whose support Czechs and Slovaks relied in their European strategy, voters are proving to be increasingly cool towards the Eastern enlargement of the Union. In Germany it is 35 per cent for enlargement and 42 per cent against while in Austria it is one-third for and half of the population against enlargement.[68]

It is in such context that the German chancellor in February 2001 asked for a seven-year transition period on the free circulation of labour from the new members after their accession to the EU. The EU Commission obliged within two months of Schroeder's speech much to the dismay of Central European candidates. The issue of the free movement within the EU is for the candidate countries a highly symbolic one: that was, with the freedom of speech, the first achievement connected with the 1989 'velvet revolutions'. The failure of the Czech negotiators to improve on what the German chancellor had asked for was seen by Czech opinion as a major setback and certainly gave amunition to critics who spoke about 'second class membership' and the need to defend national interests more vigorously. To sum up: there are three Germany-related issues (free movement of labour, the safety of nuclear plans and the abrogation of the Beneš decrees of 1945) which have been 'Europeanised' through the European Parliament, thus reinforcing the argument of oponents of the EU in the Czech Republic who suggest that the abandoning of national sovereignty required by EU accession is a means to satisfy peacefully the demands of a powerful neighbour. It was precisely to defuse such arguments that EU Commissionner G. Verheugen stated clearly in Prague in April 2002 that the EU will not open the issue of the Beneš decrees as part of the enlargement process.

To be sure, the Czech–German Declaration of February 1977, signed by the prime ministers of both countries, approved by both governments and both parliaments, contributed greatly to defusing those fears by explicitly renouncing any legal claims concerning the past and clearly pointing to European integration as the common future. The simultaneous coming to power in 1998 of Social Democrats in Prague and Berlin seemed (for a while) to remove the Sudeten German issue from the top of the Czech–German agenda and pointed rather to the potential 'Europeanising' role of Western social democracy (then a majority among the governments in the EU) *vis-à-vis* their Central European partners.

However, as the accession of the Czech Republic into the EU approaches, Prague has discovered that the attempts at 'Europeanisation' of its relations with Germany is a double-edged sword: it can help balance an asymetrical relationship and help overcome the traumas and apprehensions inherited from the past. But it can also, as more recent developments have shown, revive the apprehension that the 'European card' can be used by a powerful member-state *vis-à-vis* its Eastern neighbour which happens to be a candidate for EU membership.

SLOVAKS AND HUNGARIANS

A parallel, albeit different argument can be made concerning Slovakia's relations with Hungary, since it is is central both to the question of identity and also to the prospect of entry into the EU. Hungary, in clear contrast with its pre-war revisionist policies (which led it to eventually become Hitler's last ally), adopted a European policy for relations with neighbouring countries with significant Hungarian minorities. 'In Europe's name', Hungary seeks both the devaluation of borders, and guarantees of minority rights, in line with provisions advocated by the Council of Europe. And it is significant that, on the opening day of the 1995 European Stability Pact conference in Paris, Hungary and Slovakia signed a bilateral treaty providing for Hungarian recognition of the intangibility of their borders and Slovakia's commitment to implement the cultural and linguistic rights of its Hungarian minority.

Although Prime Minister Mečiar signed the treaty, his government did little to implement its minority provisions. For domestic purposes, he polarised relations with the Hungarian minority and with Budapest. The culminating point of that strategy of tension came in August 1997 when Mečiar told the Hungarian Prime Minister Gyula Horn (and later repeated his comment during a public meeting with his supporters in Bratislava) that the dissatisfaction of Hungarians from Slovakia could be solved by their transfer to Hungary.[69] Horn later expressed shock at the proposal and at the decision to make it public. The leader of the Slovak minority in Slovakia, Béla Bugar, called it an attempt to introduce a policy of 'ethnic cleansing'.

After September 1998, the new democratic government coalition led by Mikulas Dzurinda promptly departed from the previous confrontational policies with the Hungarian minority as with the Budapest government in favour of an inclusive policy seen as an essential part of Slovakia's European strategy. The inclusion in the government of representatives of the Hungarian minority parties (Béla Bugár), the revision of the language law and the solution of the Gabcikovo–Nagymaros dam issue through European and international court arbitration, were all meant as a new departure, internally, in the relations with Hungary, and as part of Slovakia's bid to re-join the Central European group for EU enlargement. This Central European dimension became increasingly important for Bratislava's bilateral relations with Budapest and Prague and its EU accession strategy.

Central European co-operation had been among the first casualties of the Czecho-Slovak split. Both Klaus's theory of Czech exceptionalism and the

Slovak exception under Mečiar meant that political co-operation among the Visegrád group was put on ice. The Czechs thought that regional co-operation was a substitute for the 'real' goal of 'going West'. Slovakia, the only country with borders with each of the other three, could hardly reconcile the Visegrád group co-operation with its difficult relations with Prague and Budapest. All this changed since 1998 with the departure from office of Klaus and Mečiar, and the ensuing convergent Czech and Slovak policies towards Visegrád and EU/NATO enlargements.

The Czechs were made to understand that they had better have good co-operation with Poland, the key strategic partner for the Alliance, if they wanted to join NATO. They also discovered that, given their mediocre economic performance (zero growth at the time) and their lagging behind in terms of preparation for EU accession (see the EU's critical reports of November 1998 and October 1999), they could actually benefit from the positive Central European, rather than merely Czech, image as the 'success story' of the transition. The accession negotiation process itself eventually brought Prague to increasingly co-ordinate its strategy with other Central European candidates. And the more advanced the negotiations with the EU, the more obvious it has become to the Czechs that it was also in their interest to have Slovakia included in the first wave of Central European enlargement. This, as Foreign Minister Jan Kavan pointed out, concerns more specifically the issues of borders ('It is difficult, given our common history, to imagine a standard Schengen border between the Czech Republic and Slovakia') and the customs union with Slovakia (which the Czechs wish to keep even in case of a separate accession).[70] However, under pressure from an EU increasingly concerned about illegal immigration, the Czech side attempted in the Autumn of 2001 to introduce a stricter border control with Slovakia (including a residence permit requirement after three months). This pressure for 'de-coupling' was firmly resisted from the Slovak side which rejected any talk of a visa regime between the two neighbours.[71] The controversy revealed the conflicting pressures the enlargement process imposes: dividing with one hand what it unites with the other.

Since 1998 the Czecho-Slovak rapprochement in their EU accession strategy has been closely connected with the 'rebirth' of Visegrád Four co-operation, a development of particular importance to Slovakia's new European policy. Just as Mečiar's prime interest was power rather than a European agenda, the government of Mikulas Dzurinda has established accession into the EU (and NATO) as its priority and a means to hold a fragile coalition together. After four years in office the balance sheet of that coalition is largely positive in the eyes of the EU, though not quite so in the eyes of Slovak public opinion. The glass half empty points to problematic issues such as industrial restructuring, nuclear safety, the fight against corruption, judicial reform and the management of EU funds. The glass half full reveals that the country has unquestionably made considerable efforts in establishing the rule of law. Though the efficiency and the impartiality of the judiciary is often questioned in the media, nobody challenges the rules of the game, the constitutional and institutional framework, which is a considerable departure from the Mečiar period. Secondly, the economic performance and market reforms have made considerable progress.[72] Thirdly, the inclusion of the Hungarian minority representatives in the government coalition and the much improved relations with Budapest mark a sharp departure with the previous period. Finaly, the main achievement concerns undoubtedly Slovakia's EU policy. The country opened its accession negotiations only at the beginning of 2000 and had closed twenty chapters within two years, catching up soon with the Czech Republic and with Poland.

The change of attitude towards the rule of law and an inclusive policy towards the Hungarian minority were to make up for the inherited democratic deficit. The Slovak case shows that there is no better remedy to the drawbacks of 'illiberal' or 'electoral' democracies than the electoral process itself. The heterogeneous coalition government in Bratislava has held together for four years largely thanks to a common adversary (Mečiar) and a common European goal. Just as the Zeman–Klaus pact in Prague has sometimes been justified as an expedient means for rapid adoption of a European 'legislative tornado' (Rychetsky), the heterogeneous coalition in Bratislava had essentially Europe as its common denominator.

The Slovak parliamentary elections of September 2002 can no doubt be seen as the confirmation of the country's commitment to join the European Union and NATO. Rarely has a domestic political agenda been so closely intertwined with the issue of European integration since both the EU and NATO had clearly warned that Mečiar's return to power would jeopardize Slovakia's chances to be part of the forthcoming enlargement of the two institutions. The September 2002 elections brought the Mečiar era to a close. Though his party (HDZ) did emerge with the largest share of the vote (close to 20 per cent) it has no coalition partners and will remain confined to opposition. The defeat of the populist movements (Mečiar's but also that of Robert Fico's *Smer* with 13.5 per cent) combined with that of the left-wing parties helped to bring about Slovakia's first reformist, right of centre government with a clear liberal economic agenda. The previous Dzurinda government (1998–2002) was a broad 'coalition of coalitions' with opposition to Mečiar and joining of the EU as the common denominator. This time the Dzurinda-led four party coalition is more compact, more liberal and in some ways more 'European' than its counterpart in Prague. This irony, compared to the situation in the early 1990s, was not lost on observers in Prague and Bratislava. The Czechs have noted that that the liberal Slovak Minister of finance I. Miklos has promptly announced lowering taxes for business, the privatisation of the energy sector and, most daringly, a reform of the pensions and health systems – none of which seems likely to be implemented by the social-democratic government in Prague.[73] A Slovak reformist model for Prague?

A similar reversal of roles is also to be observed in the attitudes to EU integration. While Slovak public opinion displayed in 2002 a consistent support of 65 to 69 per cent for joining the EU, Czech support for the EU has dropped to below half of the electorate during the same year.[74] Hence, the well intentioned Slovak suggestion that they should hold their referendum on EU accession first in order to 'pull into the Union the sceptical and doubting Czechs'.[75] This, of course, is an ironic overstatement related to the new self-confidence displayed by Slovak elites since the September 2002 election.

What the results of that election show in retrospect is that Mečiar's failure to pass the European test in 1997 did act as a catalyst in the rebirth of a civil society in Slovakia. External pressure, namely EU criticism of the democratic deficit of the Mečiar regime, did eventually, to use Soňa Szomolányi's phrase, 'percolate down to the population at large' and brought about the first turning point in the 1998 election.[76] Since then the fear of exclusion from the mainstream of European integration provided the chief impetus for the electoral backing of a reformist coalition. Clearly, in 2002, the issue of European integration has been directly related to, indeed turned into, domestic politics. The road to the EU has been cleared. The debate about what it actually entails can now begin.

Conclusions

1 Ten years after their separation, the return to Central European co-operation became an essential ingredient of Czech and Slovak European policy.[77] The close Czecho-Slovak relationship is clearly an important part of it. However, any suggestion that the alleged front-runners in the accession process should put to good use 'special relationships' with their Eastern neighbours, a would-be 'patronage' over their EU and NATO accession (Czechs for Slovaks, Poland for Lithuania, Hungary for Romania), is rejected both in Bratislava and Prague. Poland was called a 'strategic partner' by the Slovak foreign minister in 1998. And indeed, with Bronislaw Geremek as foreign minister in the late 1990s, Poland was aspiring to become if not a facilitator of co-operation a spokesman for Central European concerns on enlargement issues.[78] Ironically, by the time Slovakia seemed to have caught up with the Czech Republic in its accession negotiations, it was Poland which was pointed out in Brussels in 2001 as lagging behind the front-runners.

Slovakia's neighbours understand that it is also in *their* interests that Slovakia is not left out of the enlargement process. Such a hypothesis would create more problems than it would solve, leaving 'a hole in the map' of Central Europe. For example, the introduction of Schengen borders between Slovakia and the other three enlargement candidates would mean policing 1,500 km of Schengen borders as opposed to only 98 km (with the Ukraine). The meeting of the foreign ministers of the 'V4' group in Bratislava in May 1999 clearly marked the return of a Central European approach to enlargement and established a common goal of helping Slovakia 'catch up' with the EU enlargement train. The train was moving so slowly that this hope proved not to be an unrealistic one. However, the Central European co-operation also showed its limits when the V4 countries failed to establish common negotiating positions with the EU on issues such as free movement of labour. No less importantly, the endorsement in March 2002 by the then Hungarian Prime Minister Orbán of the Austro-German demand for the abrogation of the 1945 Beneš decrees prior to the enlargement of the EU has led to the cancellation of 'V4' prime ministers meeting, and more generally to a temporary suspension of co-operation vithin the Visegrád Group. These developments have made it all the more important, for both Czechs and Slovaks, to rely on a convergent if not co-ordinated Central European accession strategy.

2 The EU has played the part of an external democratiser for Slovakia, it has also provided a target for the second phase of the Czech Republic's transformation since the late 1990s.[79] Slovakia was the only country whose accession had been jeopardised by the failure to meet the democratic criteria formulated by the EU at Copenhagen in 1993. It can be argued that the defeat of Mečiar nationalist populism and the policies followed by the Dzurinda government were to large extent related to the Slovak society's response to the decision of summer 1997 to leave Slovakia out of the first wave of EU enlargement. This development, however, is by no means a linear or irreversible one. The irony of the situation four years later is that the the 'European' coalition in power in Bratislava tends now to be more popular with the Commission in Brussels than with Slovak public opinion. The new faces of populism (besides Mečiar) are called Fico or Rusko. There is an unstable, fragmented party system and the fear that the sequence between internal democratic change and European and Atlantic integration is a crucial one. The general election in September 2002 largely conditioned the decisions concerning Slovakia's fate at the NATO summit on enlargement in Prague in November 2002 and the EU final list of newcomers to the club at the end of the same year. The three elements (the general election, NATO and EU enlargements) are part of a sequence which clearly turns a domestic election into a choice with major regional and international implications for the future.

In the case of the Czech Republic, it can be argued that the EU accession process has largely contributed to setting the agenda for the second part of its unfinished transition. It focussed, as the annual reports of the EU indicate, on the rule of law and the reform of the judiciary, the privatisation of the banking system and the transparency in the way tenders are handled, the need after a decade of free market rhetoric to focus on a competent and politicaly neutral civil service.[80] The curious pact between the ruling Social-Democrats and the Civic Democratic Party has often been criticised as undermining democratic pluralism. It has, however, helped in getting the bulk of 'European' legislation speedily through parliament. That could suggest a reassuring conclusion about the the pro-european consensus in Czech politics. No political leader in Prague, whatever his or her own or party's reservations, is likely to take on himself the responsability of derailing the EU integration process. The new coalition government established in Prague in July 2002 with a tenuous majority has 'Europe' as its prime goal and only common denominator.

Yet before the post-partition European 'happy ending' is announced for both Czechs (who cultivated a premature 'eurosceptic ' posture) and Slovaks (who seem to have promptly seized upon the second chance offered to them by the enlargement process) a word of caution is in place: in both countries the elites have, sometimes reluctantly, accepted the European constraint. In building a european elite consensus they tended to forget about the public opinion drifting into an increasingly indifferent posture. Less than a half of Czechs would vote 'yes' in a referendum[81] and the situation is slightly more favourable in Slovakia. More than the hypothetical return to power of Klaus in Prague or Mečiar in Bratislava, it is the indifference or even hostility of public opinion which could, if the trend continued, undermine the two countries European prospects. In the aftermath of the collapse of the communist regime Czechs and Slovaks chose to go to Europe, separately. A decade later they both came to the conclusion that their 'return to Europe' had to start with their return to Central Europe. And jointly integrating the European Union will also be a way of overcoming the legacy and the traumas of the partition.

Notes

1 The decision announced in July 1997 concerned both the enlargement of the EU and of NATO.

2 We refer here to the standard definition of 'democratic consolidation' as formulated, among others, by J. Linz and A. Stepan, in *Problems of Democratic Transitions and Consolidations* (Baltimore: Johns Hopkins University Press, 1996), p. 3.

3 F. Zakaria, 'The Rise of Illiberal Democracies', *Foreign Affairs* (November–December 1997) 22–43 (Slovakia found itself in the company of Pakistan, the Philippines and Ghana). 'Illiberal democracies' were defined by Zakaria as 'democratically elected regmes routinely ignoring the constitutional limits on their power and depriving their citizens of basic civic rights' (p. 22).

4 C. Skalnik Leff, *National Conflict in Czechoslovakia: The Making and Remaking of a State, 1918–1987* (rinceton: Princeton University Press, 1988).

5 An IVVM poll published in *Rude Pravo* (30 September 1992). Interestingly, a 1977 poll suggests an evolution in the perceptions of history showing an improvement in the image of the first republic in Slovakia (third place) and a deterioration in the image of the Slovak state (sixth). A result of the Mečiar experience? See Z. Butorova (ed.), *Democracy and Discontent in Slovakia: A Public Opinion Profile of a Country in Transition* (Bratislava: IVO, 1997), p. 193.

6 M. Kusy, 'Slovaks Are More . . .', in J. Jensen and F. Miszlivetz (eds), *East Central Europe: Paradoxes and Perspectives* (Szombathely: Savana University Press, 1998), pp. 53–76. Kusy's essay helps to dispel such a simplified characterisation of Slovak political culture.

7 The rate of investment was relatively higher in Slovakia than in the Czech lands; see S. Wolchik, *Czechoslovakia in Transition: Politics, Economics and Society* (London: Pinter, 1991), pp. 86–195.

8 M. Butora and Z. Butorova, 'Slovakia: The Identity Challenges of the Newly Born State',*Social Research* Vol. 60, No. 4 (1993), p. 715.

9 According to opinion surveys there was, in Czech lands, a strong support for the reform even for their acceleration (2/3) while there was growing apprehension in Slovakia. See

Centrum pro Socialnu Analyzu, *Aktualne Problémy Cesko–Slovenska* (Bratislava, January 1992), p. 6.

10 The traps of constitutional continuity are clearly presented in A. Stanger's chapter in M. Kraus and A. Stanger (eds), *Irreconciliable Differences: Explaining Czechoslovakia's Dissolution* (Boulder: Rowman & Littlefield Publishers, 2000).

11 M. Kraus, 'Returning to Europe, Separately', in M. Kraus and R. D. Liebowitz (eds), *Russia and Eastern Europe after Communism* (Boulder, CO: Westview Press, 1996), p. 236.

12 In her study Abby Innes, at the risk of overstating her case, presents Klaus and the Czech right wing as the prime instigator of the divorce. A. Innes, *Czechoslovakia, The Short Goodbye* (New Haven: Yale University Press, 2001).

13 To point to the instrumentalisation of the divorce by Czech and Slovak political elites as one of its important ingredients is by no means to minimise other processes at work. Nor is it meant to suggest that elites with hidden agendas merely manipulated 'innocent' populations as is sometimes suggested by Western analysts considering that the separation was simply "a process manufactured by a ruthlessly pragmatic Czech right, abetted by a populist and opportunist Slovak leadership", Abby Innes, *Czechoslovakia, the short goodbye*, New Haven and London, Yale UP, 2001, p. x.

14 Professor Delpérée made this argument using the Belgian case as a warning in front of the MPs of the Czechoslovak Federal Parliament chaired by A. Dubček in April 1991 as part of a seminar of the East-West Parliamentary Project. See also his 'Le fédéralisme sauvera-t-il la nation belge' ('Will Federalism Save the Belgian Nation') in J. Rupnik (ed.), *Le Déchirement des nations* (Paris: Seuil, 1995), pp. 123–138.

15 Interview with *Liberation* reprinted in FMZV, *Ceskoslovenska Zahranicni Politika: Dokumenty*, 6a/1991, p. 812.

16 Quoted by Jan Obrman, 'Further Discussions on the Future of the Federation', *RFE* (20 September 1991), pp. 8–9.

17 Cf. the statement of the then Portuguese presidency of the Commission (Mr Pinheiro) in *Europe* (International Press and Information Agency) (Brussels, 22–23 June 1992).

18 Cf. R. Dahrendorf's commentary in *La Republica*, 13 June 1992, reprinted in Slovakia 'Evropa, o ktere snil Schumann se rozplyva v Praze', *Nova Evropa* (1992, 11), p. 2.

19 For a comparison of Czech and French perceptions and motives concerning EU enlargement, see J. Rupnik (ed.), *Regards communs sur l'Europe* (Prague: CEFRES, 1998).

20 Cf. among other writings of J. Patocka, *L'Idée de l'Europe en Bohême* (Grenoble: Jerôme Millon, 1991).

21 M. Kundera, 'L'Occident kidnappé: la tragédie de l'Europe Centrale', in *Le Débat* (Paris, November 1983).

22 K. Kuehnl, 'The Czech Republic is an Integral Part of European Civilisation', in W. Nicoll and R. Schoenberg (eds), *Europe beyond 2000: The Enlargement of the European Union towards the East* (London: Whurr, 1998).

23 M. Kundera, 'Le pari tchèque', *Le Nouvel Observateur* (October 1995), p. 34.

24 Klaus has used it several times since 1993; and in his television appearance cf *Pravo* (26 January 1999).

25 V. Klaus interview 'Odmitam zapirat sve vlastenectvi', *Lidové Noviny* (3 June 1999).

26 *Ibid.*

27 L. Liptak, 'Niektore historické aspekty slovensej otazky', in R. Chmel (ed.), *Slovenska otazka v 20. storoci* (Bratislava: Kalligram), p. 448.

28 *Ibid.*, p. 454.

29 In 1993 both the Czech Republic and Slovakia had to renegotiate a new association agreement with the EU which, unlike the original one in 1991, contained a suspension clause in case of violation of democratic principles and human rights. The Czech government rejected the clause on the grounds it did not feature in equivalent agreements with Poland or Hungary. The EU thus issued a unilateral declaration together with the association agreement: cf *Bulletin de l'UE*, supplement No. 3/1995, p. 15.

30 Quoted in H. Grabbe and K. Hughes, *Enlarging the EU Eastwards* (London: Royal Institute of International Affairs, 1998), p. 46.

31 According to the 1991 census there were 75,802 citizens declaring themselves as belonging to the Roma minority in Slovakia. However, according to the city summaries and reports of the municipal offices from 1999 there were 253,943 (4.8 per cent) Romas in Slovakia. A similar figure is now estimated for the Czech Republic. See Michal Vasecka, 'Put Down in the Under-class', *The New Presence* (October 1999), p. 12.

32 On 6 August 1998 Prime Minister Mečiar also suggested that the way to solve the unemployment problem among Romas was to provide 'intellectually modest work'. He added: 'Slovaks produce first-rate values, Romanies only themselves' . . . Mečiar's coalition ally, Jan Slota, chair of the Slovak National Party and mayor of Zilina declared in March 1998: 'In no case shall we agree that there is a Romany nationality. That is absolutely rubbish. They are Gypsies, who steal, plunder and loot', quoted by M. Vasecka, art. cit., p. 13.

33 Britain was the first EU member to threaten the Czech Republic with visa obligations. It imposed visa obligations on the citizens of Slovakia in October 1998. In August 1999 Finland gave a similar warning to Slovakia. Belgium decided to depart over seventy Roma to Slovakia by a special charter flight, *Le Soir* (Brussels, 6 October 1999).

34 The building of a wall in the northern Bohemian town of Usti nad Labem which would separate Czech families from their Gypsy neighbours provoked a rebuff from the head of the European Commission Romano Prodi stating that 'Europe will never accept new walls separating European citizens from one another. We have had enough walls in the past'. On 13 October 1999 (while the wall was being built) the Czech Parliament rescinded the City Council's decision, declared the action illegal and had the wall demolished. Cf 'Czech's Wall for Gypsies Stirs Protest Across Europe', *New York Times* (17 October 1999).

35 Cf. J. Grohova, 'Proc nesmeji nekteri Cesi letet z Prahy do Britanie. Vlada uzavrela s Brity dohodu', *MFDnes* (20 July 2001). The measures were opposed by the representatives of the Czech Roma community and have later been suspended. During 2000 some 1,160 Czech asylum-seekers have been repatriated from Britain.

36 G. Horvathova and K. Wolf, 'Mečiar navrhuje, aby Madari odesli', *MFDnes* (6 September 1997). Mečiar repeated the statement in a public meeting in Bratislava.

37 For details on the EU's unsuccessful democracy dialogue with Mečiar's Slovakia, see A. Dulaba, 'Zahranicno-politicka orientacia a vnutorna politika SR', in S. Szomolanyi (ed.), *Slovensko: problémy konsolidacie demokracie* (Bratislava: Slovenske zdruzenie pre politické vedy, 1997), pp. 187–203.

38 The article published in January 1996 is reprinted in V. Klaus, *Obhajoba zapomenutych myslenek* (Prague: Academia, 1997), p. 353. See also on this theme, 'Ceska republika a myslenka evropske integrace', *Lidové Noviny* (22 December 1993) or 'Pad komunismu je vyzvou i pro ES', *Cesky Denik* (9 June 1993).

39 Petr Necas, Stinovy ministr obrany na Ideové konferenci ODS (Prague: ODS 29 May 1999). For a forceful critique of the 'European super-state' and a defence of the nation-state, see the essay by Professor Vaclav Belohradsky, then associated with V. Klaus, 'Proti statu Evropa', *Literarni Noviny* Nos 51–52 (18 December 1996), pp. 1–4.

40 J. Zahradil, *Manifest ceskeho eurorealismu* (Prague: ODS, April 2001), pp. 9–10.

41 M. Plichta, 'L'Union européenne revue et corrigée par Vaclav Havel', *Le Monde* (10 March 1999).

42 CTK, 'Klaus se opet trefoval do Evropske unie', *Lidové Noviny* (26 June 2000).

43 J. Kavan, 'A Czech Perspective on the EU', lecture given at IFRI (Paris, 26 April 2001).

44 See, in particular, Havel's speech in Ottawa in April 1999 published in V. Havel, *Pour une politique post-moderne* (Paris: Ed. de l'Aube, 1999), pp. 61–70.

45 J. Rupnik, 'Na Balkane si stredni Evropa nedovedla vybrat', *MFDnes* (June 1999).

46 Quoted by S. Vaarakallio, 'Learning from history', *Europ* (May 1997), p. 86.

47 A. Vondra, 'Obcas potrebujeme supermana', *Respekt* (10–16 March 1997). Mr Vondra, the main foreign policy advisor of President Havel, became deputy foreign minister in 1993 and Ambassor to the USA in 1997. It is interesting to compare this thesis ('sometimes we need a superman') to a more recent one by the same author: 'our national interests are primarily in Europe': cf. A. Vondra, 'Svoje narodni zajmy mame v prvni rade v Evrope', *Lidové noviny* (14 August 1999).

48 *SME* (Bratislava, 2 May 1997).

49 *SME* (25 April 1997).

50 Quoted in *Pravda* (Bratislava, 30 April 1997).

51 *SME* (25 June 1997).

52 On Slovakia 'in the Russian orbit' see D. Butora, 'Na obezne draze Ruska' *Respekt* (5 November 1997). The author stresses the close economic ties particularly with Gazprom and quotes the statement of a leading HDZ member of parliament 'The defence and security of Europe should be gauranteed by Europeans'.

53 A. Cerny, 'Prague's Reality Check', *Transitions*, Vol. 5, No. 4 (April 1998), p. 53.

54 On the domestic politics of Czech exceptionalism, see J. Rupnik, 'Que reste-t-il de l'exception tchèque', *Libération* (Paris, 17 June 1996).

55 The EU Commission's assessment in November 2000 putting the Czech Republic behind its Central European neighbours provoked a sharp rebuff from Prague, which considered that gross national product (GNP) per capita should be the relevant criterion. The following year the EU dropped the ranking of candidates.

56 S. Hrib, 'Being Left Behind', *Transitions* (April 1998), p. 57.

57 B. Hronec, 'Slovak Dilemmas with Identity and Nationality: The Controversy among Slovak intellectuals in the First Half of the 19th Century', in C. W. Lowney (ed.), *Identities* (Vienna: IWM, 1998), p. 266.

58 T. Garton Ash, *In Europe's Name* (London: Jonathan Cape, 1994).

59 See point 7 of the EP resolution adopted on 15 April 1999 'concerning the progress of the Czech Republic on the way to integration', which 'invites' the Czech government to abolish the decrees of 1945, an option explicitly rejected by the Czech constitutional court in March 1995. The Czech authorities consider the decrees confiscating the property of the expellees and of collaborators as 'dead' law, i.e. not a legal reference for its current approach to citizens' rights; they refuse, however, to abolish decrees opening the way to potential legal and property claims. The European parliament has returned to the issue in a September 2001 resolution on the Czech Republic's integration progress (point 41) by 'welcoming' the decision of the Czech government to re-examine the decrees of 1945. No such decision was taken by the Prague government. For a detailed treatment of the Czech–German relationship in a wider European context, see J. Rupnik and A. Bazin, 'La difficile réconciliation tchéco-allemande', *Politique Etrangère* (2/2001), pp. 353–370.

60 This pattern in the use of the European Parliament (EP) was confirmed in the spring of 2002 at the height of the controversy over the Benes decrees: at the end of March 2002 the delegation to the joint commission between the EP and the Czech Parliament was chaired by an Austrian (ÖVP) MP with two German deputies (one of whom was B. Posselt, the chair of the Sudentendeutsche Landsmanschaft). The draft resolution concerning the Czech Republic's progress in EU accession in April 2002 was authored by MEP J. Schroeder (CDU) and devoted five out of thirteen paragraphs to the Benes decrees. The chair of the EP People's Party Club, H.-G. Poettering (CDU) proposed to his European collegues a resolution condemning the Czech Republic stance on the Benes decrees. *MFDnes* (12 April 2002).

61 In his speech at a Sudentendeutcher Tag on 19 May 2002 the leader of the German opposition stated in reference to the demand for the abrogation of the Benes decrees that 'Whoever in Europe in 2002 defends after more than 57 years expulsion and privation of rights must be asked by all Europeans to what extent he is fit for Europe (europatauglich).'

It seems unwise to speak on behalf of "all Europeans". Partly because that could only reinforce the Czechs' apprehension and turn them aginst the EU and, secondly, because most EU members are actually concerned not to see a bilateral issue of the past being raised by Germany on their behalf. This was made clear by Tony Blair during his visit in Prague in April 2002 where he clearly stood by the decisions made at Potsdam in 1945. Similarly an official statement by the French Ministry of Foreign Affairs on 19 April 2002 says: 'The [Benes] decrees . . . pre-date the treaty of Rome and a fortiori the Czech Republic's entry into the European Union and therefore bear no relation to and cannot interfere with the pursuit and conclusion of the accession negotiations of that country.'

62 Luc Rosenzweig, «Le populisme alpin phénomène transnational», *Le Monde*, 12 March 1999

63 M. Plichta, 'Une centrale nucléaire slovaque inquiète les Autrichiens', *Le Monde* (29 May 1998); see also *SME* (30 April 1999).

64 For the details of the agreement brokered by the commissioner for enlargement, G. Verheugen, see A. Leparmentier; 'L'Europe est confrontée à de nouveaux choix sur le nucléaire', *Le Monde* (2–3 December, 2001).

65 The headline in the Czech press was 'Austrians vote on the Czechlands' 'Rakusane hlasuji o Cesku, *MFDnes* (14 January 2002) quoting the Austrian economy government minister, Martin Bartenstein as saying 'Many people think they are signing against Temelin, in reality they'll sign angainst the Czech Republic entry in the EU'. It should be pointed out that the German government support for Austrian concerns over the Czech nuclear plant would probably not have been forthcoming if the Prague government had chosen Siemens (rather than the American firm Westinghouse) to complete the project and guarantee safety standards.

66 W. Baryli, 'Les Autrichiens ont peur de l'Est', *L'Européen* No. 7 (6 May 1998), p. 55; The right-wing leader Jörg Haider (27 per cent in the October 1999 elections) declared that enlargement towards the East would be a 'declaration of war' to Austria and requested a referendum on the issue. The chairman of Austria's trade unions, F. Verzetnisch, fears the arrival of 'an army of 150,000 to 500,000 people seeking work'. There is little evidence to substantiate such estimates. In the meantime, Austria's exports to Central European candidates increased by 123 per cent between 1989 and 1996. No less importantly, the experience of previous EU enlargements points less to increased labour mobility than to enhanced capital mobility.

67 Eurostat survey released in Brussels on March 1998; summary provided by CTK agency, 16 March 1998.

68 *Standard Eurobarometer* No. 55 (Spring 2001), p. 54.

69 G. Horvatova and K. Wolf, 'Mečiar navrhuje, aby Madari odesli', *MFDnes* (6 September 1997).

70 Jan Kavan, lecture at the French Institute of International Relations (IFRI), Paris (24 April 1999).

71 T. Menschik and S. Blechova, 'Slovensko nechce zavedeni viz do Ceska', *Lidové Noviny* (23 November, 2001).

72 This among others is the assessment of the FT Slovakia supplement. Cf. S. Wagstyl and R. Anderson, 'EU Membership is the Top Priority', *Financial Times* (25 May 2002). Germany is Slovakia's main trading partner ahead of the Czech Republic, Austria and Italy.

73 Cf. Jan Machacek 'Slovaci se rozjizdeji', *MFDnes* 17 October 2002.

74 The controversy with Austria and the German opposition leader over the Benes decrees during the Spring of 2002 is part of the explanation; the disclosure of the terms of entry presented in the media as unfavourable (the Czech Republic as a net contributor to the EU budget upon entry) is the main explanation for this deterioration of Czech support for enlargement.

75 Michal Fris and Roman Pataj, 'Slovaci chcu Cesko potiahnut do unie', in *SME* (Bratislava) 3 October 2002.

76 Soňa Szomolányi, 'Slovakia and EU integration', paper presented at the conference, 'Reclaiming the future: the Central European question', Dublin European Institute, 5 October 2002.

77 See the special issue of *Slovak Foreign Policy Affairs* ('Visegrád and central Europe'), Vol. 2, No. 1 (2001).

78 It is this broader role that Poland sees for itself that has also brought into the open some differences with both Prague and Bratislava on the question of visa requirements for Ukrainians. Poland insists it wants, for political as well as economic reasons, to keep an open border with the Ukraine. In contrast, Slovakia is co-ordinating with the Czech Republic on the introduction of visa obligations for the Ukraine as part of their EU pre-accession policy. Cf. Slovak foreign minister Eduard Kukan statement 'Viza pro ukrajince chceme zavest koordinovane s CR' in *Pravo* (11 November 1999). Slovakia had no visa obligations with Russia, Ukraine, Bielorussia, Bulgaria, Romania and Cuba, and decided to change its policy for reasons of EU integration, security and immigration.

79 On the EU's role as an external democratiser see J. Rupnik, 'Eastern Europe: The International Context', in M. F. Plattner and A. Smolar (eds), *Globalization, Power and Democracy* (Baltimore: Johns Hopkins University Press, 2000), pp. 57–70.

80 The Commission report pointed in November 2001 to the absence of a new civil service law as being a major drawback for the Czech Republic's preparations to join the EU. The criticism on corruption also seems corroborated by the country's drop in the transparency international rankings (corruption had previously been estimated to be on the level of Belgium; it dropped to that of Bulgaria). The sensitivity of the government on this issue showed in the prime minister's decision in October 2001 to sue the weekly *Respekt* for alleging the government not only failed to stop rampant corruption but was itself involved.

81 P. Zara and A. Volf, 'Do Unie chce jen necela polovina lidi', *Hospodarske Noviny* (27 November 2001) (44 per cent for; 14 per cent against; 26.5 per cent don't know; others don't know if they would vote).

Martin Bútora, Zora Bútorová and Grigorij Mesežnikov[1]

2

Slovakia's democratic awakening

As the clock struck midnight on 31 December 1992 and Czechoslovakia officially ceased to exist, the anthems of its two successor states, the Czech Republic and Slovakia, were played on television screens in Prague and Bratislava, respectively. The Slovak anthem, originally a patriotic song composed during the 'Slovak Revival' in the first half of the nineteenth century when Slovakia was a part of the Austro-Hungarian empire, was now sung in full, including its second stanza, depicting Slovakia as a 'Sleeping Beauty' needing to be awakened. On that night, the words of the national anthem signified the culmination of national aspirations – the creation of an independent Slovak state. Sleeping Beauty had been awakened, and now the task, metaphorically speaking, was to choose a dress for her to wear.

Five years later, in the September 1998 parliamentary elections, the citizens of Slovakia made it clear that they did not like the attire that the new state had been wearing. They rejected its authoritarian political tendencies, which included disrespect for the rule of law, favouritism, corruption, the intertwining of crime with politics, and a confrontational nationalist policy *vis-à-vis* the Hungarian minority. The voters were also expressing their dissatisfaction with a high unemployment rate (14 per cent), rising crime, the deterioration of the healthcare and education systems, and the problems young people faced in finding adequate housing. 'Change' was a key buzzword of the election campaign, which attracted a remarkably high number of voters to the polls. The turnout of 84 per cent was 9 per cent higher than that in the 1994 elections and higher than that in recent parliamentary elections in Poland and in the neighbouring Czech Republic.

The yearning for political change was a reaction against the rule of autocratic Prime Minister Vladimír Mečiar, the charismatic populist leader of the Movement for a Democratic Slovakia (HZDS). Except for a brief nine-month interruption by the government of Jozef Moravčík in 1994, Mečiar had been in power ever since the creation of the independent Slovak Republic in 1993. After the 1994 elections, Mečiar's HZDS – a broad clientelistic movement marked by nationalism, populism, and authoritarianism – ruled in coalition with the far-right nationalist Slovak National Party (SNS) and with the populist radical leftist movement, the Association of Workers of Slovakia (ZRS). According to sociological surveys the HZDS predominantly represented the older, less educated, rural, and less reform-minded part of the population.

The 1998 elections brought victory to the opposition. Although the HZDS got the most votes of any single political party (27 per cent), an alliance of four opposition parties – the Slovak Democratic Coalition (SDK), the Party of the Democratic Left (SDL´), the Party of the Hungarian Coalition (SMK), and the Party of Civic Understanding (SOP) – captured over 58 of the votes. Of the HZDS's two former allies, the SNS won 9.1 per cent of the vote, but the ZRS failed to reach the 5 per cent required to enter parliament. This time, unlike in 1992 and 1994, the votes of Mečiar's opponents were not wasted on parties that fell below the threshold.[2]

The new ruling coalition was in fact a 'coalition of coalitions' consisting of 10 parties. The SDK, the strongest party with 26.3 per cent of the vote, was originally created as a coalition of the conservative Christian Democratic Movement (KDH); the liberal Democratic Union (DU); the conservative-liberal Democratic Party (DS); the Social Democratic Party of Slovakia (SDSS); and the Party of Greens in Slovakia (SZS). It was officially registered as an 'electoral' party just four months before the elections in response to a controversial electoral law imposed by Mečiar and his allies.

The SDL´, a party of former communists and a member of the Socialist International, is the second strongest member (14.7 per cent) of the new ruling coalition. The third strongest player (9.1 per cent) in the ruling coalition is the SMK, which itself consists of three platforms: the Hungarian Christian Democratic Movement (MKDH), Coexistence, and the Hungarian Civic Party (MOS). Finally, the smallest (8.0 per cent) member of the ruling coalition is the Party of Civic Understanding (SOP), a newly created party of the centre-left.

The new governing coalition had 93 of 150 parliamentary seats, a majority that seemed large enough to make fundamental changes needed in the country after four years of 'Mečiarism'. Despite the diversity of their political programmes, ideological profiles, and approaches to societal problems, all of the coalition members were committed to democratic principles, to the rule of law, and to Slovakia's integration into the European Union and NATO. From the regional perspective, the elections have brought about hopes that Slovakia can catch the train of Euro-Atlantic integration, which has almost passed it by.

In 1998, Slovakia departed from the so-called 'South-Eastern European model' in which the country's political orientation is shaped by the vote of a large rural electorate susceptible to the appeal of authoritarian populists. It moved closer to the pattern that prevailed in Poland and Hungary, in which voter turnout is highest among the urban and better-educated population.

Although Vladimír Mečiar's style of government displayed a number of political traits similar to those of Alyaksandr Lukashenka in Belarus, Slobodan Miloševič in Serbia, and Franjo Tudjman in Croatia, while the history of Slovak nationalism bares some similarities with Serbian and Croatian nationalism, in the 1998 elections, the bulk of Slovak society resisted these tendencies.

Another crucial factor of the opposition's victory was the high turnout among first-time voters (i.e. those who have just reached voting age), which was estimated to be close to the overall turnout of 84 per cent. According to exit polls, as many as 70 per cent of first-time voters voted for the opposition, while only 24 per cent supported the parties of the ruling coalition. Only 11 per cent of these new voters cast ballots for the HZDS, as opposed to 27 per cent among the electorate as a whole; on the other hand, the radical nationalist SNS actually did better among first-time voters, winning 13 per cent of their votes, as compared to only 9 per cent in the overall electorate.[3]

Two 'velvet revolutions'

The atmosphere of Slovak elections in 1998 – intense citizen involvement, town squares filled with people, signs of post-election euphoria – was reminiscent of November 1989, when the communist regime in Czechoslovakia collapsed. Compared with the velvet revolution, however, three differences stand out.

First, in November 1989, many people in Slovakia wanted 'change', but the word meant different things to different groups. Some rejected the omnipresence of the Communist Party and the Secret Police, the lack of freedom, and the humiliating absence of citizen participation in decision-making. Others were more concerned about the malfunctioning economy, bleak shop windows, and empty stores. Some felt suffocated by their isolation and longed to travel freely beyond the Iron Curtain. Still others wanted to put an end to social injustice, the breaking of laws, the devastation of the environment, and the arrogance of a powerful bureaucracy. Nine years later, however, the situation was different. Although opposition voters still disagreed on important issues, their experience of the past few years made them more united on the need for greater democracy, which they saw as the best way to deal with their everyday economic and social problems.

Second, in 1989, the leaders of the major Slovak civic opposition group, Public Against Violence (VPN), were relatively unknown. Unlike the Czech or Polish dissidents, they did not have a track record of persevering together in opposition to the communist regime. In September 1998 however, the citizens who voted for change brought to power politicians whom they already knew, because they had watched them shape their profiles in intense political struggles that, thanks to the free media, had taken place before the public eye.

Third, in November 1989 an overwhelming majority of people in Slovakia accepted political change passively. The communist regime did not break down as a result of massive popular opposition in Slovakia; it crumbled due to the domino-effect provoked by the fall of the Berlin wall and the huge demonstrations in Prague. In September 1998, by contrast, the people of Slovakia had to put up a greater fight on their own to bring about political change.

The results of the 1998 elections were backed by a broad citizen mobilisation. The representatives of political parties, non-governmental organisations (NGOs), trade unions, independent media, and a part of the Church showed the ability to learn from their mistakes and to forge democratic alliances. Public opinion had lost its powerlessness and had become influential.

In the 1998 elections democratic changes came about primarily from within, from Slovak society's own resources. Its significance is all the greater considering that all three key political decisions since 1989 – the dismantling of the communist regime (1989–90), the launching of economic reform (1991), and the division of Czechoslovakia (1992) – caught most citizens unprepared. Their adaptation to these changes was impeded by the fact that most inhabitants of Slovakia had not been really engaged in a struggle of their own to bring down the communist regime, and that most of them did not support the transformation of the economy or the dissolution of Czechoslovakia.

On the other hand, November 1989 and September 1998 were similar in that both events represented turning points in the country's political orientation. Unlike the recent elections in the Czech Republic, Hungary or Poland, the 1998 elections in Slovakia represented a stark choice between following an authoritarian path and returning to the original ideals of November 1989 – an open society, rule of law, and the market economy. In this sense, one may call the 1998 election a 'delayed velvet revolution.'

The greater emphasis on democracy in 1998 was also due to a waning of nationalist anxieties. The alleged threats to national sovereignty, assiduously raised by the HZDS and its allies, did not evoke a great public response. Although many Slovaks were sensitive to the fact that Czechoslovakia was divided without a referendum,[4] most of them accepted the partition as a *fait accompli*. No political party, movement, or civic initiative in Slovakia has sought to revive the former common state. Some Slovaks welcomed new statehood; others gradually adapted to it. Most of them, however, shared a crucial question: What will be the nature of this new statehood? How will Slovakia's independence influence their everyday lives? Will it lead to greater prosperity, better governance, and more democracy?

The changes of 1998, however, entail new risks. The history of post-communism already contains quite a few examples of euphoria followed by unfulfilled hopes and promises giving way to disillusion. The Slovak democratic community was confronted with the difficult task of coping with the burden of its victory.

The Mečiar years

The coming to power of the HZDS–SNS–ZRS coalition after the elections of 1994 had a major impact on the quality of democracy in Slovakia. The results of its rule included the exacerbation of political polarisation in the country; a persisting confrontation between Mečiar and President Michal Kováč; efforts to concentrate power in the hands of the prime minister; repeated violations of the constitution; the politicisation of the state administration; a privatisation policy marred by clientelism; exclusion of the opposition from oversight of key executive institutions, including the intelligence service, of the publicly owned electronic media, and of the privatisation process; the frequent labelling of government critics as 'enemies', 'anti-Slovak' or 'anti-state' elements; government interference with the media, especially state-run television; a confrontational attitude toward ethnic Hungarians and a growing suspicions about ties between high state officials and organised crime. The central government's authoritarian approach was replicated throughout the country, bringing into existence a network of local autocrats and a widespread feeling of fear, especially in the countryside.

Even though Slovakia has developed instruments which made it possible to oppose these tendencies – some semblance of a separation of powers (a political opposition, the Constitutional Court, the presidency, an independent judiciary, and independent media), a diverse public opinion, and a vibrant civil society – these safeguards were not sufficient to meet the criteria for inclusion into the first group of candidates for NATO and EU membership. After succeeding to the treaties made by the former Czechoslovakia, Slovakia had every chance to continue its integration process into NATO and EU along with its neighbours from the Visegrád Four (Poland, Hungary, and the Czech Republic). But it was due to domestic policy trends, following the 1994 elections, that Slovakia under Mečiar disqualified itself and wound up among the 'outs' when the list of front-runners for EU enlargement was announced in July 1997.

However, the government's growing authoritarian tendencies also had unintended positive outcomes. Slovakia's citizens began to regard the issue of democracy with greater care. Their understanding of the importance of political rights and freedoms increased. On the eve of the 1998 elections, Slovak intellectual circles began to speak of founding the state anew (i.e. endowing the state with new and democratic content).[5] Perceptions of crucial social problems also changed. While in the first years of post-communist transformation people were most concerned with problems of living standards, social insecurity, unemployment, crime, and health care, since 1994 issues of political culture, democracy, and rule of law have become increasingly prominent. People put more emphasis on pluralism, compliance with the law, the search for consensus, and respect for minority rights.[6]

Political polarisation of Slovak society increasingly came to reflect sociocultural differences. Younger, better educated people in the larger cities were more sensitive to deficiencies in democracy, more critical of authoritarian politicians, more reluctant to adopt an attitude of passivity and resignation – and were thus more prepared to support the opposition. According to exit polls conducted during the 1998 elections, opposition voters included more people with higher education; young people, students, entrepreneurs, professionals, and inhabitants of big cities than those of HZDS.[7] Since the 1992 elections, the electorate of HZDS and SNS has become more rural, while that of the opposition is predominantly urban.[8]

Obviously, shifts in people's attitudes captured by opinion polls do not necessarily guarantee political change. Increased public discontent becomes an impetus for political change only when groups of people take a particular issue in their hands, publicise it in the media, create forums where it can be discussed, organise themselves and formulate their position, engage in pressure or lobbying activities, and establish alliances to obtain political backing. By doing so, they push forward a change aimed at solving the problem. And this was precisely the road the Slovak civil society has taken.

The turning point

One of the most important political events after the 1994 elections was the run up to, and the conduct of, the May 1997 referendum on NATO membership and direct presidential elections. The presidential election issue arose in December 1996, when representatives of several opposition parties introduced a bill to amend the constitution to provide for direct presidential elections. After the speaker of parliament refused to schedule a debate on their proposal, the opposition parties launched a petition drive for a referendum, eventually gaining over 500,000 signatures. The public found the idea of direct presidential elections attractive. According to a March 1997 survey, 57 per cent of respondents intended to take part in the referendum, and 76 per cent of them would have voted for direct presidential elections.[9]

The situation became even more complicated, after parliament passed a resolution directing President Kováč to call a referendum on Slovakia's membership in NATO – even though Slovakia had not been invited to join the alliance. Government critics believed that this referendum was an obvious attempt to shift responsibility for the looming failure of the government's integration policy to the citizens themselves.

President Kováč decided to combine the two referendums on a single ballot. This was vigorously opposed by the government, which finally instructed Interior Minister Gustáv Krajči to remove the question about presidential elections and to reprint the ballots. The chairmen of the opposition parties appealed to citizens not to vote under these circumstances. Less than 10 per cent of the people went to the polls, and the Central Referendum Commission declared the referendum invalid. The obstructed referendum proved to be a political turning point, serving as an impetus for the formation of the Slovak Democratic Coalition.

In the years following the 1994 elections, the Slovak political scene presented a paradox, though one far from unique in the post-communist countries. Popular support for the opposition was significantly higher than support for the ruling coalition, but the fragmented opposition was unable to take advantage of this favourable position. Part of the problem was its failure to co-operate – a consequence of the opposition's heterogeneity and of continuing efforts on the part of various opposition groups to define their own identities. Eventually, however, opposition leaders came to realise that their differences were outweighed by the need to resist the ruling coalition's authoritarian politics. They decided to form a broad coalition of democratic parties covering a range of conservative, liberal, social-democratic, and ecological values.

In July 1997, after the obstruction of the referendum, the chairmen of the KDH, the DU, the DS, the SDSS, and the SZS signed an agreement pledging to contest the 1998 parliamentary elections as a unified bloc, the SDK. The coalition chose as its spokesman (later, its chairman) Mikuláš Dzurinda, a representative of the younger generation of 'pragmatists' within the KDH, who was expected to garner the widest support in the challenge to Mečiar. The formation of SDK offered a way to prevent a repetition of the traumatic experience of the 1992 and 1994 elections, when the votes of supporters of smaller opposition that did not reach the required 5 per cent threshold for getting into the Parliament were wasted.

Due to the restrictive election law (according to which *each* party within an electoral coalition had to receive 5 per cent of the vote to qualify for seats), private electronic media were not permitted to broadcast activities relating to political campaigns during the official campaign period. The state-owned media (especially television) clearly displayed pro-government bias. During the first two weeks of the election campaign, state-owned television devoted 61 per cent of its news coverage to the government and its coalition parties and only 15.2 per cent to the opposition. Unlike in previous elections, however, Slovakia now had well-established independent print media and private electronic media, whose news coverage compensated for the bias of state-run television.

A 'civil archipelago'

In contrast to the elections of 1994, the challenge in 1998 was to ensure their free and fair character. There was widespread concern about the possibility of unfair party competition, and that the obstruction of the referendum had been a dress rehearsal for the manipulation of the upcoming parliamentary elections.[10]

In this context NGOs became involved in an attempt to counter this mounting public concern. They established Civic Campaign (OK) '98, an open, non-partisan initiative designed to help ensure free and fair elections. Within the framework of OK '98, dozens of NGOs prepared educational projects, cultural activities, get-out-the-vote concerts, brochures, TV films, videoclips, analytical materials, and discussion forums open to candidates from all political parties. 'Road for Slovakia', the trek in which mostly young volunteers visited more than one thousand villages and towns, became one of the crucial projects within OK '98. In ingenious TV spots produced by 'Head 98', popular music, sports, and entertainment personalities addressed young people with the message 'I vote, therefore I am'. Several independent think tanks and expert groups published analyses of the government's performance since the 1994 elections. These kinds of activities reached hundreds of thousands of citizens and helped to boost voter turnout to 84 per cent of eligible voters. They were particularly instrumental in raising the participation of first-time voters from around 60 per cent in 1994 to over 80 per cent in 1998.

NGOs monitored key electronic and print media to assess their objectivity and political independence (Project MEMO '98); helped the opposition to organise a parallel vote count; trained members of electoral committees (the Anton Tunega Foundation); and organised domestic election observers (Project OKO '98 carried out by the Association for Fair Elections). These activities contributed significantly to the fairness of the elections and helped to prevent interference in the electoral process.

While most citizens approved these activities,[11] some government politicians accused NGO leaders of being paid from abroad, of serving the "enemies of Slovakia's independence" and democracy, and of campaigning in favour of the opposition. In the end, however, these assaults backfired by raising interest in OK '98 initiatives. Hardened by many clashes with authorities, Slovakia's NGOs appeared to be much more than the 'islands of positive deviants', as independent civic activists had been called by Slovak sociologists in the late 1980s. Instead, they constituted a 'civil archipelago' of positive action.

Among the most important initiatives was the 'Democratic Round Table', formed in reaction to the need to prevent electoral fraud, and to secure a smooth transfer of political power after the election. This informal gathering first met in June and was attended by four democratic opposition parties (SDK, SDL', SMK and SOP) and four non-partisan actors (Assembly or Co-ordinating Committee of the Third Sector, the Confederation of Trade Unions, the Union of Cities and Villages, and the Youth Council of Slovakia).[12] The Democratic Round Table was a symbolic embodiment of one of the main achievements of the campaign – the ability of democratic forces to form alliances. It became increasingly clear that this semi-institutionalised grouping, which brought together leaders of representative democracy with those of participatory democracy, was ready to defend the democratic character of the elections and, should the opposition succeed, to help form a cohesive base for a new government.

Slovakia's NGOs now constitute a vibrant and efficient 'civil archipelago', whose potential became important as the society started to deal with the legacy of the Mečiar's government and become a partner that the new government had to reckon with, both as a prospective collaborator and as a potential opponent.

Overcoming illiberalism

The international environment, the communication with Western democracies also played a role in the political change. The assessment of developments in Slovakia by Western institutions, politicians, experts and independent organisations concerned made an impact. The domestic political opposition was able to refer to them and invoke commonly shared values because, unlike the parties in Mečiar's coalition, it had ties to a variety of international partner organisations. They also learned how to seek international support, including financial assistance, from institutions in the United States and in the EU countries designed to promote democratisation. For civic activists in Slovakia, the involvement with an emerging 'global civil society' was not a mere phrase.

The West's open emphasis on the need for democratisation was of great importance in the evolution of public opinion. Research data repeatedly showed that a substantial segment of the population considered the criticism from abroad to be justified and saw democratisation as a prerequisite for the integration of Slovakia into the European and Atlantic structures. The international democratic environment has impacted on the domestic process. The success of the democratic opposition in Slovakia can thus be seen as an argument for long-term assistance aimed at fostering the growth of civil society, the rule of law, and democratic culture.[13]

Foreign assistance to new democracies had been questioned by Fareed Zakaria in a controversial *Foreign Affairs* article on 'The Rise of Illiberal Democracy'. The article struck a responsive chord in Slovak intellectual circles, as the author placed the Slovak Republic among the countries where free elections bring to power politicians who do not adequately respect the rule of law, the separation of powers, and the protection of basic liberties; where 'democracy is flourishing, [but] constitutional liberalism is not'. Zakaria did not see any great difference between the nature of the regime in Slovakia and in Sierra Leone, Pakistan, or the Philippines; for him, they were all illiberal democracies 'routinely ignoring constitutional limits on their powers and depriving their citizens of basic rights and freedoms'.[14]

It is no doubt justified to note the shortcomings of third-wave democracies, which frequently tend to be only 'procedural' or 'delegative' democracies or even 'pseudodemocracies' or 'semidemocracies'.[15] Indeed, they often tend to be 'electoral democracies' rather than 'liberal democracies' – to use the terms of Larry Diamond who pointed at 'increasing shallowness' of democratisation in the latter part of the third wave: 'Electoral democracies have governments resulting from reasonably free and fair elections, but they lack many of these other safeguards for rights and liberties that exist in liberal democracies'.[16] The crucial question, however, is how to *stem* the rise of illiberal democracies, and in particular, whether the trend toward illiberalism can be stopped or reversed through free elections. The Slovak experience confirms that this is indeed possible. As Carl Gershman recently observed, the virtue of relatively free and fair elections is that they 'allow political and civic groups to fight for more space and more accountability. The process itself offers citizens an opportunity to gain experience and confidence'.[17]

The prospects for overcoming illiberalism are better when the following conditions exist: (1) at least some of the elements of liberal constitutionalism are present (such as a relatively independent judiciary and reasonably autonomous social institutions like universities and trade unions); (2) the separation of powers is not completely suppressed and those attempting to wield authoritarian power are at least partly contested by other legitimate actors; (3) at least some elements of a market economy are in place and the private sector has attained a certain degree of development; (4) some free space exists for the independent media enabling them to monitor and comment on the struggle between authoritarian and democratic political cultures; (5) there is no sharp domestic (ethnic, for example) strife that significantly distracts the society's attention; (6) economic hardships are not so severe as to prevent people from taking part in political life; (7) opposition political parties and elites have earned enough from their previous defeats to enable them to coalesce; (8) the opposition at least partially succeeds in determining the topics of public discourse; (9) civil society has attained at least a certain degree of development, and there are the sources of citizen participation that can be mobilised; (10) pro-democratic alliances have been created; (11) the illiberal government makes political mistakes.

The new government

Most citizens welcomed the 1998 change in government. According to a November 1998 survey by the Institute for Public Affairs conducted immediately after the elections, 62 per cent of people expected that the state of democracy in Slovakia would improve after the elections. As many as 57 per cent of respondents expressed confidence in the new parliament. Fifty-two per cent of people believed that the chance of Slovakia's admission to the EU improved after the 1998 elections and, according to 42 per cent, so did its chance of NATO membership. The new government enjoyed the trust of 55 per cent of citizens, while 33 per cent expressed their mistrust.

In contrast to Mečiar's government, half of the 20 members of the new cabinet (including Prime Minister Dzurinda) have never been members of the Communist party, and all the cabinet ministers speak at least one Western language. In sharp contrast to the previous ostracism, representatives of the Hungarian minority held three ministerial positions. It is hardly possible to overestimate the significance of this change. For the first time since the creation of Czechoslovakia in 1918 (not to mention the creation of a Slovak republic in January 1993), members of Slovakia's largest ethnic minority have an opportunity to be partners in governing the country. The new cabinet was a 'grand coalition' government resembling the model of consociational democracy described by Arend Lijphart. This 'grand coalition' makes it possible to secure an adequate representation of as many important segments of society as possible, including the minorities.[18]

The complex search for consensus among the four parties making up the government foreshadowed the difficulties that the new ruling coalition was to face in office. To stay in office the entire four-year period the government had to find effective and generally accepted mechanisms to resolve these difficulties. The ability of the new governmental coalition to keep the opposition, which received 36 per cent of the vote, involved in the political system was also of considerable importance. In the new parliament headed by Speaker Jozef Migaš, the SDL′ leader, the opposition was offered one of the four deputy speakerships, and one third of the committee chairs, but the HZDS declined the offer. Its chair, former Prime Minister Mečiar, has renounced his parliamentary seat raising questions about the kind of opposition the HZDS was likely to be. On the whole, it seems that the new style of government and a degree pragmatism within the HZDS contributed to alleviating the deep political polarisation in the country.

Democracy and the 'Slovak question'

The government coalition which came to power in 1998 faced major challenges at three different levels. Some of problems are present in a number of Western countries as well, such as the ageing of the population and the resulting need to reform the pension system and to improve the treatment of the elderly. Second, Slovakia faces a set of problems more or less common to all the post-communist countries: unfinished reforms in society and in the economy and changes in people's mindsets and behaviour. Third, the country must come to grips with a specifically Slovak problem – the legacy of Mečiarism, which has left a deep imprint on the country's political culture. The problems of ethnic minorities (Hungarian and Roma) were potentially explosive at the end of the Mečiar era. The new government attempted political inclusion for the Hungarians and social inclusion for the Roma. The improvement on the former was almost immediate, much more difficult and long-term for the latter.

There are no simple recipes for such a situation. The anticipated negative impact the delayed economic reforms have on the standard of living of many people has been a test of social and political cohesion of the population.

Mečiar-style 'goulash nationalism', the post-communist successor to Kádár-style 'goulash socialism', rested on the idea that, to attain economic prosperity, it would be sufficient for the Slovaks to rule in their own independent state, and that the ruling party and its allies were the best guarantor of both national sovereignty and prosperity. It rested on the assumption that it was possible to achieve prosperity without respecting the principles of democracy and the rule of law. As the elections drew closer, it became evident that it was not.

Ever since the emergence of modern Slovak national awareness in the middle of the nineteenth century, the 'Slovak question' had been perceived in several dimensions – from the national, social and democratic perspectives. An anthology of Slovak political thinking, *The Slovak Question in the 20th Century*, documents how each of the past attempts to solve the Slovak question non-democratically has turned out to be problematic.[19] That applies as much to the autocratic war-time Slovak State (1939–45) as to the Stalinist and post-Stalinist eras. For most of the twentieth century, the aspirations to nationhood have been the leitmotif of the Slovak question. In the early years of the century, when Slovakia was a part of Austria–Hungary, the 'Slovak question' meant the struggle of Slovaks against Magyarisation; since the foundation of the Czechoslovak Republic in 1918, it meant striving for an equal partnership with the Czechs. The breakdown of Communism in 1989 opened new opportunities to address the Slovak question. After the national dimension was resolved by Slovakia's gaining independent statehood in 1993, the need for democracy has become the priority. As interpreted by Peter Zajac, a leading Slovak intellectual and politician, the Slovak question has now ceased to be a matter of contention between Slovaks and Hungarians or Czechs paradoxically, it has become a Slovak 'family quarrel'. Zajac views the current task as a complex of several challenges: to build Slovak statehood as an open process; to cultivate constitutional patriotism instead of defensive-aggressive nationalism; to assume individual responsibility and to accept pluralism of opinions as a guarantee of national dynamics and progress.[20] While the 1998 elections brought to the fore an intellectual and political elite more likely to act in accordance with modern democratic standards, creating a consensually unified national elite that backs democratic procedure as the only game in town will take more time. According to Soňa Szomolányi, a prominent Slovak political scientist, at least two electoral cycles will be required to assure democratic consolidation.[21]

A new reading of the Slovak anthem and the European agenda

Since November 1989, it had become customary to conclude political rallies by singing the Czechoslovak national anthem. Protest rallies against Mečiar, held during the first years of Slovakia's independence, concluded with a song written by the late Czech dissident singer Karel Kryl instead of the Slovak anthem, which at the time was a source of embarrassment to many Slovak democrats.

After a while, however, participants of such rallies began to sing the Slovak anthem. It was sung by Slovak politicians, students, NGO representatives, actors, members of the Church, academics, trade unionists, representatives of the Hungarian parties, all determined to stand up to Mečiarism. This represented a symbolic turning point, demonstrating the seriousness of the struggle being waged by the opposition in the name of constitutional patriotism. The anthem, resounding from opposition rallies in public squares in Bratislava,

Košice, Prešov, Banská Bystrica, began to be regarded as something natural; people sang it with greater confidence than before. And the second stanza suddenly acquired new meaning. Awakening Sleeping Beauty no longer meant awakening to national independence. That has already been achieved. It meant awakening Slovakia to democracy and an open society. The election 'alarm clock' went off on schedule.

Between 1999 and 2002, Slovak society continued to develop towards the overall strengthening of reformist and democratisation trends. In the field of domestic politics, the country experienced a significant institutional stabilisation; important laws were incorporated into its legal system, which enhanced stability of its political system; the environment, for an implementation of human and minority rights, also became more favourable. A culture of negotiation continued to be increasingly firmly embedded in Slovakia's political and social life, thus defusing the risks of serious social conflicts in conditions of socio-cultural, ethnic, regional and confessional diversity.

Following the 1998 parliamentary elections, the pro-democratic political elite was confronted with several crucial challenges in domestic and foreign policy. With some of these challenges the new government managed to cope rather well and relatively swiftly. However, with some others, it devoted more time to seeking compromises that would be acceptable to all members of the broad ruling coalition than to actually implementing necessary measures. That accounts in part for the mixed balance sheet of Mikuláš Dzurinda's administration on the eve of the September 2002 elections.

After 1998, there was great expectation of positive changes in Slovakia. Within months, however, it turned out that this optimism was unrealistic given the depth of problems inherited from the Mečiar period. Consequently, the disillusionment of a significant proportion of citizens has gradually grown into severe criticism. This disenchantment stemmed from fact that some of the most pressing social issues were still persisting: high unemployment, deterioration in healthcare and education, widespread corruption, and the persistently high crime rate. The current state of the society was perceived as unsatisfactory not only by politicians (including those belonging to the ruling coalition), but also by civic activists, intellectuals, and the media. Nevertheless, one could hardly deny that positive fundamental changes have been introduced in Slovakia after the 1998 elections.

In the period 1999–2002, the ruling coalition accomplished some of its most important achievements in foreign policy. Breaking the barriers of Slovakia's international isolation from the 1994–8 period, resuscitating the country's integration ambitions and chances, improving the quality of bilateral relations with its Visegrád neighbours – all this could be added up to the list of the country's achievements. The improved relations with the Visegrád partners were put to a severe test when the Hungarian Prime Minister Viktor Orbán, called in March 2002 in Brussels, for the abrogation of the Beneš decrees of 1945 concerning the confiscation of the property of German and Hungarian citizens of Czechoslovakia prior to the enlargement of the EU. The moderate response of the Slovak authorities and mainly Orbán's defeat in the general election in the Spring of 2002 have preserved the prospects of future co-operation within the Visegrád Group.

Thanks to favourable domestic political developments and clearly articulated pro-european and pro-Atlantic foreign policy, the Slovak Republic was able to stick a foot in the door leading to European Union and NATO membership. Inviting Slovakia to join the OECD in September 2000 and the EU assessment a functioning market-oriented economy in the 2001 evaluation report may serve as a confirmation of the shift in the country's international position. This movement has occurred as a direct result of reformist political and economic measures adopted in Slovakia combined with a diplomatic offensive abroad. By mid-2001, Slovakia caught up with its Visegrád neighbours in the accession negotiations with the European Union. It has opened all twenty-nine chapters of the acquis communautaire (over twenty of them were already closed, on par with those who had been negotiating with the Union since 1998). At the same time, public support to Slovakia's EU membership continues to be well over 60 per cent.

A profound change also occurred in the domestic policy. The parliament rectified a number of legislative anomalies inherited from Mečiar administration's term in office, mostly in the election legislation. In May 1999 the citizens elected a new head of state in the first direct presidential elections ever held in Slovakia. The parliament also approved a new judicial code and passed the important Act on a Free Access to Information. Independent media became yet another important catalyst of positive changes within society. The progress in freedom of the press in Slovakia was praised by a number of international institutions (e.g. Freedom House in *Freedom in the World*, US State Department in *Human Rights Report*). Of major importance were the newly adopted legal norms such as the Act on the Use of Languages of Ethnic Minorities, and the ratification of the Charter of Minority and Regional Languages. Both have substantially improved conditions for implementing minority rights. In sharp contrast to the previous period, they have considerably improved ethnic relations in the country but also its relations with Hungary, particularly sensitive to the situation of the 650,000 Hungarians in Slovakia.

The new approach to minority rights and the amending of the Slovak constitution in February 2001 strengthened country's democratic character and created more favourable conditions for its joining the European Union. The approved amendment, concerning more than a half of all the constitution's provisions, amounted to a thorough revision. It created the institution of a public human rights defender (ombudsman), anchored the possibility of transferring the performance of sovereign rights of the Slovak Republic onto the European Union, and gave precedence to legally binding acts of the EU over Slovak laws. According to the amendment, Slovakia may join any organisation of mutual collective security. These changes were further enhanced after the public administration reform was launched and the first elections to regional parliaments were held at the end of 2001. The constitutional amendment also strengthened the status of the constitutional court and laid down provisions that pave the way to important goals: to create self-governed regional administration and to guarantee the basic powers of elected regional self-government bodies.

After the 1998 elections, the country's economic policy was also redefined. Through macroeconomic stabilisation the government managed to reduce the external imbalance of Slovakia's economy. Public finances experienced a positive development after the cabinet decided to champion modern approaches to drafting the state budget. However, economic experts maintain that if the country's macroeconomic stability is to have a long-term character, it has to be supported by the completion of structural changes, such as restructuring of the banking sector, the denationalising of monopolies and major reforms in social security, taxation, health care and education. In the period of 2000–2002, Slovakia attracted considerably larger amounts of foreign direct investments than during the previous decade, which further enhanced optimistic prospects of its economic development.

The irreversibility of these changes depended on their protagonists' ability to implement them and administer the country also after the next 2002 elections. Their outcome was likely to be influenced by a number of factors. People traditionally tend to perceive problems much more sensitively (especially if they directly affect them) than actual achievements (which they tend to take for granted). The high unemployment rate, reaching 18 and 19 per cent, problems haunting the health service and educational systems, widespread clientelistic practices and corruption scandals involving high-ranking government officials, permanent discords within the ruling coalition, and unsatisfactory attempts to deal with the so-called Roma issue are just some examples of problems which fostered the citizens' criticism of the Dzurinda government's performance.

Four years after the 1998 elections, the political landscape considerably changed. Although the opposition parties of the HZDS and SNS did not manage to broaden the ranks of their followers, the parties of the ruling coalition lost a considerable share of their support. Consequently, riding the wave of citizens' disillusionment were newly formed parties with hazy ideological and political programmes combined with elaborated media and communication strategies of addressing voters. Before the 2002 elections, one of these so-called 'alternative' parties, namely Smer (Direction) founded by Robert Fico, a former vice-chair of SDL′, who defected from this party, became the second strongest political party after the HZDS. Another 'alternative' party called Alliance of the New Citizens (ANO) was founded by a media magnate and co-owner of the largest private TV Markíza Pavol Rusko. Since its founding, it has been credited with attracting around the 5 per cent threshold of popular support at the expense of the government coalition.

Paradoxically, well-established political parties with a history of more than ten years – KDH, SDL′ and DS – were struggling to reach this 5 per cent limit required for parliamentary representation. It can be assumed that the decline of political parties with clearly defined programmes is due to the fact that they are the chief protagonists of necessary but unpopular socio-economic measures. Furthermore, they are burdened by internal disputes, which frustrate their stalwarts and repel potential voters. In this situation the 'alternative' parties, without clearly professed political values and programmes, are benefiting from voters' disenchantment of coalition voters who do not wish the authoritarian politics of Vladimír Mečiar to return.

In recent years, Slovakia's system of political parties experienced a complex development. Expectations of many observers that the country's political landscape might become more 'standardised' have not materialised. The HZDS remained the largest party whose electoral preferences were steadily hovering at or above its 1998 election result. On the other hand, all parties of the ruling coalition (except of the Party of the Hungarian Coalition) experienced a decrease in popular support, internal conflicts and fragmentation.

This applied to the situation in the non-leftist segment of the political spectrum. Following a promising launch, Slovak Christian and Democratic Union (SDKÚ), a new political formation of Prime Minister Mikuláš Dzurinda at the beginning of 2000, began to drop in the polls. Similarly, the main left-wing component of the coalition was divided, forcing the resignation from the government of its most prominent moderate B. Schmögnerova. Although it was clear that a possible competitor of Mečiar and Fico in the 2002 elections had to muster at least 20 per cent of popular support and that the basic precondition for founding such a subject is reaching a political compromise by several parties, their representatives continued to champion their mutually unacceptable ideas or pre-conditions for fusion. The ruling coalition, on the whole, came through repeated disputes and conflicts. Instead of providing a strong, coherent, democratic counterbalance to their populist rivals, the ruling parties bickering over the governmental agenda undermined their credibility.

So, what are the prospects for the country's following the 2002 parliamentary elections? Most analysts agree that the HZDS electorate is so stable that the party will reach its highest voter support. However, the real question is: could the HZDS headed by Mečiar forge a new Slovak government. On the eve of the September 2002 election, Mečiar's coalition potential was close to zero, which means that no party (except the SNS) was willing to form the future ruling coalition with the HZDS under its current leadership. Much depended on the turnout of the urban electorate, which in the 1998 elections voted against the HZDS for a heterogeneous 'pro-European' coalition. Four years later the dividing lines became somewhat blurred but Slovakia faced basically a similar dilemma.

Bearing in mind the emerging consensus on Slovakia's foreign policy aims (even HZDS belatedly joined the ruling coalition parties in their support of Slovakia's EU and NATO membership), it was likely that continuity would prevail in any future coalition government's foreign policy orientation for the country. It could also be expected that the new government will continue the reformist course in some fields of domestic policy though it could also be anticipated that certain reforms launched since 1998 might be inhibited after the 2002 elections. Thus the main challenge for the representatives of the new ruling coalition was to build on the positive developments inherited from its predecessors and to ensure the continuation, after the Autumn of 2002, of those reformist policies deemed necessary not to jeopardise Slovakia's chances to meet the 2004 target for the enlargement of the European Union.

The results of the 20–21 September general election in Slovakia came as a relief to those concerned that the country might be shut out of the EU and NATO enlargement announced in the Autumn of 2002 in case Mečiar had returned to power. Mečiar's Movement for Democratic Slovakia did come out first in the election with almost 20 per cent of the vote (a sharp drop from the 27 per cent in the previous election) but with no coalition potential. The voters returned to power a coalition led by prime minister Mikuláš Dzurinda which received 42.5 per cent and a total of 78 seats in the 150-member Parliament. The four-party coalition is composed of Dzurinda's Slovak Democratic Christian Union which received 15 per cent of the votes, the Party of the Hungarian minority led by Béla Bugár (11 per cent), the Christian Democratic Movement (8 per cent) and the Alliance of New Citizens (8 per cent) led by Pavol Rusko.

The results are significant in two respects. First, there are not many examples in East-Central Europe where a reform government has been re-elected with the same prime minister and a similar, though not identical, coalition of parties. Usually they pay the price for unpopular economic policies. In Slovakia, Dzurinda's government has been re-elected and even given a stronger mandate to pursue its reformist agenda. Second, the elections show that the Slovak voters had matured and broken out of the isolation in which Mečiar had left them. The external pressure, the warnings by NATO Secretary General George Robertson and the US Ambassador in Slovakia against support of Mečiar seen as an authoritarian and anti-Western leader, did not prove to be counter-productive. They were seen as expressions of concern and clearly helped focus the electoral debate on the longer-term implications of domestic political choices for the EU and Euro-Atlantic integration.

Notes

1 This chapter represents a revised and updated version of an article by Martin Bútora and Zora Bútorová published in the January 1999 issue of the *Journal of Democracy*.

2 Only 6 per cent of votes in 1998 went to parties that did not qualify to enter parliament, and most of them (4 per cent) came from supporters of the Communist Party of Slovakia and the ZRS. In the previous elections, the number of votes cast for parties that did not meet the 5 per cent parliament-entry threshold was much higher. In the 1992 elections, as many as 24 per cent of the votes were lost; in 1994, the portion of lost votes constituted 13 per cent. In both cases, most of these lost votes supported non-Mečiar or anti-Mečiar parties. See V. Krivý, 'Voliči' ('Voters'), *Domino-fórum* (Bratislava, 2, 1998), 7–9.

3 *Parlamentné vol´by '98. Výskum pre International Republican Institute (Parliamentary Elections '98. Survey for the International Republican Institute)* (Bratislava: Focus, 1998).

4 See M. Bútora and Z. Bútorová, 'Slovakia: The Identity Challenges of the Newly Born State', *Social Research* Vol. 60 (Winter 1993), 705–736.

5 M. Šútovec, 'Kam povedú tie dial´nice?' ['Where Do Those Express Highways Lead?'], *Domino-fórum* (Bratislava, 1, 1997).

6 For a detailed analysis of these trends, see Z. Bútorová (ed.), *Democracy and Discontent in Slovakia: A Public Opinion Profile of a Country in Transition* (Bratislava: Institute for Public Affairs, 1998).

7 *Parlamentné vol'by '98. Výskum pre International Republican Institute (Parliamentary Elections '98: Survey for the International Republican Institute)* (Bratislava: Focus, 1998).

8 V. Krivý, 'Mestá a obce vo vol´bách. Ako volili?' ['Towns and Villages in the Elections: How Did They Vote?'], *Domino-fórum* (Bratislava, 2, 1998), 6.

9 See *Názory. Informačný bulletin* [*Opinions. Information Bulletin*], 8 (Bratislava: Public Opinion Research Institute, Statistical Office of the Slovak Republic, 1997, No. 1).

10 In January 1998, only 41 per cent of respondents believed the elections would be free and fair. See Z. Bútorová (ed.), *Democracy and Discontent in Slovakia: A Public Opinion Profile of a Country in Transition* (Bratislava: Institute for Public Affairs, 1998).

11 See Z. Bútorová ['Public Opinion'], in M. Bútora (ed.), *Slovakia 1997: A Global Report on the State of Society* (Bratislava: Institute for Public Affairs, 1998).

12 P. Demeš, 'OK '98 Campaign of Slovak NGOs for Free and Fair Elections' (Bratislava: Slovak Academic Information Agency, 1998). Since 1996, the Confederation of Trade Unions (KOZ), Slovakia's strongest labour organisation, has assumed an increasingly political and explicitly pro-democratic character. The KOZ criticised the government for its reluctance to conduct a dialogue with trade unions and employers, and it supported public protests against some government decisions. Shortly before the elections, the KOZ conducted an analysis of how parliamentary deputies had voted on various important bills. Based on this analysis, it concluded that the opposition parties (SDL, SDK and SMK) best represented the people's interests and urged voters to support them.

13 See J. Shattuck and J. B. Atwood, 'Defending Democracy: Why Democrats Trump Autocrats', *Foreign Affairs* Vol. 77 (March–April 1998), 167–170.

14 F. Zakaria, 'The Rise of Illiberal Democracy', *Foreign Affairs* Vol. 76 (November–December 1997), pp. 22–23.

15 S. P. Huntington, 'Twenty Years: The Future of the Third Wave', *Journal of Democracy* Vol. 8 (October 1997).

16 L. Diamond, 'Is the Third Wave Over?', *Journal of Democracy* Vol. 7 (July1996), 20–37.

17 C. Gershman, 'Democracy for All?', Speech for the Council on Foreign Relations (New York, 19 May 1998).

18 G. Mesežnikov, 'Vláda "vel´kej koalície"' ['Government of the "Grand Coalition"'], *Mosty* (Bratislava, 7, 1998), 8.

19 R. Chmel, 'Introduction', in R. Chmel (ed.), *Slovenská otázka v 20. storočí* (*The Slovak Question in the 20th Century*) (Bratislava: Kalligram, 1997).

20 P. Zajac, *Sen o krajine* [*A Dream about a Country*] (Bratislava: Kalligram, 1996).

21 S. Szomolányi, 'Identifying Slovakia's Emerging Regime', in S. Szomolányi and J. Gould (eds), *Slovakia: Problems of Democratic Consolidation and the Struggle for the Rules of the Game* (Bratislava: Slovak Political Science Association and Friedrich Ebert Foundation, 1997).

Steven Saxonberg[1]

3

The Czech road towards a consolidated democracy

Developments in the Czech Republic since 1996 have made many Czechs fear that their young democracy is already experiencing signs of crisis or democratic fatigue. This contrasts sharply with the atmosphere during the first half of the 1990s, when Czechs were proud to live in the country that was considered the region's model for transformation to democracy and market economy.

During the 'velvet revolution' of 1989, the famous dissident-playwright Václav Havel successfully negotiated the peaceful transfer of power from the Communist party to a coalition government that included members of the Czech opposition group Civic Forum, the Slovak opposition group Public Against Violence, Communists, and members of the former Communist support parties (the Socialist Party and People's Party). When the playwright became president, he asserted tremendous moral authority, as a man who had spent time in prison and working at various manual labour jobs because of his unrelentless opposition to the communist regime.

Czechoslovakia had several advantages over its neighbours during the initial phase of transformation, besides having the leader with the highest moral authority.[2] It had the strongest democratic legacy, being the only country in the region to have had democratic rule during the entire period between the two world wars.[3] The economy was also in better shape than its neighbours. Per capita debts were about one-third the size of Hungary and one-fifth the size of Poland.[4] With the exception of former East Germany, it was also the most industrially advanced country in the region and had the highest proportion of capital goods exports to the industrialised capitalist countries.[5] The economy did not suffer from hyperinflation (as in Poland) or high rates of inflation (as in Hungary). In contrast to Poland, the first elections in 1990 led to a stable government that lasted its full term until 1992.

By the June 1992 elections, the Czech Civic Forum and Slovak Public Against Violence had both split into several competing parties. Former federal

Finance Minister Václav Klaus of the market liberal ODS and Slovak Prime Minister Vladimír Mečiar of the left-populist HZDS came out winners of the 1992 elections. These two leaders with sharply contrasting views on policy issues were not able to agree on constitutional reform that would clarify the powers of the Czech and Slovak republics within the federation. However, the two men were able to agree on the peaceful separation of the country (known as the 'velvet divorce').

Afterwards, Klaus, as prime minister of the Czech Republic, presided over a centre-right coalition government of the market liberal ODS and ODA and the Christian Democratic KDU-ČSL. which was able to sit out its entire four-year term without any threats to governmental stability. Klaus introduced a voucher-privatisation scheme that led to the fastest denationalisation of state property in the region. He managed to keep unemployment levels around 3 per cent in a region where double-digit unemployment abounded; the budget was in balance and inflation was the lowest in the region.

In the 1996 elections, Klaus's centre-right coalition returned to power: for the first time in the region, a government was re-elected. In Hungary, every government has been stable enough to govern for its entire legislative period, but no ruling party has ever been re-elected or even returned to power after a period in opposition.[6] Poland has had relatively stable governments since its electoral reform in 1993, but each election brought a different government: first a socialist-peasant coalition, then a Solidarity-liberal coalition and , since 2001 a social-democrat government again. In Slovakia, Mečiar ruled from the entire period from June 1992 to September 1998 with a seven-month exception in 1994.[7]

Consolidation of a stable party system

Until 1997, the Czech Republic's party-political development also appeared as the most stable and 'Western-like' of the region. Jack Bielasiak considers three stages to the development of stable party systems in the former communist countries. First, a *polarised party system* emerges, in which the main political cleavage is between regime and society. After the communists were defeated, the anti-communist ruling coalitions split up into competing groups that have different notions of how to carry out the transformation. At this stage, clear economic interests have still not developed among the electorate, because voters cannot be sure how their situation will change after the economic reforms are carried out – they cannot even know what the reforms will be. Consequently, an 'open political space' develops that allows newly emerging political organisations to appeal to many types of issues (such as national, ethnic, religious, cultural and political dimensions). During this period, voters have not yet developed loyalties to existing parties, so no party system has yet crystallised. Thus, the system becomes *fragmented*. Finally, a *pluralist party system* arises, as voters become more cognisant of their interests and the electoral system filters out weak parties.

In the polarisation phase, Civic Forum in the Czech lands and Public Against Violence in Slovakia became the dominating anti-communist movements, although several smaller parties also obtained the necessary 5 per cent of the votes to enter parliament. As can be seen from table 3.1, the Czech society was more polarised than the Slovak one. There were several more Slovak parties than Czech parties in both houses of the Federal parliament and the main Czech opposition movement gained a larger share of the votes than their Slovak colleagues. The same holds true for the national parliaments in the Slovak and Czech Republics.

Table 3.1 The 1990 election results (%)

Parties	*Federal Assembly: House of the People*	*Federal Assembly: House of Nations*	*Czech/Slovak National Councils*
Czech Republic			
Civic Forum	53.1	50.0	49.5
Communist Party	13.5	13.8	13.3
KDU (Christian Democratic Union)	8.7	8.7	8.4
HSD-SMS[a]	7.9	9.1	10.0
Slovak Republic			
Public Against Violence	32.5	37.3	29.3
Slovak National Party	13.8	13.4	13.3
Christian Democratic Movement	19.0	16.7	19.2
Communist Party	11	11.4	13.9
Hungarian Movement[b]	8.6	8.5	8.7
Democratic Party	4.4	3.7	4.4
Green Party	3.2	2.6	3.5

Notes: [a] Movement for Self-government Democracy–Society for Moravia and Silesia.
[b] Coexistence and the Hungarian Christian Democratic Movement.
Source: Abby Innes, 'The Breakup of Czechoslovakia: The Impact of Party Development on the Separation of the State', *East European Politics and Societes*, Vol. 11, No. 3 (1997), 396.

Shortly after the first free elections in 1990, the political scene became more fragmented. Federal Finance Minister Václav Klaus got elected chair of the Civic Forum in the following autumn. Once he assumed his new post, he favoured splitting the forum and establishing a traditional right-wing political party. He founded the ODS (Civic Democratic Party) while the intellectual faction that had dominated the Forum's leadership established the social-liberal OH (Civic Movement). Another smaller right-wing party, the Civic Democratic Alliance (ODA), had already emerged from the Forum. This party did not differ much ideologically from ODS, but it had a more intellectual profile. The ODA intellectuals wanted to remain outside the ODS, less for ideological reasons, than because Klaus already completely dominated his party.[8] Some of Civic Forum's former members also joined the small Czechoslovak

Social Democratic Party (ČSSD), that had failed to enter parliament in the 1990 elections.

Meanwhile, the two parties that had existed as 'satellites' of the ruling Communist Party, hoped to revive their chances to influence Czech politics by entering into alliances with other parties. The Socialist Party joined forces with the Greens and the Peasant Party and formed the Liberal Social Union (LSU). The Peoples Party merged with the Christian Democratic Union and became the KDU-ČSL. Even the communists led an electoral alliance, by co-operating with a small socialist group under the name Left Bloc (LB).

All of these parties made it into parliament except for the social-liberal OH. As table 3.2 shows, there were eight groups that made it into parliament in the Czech lands, including the right-wing populist Republicans. If one considers the parties that came in as part of alliances, then there were twelve parties in all. Although the results of the elections to the federal assembly are not mentioned, the results for the Czech parties were basically the same there.

Table 3.2 The 1992 election results for the Czech National Council

Parties	*% of votes*	*Seats*
ODS-KDS	29.7	76
LB	14.1	35
LSU	6.5	16
ČSSD	6.5	16
KDU-ČSL	6.3	15
Republicans	6.0	14
ODA	6.0	14
HSD-SMS	5.9	14
Other parties	19.0	0
ODS-KDS+ODA+KDU-ÄSL	42.0	105 of 200

Source: Innes, 'The Breakup of Czechoslovakia', p. 431.

Several kinds of cleavages emerged from the 1992 elections. The HSD-SMS and the Peasant Party of the LSU alliance both represented geographical and urban–rural cleavages. The Republicans and Communists of the Left Bloc added an authoritarian–democratic tension (the anti-Romany Republicans also added a nationalist dimension). To some extent, the Christian democratic KDU-ČSL group revealed a (weak) religious–secular cleavage; the party profiled itself as 'Christian' mainly on the question of restitution of Church property. On other issues, it often swings from conservative market-oriented to social liberal stances.[9]

The main parties came closer to the traditional Western party-system than in many other former communist countries. The ODS is a free market liberal party, while the ČSSD is the only social democratic party in the region that is not a reformed communist party. So three of the most important parties have traditional Western ideological profiles. In both Hungary and Poland, the social democratic parties are ex-communist parties which do not have a clear ideological profile, because their power base was the old nomenklatura from the communist era. Many of their clientele are former state or party officials who have become private entrepreneurs by taking control of state property. Consequently, the Polish and Hungarian parties often pursue pro-business policies that are more market-liberal than the centre-right parties. Similarly, the centre-right parties in other former communist countries are often based on personal contacts rather than ideology. For example, in Hungary, the Democratic Forum had its base in former 'populist' dissidents, the Free Democrats in 'urban' dissidents, while the Young Democrats emerged from an anti-communist student union. All three parties changed (albeit to different degrees) their ideological profile several times since their foundation. So the Czech Republic had already come closer to establishing a stable plural party system than most of its neighbours.

The movement towards consolidation of a pluralist party system was further helped by the division of Czechoslovakia. After the 1992 elections, president Havel asked Václav Klaus to form the new government. However, his Slovak counterpart, Vladimír Mečiar had very different views than Klaus on economic and constitutional issues (the status of the two republics within the federation). They both agreed to divide the country, rather than compromise on these issues. This made it easier for Klaus to pursue market-liberal policies, while Mečiar could gain more power in an independent Slovakia than in a continued federation.[10] Since there were no cross national parties, the Czechoslovak parliament was composed of Czech and Slovak parties. A split meant that the number of parties for each separate country would be less than if the parties of both the Czech and Slovak Republics were part of one federal parliament.

The 1996 elections: the crisis begins

The centre-right coalition of ODS, ODA and KDU-ČSL ruled without any important problems until the 1996 elections. That election moved the country even closer to the traditional type of Western parliamentary system, with fewer cleavages and more clearly defined interests. As table 3.3 shows, the geographical cleavage disappeared, as both the HSD-SMS and Peasant Party (as part of the LSU) left parliament. The number of parties further decreased as the ODS absorbed the Christian Democratic Party (KDS). Furthermore, the Left Bloc dissipated, leaving the Communists to fend for themselves. Thus, the number of parties in parliament declined by half to only six parties.

The electoral system also appeared to be among the most stable in the region, as the centre-right coalition received nearly the same amount of votes as in the last election (it increased its total by about 2 per cent). In comparison, the winners of the first free elections in Hungary, the Hungarian Democratic Forum, became so unpopular that it became an insignificant party after its first term of office.

Table 3.3 The 1996 election results

Party	*% of votes*	*Seats*
ODS	29.6	68
Social Democrats	26.4	61
Communists	10.3	22
KDU-ČSL	8.1	18
Republicans	8.0	18
ODA	6.4	13
ODS+KDU-ČSL+ODA	44.1	99 of 200

Sources: The % of votes is listed in Pavel Machonin *et al.*, *Strategie Sociální Transformace České Spole Čnost* (Brno: nakladatelství Doplněk, 1996), 114; I calculated the numbers of seats in parliament from a list of parliamentary members printed *in Parlament zpravodaj* (06/96–97): 229–231.

Another indication that the system was becoming more stable was the consolidation of the centre-left. OH , which had barely missed the 5 per cent barrier in the previous elections, and the LSU did not make it into parliament. Many of these parties' voters switched over to the ČSSD. Thus, the social democrats quadrupled their totals from the last election. There was now a strong centre-left opposition that was not overshadowed by the communists.

With the decrease in the number of parties and the resulting decline of cleavages, the political spectrum came close to the traditional Western system with class-based voting political contention centring around economic policy. The social democrats received most of their votes from blue-collar and white-collar workers, while the market-liberal ODS and ODA were much more dependent on the self-employed, managers, technicians and those doing intellectual work.[11] Klára Vlachová writing after the 1996 elections concludes: 'The dominant axis of the Czech political system is the classical socio-economic dimension of left–right. This means that the main political conflicts in society are over the economy, the role of the state in the economy and social inequality, i.e. the conflict between redistribution and the market'.[12]

Despite this movement toward consolidation of a stable, pluralist party system, some warnings arose with the 1996 elections. Although voting patterns stabilised and the centre-right was able to maintain its support and even add 2 per cent, it now lost its absolute majority in parliament. As part of this consolidation process, votes that previously had been 'wasted' on small parties that failed to enter parliament, now went to parliamentary parties – particularly the ČSSD.[13]

As Kieran Williams points out, government instability is often a large problem when over 15 per cent of the vote goes to extremist parties. In the 1996 elections, the Republicans and Communists received over 18 per cent of the vote, which meant that a significant fraction of the parliamentary deputies were automatically outside of the coalition 'game'. This meant that the democratic parties had 'to operate within a restricted political space'. [14] In this sense, the Czech political scene became more fragile than in Hungary or Poland, where no 'untouchable' parties have entered parliament since the first free elections. In both countries, the former Communist Parties transformed themselves into social democratic parties and no right-wing extremist parties had entered their parliaments. The situation had been reversed after 1998 when the Republicans did not enter the Czech Parliament while Czurka's far right nationalist Party entered the Hungarian Parliament.

As the political situation became less stable, so did the economic situation. Statistics released in 1997 showed that the balance of trade and balance of payment deficits turned out to be much higher than expected. Both of these deficits were then higher than in Poland and Hungary.[15] In response, the formerly popular Trade Minister Vladimír Dlouhý resigned and the National Bank was forced to let the Czech crown float. Until then, Klaus had succeeded in keeping the Czech crown as not only the most stable currency in Central and Eastern Europe, but also one of the most stable in *all* of Europe. During the following year, unemployment and inflation also increased. Foreign investors and Western governments complained over the lack of transparency on the stock and bond markets. Economic and business analysts concluded that the voucher privatisation scheme had failed. Most citizens had sold their vouchers to investment funds, which bought shares in state firms. These funds, in turn, were often owned by state-controlled banks. These banks did not pressure the newly privatised firms into restructuring and modernising themselves. Instead, they continued to subsidise the enterprises by giving them loans. Consequently, Czech industrial restructuring was falling behind Polish and Hungarian industry.[16]

Not surprisingly, Prime Minister Klaus received much of the blame for the situation. His popularity fell from 71 per cent in January 1994 to 33 per cent in November 1997.[17] To make matters worse, the press began reporting about alleged illegal practices in the financing of Klaus's party, the ODS. In October 1997, ODS co-founder, foreign minister Zieleniec, resigned, claiming that Klaus knew about the true source of anonymous donations. When the mass media in late November also alleged that the party had a secret bank account in Switzerland, the ODS leadership turned against Klaus. Finance Minister Ivan Pilip and former Interior Minister Jan Ruml openly called for Klaus's resignation.[18] At the same time, the two junior coalition partners, ODA and KDU-ČSL announced they were leaving government.

Ruml promptly announced that he would run for the chair against Klaus at the extraordinary ODS conference. Although all the former ODS ministers opposed Klaus, he gained around 70 per cent of the vote and thus, maintained his hold over the party.[19] Ruml, Pilip and several other prominent ODS members left the organisation to found a new party. Four members of this new party, Freedom Union (US), joined the new caretaker cabinet led by National Bank Chairman, Josef Tošovský. The social democrats agreed to support this coalition of independent technocrats as long as it agreed to hold new elections in June.[20]

The US wanted to rejuvenate and reshape the right by bringing young intellectuals without previous political experience into its leadership.[21] The first polls gave reason for optimism. The US continuously had the support of more voters than the ODS. By mid-spring, one poll gave the US the support of 18.3 per cent of the populace, while the ODS sank to 11.4 per cent.[22] However, during the campaign Klaus regained lost ground against the defectors from his party by using scare tactics about the 'return of socialism'. The latter seemed to have little credibility, as the ČSSD eventually did much better than the pre-election polls indicated, with over 32 per cent over the votes. Klaus polarisation attempts did succeed, though, in mobilising right-wing voters behind him. The ODS received nearly 28 per cent of the votes, while the US did not even gain 9 per cent (see table 3.4). Thus, the US became more like a replacement for ODA than ODS.

Table 3.4 The 1998 election results

Party	*% of votes*	*Seats*
Social Democrats	32.3	74
ODS	27.7	63
Communists	11.0	24
KDU-ÄSL	9.0	20
US	8.6	19
Republicans	3.9	0
Pensioners Party	3.1	0

Source: *ČTK*, internet address: www.ctknews.com/archiv/volby.htm

After winning the elections, the ČSSD now had the difficult task of forming a government. The party had originally hoped to form a coalition with the Christian Democrats. KDU-ČSL leader Josef Lux had given indications that such a coalition would be possible during the fall of 1997,[23] and supporters of such a coalition noted that a Christian democratic-social democratic alliance had been successfully ruling neighbouring Austria for quite a while. The social democrats hoped that if the 'Austrian solution' could not produce a majority, then the Christian democrats might accept an 'Italian' solution, in which a centre-left coalition gained the passive support of the Communist Party. But in the anti-communist atmosphere that dominated Czech politics, it is still unthinkable for any right of centre party (even for the social-democrats) to co-operate with the communists.

When president Havel gave Zeman the task of forming a new government, the social democratic leader tried to induce US leader Ruml into joining a Christian-social democratic alliance. Zeman even offered to step down as the prime ministerial candidate in favour of Lux wih the US in charge of four cabinet posts. Although Ruml admitted this was a generous offer, he insisted that he could never support a government with social democrats.[24] (Four years later, after the June 2002 elections, his party joined exactly such a coalition though on much less favourable terms: four years to move from considering the right–left divide as paramount to considering the pro-EU stance of the social democrats as a proper base for joining the government coalition facing a 'eurosceptic' opposition of Klaus, on the one hand, and the communists on the other.)

Klaus and Zeman separately reached the conclusion that they were not willing to become hostages of the two small centre-right parties. Instead, the hitherto arch-rivals entered negotiations on the terms of the ODS tolerating a minority social democratic government. They also concluded that electoral reform was necessary in order to strengthen the power of the largest parties. Together, the two parties held two-thirds of the seats in parliament, which gave them enough votes to change the constitution. Besides electoral reform the ODS agreed not to support any no-confidence motions proposed by the other parties. In return, the social democrats agreed to give the ODS the main post in parliament, including its chair, to Vaclav Klaus. They would also consult the ODS on all important decisions. Although the agreement was for an indefinite period, either side could cancel it. According to the agreement, the ODS would abstain on the budget but was under no obligation to support any social democratic proposals; so the social democrats might still have to co-operate with the other parties to pass its bills.[25]

Not surprisingly, the US and KDU-ČSL immediately criticised the deal for being 'unconstitutional'. Havel was also sceptical of the 'unholy' alliance and declared that his lawyers would examine the constitutionality of the scheme.[26] Some political commentators even expressed alarm over the country's democratic future. Some went as far as to compare the agreement to the legacies of previous communist-led regime.[27] According to the sceptics the two main parties had united to sidestep the established norms of democratic decision making.[28] Moreover, the social democratic government would probably be extremely weak and unable to take any important measures for solving the country's economic problems. Zeman, himself, admitted that he was forming a 'suicide cabinet'.[29] For the second time in two years, elections have failed to produce a government with a parliamentary majority. Hungary has never needed to have an early election, since each election has produced a stable government. Once Poland reformed its electoral system in 1993, the country has also had much more stable governments. A socialist-peasant coalition ruled the country from 1993 until 1997. The Solidarity-liberal coalition has been able to last for its entire mandate. Despite the fears that a section of the Czech political and intellectual elites had over their country's future, I argue below that *the elections have actually brought the country much closer to the consolidation of democracy.*

The decline of populism

Even the pessimists have admitted, the failure of the main populist movements to reach parliament was a victory for democracy, leaving parliament over 'standard' parties. Both the right-wing extremist Republicans and the left-wing populist Pensioners Party received less than 5 per cent of the vote in 1998. The failure of these two populist parties to enter parliament has undoubtedly made the democratic institutions more stable. The communists were the only extremist party that remained in parliament with 22 seats. The demise of the xenophobic Republicans also meant that the country moved closer to the establishment of a more stable pluralist party system, as the nationalist-cosmopolitan cleavage receded from the political scene.

The democratic transfer of power

In a well-functioning democracy, the transfer of power from the government to the opposition is a normal occurrence. As Samuel Huntington notes, for a new democracy, the first change of government through an election has symbolic significance and shows that a country is becoming a normal democracy. He sees change of governments through elections as one of the most important criterions for measuring consolidation.[30] In the Czech Republic this alternation of power represented an important landmark for the young democracy. Since the split of Czechoslovakia, the country has only experienced centre-right governments. In contrast, neighbouring Poland has already experienced five governments since the break-up of the Solidarity coalition, while Hungary has had three different administrations. Even Slovakia, which has been dominated by the authoritarian Mečiar, experienced a seven-month period in 1994 when the autocrat was deposed from office.

Czech voters are probably the most anti-communist in the entire region. As already noted, the ODS used this atmosphere to its advantage by playing the 'red-scare' card. Even the idealistic students, who comprise the next generation's political and economic elite, have sometimes been prone to an intolerant tendency.[31] This became apparent when students were allowed to question Zeman on the TV show Na hraně, in March. Journalist Daniel Kumermann summarised the students behaviour: 'With few exceptions, every student who spoke stuck to one very simple tune: If the ČSSD wins the parliamentary elections in June, it will be the end of any positive economic and social development in this country – if not the end of democracy itself.'[32]

Under these circumstances, the ascendance of a social democratic government represented an important step to the consolidation of democracy. It need not be a particularly successful government. Social democratic rule, without damage to either democratic institutions or the economy, can be considered a victory for democracy. This insight will add to the tolerance that is necessary for a democratic political system to function properly. Furthermore, after the ODS had given for four years its tacit support to the social democrats in government, it can no longer repeat its red-scare campaign of 'Klaus or the Left'.

The rise of the region's only 'genuine' social democratic party

Another factor leading to the consolidation of democracy is the rise of the region's only 'genuine' social democratic party. Poland, Hungary and Slovakia all have large social democratic parties.[33] In Poland and Hungary, the social democrats have even ruled for one mandate period. These parties, however, have in common their communist heritage. All three parties emerged from the former communist parties, which attempted to reform themselves during or after the collapse of the previous regime. Compared to the Czech social democrats, these parties have the advantage of the vast resources and organisational networks that remained intact after the collapse of the Soviet bloc. As former ruling communist parties, they also have a different constituency from the Czech social democrats. The reformed communists gain much of their support from former party or state functionaries and party members from the old regime. Some of them are simply nostalgic for the past, some are state employees who are worried that a non-socialist government might fire them for their communist past. A third group is the *apparatchik*-turned-entrepreneur. Many of them gained control of state property through dubious means. In Poland and Hungary 'spontaneous privatisations' were common. Managers of state firms or party officials at these firms took control of the enterprise's assets to start their own private companies. The communist regimes hurried to legalise these moves before handing over power. Other former officials hope that reformed communist governments will favour them when privatising state property or passing legislation that affects their enterprises. These groups of *nomenklatura* entrepreneurs and party members nostalgic for the *ancien regime* are absent from the Czech social democratic party. Instead, the latter tend to favour the only remaining non-reformed communist party in Central or Eastern Europe. Thus, the social democrats have the traditional social democratic voting base of industrial workers, public employees, left-leaning intellectuals and pensioners.

The rise of the Czech social democrats has been quite impressive. The party had to be built up from scratch, without the support of the communist old-boy network. In the first post-communist elections in 1990 the social democrats did not meet the 5 per cent threshold for entering parliament. In the 1992 elections they only received 6.5 per cent of the vote.[34] Shortly after assuming chairmanship of the party, Zeman succeeding in building popular support. With 26.4 per cent in the 1996 election the democratic left became strong enough to be a serious contender for power. It fulfilled this potential with convincing victories in 1998 (32 per cent) and in 2002 (30 per cent) which led the party to government.

Ironically, the man who built up the party has become a main handicap. Milos Zeman has been criticised, especially during his term at the head of the government, of being populist and authoritarian.[35] The next generation of social democratic leaders show great potential. Polls give consistently Gross, Buzková and Špidla the highest approval ratings of all Czech politicians.[36] If they show themselves to be capable ministers in the new government, though, then the social democrats could potentially reach a comparable position in Czech politics of the Swedish social democrats and Britain's 'New Labour'. Why is the emergence of a strong social democratic party good for democracy? A key component to a functioning democracy is that the opposition can provide a viable, democratic alternative. As long as the social democrats were small and the largest opposition group was the communist party, the centre-right coalition faced no credible alternative. The recent social democratic electoral victories shows that a centre-left alternative does exist.

Constitutional changes will probably increase stability

The US, KDU-ČSL and President Havel have raised fears that the two largest parties will shape the constitution to their advantage by instituting a majoritarian system. This criticism is hard to understand, since both the US and President Havel claim to support majoritarian voting system.

Havel has also added that, although he supports majoritarian rule, he is afraid it could lead to a two-party system, which would make the country less pluralistic.[37] Certainly, pluralism provides a good argument for favouring a proportional system over majoritarian system *when it works*. For example, Germany, Austria and Sweden have long combined stable governments and a proportional electoral system. These countries have succeeded in electing stable governments because the largest parties have always found reliable allies that have joined them in forming coalition cabinets. Or one of the smaller allies has tolerated the largest party by supporting it in important parliamentary votes. Such co-operation is necessary for stable governments. For under proportional electoral systems, one party rarely gains a majority in parliament.

If the political elite is not able to co-operate, then the 'first-past-the-post' elections usually produce more stable governments, because one party can gain more than half of the seats in parliament without winning anywhere near 50 per cent of the total vote. For example, in the UK the Tories were able to hold power for nearly two decades without ever gaining more than 45 per cent of the votes. In Hungary, where half the seats are allocated on a majoritarian basis and half on a proportional, the socialists gained an absolute majority of seats, even though they only won 32.6 per cent of the votes.[38]

In the Czech Republic, no formal institutions prevent the kind of co-operation that leads to stable governments. The proportional system could not make up for unwillingness of the politicians themselves to co-operate with each other. Personal differences have become one of the most important issues in political bargaining. Understandably, many Czechs are concerned about the prospects of having their constitution changed. First, they had to amend the communist constitution, then they had to create a new one after the break-up of Czechoslovakia. The joint ODS-social democratic proposal put forward at the end of the 1990s raised a broader issue about the wisdom of periodic changes in the constitution.

During transitions from authoritarian to democratic rule, the new constitutions result from bargaining between the old regime and the opposition.[39] As Przeworski *et al.* note: 'Conflicts over institutions are likely to be protracted. The actors bargaining over the institutions are unlikely to "get it right" the first time: it often takes several attempts before a stable framework emerges.'[40] In his classic book *Democracy in Plural Societies*, Arend Lijphaart asserts that proportional systems work best in plural societies, in which ethnic and/or religious cleavages are as important as class cleavages.[41] Under such conditions, it is good for democracy if there is a coalition government that includes members of all ethnic and/or religious groups. Otherwise, a majoritarian system makes it easy for the largest ethnic or religious group to exclude the minority group from the political decision-making process, which in turn can potentially lead to violent conflicts and movements for national independence. However, this type of 'consociational democracy' only functions well if the elites are willing to co-operate well. Finally, Lijphart concludes that majoritarian systems function best for homogeneous societies.[42]

In the Czech case, the political elites negotiated a democratic transition with the communist regime when Czechoslovakia was a plural society that included Czechs, Slovaks and a sizeable Hungarian minority. The new democratic Czechoslovakia took over the consociational elements of the old communist constitution. There were two houses of parliament: the House of the People, based on proportional representation and the House of Nations, in which both the Czech and Slovak Republics were allocated an equal number of seats, although there were nearly twice as many Czechs as Slovaks in the country. When the country divided, the Slovak and Hungarian minorities became negligible in the new Czech Republic. According to Lijphart's criteria, it was no longer a plural society; therefore there was no longer such compelling need to have a proportional electoral system. The Czech Republic kept the proportional system for several reasons. The country, as part of Czechoslovakia, had a tradition of proportional representation dating back to the First Republic of the inter-war period. Second, the newly established country had to pass a new constitution very quickly after the 'velvet divorce'. Thus, it was easier to continue the old tradition, rather than have a long protracted debate over a new system. Finally, the constitution was a result of political bargaining and the ruling ODS needed the support of smaller parties to pass the new constitution. None of these parties could have expected to do better under a majoritarian system. Once the social democrats became large enough to believe that they could benefit from a majoritarian system there was a temptation to make a deal with the ODS and change the electoral system. In the end the opposition of the smaller parties, of the senate and of the president avoided major constitutional changes.

Conclusion

There have been somewhat exaggerated concerns voiced among some Czech political analysts concerning the evolution of the country's democratic institutions after the unholy alliance of a minority social-democratic government and its main rival, the ODS of Vaclav Klaus. In contrast, I have argued, the Czech Republic has moved closer to consolidating its democracy. The 1998 elections had strengthened the country's democratic development for four reasons. First, contrary to the pre-election polls the two populist parties, the republicans and Pensioners' Party, failed to enter parliament. Second, there has been a change of government from the centre-right to the left. Democracy cannot be consolidated until the citizens accept that it is perfectly normal for government to change hands. Once right-wing voters realised that the democratic left was not a threat to the consolidation of political democracy and a market economy, the political atmosphere became more tolerant and political debates tend to become more issue-oriented. Third, the swift rise of the Social Democratic Party has meant that the electorate did finally have a viable alternative to the ruling centre-right coalition. This has also improved the quality of democracy. As long as the communists were the largest opposition party, a change of government was not possible. Moreover, the Czech Social Democratic Party has the strongest democratic credentials of any party in the region, because it is the only one without a Stalinist past.

Reflections on the first social democratic government

When I first wrote on this subject a few years ago, I claimed that despite widespread criticism of the opposition agreement between the Social Democrats and ODS, several important positive results would come out of the election. Specifically, I mentioned: (1) the decline of populism; (2) the democratic transfer of power; (3) the rise of the region's only social democratic party that is without a communist past; and (4) the desire of the ODS and ČSSD to reach constitutional changes in the electoral system, which would increase political stability.

Of these four issues, the last one remains the greatest problem. The two largest parties agreed to a reform that would keep proportional representation, but would increase the number of districts from 8 to 35 and thus radically decrease the number of MPs that could be elected in each district. Most districts would only have 5–6 representatives, compared to an average of 16–17 at present. Consequently, small parties would have trouble reaching the 15–20 per cent threshold required in each district for sending candidates to parliament. The two parties had hoped that a two-party system would consolidate their dominance. Instead, the ČSSD and ODS tried to push through their reforms against the vicious opposition of the other parties. However, the supreme court has ruled most of their reform to be unconstitutional. The only portion of the reform that the court kept was a law requiring electoral coalitions to gain 5 per cent of the vote for each party. That is, for example, the four-party coalition would need to obtain 20 per cent of the vote, since it represents four parties.[43]

Concerning the other three points, populism on the far right seems to be dead, as the Republicans have continued to decline into obscurity. On the other hand, Zeman's behaviour as prime minister (1998–2002) has led to accusations of populism among the ruling party. His relationship with the press has especially created cause for concern. On one occasion, he claimed that Czech journalists are 'largely amateurs and liars' and added that many journalists are corrupt.[44] As the American journalist Andrew Stroehlein noted, most of

Zeman's accusations in this case were actually to some extent true. Being a former editor of the *New Presence* and later editor of *Central European Review*, and having written for several Czech language newspapers and journals, he had first-hand experience of 'amateurism and corruption' ; nevertheless, he argued, it is not exactly statesmanlike to make such claims without having evidence to back it up.[45]

Regardless of the charges of populism against Zeman, the government has definitely removed all fears that a social democratic government could reinstate communism. On the contrary, the social democrats have won praise for their efforts in privatisation. While Klaus agreed with Lenin that banks provide the 'commanding heights' of the economy and therefore, must be in state hands, the social democrats have privatised all the major banks. While Klaus wanted to keep Czech firms in Czech hands by spreading ownership through coupon privatisation, the social democrats have openly sought large foreign multinational corporations as owners for privatised firms and they have even hired the most prestigious brokerage firms, such as Goldman and Sachs, to advise them on the privatisations. They have also placed great emphasis on transparency, so that accusations of corruption and 'tunnelling' cannot emerge as in the original Klaus privatisation scheme.[46]

After the EU annual report on accession sharply criticised the Czech Republic in 1999, Klaus had suggested forming a grand coalition. Once that offer failed, he decided to strengthen the opposition pact with the ČSSD, by agreeing to take a more active role in negotiating on policy proposals, such as the annual budget and adopting laws to EU standards. In return, the ČSSD had to support electoral reform and had to sack several ministers, whom the ODS found unpalatable.[47] Of course, the unwritten price of co-operation with the ODS is that the government can hardly fulfil its promise of fighting previous corruption with its 'clean hands campaign', since such actions would have to be largely directed against the ODS. Nevertheless, the social democrats have achieved some success in making current transactions more transparent, especially by allowing greater openness in the privatisation process. After the strengthened co-operation with the ODS, the government has made considerable progress in the privatisation process and the economy has begun to recover. Foreign investments are at an all-time high (partially through the sell-offs of state firms to foreign companies), growth has increased and unemployment is declining. The major economic concern is the budget deficit, which has grown to over 5 per cent and problems in deregulating the telecom industry. But the overall economic situation appears to be better than when the social democrats came to power.

Despite the praise that the social democratic government received for its privatisation policies, the party does not operate yet as a traditional Western social democratic party. The media used to emphasise a split in the party between 'traditionalists' around Zeman and 'modernisers' around Buzková and Gross. The ideological lines, however, are not so clear. It seems more relevant to divide the party into 'populists', who actually tend to be disliked among in the population (which includes people such as Zeman and Gregr) and a those who are extremely competent ministers, and have won the respect of the middle-class voters, regardless of their political opinions. This latter group of 'modernists' is led by former Labour and Social Minister Vladimír Špidla who has become much more popular than Zeman.[48] Zeman, interestingly, made Špidla his choice to succeed him as party leader. Špidla seems be able to gain the respect of the voters and , no less importantly of the smaller centre parties (the Christian KDU and the liberal US) with whom the social democrats formed a new coalition government in July 2002. Thus a clear break with the previous policy of tacit alliance between the main parties of the left and the right, the social democratic government and the ODS, has taken place, opening the way for democratic pluralism. The new coalition's explicitly stated common denominator is: the completion of the country's preparation for entry into the EU.

Notes

1 An earlier version of this chapter was published in the January 1999 issue of the *Journal of Democracy*.

2 Czechoslovakia contrasted strongly with Poland, where Lech Walesa also enjoyed tremendous moral authority, but the former Solidarity union leader refused to become prime minister in the coalition government between Solidarity, the Communists and former Communist support parties.

3 See, for example, J. Batt, 'Czechoslovakia', in S. Whitefield (ed.), *The New Institutional Architecture of Eastern Europe* (New York: St Martin's Press, 1993), 35, and G. Golan, *Reform Rule in Czechoslovakia. The Dubček Era* (Cambridge: Cambridge University Press, 1973), 1.

4 See the graph in S. Saxonberg, 'The Fall: Czechoslovakia, East Germany, Hungary and Poland in a Comparative Perspective' (doctoral dissertation, Uppsala University, 1997) 54.

5 For statistics on the exports of capital goods, see H. Wienert and J. Slater, *East–West Technology Transfer: The Trade and Economic Aspects* (Paris: OECD, 1986), 223–225. Czechoslovakia ranks second after East Germany. However, in the Czech lands, which later became the Czech Republic, the proportion of capital goods exports was probably higher than in East Germany, since Slovakia was much less industrialised than the Czech lands.

6 The first elections were won by the Hungarian Democratic Forum, which entered into an alliance with several small parties. Then the socialist party won an absolute majority, but chose to govern in a coalition with the liberal Free Democrats. After the 1998 elections, the liberal-conservative Young Democrats became the largest party of the new coalition government.

7 S. Fisher, 'Slovakia: The Firs Year of Independence', *RFE-RL Research Report*, Vol. 3, No. 1 (1994), 87–91.

8 K. Dahl Martinson, 'Václav Klaus und die politische stabilität in der Tschechischen Republik', *Osteuropa*, Vol. 44, No. 11 (1994), 1,058.

9 See, for example, S. Saxonberg, 'Konzervativní strana? Pouze KSČM', *Listy*, Vol. 28, No. 4 (1998), 8–12.

10 A. Innes, 'The Breakup of Czechoslovakia: The Impact of Party Development on the Separation of the State', *East European Politics and Societes*, Vol. 11, No. 3 (1997), and G. Wightman, 'The Development of the Party System and the Break-up of Czechoslovakia',

in G. Wightman (ed.), *Party Formation in East-Central Europe* (Aldershot: Edward Elgar Publishing, 1995), 79–106.

11 P. Machonin *et al.*, *Strategie sociální transformace České spolecnosti* (Brno: Nakadatelství Doplněk, 1996) 122.

12 K. Vlachová, 'Czech Political Parties and Their Voters', *Czech Sociological Review*, Vol. 5, No. 1 (1997), 50.

13 This point has been made by F. Turnovec, 'Votes, Seats and Power: 1996 Parliamentary Election in the Czech Republic', *Communist and Post-Communist Studies*, Vol. 30, No. 3 (1997) 295, and M. Novák, 'Is There One Best "Model of Democracy"? Efficiency and Representativeness: "Theoretical Revolution" or Democratic Dilemma?', *Czech Sociological Review* Vol. 5, No. 2 (1997), 152.

14 K. Williams, 'Blame It on the Extremists', *New Presence*, January (1998).

15 V. Nikolski, 'Současné postavení České ekonomiky', *Mezinárodní politika*, Vol. 22, No. 1 (1998), 17.

16 See, for example, S. Kettle, 'Of Money and Morality', *Transition* (15 March 1995), 37, Orenstein, 'Václav Klaus: Revolutionary and Parliamentarian', *East European Constitutional Review*, Winter (1998) 53–55, Václav Žák, 'Křižovatky naší privatizace', *Listy*, Vol. 27, No. 3 (1997), 13–22 and *Prague Post* (30 April 1997). For a summary of the state of the economy at the end of 1997, see M. Geussová, 'Ekonomika stagnuje', *Tyden*, No. 1 (1998), 61.

17 *Mladá fronta dnes* (19 November 1997).

18 *Mladá fronta dnes* (29 November 1997).

19 *Lidové noviny* (15 December 1997), reports that Klaus received 227 of 314 votes.

20 See, for example, B. Pecinka, 'Bez Klause', *Respekt*, Nos 1–2 (11 January 1998). The dissident ODS members did not officially establish the US until its congress in February. For reports on this congress, see, for example, *Hospodářské noviny* (23 February 1998).

21 See the interview with Jan Ruml in *Hospodářské noviny* (23 February 1998).

22 The poll was taken by the organisation STEM. See *Právo* (16 March 1998).

23 In the words of Jiří Pehe, writing in late 1997: KDU-ČSL leader Lux 'is and isn't trying to appear like a potential partner for the ČSSD'. J. Pehe, 'Krize politiky a politika krize. Ohlédnutí za odcházejícím rokem 1997', *Nová Přitomnost* (December 1997).

24 *Mladá fronta dnes* (2 July 1998).

25 The agreement was reprinted in *Právo* (10 July 1998).

26 For example, *Lidové noviny* (10 July 1998).

27 For example, Ondrej Štindl, writing in *Lidový noviny* (10 July 1998).

28 For example, J. Macháček and P. Holub, 'Země dvou Mečiarů', *Respekt*, No. 29 (13 July 1998).

29 For a discussion of this, see, for example, J. Leschtina, 'ČSSD na konci spasitelských snů', *Mladá fronta dnes* (29 July 1998).

30 S. P. Huntington, *The Third Wave: Democratisation of the Late Twentieth Century* (Norman: University of Oklahoma Press, 1992), 266–267.

31 For a discussion of this phenomenon, see S. Saxonberg, 'Nesnášenliví čeští studenti. Ekonomičtí liberálové, intelektuální dogmatici', *Nová přitomnost* (August, 1998).

32 D. Kumermann, 'ČSSD Feels Intolerance of Youth', *Prague Post* (25 March 1998).

33 In Slovakia the party officially calls itself the 'Party of the Democratic Left'.

34 The statistics come from P. Machonin, 'Socio-economic Changes in the Czech Republic: With an Appendix Concerning the 1996 Elections' Result', *Working Paper 96:10*, 1996 (Institute of Sociology, Academy of Sciences of the Czech Republic), 35.

35 See, for example, P. Fiala and F. Mikš, *Úvahy o České politické krizi* (Brno: CDK, 1998), 26.

36 For example, a poll taken in February 1998 showed that 70 per cent support Buzková and 65 per cent Gross, compared to only 38 per cent for Zeman ad 17 per cent for Klaus. See *Pravo* (17 February 1998).

37 He was also afraid that a proportional system with a high threshold – such as 15 per cent – would lead to a two-party system. This alternative is more likely to lead to a two-party system than purely majoritarian elections. For although the KDU-ČSL and US both received under 15 per cent of the vote, they do have well-known, popular politicians who would be likely to win some districts in a majoritarian system. In fact, the ODA and KDU-ČSL did in fact win a large proportion of seats in the senatorial elections, where, as in America, citizens vote for persons rather than parties on a 'first-past-the-post' basis.

38 The statistics on Hungary come from the Internet address: http://-public.rz.uni-duesseldorf.de/~nordsiew/hungary.html

39 S. Haggard and R. R. Kaufman, *The Political Economy of Democratic Transitions* (Princeton: Princeton University Press, 1995), 118.

40 Przeworski *et al.*, *Sustainable Democracy* (Cambridge: Cambridge University Press, 1993), 49.

41 A. Lijphart, *Democracy in Plural Societies: A Comparative Exploration* (New Haven: Yale University Press, 1977).

42 A. Lijphart, *Democracies: Patterns of Majoritarian and Consensus Government in Twenty-one Countries* (New Haven: Yale University Press, 1984).

43 See, for example, *Lidové noviny* (25 January 2001), whose headline reads 'Havel wins fight over electoral law'.

44 ČTK (6 July 1999).

45 A. Stroehlein, '"Scum" Writer Comes Clean', *Prague Post* (14 July 1999).

46 I am basing this account on the EU Progress Report available at http://europa.eu.int/comm/enlargement/czech/index.htm entitled *2000 Regular Report from the Commission on the Czech Republic's Progress towards Accession* and interviews with officials from the Finance Ministry and National Property Fund, as well as articles in business journals. For example, *Business Central Europe* (*The Annual 2001*), 23, reports that growth increased from –2.2 per cent in 1998 to 2.5 per cent in 2000, while inflation decreased from 10.7 per cent to 3 per cent and unemployment increased from 1998, but decreased from 9.4 per cent in 1999 to 9 per cent in 2000. However, the budget deficit has increased from 1.6 per cent of GDP to 5.1 per cent.

47 See, for example, *Lidové noviny* (27 January 2000) and *Mladá fronta dnes* (26 January 2000).

48 Interestingly, the social democratic party's homepage mentions that a survey taken by the Institute for Public Opinion (IVVM) on 20 October 2000, shows that Buzková had the sympathy of 65 per cent of the citizens, with Bross receiving 62 per cent, Špidla 49 per cent and Mertlík over 40 per cent. However, the party did not want to mention the showing of its leader, Prime Minister Zeman, whose ratings have consistently been around 20 per cent. See http://cssd.cz/aktuality/a_145.htm. For example, *Lidové noviny* (26 September 2000) reported that Zeman had the trust of 23 per cent of the populace (up from 20 per cent).

Michael Leigh

4

The Czech Republic as an EU candidate

Strengths and weaknesses

Introduction

From the start of the transition process with the 'velvet revolution' of 1989, there has been every reason to expect the Czech Republic to be among the first countries in Central and Eastern Europe to join the European Union. The first Czechoslovak Republic, established in 1919, gave the country a solid democratic tradition that sustained the dissident movement during the cold war and the restoration of democratic institutions following the 'velvet revolution' of 1989. The 'velvet divorce' between the Czech and Slovak Republics in 1993 further confirmed the Czechs' reputation for moderation and orderliness. The Europe Agreement, renegotiated after separation from Slovakia, provided the initial framework for the transposition of EU legislation. Accession to NATO sealed the Czech Republic's standing among the most advanced of the Central and East European countries.

In the economic sphere, the early years of the transition process reinforced the overall impression of maturity. The country's industrial traditions and well-qualified labour force appeared as the economic counterpart of its earlier democratic experience. The main macroeconomic indicators were reassuring. The shift to a market system seemed to be occurring with a minimum of social and economic disruption. Ministers reeled off statistics to visitors which apparently showed that it was possible to move to a market system, while keeping down inflation and unemployment, maintaining price stability, absorbing a significant currency devaluation and achieving a respectable rate of growth.

Yet by 1997, there were considerable doubts in the Czech Republic about whether the country could maintain its place among the front-runners for EU membership. These doubts were confirmed by critical reports from the European Commission on difficulties encountered by the Czech Republic in preparation for EU membership.[1] What had occurred since the heady days of November 1989 to raise such doubts and to what extent had the country's problems been overcome by 2001? This chapter looks at some of the strengths and weaknesses of the Czech Republic in the accession process and the circumstances which underlie shifting perceptions of its performance. It does not reproduce or summarise the detailed analyses in the European Commission's regular progress reports but rather presents an analysis of the factors influencing the country's efforts to complete the transition and to prepare for EU membership. It takes into account developments until early 2002.

Czech traditions and the start of the transition process

One of Czechoslovakia's main advantages in the transition process, which began in 1989, was the country's democratic and business traditions. Memories of the prominent role played by the Czech lands during the Austro-Hungarian empire and of the first republic of Tomas Masaryk, the consecration of the Czech national revival, sustained the dissident movement and much of the silent majority during the Communist regime. There was considerable pride in the country's achievements in the 1920s and 1930s, with the success of the Czech shoe industry often cited as emblematic of the development of a particularly Czech brand of enlightened capitalism.

In the inter-war period, 'the Czech lands had all the accoutrements of a modern civil society: large cities and abundant middling-size towns, a literate public, established political parties, trade unions and chambers of commerce, a multitude of voluntary clubs and societies, a vigorous press, high schools, theatres, art galleries and so on'.[2] The strong middle class, entrepreneurial spirit and democratic institutions, in the pre-Munich period, were remembered as proof of Czechoslovakia's underlying strength, which the Nazi and Communist periods could not extinguish. The country's civil society tradition was frequently evoked by President Havel.

Czechoslovakia's main trading partners, in the inter-war period, were the present members of the European Union. The Comecon system, imposed by the Soviet Union, distorted the country's comparative advantages and forcibly reoriented its economy towards the East, providing a cover for the theft of its natural resources and despoiling its natural environment. The communist regime benefited from some initial legitimacy in the eyes of the Czech people, on the basis of residual pan-Slav leanings, and the rather wide membership of the Communist party before the 1948 coup. This was based on the nationalist, anti-German feeling that sustained many post-war communist parties in Central and Eastern Europe. However, any legitimacy was eroded, gradually at first, as internal dissent was repressed, and, more rapidly, after the failure of the 'Prague Spring' which was followed by a brutal suppression of human rights and systematic erosion of civil society. A pronounced bias in favour of the less numerous and less prosperous Slovaks in the leadership of communist Czechoslovakia added to the regime's illegitimacy in the Czech lands. But relatively high living standards in Czechoslovakia, by comparison with other Soviet-dominated countries, helped to blunt popular resistance to the regime.

The country's Western-oriented traditions and earlier successes created fertile ground for the transition, once the communist regime began to crumble. Identification of the transition with a 'return to Europe' evoked long-cherished memories, even if these were somewhat abstract for the younger generations. For Czechoslovakia's first democratically elected government, the Civic Forum government of June 1990 to June 1992, this identification with the inter-war period and with a 'return to Europe' was central. But subsequent governments drew only selectively on earlier traditions.

The country's early post-communist leadership enjoyed widespread popular support, as it could claim implicitly to be the incarnation of the national spirit and tradition. This created a widespread assumption that the people could count on the authorities for good and wise government.

The conditions of everyday life at first seemed to confirm the validity of this assumption. The opening up of the economy brought immediate improvements in the quality and variety of goods available to the population. Macro-economic stability was maintained, without the draconian effects of 'shock therapy' which were felt in some other transition countries. There was scarcely any increase in unemployment; inflation, after an initial jolt from the November 1990 devaluation, remained low and everyday life continued very much as before. Gradually, however, the population became alarmed as their purchasing power declined. There were more goods and services available in the cities, but many Czechs felt that they could afford less. Still, the atmosphere of political and economic freedom was a breath of fresh air to a population that had become inward-looking and defensive.

Even privatisation, which might have upset this rather comfortable 'velvet' transition, seemed remarkably painless. Many potential stakeholders preferred to cash in their vouchers for a small windfall gain. For quite some time privatisation without significant restructuring did little to disrupt the way of life of most workers and their families. When separation from Slovakia became effective on 1 January 1993, with minimal effects on the life of most Czechs, but with general relief at a lightening of the country's burden, it really did seem as though wise leadership had enabled the country to have its cake and eat it too.

Problems

Needless to say, the reality was more complex and the Czech people were soon to find that, changing somewhat the figure of speech, there is no free lunch. Charismatic leadership on the part of President Václav Havel from November 1989 and Prime Minister Václav Klaus from June 1992, was reassuring at a time of major upheaval. However, it needed to be backed by an effective economic reform strategy.

The 'Czech way', which resulted from bargaining among the country's new economic leaders whom the President had summoned to office after the velvet revolution, consciously rejected 'shock therapy'. It focused at first on 'small' privatisation, involving retail outlets, restaurants, and other small enterprises, followed by larger-scale privatisation, without significant prior restructuring. This privatisation was to be achieved through the free distribution of vouchers to the population and through credits provided by the still state-owned Czech banks.

The 'Czech way' worked well enough at first for small firms, although there was less than full transparency as to the origin of the finance for many new enterprises. It became increasingly difficult to found small businesses because of prohibitive interest rates and bank unhelpfulness. The banks seemed more inclined to provide large unsecured loans to major, loss making enterprises than to make modest loans to small potentially profitable businesses. The privatisation of larger firms through the voucher scheme brought little or no new capital, technology or management skills and was largely driven by more political concerns. As the privatisation process was designed to retain control of enterprises in Czech hands, avoiding the sale of most jewels of Czech industry to foreign companies, the state owned banks were encouraged to provide finance to supplement the voucher scheme. But they did not exercise normal economic discipline through the careful scrutiny of business plans, restructuring requirements and potential rates of return. As a result, huge portfolios of bad loans accumulated, which still burden public finances today. Many enterprises were privatised without significant restructuring, and continued to function without making a profit.

The combination of easy finance and lack of any effective control of management encouraged wholesale asset stripping, known as 'tunnelling', by managers who were able to exploit the ignorance of the many small shareholders and amass considerable private wealth without creating any additional value for the economy. Suspicions that such practices were condoned by the authorities, or even encouraged by lax enforcement of existing legislation, led to considerable popular disenchantment and a gradual change in the international perception of the Czech economic transition. Problems included an inadequate legal framework for privatisation and inadequate state oversight of the financial sector.

In the mid-1990s, the government referred openly to 'cushions' which were needed to sustain popular support. These included delays in the shift to market-based pricing in such key sectors as housing and energy supply. The restructuring and effective privatisation of the banking sector, utilities and much of industry were put off, avoiding unemployment but also the exercise of normal market discipline on the economy. The availability of new goods and services as a result of the 'small' privatisation further 'cushioned' the population from fundamental economic change.

The perspective of early accession to NATO and progress towards EU membership seemed to confirm the perception that the country was on the right track. Indeed, the Czech Republic was moving forward along the track of political and economic reform throughout the 1990s, even though the pace was somewhat uneven. A relatively cautious approach had the advantage of allaying the fears of the population.

The inheritance of the first republic, in which political parties were used as a means of political patronage, and of the communist period, in which some parties continued to exist merely as a token pretence at legitimacy, had robbed the notion of political 'parties' of popular legitimacy, and led to widespread early acceptance of the dissident-based citizens' movements that contributed to the overthrow of communism. However, as vehicles for the development of a democratic system, these movements were abandoned in favour of the creation of more classical parties.

Given popular inexperience with the party system, links between political parties and the citizens were uneven, with, for example, the beneficiaries of the privatisation programme exercising a strong influence on the right-wing parties, and the continued existence of an unreformed communist party, hobbling the development of the left-wing parties. Despite lively and often sensational coverage in the media of politicians' foibles, little discontent with the slow pace of reform found its way into the political system.[3]

Other transmission belts, outside the political system, were slow to form. Non-governmental organisations, voluntary associations and other manifestations of 'civil society', which had thrived during the first republic but were dismantled under communism, received little official encouragement. Yet these were much needed both to fill the gaps in the formal political process and to address specific issues, such as the condition of the Roma or the protection of the environment. Czechoslovakia had missed out on the efforts made over a generation by voluntary groups in Western Europe or the United States to raise awareness about the unacceptability of public expressions of racism and xenophobia, or about other public policy issues.

The nascent NGO sector in the Czech Republic depended to a considerable extent on foreign support. Foundations in Western Europe, sometimes linked to political parties, as well as private sponsors, played a major role in nurturing voluntary bodies in the Czech Republic. The efforts of such international sources of support, including the European Union, appeared at times as a substitute for civil society in the Czech Republic itself.

Even the business community, which can be relied upon in most countries to lobby for policy initiatives which it favours, was too permeated by officials of the former regime, who benefited from privatisation without restructuring and without legal oversight, to bring much pressure to bear for quicker and more comprehensive reform. Indeed the intimate links in the mid-1990s between the state-owned banks, the investment funds, and enterprise meant that important parts of the business community had a vested interest in the status quo. Small and middle-sized firms contributed increasingly to national income but were, on the whole, too dispersed and focused on immediate concerns, to bring their influence to bear on the political system. As a result, the returns on investment remained very low, and the economy consistently under-performed.

Against this background, 'institution-building' became a major focus of the European Union's efforts to help the Czech Republic prepare for membership. To be sure, most of the institutions concerned are specialised, working to implement public policy in areas covered by the *acquis* of the European Union. But institution building, in the wider sense of recreating the profusion of autonomous bodies which form an independent support structure for the political system, also became a priority for foreign providers of assistance. This was evident, for example, in efforts to set up organisations to help overcome the marginalisation of the Roma community. Institution building primarily covers the reform of the public administration and the judiciary. Here, too, half a century of authoritarian rule had left a major gap to be filled with foreign advice and assistance. The country's needs ranged from the establishment of a proper statute for civil servants to the training of judges and the acceleration of judicial procedures. There was a certain reluctance to guarantee, through a proper civil service statute, the jobs of the many officials at all levels who had been employed by the state before 1989. But there was also reluctance to give up the opportunities for patronage provided by a more flexible system. By early 2002 there still were no 'civil servants' as such in the Czech Republic. Officials were merely employees of ministries, municipalities and so on. Delays in reform of the public administration and the judiciary inevitably had an impact on the country's preparations for EU membership and were regularly pointed out in the annual reports drafted by the Commission.

Often draft laws proved unsatisfactory because it was hard for ministries to recruit and retain sufficiently well-qualified staff. Poor remuneration, compared with the private sector, was part of the explanation. But the early introduction of a civil service statute might have produced incentives in the form of job security and other benefits which would have improved the quality of the public administration. In the event, the creation of a modern civil service became unnecessarily caught up in the introduction of new regional administrations, leading to further delays.

Institutions also needed to be strengthened to regulate newly liberalised sectors, such as telecommunications and broadcasting as well as financial markets. Progress eventually speeded up in these areas, largely under the influence of the accession negotiations and as a result of diminishing returns for the dominant foreign players of a closely regulated market.

The need to make greater efforts to prevent economic crime and corruption was a recurrent theme in the Commission's progress reports between 1998 and 2001. The problem was not peculiar to the Czech Republic, but, rather, an issue in most candidate countries. This should have enabled the political authorities to take up the question boldly, without implying any particular negligence in the Czech Republic. Such an approach would have helped overcome public disenchantment with the political process and could even have become a popular electoral theme. The problem was, indeed, acknowledged by the country's new political leadership in 1998. There were a number of false starts at launching an Italian-style 'clean hands' campaign. But the police and judicial authorities often lacked the capacity or the technical means to track down those at the origin of complex activities in the black and grey economy. Above all, political will was lacking to create a determined national strategy to fight corruption and economic crime.

The Czech Republic and the EU accession process

The years 1997 and 1998 marked a sea-change in the EU's approach to enlargement and subsequently in the Czech Republic's preparations for EU membership. In July 1997, the European Commission published Agenda 2000, incorporating its Opinions on the applications for membership of the Czech Republic and the other candidates in Central and Eastern Europe. The Commission's recommendations were endorsed in December by the Luxembourg European Council. These recommendations coincided with the attempt by rebels within the dominant right-wing party to remove the leadership and to adopt a more consistent pro-European line, less linked to business lobbies that saw an interest in postponing reform. This attempt resulted in the fall of the government and the establishment of a new centrist party, the Freedom Union.

The prospect of the imminent formal opening of the accession negotiations and the start of the 'screening' operation, by which the existing laws and legislative plans of the candidates were compared with the requirements of the *acquis* of the European Union, did much to focus minds in the Czech administration. This was in the hands of a caretaker government that ruled the country from December 1997 to June 1998 under the leadership of the former central bank governor Josef Tosovsky. The Tosovsky government approached pre-accession preparations in a non-political, pragmatic way.

The Foreign Ministry was given responsibility for conducting the negotiations. This implied co-ordination of the work of the specialised ministries which possessed expertise in the twenty-nine substantial 'chapters' into which the *acquis* had been divided for the purposes of the negotiations. (The other two chapters cover institutional and miscellaneous questions.) Political considerations were swept aside in the appointment of a small team in the ministry under well-qualified, firm, young leadership. This team bore a heavy responsibility in persuading other ministries to deliver timely and well-conceived negotiating positions. This was not always easy, given the highly technical nature of the acquis, the uneven quality of the public administration, and remaining scepticism in some quarters of the government and administration.

The minority social-democratic government led by Prime Minister Milos Zeman, came to power under an agreement with the ODS following the June 1998 elections. This agreement, which was signed between the Social Democratic Party and the ODS, functioned much like a power-sharing agreement. The Zeman government preserved the structure for co-ordinating the negotiations, established by its predecessor, centred on the Foreign Ministry. The appointment of a separate deputy prime minister charged with the co-ordination of efforts to prepare for membership was not a success, and the function reverted to the foreign minister who was, himself up-graded to the rank of deputy prime minister. A deputy finance minister was the contact point for financial assistance. The government adopted an ambitious legislative programme and undertook to tackle vigorously bank privatisation and other long-stalled reform measures. Nonetheless, it took time for its good intentions to be transformed into action and the Commission was rather critical of the progress achieved in its 1998 and 1999 reports.

In these years, the Czech Republic presented the paradox of a country making good progress in the negotiations, while receiving rather critical reports from the Commission on actual progress within the country in preparing for membership. The paradox is explained by the fact that the provisional closure of 'chapters' in the negotiations, at least in the early stages of the process, was based on promises by the candidate, undertakings as to the future transposition of EU legislation and the creation of the necessary administrative structures to implement and enforce it properly. In addition, the negotiations were structured so as to deal at first with the less technically and institutionally demanding chapters, leaving more difficult issues, such as environment and energy policy, to a later stage. The Commission's reports, however, recorded real progress actually made during the past year.

As the accession process reaches its conclusion the results achieved in the negotiations and in substantial preparations for membership should converge. But this was not yet the case in 1998 and 1999 when the Czech Republic's honourable record in the negotiations was not fully matched by achievements in the reform process itself. With the EU's increased insistence on careful monitoring of the carrying out of commitments, this situation would indeed have slowed the country's progress towards membership if not remedied in time. Fears were expressed in the press that the Czech Republic might even drop out of the first wave of likely new EU members.

Improvement

Between 2000 and 2002 the economic situation improved considerably, with clear signs that the recession which began in 1997 had bottomed out. There was a return to positive growth, strong inflows of foreign direct investment, and a determined effort to address long-standing needs for structural reform. The fiscal position remained fragile, however, because of the continued weight of past structural problems, and a commitment by the social democratic government to maintain, or indeed expand, fiscal transfers to the population. The key issue became one of sustainability, depending largely on the political system's capacity to deliver good governance, legal certainty, and sound economic management. The record had also improved in the transposition of the *acquis* into Czech law and arrangements for its proper implementation.

The quality of draft legislation submitted to parliament by the government improved through the efforts of the responsible deputy prime minister and a legislative council, which now consisted of independent experts, whose job was to scrutinise bills for compatibility with the *acquis*. Despite the priority given to EU legislation, amendments were frequently tabled and sometimes adopted which were out of line with aspects of the *acquis*. A notable case was the law on the National Bank which, in the view of EU and other experts, failed to ensure sufficiently the bank's independence. On the whole, however, the 'whirlwind' of legislation promised by the government in 1998 brought results, as reflected in the Commission's 2000 regular progress report.

By 2002 the Czech Republic had made up for earlier delays in legislative preparations for membership, with particularly strong progress in areas related to the free movements of goods, intellectual property and data protection, the liberalisation of capital movements and the control of state aids. In some of these areas, such as safety standards for toys and industrial standards in general, the Czech authorities could draw on the country's traditional strengths. But a firm grasp of the *acquis* on state aids took some time coming, as a result of the mindset created by the communist command economy, as well as subsequent politically motivated aids for industry. New laws have now adopted the EU's market-oriented approach in this area as well.

Work still to be done

Despite certain persistent shortcomings, by 2001 the Czech Republic was generally back on track in readying itself for EU membership. There was no further speculation about the Czech Republic dropping out of the likely first wave of EU enlargement. Nonetheless reaction in political circles in Prague to the Commission's November 2000 assessment focused somewhat disproportionately on the report's conclusions about the Czech Republic's capacity to cope with competitive pressures and market forces in the European Union[4].

The report, in fact, indicated a marked improvement in this area. The assessment was made in terms of the benchmarks used in the 1997 opinions on the candidates' applications for membership. What caused concern in Prague, however, was not so much the assessment itself but an apparent rank-ordering among the candidates in terms of the economic criteria for membership set out by the 1993 Copenhagen European Council. This appeared to place the Czech Republic in a third tier after not only Cyprus and Malta, functioning market economies, able to cope with competitive pressures and market forces in the European Union, but also after Estonia, Hungary and Poland. The Czech Republic appeared to be ranked together with Slovenia and ahead only of the other countries, which began negotiations in 2000, two years after the Czech Republic.[5]

Although this apparent rank-ordering under the economic criteria for membership in the Commission's Enlargement Strategy Paper, which accompanied the 2000 progress reports may have been somewhat infelicitous, official reaction in Prague erred in unduly accenting the negative. Indeed governments of several candidate countries often choose to question critical aspects of the Commission's reports, rather than vaunting their achievements, in order to preempt attacks from their political opponents. On balance, it was evident by the time the following progress report was released at the end of 2001 that the Czech Republic was also on track to satisfying the economic criteria for membership in the near term, a clear improvement over the three previous years' assessment.

Thus the accession negotiations, based on commitments concerning the country's capacity to implement the *acquis* and the monitoring of actual achievements in the Czech Republic's preparations for membership had begun to converge by 2001. A reassessment by the government of requests for transitional periods, in the light of progress made in putting into place the necessary laws and administrative arrangements for implementing the *acquis*, gave reason to expect that the Czech Republic would be able to keep up with the Commission's 'road map' for completing the negotiations.

One cloud on this relatively serene horizon appeared in 2000 in the form of relations with Austria. The most conspicuous difficulty concerned opposition in Austria to the Temelin nuclear power plant. Demonstrations by opponents of this project led to the blockading of border crossings and a chill in bilateral relations. This also threatened to affect the accession negotiations on energy policy, which include in rather broad terms the question of nuclear safety. Tensions were partly defused by the Czech authorities' agreement to carry out a new environmental impact study and by the Prague and Vienna governments signing at the end of 2001 of an EU-brokered compromise agreement. The issue, however, remained highly politicised in Austria.

On the Czech side there were suspicions that the demonstrations had been encouraged by political groups in Austria opposed to enlargement and by economic interests in the power industry which were less concerned with the safety of the Temelin nuclear power plant than with the competitive challenge it posed. In any event, the issue placed a strain on bilateral relations at a time when the Czech Republic's overall standing in the accession process was improving.

These relations also came under pressure from calls in Austria for the Czech Republic to address the question of the transfer of 'Sudeten Germans' from Czechoslovakia to Austria and Germany after the Second World War. Austrians repeatedly called for the rescinding of the 'Beneš decrees', to which they traced the transfer, while Czechs relied on the protocol to the Potsdam Conference of August 1945, as providing a legal basis for the transfer. Such issues draw attention to the importance of good neighbourly relations among present and future EU members.

Conclusion

The prospect of EU membership has provided a necessary boost to efforts to complete the political and economic transition process in the Czech Republic. Earlier delays in this process are now being overcome, largely as a result of the determination of Czech political leaders to ensure that their country realises its potential to be among the first to enter the Union. The overwhelming majority of the legislative and administrative reforms needed to prepare for membership would have formed part of the transition process under any circumstances. The *acquis* has provided a model for reform efforts which is logical in terms of existing economic inter-dependence and the perspective of accession.

Notes

The views in this chapter commit only the author and are not necessarily those of the European Commission.

1 *Regular Reports from the Commission on the Czech Republic's Progress towards Accession 1998, 1999, 2000*, European Commission, Brussels, http://europa.eu.int/comm/enlargement.htm
2 D. Sayer, *The Coasts of Bohemia: A Czech History* (Princeton, NJ: Princeton University Press, 1998).
3 M. A. Vachudova, 'The Czech Republic: The Unexpected Force of Institutional Constraints', in A. Pravda and J. Zielonka (eds), *Democratic Consolidation in Eastern Europe* (Oxford: Oxford University Press, 2001).
4 See note 1.
5 *Enlargement Strategy Report 2000*, European Commission, Brussels, http://europa.eu.int/comm/enlargement..htm, 2000.

Darina Malová and Marek Rybář

5

The European Union's policies towards Slovakia

Carrots and sticks of political conditionality

Introduction

Since 1993 Slovak politics has evolved around the building of the new state, covering such fundamental issues of statehood as territory, citizenship, constitution, administration and foreign and security policies. All these matters were connected with political struggle over the rules of game and the shape of the regime. The conflict-ridden nature of these issues has circumscribed the very substance of Slovak politics, full of dogged and protracted fights over constitutional matters, the rights of the opposition, and the rights of minorities. Shortly after the peaceful division of the Czechoslovak federation, there were some concerns about the democratic nature of the political regime in newly independent Slovakia, due to the nationalist appeals of the strongest party in Slovakia, the Movement for Democratic Slovakia (HZDS), led by Vladimír Mečiar. However, it was only the early elections in 1994 that started an era of serious political backsliding in democratic institutionalisation and practices. The period of 1994–98 also witnessed the most intensive diplomatic engagement in, and criticism of, the political situation in Slovakia by the representatives of west European and transatlantic international organisations (the European Union, NATO).

The aim of this essay is to illuminate the character of the European Union's political conditionality and to illustrate the role it has played in political development in Slovakia. We argue that EU political conditionality does not work formally, i.e. stability of institutions cannot be achieved only by establishing legal changes of a political system, it also requires a corresponding set of political actors, who comply with democratic rules and procedures. We examine how in Slovakia EU political conditionality has facilitated political co-operation between non-nationalist political parties and shaped the nature of party competition. In turn, the political changes after the 1998 elections stimulated institutional improvements by refining the constitutional framework, improving administration and rights of opposition and minorities.

The main body of the chapter is structured into three parts. First, we describe the scope and nature of EU political conditionality with regard to the candidate countries from Central and Eastern Europe (CEE). Second, we show the ways EU political conditionality influenced Slovakia's internal political development, and we argue that despite the minimalist (electoral) conception of EU political criteria, these were, in fact, more precisely defined in the political dialogue, which put greater emphasis on the behavioural and normative aspects of democracy. In the third part we describe the turn in the political processes after 1998 as well as recent constitutional and administrative changes that were to clarify the rules of the political game and were in part motivated by Slovakia's aspiration to eventual full membership in the EU.

Defining EU political conditionality

How are we to understand the meaning of conditionality? In general, international institutional lenders, such as the IMF, World Bank and ECDR have frequently practised conditionality in the pursuit of neo-liberal fiscal policy during regime change. Therefore, it is often understood and defined as an international pressure that involves certain institutional preferences.[1] Pridham defines it as a process that 'requires specifying conditions or even preconditions for support, involving either promise of material aid or political opportunities, and it usually includes political monitoring of domestic developments in the countries under discussion'.[2] Thus, concrete *conditions* to be fulfilled; *rewards* for complying with them, and a mechanism for monitoring and *evaluation* are the three constitutive elements of any conditionality.

As we focus on political conditionality, we analyse the EU's basic political conditions towards the applicant countries, the rewards being the prospect of eventual membership in the EU and the monitoring system embodied primarily in the political dialogue set up in the association agreements and in the European Commission's annual evaluations of the candidates' progress. Besides the incentives, we have to point out the limits of political conditionality, as this policy is based primarily on influencing and persuading the countries in question. Bilateral EU-candidate country meetings, expressing concerns, resolutions, diplomatic notes, demarches and other opinions are traditional methods of diplomatic influence and in principle do not have coercive character. As such, their impact may be rather limited, depending on the depth of commitment of the candidate's political representatives. Thus, in order to assess the independent impact of EU conditionality, we have to take into account the internal dynamics of the political situation in a candidate country. As support for democracy became one of the main priorities of Eastern enlargement, the EU issues regular reports on political developments in applicant countries, presents requirements and recommendations, and launches programmes that offer financial aid for strengthening democracy. In addition to being the first criterion for membership, 'stable democracy' has been a precondition for starting accession negotiations with the EU. The European Council's strategic decisions on general policies towards the candidate countries, based on the Commission's annual reports, together with the threat to suspend the association agreements with the candidates are the only tools with direct policy impact used in EU political conditionality. It was the European Council meetings in Luxembourg and Helsinki that have been of primary importance, with the former dividing candidates into the fast track and the slow track groups and the latter changing the system and introducing the so-called regatta system.

Setting political criteria

Even though the European Union increased the number of its member states from the original six to the current fifteen, until recently formal political conditions for membership had not been explicitly stated. EU political criteria for membership were formally set up only when the question of admitting post-communist countries was opened. These conditions were introduced only later, after the first Europe Agreements (EAs) were signed in 1991. At that time, the name 'Europe Agreements' should stressed a difference between the new association agreements and those concluded with Turkey, Malta and Cyprus. This so-called second generation of agreements provided a more comprehensive form of partnership than previous styles of association. Only the Treaty of Amsterdam in 1997 made the political criteria explicit conditions for EU membership, stressing that any European state may apply to become a member of the Union, but must respect 'the principles of liberty, democracy, respect for human rights and fundamental freedoms, and the rule of law' (Art. 6). Moreover, it provided for a mechanism that enabled suspension of the rights of a member state if these principles were not upheld therein (Art.7).

The first EAs had been signed with Hungary, Poland and the former Czechoslovakia in 1991; at that time only the preamble of the EAs mentioned the political dimension of the integration by referring to 'common values', such as the support for a pluralistic democracy, the rule of law, the respect for human rights and political freedoms, as well as a multi-party system with free and democratic elections and the principles of market economy and social justice. Only later, in May 1992, the EU strengthened this rather vague commitment to democracy by attaching a suspension clause that linked trade and co-operation agreements to the achievement of democratic principles, human rights and a market economy. Moreover, since then on all Europe Agreements included a special article concerning the respect of the principles of democracy and human rights. The renegotiated agreement concluded with Slovakia in 1993 (following the break-up of Czechoslovakia) also contains this article and the suspension clause. EAs set up five conditions for EU accession: the rule of law, human rights, a multi-party system, free and fair elections, and a market economy. The second generation of association agreements changed EU policies toward a future enlargement, which now clearly depends also on political conditions. This decision differs from the response of the EU toward the Southern European countries, when authoritarian regimes had collapsed in Greece, Portugal and Spain. They became members of the EU without stipulating political conditions as the explicit requirements. On the contrary, at that time one of the goals of EU enlargement was to support consolidation of democracy in these countries. Now, applicants are expected to meet all the conditions before accession.

The Copenhagen European Council in 1993 further elaborated political, economic, and administrative conditions for EU accession. With respect to political conditionality the Copenhagen summit stipulated that membership requires that 'the candidate country has achieved stability of institutions guaranteeing democracy, the rule of law, human rights and respect for and protection of minorities'. These conditions were followed by a 'pre-accession strategy' that was launched at the Essen European Council in December 1994. The decision incorporated the Europe Agreements and the PHARE aid programme as a special EU policy toward CEE applicants. Copenhagen political requirements do not substantially differ from those that are stipulated by the Council of Europe or by the OSCE. They are based on the minimalist, electoral conception of democracy and the idea of protection of human and minority rights, therefore allowing individual countries to opt for different institutional solutions. Since launching the pre-accession strategy the European Commission had been screening the process of the implementation of all Copenhagen conditions. In July 1997 the Commission published its views on the progress of the applicant countries, assessing how individual countries had been fulfilling the Copenhagen conditions and whether they were able to assume the obligations of membership. All applicant countries with the exception of Slovakia were judged to meet the political criteria. Their fulfilment was considered to be necessary, though not sufficient, for beginning negotiations about the eventual accession to the EU as the example of Bulgaria, Latvia, Lithuania and Romania illustrated. These countries did not meet economic conditions. Thus, from among the post-communist candidates, the Commission proposed to start negotiations with the Czech Republic, Estonia, Hungary, Poland and Slovenia, i.e. countries that met political as well as economic conditions. The Commission's document *Agenda 2000* set up also the Accession Partnerships (APs) by merging all EU demands and assistance within a single framework. Since the EAs were signed, political criteria have not substantially changed in general, but they were elaborated in individual discussions, reflecting the different conditions of each applicant country. Structured dialogue functioned as the main channel for mediating EU conditionality. CEE countries had already learned during the EAs negotiations that 'the Community understands political dialogue as a channel to transmit its common positions and interests to like-minded third countries, rather than to initiate a real two-way-dialogue on a jointly set agenda'.[3]

The Luxembourg European Council in December 1997 basically confirmed the Commission's view. Even though it decided *formal* accession talks would involve all candidates, individual negotiations would start only with the most advanced countries. The Luxembourg decision was the first application of the EU political conditionality with direct policy impact. Slovakia, though judged relatively favourably in meeting economic criteria, was not considered for accession negotiations because of its failure to comply with EU political conditions. The 1998 Accession Partnership on Slovakia in a way stressed the political dimension of Slovakia's failure, as it emphasised short-term priorities (political criteria) for the country. These included free and fair elections (parliamentary, presidential and local), the need to involve political opposition in decision-making and control procedures, and the necessity to enact legislation on the use of minority languages. Two groups of candidates were created as a result of the Luxembourg decision; while the countries in the first group started direct negotiations on the EU accession in March 1998, the second group countries were to get prepared within the framework of Accession Partnership and the reinforced pre-accession strategy. It was also decided that the Commission would prepare annual reports on candidate countries' progress. The Commission's opinions published in November 1998 highlighted some progress in Latvia, Lithuania and Slovakia. Consequently, the Commission proposed to change the overall strategy towards candidates in October 1999. The Helsinki European Council in December acknowledged the progress of the second group candidates and direct negotiations with them started in February 2000. The EU political conditions were considered to be met by all CEE candidates, even Slovakia, after a change in the 1998 elections allowed them to qualify politically.

Monitoring the candidates: the institutional framework and events

The Europe Agreement concluded in October 1993 between the European Community and its member states on the one hand and the Slovak Republic on the other provided for a framework for economic and political relations between the SR and EU, and set up political dialogue. Among the essential preconditions to the conclusion of any such a treaty is identified 'respect for the democratic principles and human rights established by the Helsinki Final Act and the Charter of Paris for a new Europe, as well as the principles of market economy'. The political dialogue is to support economic and political transformation in the Slovak Republic and to start both economic and political convergence of the two parties. It is to embrace regular bilateral consultations and meetings at the highest political as well as ministerial level involving all topics of common interest. At ministerial level, political dialogue takes place within the Association Council, whereas at parliamentary level it shall take place within the framework of the Association Parliamentary Committee.

The Association Council meets at least once a year at ministerial level. The Council supervises the implementation of the Europe Agreement. It is composed of the members appointed by the Slovak government as well as by the members of the Commission and the Council of the European Union. The Association Council is in its work assisted by the Association Committee (composed according to the same criteria as the Council itself) that is to prepare the meetings technically. The Association Parliamentary Committee is a joint parliamentary body composed of an equal number of members of the European parliament and the Slovak parliament. The APC meets twice a year, once in the country of the associated parliament and once in Brussels. Although the joint parliamentary committee's role is limited (it is 'informed' of the decision of the Association Council and may only 'make recommendations' to the Association Council), its activities were more resonant in the Slovak media and public. The main reason is the fact that the Association Council is mostly an expert body engaged predominantly in solving technical economic problems, whereas the Association Parliamentary Committee has been very open and critical about the EU political conditions and Slovakia's difficulties in meeting them. During the period before the 1998 elections it provided the opposition parties with a forum where it could have voiced its concerns to the international audience. Several resolutions of the Association Parliamentary Committee (proposed mostly by the opposition deputies together with the MEPs) called for the improvement of the democratic practices in Slovakia. These were important signals to the Slovak public showing that the opposition's criticism of the government was justified and supported by a third party (the EU).

While the provisions of the EA political dialogue institutionalised the relationship between the EU and Slovakia and thus served as a channel for transmitting and reminding Slovakia about its commitment to democracy, it was the Commission's official evaluations of the candidates that had the major impact even on the internal political situation. The first opinions (*avis*), especially, formally included into the document Agenda 2000, played an important role in Slovak political struggles. These documents were based on a whole range of information sources. In part they drew from the questionnaire each applicant had to submit, but attention was also paid to the results of the bilateral consultations between the EU and the candidates (including, but not limited to, the institutions of the EA's political dialogue). Reports from the Delegations of the European Commission as well as of other international (the Council of Europe) and non-governmental organisations were also taken into account. As we have already mentioned, the Commission's *avis* of 1997 served as the basis for the Luxembourg European Council decision to divide the candidates into two groups. Moreover, since then the Commission's evaluations are published annually and again serve as the basis for the European Council's conclusions about the enlargement process. As from February 2000, all CEE candidate countries directly negotiate about their membership in separate intergovernmental conferences. At this stage, however, their democratic character and stability (i.e. complying with the political criteria) are beyond question and the attention is given to substantive policy areas.

The EU's impact on Slovakia, 1994–98

In the period prior to the general election of 1998, the EU criticism of Slovakia had focused on three broad political issues: respect for the rights of the parliamentary opposition, protection of minority rights, and stability of its institutions. After the 1994 elections the coalition of three parties (the Movement for a Democratic Slovakia – HZDS, the Workers' Association of Slovakia – ZRS, and the Slovak National Party – SNS) formed a new government. This new government had substantially influenced the performance of parliamentary democracy and functioning of the separation of powers: namely the ruling majority succeeded in the full marginalization of the opposition.[4] The country's political discourse had dramatically changed in favour of a majoritarian interpretation of democracy. Political leaders of the ruling parties defended their distorting actions by apologetic rhetoric based on the principle of majority rule, asserting that, 'it is after the elections you [the opposition] should get used to it [arbitrary and unlimited rule of majority]',[5] or 'democracy is the terror of the majority',[6] or 'the winner takes it all'.[7]

Immediately, after the first session of the 1994 elected parliament, the ambassadors of the EU troika delivered a diplomatic demarche to the president, the prime minister and the speaker of the parliament. The EU pointed out that an ongoing process of Slovakia's integration into the EU brought about not only advantages but commitments as well. The EU presented 'its concern about some facts of the political life after the elections of 1994 and expressed its hopes that Slovakia, carefully considering its own interests, will continue on the way of democratic reforms' (*SME*, 28 November 1994).[8] In other words as early as late 1994 the EU warned that Slovakia could be invited to accession talks only after it met and respected all general democratic norms and conditions. In its official reaction, the Slovak government did not respond to the concerns of the demarche and only expressed 'its appreciation to the EU for attention paid to the developments in the Slovak Republic'.[9]

More importantly, the government's general policy towards its opponents had not changed substantially. Due to growing tensions between the cabinet and the president, verbal attacks on the Constitutional Court (which overturned several controversial laws passed by the parliamentary majority), and a suspicion that the Slovak Intelligence Service organised an abduction of a Slovak citizen, the EU had undertaken additional formal diplomatic steps. A 'second wave' of diplomatic demarches followed in October 1995, when the EU and later also the USA displayed their concern about the political situation in Slovakia. The EU again reminded Slovakia of its obligation to respect the political criteria set up by the Copenhagen Summit as well as stated in the association agreement. The reaction of the Mečiar administration was similar as in the previous case. It denied any responsibility for the issues criticised. It even spoke about the EU's unfair attitude to Slovakia, and allegedly different standards applied to Slovakia in comparison with other applicants. The demarches in 1995 were followed by a resolution by the European Parliament calling for respect to democratic procedures and minority rights in Slovakia. The resolution warned that if the Slovak government 'continues to follow policies which show insufficient respect for democracy, human and minority rights and the rule of law, it will be necessary for the European Union to reconsider its programmes of assistance and co-operation under the Europe Agreement which might have to be suspended'.[10] The importance and political significance of the demarches and resolution even increases when taking into account that no other EU candidate country received comparable concerns and warnings.

However, Mečiar-led government even escalated its policies against the president, opposition and ethnic minorities. Among other decisions, the parliamentary majority violated the civic rights of an MP, who was stripped of his mandate; later it ignored the Constitutional Court's ruling calling for a remedy. The cabinet disregarded the powers of the Constitutional Court as well as of the Central Referendum Committee and thwarted a referendum on the direct presidential election and NATO membership in 1997.[11]

During an official visit to Slovakia just two days after the referendum, the EU Commissioner Hans van den Broek again stressed the need to strengthen democratic institutions and procedures and again reminded Slovak political representatives about EU political conditions. In a reaction to the referendum affair he labelled the integration chances of Slovakia as 'politically controversial'. In mid-June 1997 the meeting of the Joint Parliamentary Committee (JPC) took place in Bratislava, the Slovak capital. It was the last official meeting within the framework of EA political dialogue taking place before the Commission's avis were to be published. After three days of negotiations the Committee adopted a 'last chance' resolution recommending adoption of legislative norms and executive acts that would improve the functioning of the democratic system. In order to meet the political criteria no later than in November that year (i.e. still before the Luxembourg summit), it recommended the re-creation of parliamentary committees on a proportional basis, increasing chances of the opposition to control the intelligence services, and also urged a consensual preparation and adoption of a law on minority languages (*SME* 20 June 1997). It basically repeated what the JPC had stated in its conclusion a year before, when it specified thirteen problematic areas of Slovak politics were and called for the improvement. However, even these recommendations proved futile, as Slovakia's ruling majority basically ignored the JPC conclusions.

The results of the referendum, together with the ongoing EU concerns about the democratic character of the political regime in Slovakia, prompted five opposition political parties to create an alliance called the Slovak Democratic Coalition (SDK). The SDK also decided to deepen its co-operation with the three parties of Hungarian minority. They aimed to present themselves as a trustworthy alternative to the existing government. The 'EU factor' was strongly felt in the process, as the SDK emphasised many times the need to break Slovakia's growing international isolation and to improve relations with the EU in order to increase its chances of early accession. 'Appeals of opposition parties to voters have been increasingly typified by their stressing their "European compatibility", and their coming to power was presented as the only possibility of salvaging the country's weakened integration chances'.[12] Moreover, the co-operation of the SDK with the Hungarian parties was to indicate that the minority problems, a major weakness of the Mečiar administration, could be solved in a consensual way, i.e. by involving the minority representatives in the decision-making processes. In addition, the parties of the opposition succeeded in attracting the attention of other civil society actors in organising the so-called 'democratic roundtable discussions', such as the trade unions, representatives of churches, non-governmental organisations and with the association of local self-governments. The meaning of these meetings was largely symbolic; they had to show that the opposition was able to talk and agree with the forces that were marginalised by the Mečiar administration.

The opposition co-operation even increased after the Luxembourg European Council in December 1997 did not invite Slovakia to the first group of countries directly negotiating on the accession. The opposition blamed the government for violating the democratic norms and criteria that led the EU to leave Slovakia. The Slovak Democratic Coalition pledged after the Luxembourg summit to fulfil all political criteria required by the EU of applicant states within one hundred days after its supposed coming to power (*SME* 15 January 1997). The opposition co-operation was also prompted by the fact that parts of the ruling coalition used to look for an alternative foreign policy orientation. This was demonstrated by a famous Mečiar statement to the German press in autumn 1995 saying: 'If they do not want us in the West, we will turn to the East' (*SME* 14 July 1997). However, there were more substantial grounds for this kind of speculation. Mečiar's administration concluded a whole range of bilateral Slovak–Russian treaties that with respect to energy resources effectively rendered Slovakia dependent on Russia. Moreover, in 1996 the government even seriously considered conclusion of a treaty on a free trade area with Russia, even though such a treaty clearly contradicted the Europe Agreement.[13] The opposition parties feared that Slovakia's isolation from the mainstream integration processes could lead to a closer alliance with Russia and to further decay of democratic regime. Thus, for them the EU integration had to play a dual role of a means as well as an end. As a means it was to integrate the country to an organisation whose political environment would be favourable to democracy. In other words, the EU membership was valuable because it contributed to the consolidation of democracy. As an end, economic, political and cultural benefits of the EU membership were most often stressed.

The Constitutional Court in February 1998 ruled that the Interior Ministry infringed the citizens' constitutional rights, as they could not have taken part in a lawfully called referendum with four questions. In response, the President called a new referendum with the original questions. However, before it was to take place, the five-year term of Michal Kováč in presidential office expired and the government (the prime minister) assumed some of the presidential prerogatives. The government immediately cancelled the referendum called by the former president. Moreover, the prime minister used his temporary presidential powers to declare an amnesty on persons associated with the thwarted referendum in 1997. The measures were clearly politically motivated and aimed at protecting the interior minister. In addition, the prime minister also declared an amnesty on the persons who were involved in kidnapping a Slovak citizen to neighbouring Austria. There was strong evidence that it was initiated, if not carried out, by the Slovak intelligence service. An official reaction from the EU followed a week later. The EU presidency issued a statement in which it clearly expressed that the Mečiar administration was not perceived as a reliable and committed partner: 'The decision by Prime Minister Mečiar to exercise the presidential powers to grant amnesties [. . .] brings into questions his commitment to commonly accepted principles of good governance and the rule of law.' With the Slovak general elections scheduled for September in mind, the EU further claimed: 'The EU regrets that such steps might represent a set-back to the legitimate aspirations of the Slovak people to international respect and progressive integration into European structures. [The EU] will continue to support these aspirations and to follow developments related to their fulfilment closely'.[14] By carefully distinguishing the Slovak population and its government, the EU representatives tried to support the opposition forces that would be able to carry out a domestic political change.

EU conditionality and political changes after the 1998 election

The second general election since independence was scheduled for September 1998. It was held under the supervision of the delegations from the OSCE, and the Council of Europe. Several observers from the European Parliament also took part in the supervisory teams. The four opposition parties emerged victorious, gaining together 58 per cent of the votes and obtaining 93 of the 150 seats in parliament. Mikuláš Dzurinda, the leader of the Slovak Democratic Coalition (SDK), was designated to form the government. At the end all four formerly opposition parties, including SDM, Hungarian Coalition Party (SMK), Party of Civic Understanding (SOP), and the Party of the Democratic Left (SDL′) formed the new coalition cabinet. Although the new coalition was very broad in terms of political ideology and policy priorities, all these parties shared the priorities of the foreign policy orientation towards the EU and NATO. In particular, the inclusion of a Hungarian party in the oversized cabinet was an important step in changing country's policy toward ethnic minorities and carrying out significant political reforms stabilising the democratic regime, thus strengthening Slovakia's chances of EU accession.

The newly formed ruling coalition also tried to take a conciliatory stance towards the HZDS and SNS, parties of the opposition, and offered them a roughly proportional share of the posts in the parliament as well as in other important semi-governmental control bodies. Candidates of the opposition were elected into new controlling bodies supervising the broadcasting of the public radio and television. It also nominated its candidates into the controlling bodies of the National Property Fund. However, the strategies of the two opposition parties varied considerably. While the HZDS declined to nominate its candidates into the parliamentary committees' chairship, the SNS accepted these offers and submitted its nominees. Only in the EU–Slovak Joint Parliamentary Committee did the HZDS make an exception and nominate a vice-chair of the committee.

The representatives of the EU welcomed the peaceful and fair character of the elections as well as their results. There were even signs that Slovakia could be invited to the first group of candidates for EU accession.[15] Moreover, European Parliament issued a resolution appealing to the Commission to take the new situation in Slovakia into account in preparing further strategy towards the candidate countries. However, the European Commission was more cautious. In its second Report on Slovakia in 1998 it noted that 'a different political climate is emerging and a window of opportunity exists for a new government majority to address the … [previously existing] … shortcomings … The new government now has an opportunity to demonstrate Slovakia's commitment to democratic principles, respect for human rights and the rule of law'.[16] Even though the expectations of the new administration for Slovakia's early inclusion into the first group proved too optimistic, EU – Slovak co-operation regained momentum. For example, in November it was agreed that a high-level working group composed of experts from the EC and Slovakia would be created to help Slovakia to enter the accession negotiations.[17]

Dzurinda's cabinet focused on those reforms that are key to the EU accession process. First, since Slovakia had been without a head of state for a long time, the coalition parties agreed on amending the constitution to allow for a popular presidential election. In May 1999 Rudolf Schuster, the chairman of the governing SOP, supported by all coalition partners became the new president. Thus, Slovakia's institutional system found renewed stability. Parliament adopted legislation that permitted the minority schools to issue grade certificates in minority languages, a policy they were denied during the previous government. Long-awaited legislation on languages used in the state administration, enabling persons belonging to the ethnic minorities to use their own language, was also approved by Parliament in July 1999. In December 1999 Parliament issued a declaration expressing regret that Mr Gaulieder was stripped of his mandate by the previous Parliament.

The representatives of the European Union carefully observed the government's steps. In its report on Slovakia issued in October 1999, the Commission concluded that Slovakia fulfilled basic political criteria for opening negotiations on EU accession, including institutional stability, the rule of law and respect for human and minority rights.[18] Based on favourable reports on other candidate countries as well, the European Council meeting in Helsinki in December decided to start direct negotiations not only in Slovakia but also with other countries of the second group created in Luxembourg. In Slovakia the decision was welcomed as a clear signal that the country had broken with its controversial political past of the 1994–98 period. The Commission, assessing the situation in Slovakia in 2000, concluded 'Slovakia continues to meet the political criteria which the last report had recognised, for the first time, as having been fulfilled. Slovakia has further advanced in the consolidation of its democratic system and in the normal functioning of its institutions'.[19] Even, if some policy measures presented in the 1998 Government Manifesto were implemented at a slower pace than was expected,[20] the EU–Slovak relations have substantially improved. After political problems had been overcome, relations between the EU and Slovakia have focused more on concrete technical problems connected with accession to the Union.

However, in Spring 2001 the EU employed a new policy measure from the 'conditionality package' toward Slovakia. The European Commission temporarily suspended the preparation of new projects as well as tenders financed from EU development funds in Slovakia. This decision was a reaction to the allegations about the misuse of EU funds. Deputy prime minister for European Integration, Pavol Hamžík, informed the EC about some suspicions against one government official responsible for the EU funds. He immediately dismissed that official and asked for an investigation into the case. Prime Minister Dzurinda apparently in an effort to follow 'informal rules, which are standard in Western democracies' overreacted and dismissed the deputy prime minister, blaming him for not promptly informing the government about the case. Moreover, the EU's reaction was too hasty. In particular, the European Parliament got seriously involved in this case and delegated the EP's Budget Control Committee to Bratislava to examine the allegations about the EU funds mismanagement. The committee stated, 'Slovakia has weak spots in state administration, in independent financial inspection, and in the effective fight against fraud and corruption',[21] however the following investigation did not confirm abuse of EU funds. Only in December 2001 did the European Parliament's Budget Commission reverse its previous decision to cut the aid package for Slovakia and to allocate the full amount of funding. The Commission concluded that Slovakia had improved its system of financial checks, thus reinforcing its policies against corruption.

The whole case, despite its extensive publicity has not affected Slovakia's negotiations to join the EU. It only confirmed the democratic commitment of the current government, that acted pre-emptively and dismissed all the officials and politicians, since it had become suspicious about this 'corruption affair'. Slovakia, in spite of starting later with EU accession talks has made enormous efforts to catch up with the front-runners. In 2001 its negotiating team concluded most of the negotiating chapters among the second-wave candidate countries. Although the number of closed negotiating chapters does not represent a foolproof measure of real progress, it offers a useful indication of how far a candidate has moved on the road toward incorporating EU regulations.

Thus, Slovakia has a very good chance of joining the EU together with its three Central European neighbours Hungary, the Czech Republic and Poland.

Conclusion

Even though the political conditions of the EU were often criticised for being very broad and difficult to measure,[22] their application to Slovakia played a major role in turning the country's regime back on the road to consolidated democracy after the 1998 elections. Applying EU democratic conditionality to the Slovak case also meant a more precise elaboration of the very notion of 'democracy', though it remains difficult to be measured. EU minimalist definition included rights of opposition, constitutionalism, and ethnic minorities rights.

The European Union reacted to the violation of democratic rules by the Slovak government between 1994 and 1998 by issuing several diplomatic demarches, presidency statements, and resolutions of the European Parliament. Official channels through institutions of the Europe Agreement, political dialogue plus personal letters and declarations were used to voice the EU's concern. On numerous occasions the representatives of the EU warned that the political criteria, namely the rule of law, stability of the institutions and respect for human and minority rights, constituted an absolute requirement for entering into accession talks with a candidate country. Besides these diplomatic tools, the Commission's regular reports and the European Council's decisions constituted major leverage for influencing the political situation in Slovakia. However, the direct impact of the EU political conditionality approached its limits, as the previous Slovak government (1994–98) representatives did not respect EU recommendations.

The impact of EU political conditionality increases, however, if we shift from its conventional understanding as a bilateral international issue (involving the EU and Slovakia) towards understanding it as a trilateral dialogue taking place between the EU, the Slovak government, and the Slovak opposition. Within this framework we can better understand the careful distinction made by the EU between Slovakia's political representation and its population.[23] The EU's reactive involvement especially in 1997 (the thwarted referendum, EU reactions, the Commission's avis) and its Luxembourg European Council decision functioned as a catalyst prompting the co-operation of the opposition and increased the general public's awareness of danger of Slovakia's international isolation. The EU's political criteria even played a role of guidance for the acts of the new parliamentary majority after the 1998 elections. In a relatively short period of time it fulfilled all the political conditions of accession. The new government's attitude towards the opposition and ethnic minorities contrasts with the previous oft-criticised practices. The constitutional amendments of 1999 and 2001 increased the overall institutional stability of Slovakia and also included new provisions that allow Slovakia to enter the European Union.

As the case of Slovakia illustrates, the 'success' of EU political conditionality depends mainly on the domestic political situation. It can work in countries whose overall institutional structure remains democratic even though some features of substantive democracy are violated. Political conditionality can have a major impact on the internal political development of the country in question if there is a viable political alternative to the existing government and if the opposition can mobilise the population and use the government's foreign policy failure as a political weapon.

Notes

1 P. Schmitter, 'The Influence of the International Context upon the Choice of National Institutions and Policies in Neo-Democracies', in L. Whitehead (ed.), *The International Dimensions of Democratization, Europe and the Americas* (Oxford: Oxford University Press, 1996).
2 G. Pridham, 'Complying with the European Union's Democratic Conditionality: Transnational Party Linkages and Regime Change in Slovakia, 1993–1998', *Europe–Asia Studies*, Vol. 51, No. 7 (1999), 1222.
3 B. Lippert, 'Shaping and Evaluating the Europe Agreements: The Community Side', in B. Lippert and H. Schneider (eds), *Monitoring Association and Beyond: The European Union and the Visegrád States* (Bonn: Europa Union Verlag, 1995), p. 29.
4 D. Malová and M. Rybář, 'The Troubled Institutionalization of Parliamentary Democracy in Slovakia', *Politicka misao: Croatian Political Science Review*, Vol. 37, No. 2 (2000), 99–115.
5 Vladimír Mečiar, HZDS Chair, at the first session of the parliament.
6 Daily *SME* cited Eva Zelenayová, HZDS MP. *SME* (7 June 1995).
7 Daily *Pravda* cited Vít'azoslav Móric, MP of the Slovak National Party (*Pravda*, 7 February 1997).
8 Slovak daily newspapers *SME* and *Slovenská republika.*
9 A. Duleba, 'Democratic Consolidation and the Conflict over Slovak International Alignment', in S. Szomolányi and J. A. Gould (eds), *Slovakia: Problems of Democratic Consolidation* (Bratislava: Slovak Political Science Association, 1997), p. 215.
10 'Resolution of the European Parliament on the Need to Respect Human and Democratic Rights in the Slovak Republic', *Official Journal* C 323, 1995.
11 Malová and Rybář, 'The Troubled Institutionalisation of Parliamentary Democracy in Slovakia'.
12 P. Učeň, 'Implications of Party System Development for Slovakia's Performance in European Integration', unpublished manuscript (European University Institute, 1998), p. 48.
13 Duleba, 'Democratic Consolidation.
14 'Presidency Statement on behalf of the EU on the Situation in Slovakia', *Bulletin of the EU*, 3/1998 Common foreign and security policy (15/16), ECSC-EC-EAEC, Brussels – Luxembourg 1998, www.europa.eu.int/abc/doc/off/bull/en/9809/p103022.htm
15 J. Marušiak, J. Alner, P. Lukáč, R. Chmel, I. Samson and A. Duleba, 'The Foreign Policy and National Security of the Slovak Republic', in G. Mesežnikov, M. Ivantyšyn and T. Nicholson (eds), *Slovakia 1998–1999* (Bratislava: IVO, 1999), pp. 167–196.
16 *Commission Report: Slovakia*, Brussels: The European Commission, 1998.
17 V. Bilčík, M. Bruncko, A. Duleba, P. Lukáč and I. Samson, 'Foreign and Defence Policy of the Slovak Republic', in G. Mesežnikov, M. Kollár and T. Nicholson (eds), *Slovakia 2000* (Bratislava, 2000), pp. 233–296.

18 *Regular Report on Slovakia's Progress Towards Accession* (Brussels: European Commission, 1999).
19 *Regular Report on Slovakia's Progress Towards Accession* (Brussels: European Commission, 2000).
20 Namely, the complex amendment of the constitution and administrative and regional reforms were passed only after protracted negotiations in 2001.
21 Slovak press agency *SITA* (22 June 2001).
22 H. Grabbe and Hughes, *Enlarging the EU Eastwards* (London: Royal Institute of International Affairs, 1998).
23 E.g. EU presidency statement in 1998 after Mečiar's amnesties.

Susan Senior-Nello

6

The economic criteria for EU accession

Lessons from the Czech and Slovak Republics

Introduction

Transition in Central and East European countries has been underway for over a decade. As early as 1995 Václav Klaus announced that transition was complete in the Czech Republic, and a central question several years later is whether this is in fact the case. Certainly the achievements of transition in both the Czech and Slovak Republics are substantial: most output is exchanged in markets and is produced by private firms, while free elections have led to democratic changes in government.

Increasingly, economic and political transition have become fused with another task: that of preparing for EU accession. In many ways the prospect of EU membership has helped to accelerate the transition process. The market has anticipated enlargement, and trade reorientation and foreign direct investment (FDI) have proceeded rapidly. However, preparing for EU membership has imposed a type-cast on transition, requiring that it follows a specific pattern.

In theory, preparing to join the EU is said to be a question of progress in meeting the Copenhagen accession criteria. In practice as soon as accession negotiations started (in 1998 for the Czech Republic, and 2000 for Slovakia) the Commission began a process of screening the applicant countries to assess their progress in taking on the 'obligations of membership'. The requirement that the applicant countries are able to assume the 'obligations of membership' is generally taken to mean their ability to adopt the *acquis communautaire*.[1] This criterion has meant a shift away from the other Copenhagen conditions. The speed and progress of accession negotiations now appears to depend primarily on the process of legal approximation and the ability of a country to introduce the judicial and administrative capacity to implement the *acquis*.

While these are central elements of the process of preparing to join the EU, the aim here is to return to the wider spectrum and see how far the Copenhagen criteria are useful in assessing progress in economic transition and in preparing the Czech and Slovak Republics for operating in an enlarged EU. This will also help in addressing the question of whether transition is effectively over.[2]

We set out general considerations on the Copenhagen criteria and the way in which they are being applied. Next, we provide a brief summary of recent macro-economic developments in the Czech Republic and Slovakia. There follows a discussion of the, unexpected consequences of privatisation, the weakness of the financial sector and the shortcomings in corporate governance which have proved major obstacles to introducing a *'functioning market economy'* in the two countries. Given the difficulties of assessing whether a country is able to *'cope with competitive pressures and market forces'* in an enlarged EU, we then analyse the degree of current integration between the Czech and Slovak economies and the EU as, it is argued, this may prove a useful indicator of their present and future performance. We go on to discuss the applicability of the Maastricht criteria to transition economies, and consider appropriate policies in preparing for membership of Economic and Monetary Union (EMU), before drawing our conclusions.

The Copenhagen criteria

The Copenhagen accession conditions require that:

- the applicant state must have a functioning market economy with the capacity to cope with competitive pressures and market forces within the Community;
- the applicant state must have achieved stability of institutions guaranteeing democracy, the rule of law, human rights and respect for and protection of minorities;
- the applicant state must be able to take on the obligations of membership, including adherence to the aims of political, and economic and monetary union.

At the Copenhagen Summit it was also stipulated that enlargement is subject to the condition that the EU is able to absorb new members and maintain the momentum of integration.

The criteria are generally divided into political criteria, economic criteria, and ability to take on the *acquis* and to establish the administrative and judicial capacity to ensure its effective implementation.[3] There are three political criteria:

- stability of institutions guaranteeing democracy, the rule of law, human rights and respect for and protection of minorities;
- adherence to the objective of political union, and
- maintaining the momentum of integration.

The economic criteria are similarly divided into three:

- the existence of a functioning market economy;
- capacity to cope with competitive pressures and market forces within the Community, and
- adherence to the aim of economic and monetary and union.

The accession criteria are presumably intended to provide some kind of objective basis for selecting those CEECs ready to join the EU, as well as indicating to the applicant countries the tasks they are expected to perform. The introduction of the Copenhagen criteria would therefore seem aimed at replicating the experience of the Maastricht criteria, but in a different field, that of enlargement.

However, although there is a certain flexibility and political leeway in deciding whether the Maastricht criteria have been met, this is far more the case for the accession criteria. This arises from the number of these, and, in some cases from the vague and imprecise nature of the concepts involved. This is the case, for instance, in deciding whether a country has 'a functioning market economy' or the 'capacity to cope with competitive pressures'. For other criteria, such as taking on the objective of political union, or the requirement that the momentum of integration can be maintained (which presumably requires some form of flexibility or enhanced co-operation)[4] the objectives in question have yet to be fully defined in practice. The simple rule 'when a CEEC meets the accession criteria it can join the EU' is misleading given the degree of discretion in deciding whether the accession criteria have been met.

The European Commission maintains that a country must fulfil the political criteria before joining and must be making substantial progress towards meeting the economic criteria. The 1997 Opinion on Slovakia confirmed that political criteria carry more weight than economic criteria, and Agenda 2000 stresses that 'the effective functioning of democracy is a primordial question in assessing the application of a country for membership of the Union'.[5]

According to the 2001 Regular Reports, both the Czech Republic and Slovakia had functioning market economies, and provided reforms were continued, both should be able to cope with competitive pressures and market forces within the EU in the near term. However, Slovakia's performance was judged rather more negatively, and it was emphasised that 'substantial efforts' were required.[6]

Recent macroeconomic developments

The Czech Republic

In 1997 the Czech Republic suffered a severe currency crisis, which was largely due to a combination of poor regulation of financial markets, relatively easy access to the credit provided by state-owned banks, and weak corporate governance (as described below). In this situation Czech firms delayed restructuring and lost competitiveness, bringing about deterioration of the external balance and speculative pressures against the currency. To meet this crisis, in May 1997 the Czech authorities were forced to abandon the fixed exchange rate regime, move to inflation targeting, and to introduce tight fiscal and monetary policies and structural reforms.

Macro-economic restraint and the repercussions of the Russian and Asian crises led to the 1997–99 recession, but growth had recovered by 2000. However, recovery could be jeopardised by the slowdown in the EU, and in particular Germany, the destination of 40 per cent of Czech exports. Exports have been increasing, though imports (including those of capital equipment) remained high, which accounts for the expected trade deficit of –$3.1 billion in 2000. High levels of FDI contributed to currency appreciation, which could threaten export performance. As shown in table 6.1, the fiscal deficit also remains a problem.

Per capita income was second only to Slovenia among the CEECs.[7] Unemployment rose from 2.1 per cent in 1995 to 8.8 per cent in 2000, but jobs were being created faster than predicted in the Prague area.

The Slovak Republic

GDP growth in Slovakia resumed in 1994, and generally remained relatively high. The Mečiar regime left large fiscal and current account deficits (of 5.8 per cent and 10 per cent of GDP respectively in 1998); a rapidly growing external debt (of $11.9 billion or 58.5 per cent of GDP in 1998); over-extended state banks; and a corrupt privatisation programme.[8]

Following a decision to float the currency in October 1998, the Dzuringa government announced its economic programme in December of that year, which entailed reducing the fiscal deficit, raising regulated prices to international levels, and accelerating the restructuring of banks and enterprises. Measures were also introduced to correct some of the abuses of the earlier privatisation process and attract foreign direct investment. However, the heterogeneous nature of the government coalition has at times slowed down implementation of such measures.[9]

The government succeeded in reducing both the fiscal and current account deficits in 1999 (see table 6.1). Although growth slowed in the 1999–2000 period, it remained positive and is expected to increase in 2001. However, the increase in bankruptcies associated with the restructuring process pushed unemployment up to 19.2 per cent in 1999, and in some districts it was estimated to be as high as 40 per cent.[10]

An IMF staff monitored programme was agreed in May 2001which entailed privatisation revenues being earmarked for debt repayment and pension reform rather than assistance to ailing industries. The programme should help to avoid relaxing of fiscal discipline before the 2002 elections.

Table 6.1 Main macroeconomic indicators for the Czech and Slovak Republics

	Czech Republic				*Slovakia*			
	1998	*1999*	*2000*	*2001*[a]	*1998*	*1999*	*2000*	*2001*[a]
Total GDP (Czech and Slovak koruna bn)	1,820.7	1,854.8	1,976.8		717.4	779.3	887.2	980.5
GDP growth (real annual per cent change)	–2.2	–0.2	3.1	3.5	4.4	1.9	2.2	2.7
GDP per capita ($)	5,479	5,242	4,981	5,449	3,795	3,489	3,557	3,940
Population[b]			10.3				5.4	
Inflation (annual per cent change in CPI)	10.7	2.1	4.0	4.8	6.7	10.6	12.0	7.5
Unemployment rate (per cent workforce)	7.5	9.4	8.8		15.6	19.2	17.8	18.0
Government budget balance (% GDP)	–1.6	–3.8	–4.9	–9.2	–5.8	–3.6	–4.3	–4.7
Current account balance ($ bn)	–1.3	–1.1	–2.3	–3.7	–2.1	–1.1	–0.7	–1.0
Merchandise exports ($ bn)	26.3	26.8	29.1	33.0	10.7	10.2	11.9	13.2
Merchandise imports ($ bn)	28.9	28.9	32.2	38.0	13.0	11.3	12.7	14.4
Trade balance ($bn)	–2.6	–2.1	–3.1	–5.0	–2.2	–1.1	–0.9	–1.3

Note: [a] estimate, [b] end 2000

Sources: European Bank for Reconstruction and Development (EBRD), Financial Times Survey, *Slovakia*, 25 May 2000 and 4 July 2001, Financial Times Survey, *The Czech Republic*, 26 September 2000 and 12 December 2001.

How far the applicant country has a functioning market economy

The 2001 regular reviews maintained that both the Czech and Slovak Republics have functioning market economies. However, in various assessments by the EC Commission, attention has been drawn to shortcomings in the privatisation process, and the financial system in each country, so it is useful to consider these in more detail.

Introduction of a functioning market economy: the Czech experience

PRIVATISATION AND THE PROBLEM OF CORPORATE GOVERNANCE

The operation of the Czech economy is profoundly affected by a system of complex and confused ownership relations which emerged with the privatisation process, and were shaped by the predominant role played by the banks in the Czech economy.

In the Czech Republic privatisation relied on a variety of techniques including property restitution, direct sales, auctions and public tenders, as well as the mass privatisation scheme through the voucher system. The privatisation of most large-scale state enterprises took place in two waves. The first was launched in the former Czechoslovakia in 1992 and was complete by mid-1993. In the Czech Republic it involved sales of shares as well as the transfer of shares in 988 firms through a voucher scheme.[11] The second wave began in the Czech Republic in 1994 and aimed at privatising a further 2,000 firms through a mixture of sales and a voucher scheme. It is estimated that there were some eight million participants in the mass privatisation voucher schemes.

From being one of the most state-dominated economies of the Eastern bloc (together with the former GDR) by mid-1999 the private sector accounted for some 80 per cent of Czech GDP. In 2002 the government planned privatisation in sectors where the state retained large ownership stakes, such as telecommunications, petrochemicals and energy. According to the Finance Minster, Rusnok, this could yield revenues of roughly 15 per cent of GDP.[12]

Initial fears that voucher privatisation would lead to excessive dispersion of ownership were not borne out, due largely to the role of the Investment Privatisation Funds (IPFs, also referred to as mutual funds). It is estimated that some 70 per cent of privatisation vouchers were placed with the IPFs and used to buy shares. Most of the investment funds were held by state-dominated banks and insurance companies. After the first wave of voucher privatisation, the IPFs become shareholders of a large number of enterprises, including financial companies and each other.[13] Cross-ownership was widespread, and this together with legal loopholes tended to encourage insider trading and fraud.[14]

Privatisation has profound consequences for the corporate governance of firms. In the case of small firms the owner is generally also the owner, so corporate governance is relatively straightforward. The difficulty arises with larger firms where there is a divorce between ownership and control, so monitoring is necessary to ensure that the managers act in the firm's best interest. The ability of owners to remove managers may also be required to ensure the efficient operation and restructuring of the firm.

There are two main models of corporate governance.[15] The Anglo-American model relies on efficient financial markets, with shareholder bids, and the prospect of takeovers as a means of disciplining managers. The German–Japanese model relies more on the relations between firms and their owners (and, in particular, banks which may hold a significant amount of shares) to monitor the behaviour of managers and the performance of the firm.

The pattern which has emerged in the Czech Republic failed to correspond to either of these models. Lack of transparency meant that trading on the Czech stock exchange was thin. As in Slovakia the local capital market fails to serve as a source of capital for most enterprises so discipline operating through transactions on financial markets is slow to emerge. Complex ownership relations and weak regulation meant that in practice there were few checks on the activities of the IPFs, though in 1998 legislation covering these funds was tightened. The managers of investment funds were often less concerned with the profit maximisation and restructuring of the firm in which they own shares, than with siphoning off capital and appropriation of profit. In 2000 legislation was introduced to strengthen minority shareholder and creditor rights, to tighten up on bankruptcy proceedings and to improve judicial capacity in this area.

The lesson to be learnt from the Czech experience is not that voucher privatisation per se leads to problems of corporate governance. Countries such as Poland, Hungary or Croatia which have relied more heavily on direct sales have not achieved substantially better results. In general shortage of domestic capital meant that sales took place at preferential conditions, often to employees. At times these were less concerned with profit maximisation than with 'entrenchment' aimed at ensuring the survival of their firm, and their own position, if necessary by lobbying politicians and bureaucrats.

The lesson is, rather, that until the financial system is adequately developed and an effective regulatory system is in place, it is premature to argue that economic transformation is over.

THE IMPLICATIONS OF SLOW TRANSFORMATION OF FINANCIAL AND CAPITAL MARKETS

Reform of the financial system in a transition economy entails the creation of a two-tier banking system, with the establishment of independent central banks, a commercial banking system, and financial markets for bonds and shares. In 1990 legislation was introduced to end the mono-bank system in the former Czechoslovakia, and in 1993 the Czech National Bank was established to replace the former state bank of Czechoslovakia.

The Czech banking sector has grown rapidly, and in 1996 included 55 licensed commercial banks.[16] However, between 1994 and 1996 11 Czech banks failed. There have also been numerous financial scandals and instances of negligence and fraud, leading to the resignation of Václav Klaus in late 1997. Two main causes for the fragility of the financial system can be identified:

- the failure to introduce much-needed regulation of the emerging financial market, in part because of the ideological commitment of the Klaus government to the free market, and
- the unclear pattern of ownership in the partially privatised system, which led to perverse incentives and conflicting objectives.

Commercial banks in the Czech Republic consist of banks created through the separation of commercial activities of the former central bank, and of smaller, new banks frequently set up by enterprises at least in part to meet their own financial requirements.

A risk for the small, new commercial banks was that their management was sometimes 'more interested in the financial problems of the enterprise which owns the bank than in preserving the bank's viability and increasing its profits' (OECD, 1996, p. 51). The slow development of sound accounting practices and the absence of an effective supervisory system meant that the precarious situation of some of these banks was not always immediately realised.

The banks emerging from the former mono-bank system were partially privatised, but the state continued to play an important role in the largest of these banks through the National Property Fund (NPF), or state agency responsible for privatising state assets.[17] As a result, until the late 1990s these banks remained in a limbo between state control and effective market discipline.

A major problem faced by the banks emerging from the mono-bank system was the legacy of 'bad debts' of state enterprises that these banks inherited.[18] Moreover, during the early years of transition all banks tended to take on dubious assets in order to increase their market share.[19] The banks provided entrepreneurs with soft loans both to buy firms and to continue operating.[20] Banks were reluctant to force companies controlled by their funds into bankruptcy, while investment funds hesitated selling companies in case contracts and loans were lost for their bank. The easy credits enabled firms to postpone restructuring and fund repeated losses, so they were able to continue granting wage increases in excess of productivity gains, and delay cuts in overstaffing.

Widespread diffusion of bad debts may also render the instruments of monetary policy less effective. Even when monetary policy is tightened, the banks may continue to support state enterprises which are backed by government guarantees. Substantial increases in the price of credit may therefore fail to limit credit expansion and may mean that small private firms are crowded out as an increasing share of credit goes to the large state enterprises, thereby slowing down the transition process.

There have been various interventions by the Czech authorities to meet the problem of bad debts including a 1995 law allowing banks to obtain tax relief on provisions against bad loans.[21] Apart from their high budgetary cost, these interventions encountered the problem of *moral hazard* in that the reluctance of banks to take on bad assets may be lessened by the prospect of being bailed out.[22]

In 1991 the Consolidation Bank (KOB) was set up as a state-owned depository for bad loans. This initially adopted a twin-pronged approach: auctions of packages of small loans, and a revitalisation programme to deal with large debtors. An auction of a package of 500 loans in February yielded only 11 per cent of its book value.[23] The revitalisation programme to restructure and sell larger enterprises also ran into difficulties as a result of political interference, and obstruction by owners, managers and creditors. The activities of the Revitalisation Agency which had been set up in 1999 were again taken over by the KOB. Both these programmes were put on hold following the resignation in April 2001 of the Finance Minister, Merlik. In 2001 it was estimated that the Consolidation Agency (CKA) had an unconsolidated loan book of 185 billion korunas (kcs), equivalent to $5 billion, which the IMF estimated could rise to 432 billion kcs when the transfers from *Investicni a Postovni* and other banks were completed.[24]

Since 1998 the Czech National Bank has tightened provisioning rules, and has urged banks to be more assertive towards debtors and write off more loans. Banks were also required to increase their share capital to cover problem loans. A Securities and Exchange Commission was set up in April 1998 to bring greater transparency to the stock exchange and reduce the opportunities for insider trading, though there are doubts about how far it will be able to assert its independence.[25]

Amendments to the investment fund laws were also introduced. In 1998 an amendment to the Bank Act was passed which expressly prohibits banks from exercising direct or indirect control over any legal entities other than banks or financial institutions. However, the most crucial step in improving corporate governance is probably bank privatisation.

All the main banks have now been privatised. The state's share in CSOB (Ceskoslovenska Obchodny Banka) was sold to the Belgian KBC (Bancassurance Holding) in 1999, while the Erste Bank of Austria bought 52 per cent of Ceska Sporitelna in February 2000. In June 2000, IPB (Investicni a Postovni Banka) in which Nomura Securities of Japan held a 46 per cent stake collapsed. The Czech authorities intervened transferring IPB assets to CSOB. A deal with Societé Générale for Komercni Banka was reached in 2001.

A question linked both to the issue of corporate governance and to the role of the banks in the economy is the extent to which there are significant barriers to market entry or exit. Anti-trust measures can play an important role in this context. The Europe Agreements committed the CEECs to adopting competition policies compatible with those of the Community and this objective was further specified in the 1995 White Paper.[26] External pressure to force measures which are unpopular, but essential to the transformation process, may provide a useful scapegoat. The need to bring legislation into line with that in EU countries in areas such as the control of state aids can provide CEEC governments with a strong justification for resisting excessive rent-seeking on the part of producers.

Introduction of a functioning market economy: the Slovak experience

Although traditionally Slovakia was predominantly an agrarian country, during the communist era emphasis was placed on industrialisation and catch-up policies. By 1989 much heavy industry (including defence production) was located in Slovakia, but it was highly dependent on Eastern markets for energy, raw materials and outlets. The break-up of the Soviet Union therefore hit Slovakia more than the Czech lands, causing differences in attitudes concerning the nature and pace of economic transformation, and this was one of the factors contributing to the split of Czechoslovakia in 1993.

Although Slovakia inherited a low foreign debt, relatively low inflation and a tradition of fiscal orthodoxy from the former Czechoslovakia, separation added to economic difficulties by creating political uncertainty, ending the transfers from the Czech Republic and disrupting trade between the two countries.[27]

The main criticisms of Slovakia in the 1997 Opinion and subsequent Regular Reports concerned the need to introduce more 'transparent and market-based policies'. Also, in this case, perverse effects of the privatisation process, and the weakness of the financial system were among the major shortcomings.

Though a first wave of voucher privatisation was concluded before separating, the Slovak Republic decided to cancel the second wave to avoid excessive dispersion of ownership. Instead privatisation proceeded largely to the benefit of 'insiders', with preferential sales to management and employees. Political uncertainty meant that foreign direct investment was low. In 1995 a law excluded certain 'strategic' enterprises such as infrastructure companies and major financial companies from privatisation. In 1999 this law was cancelled and replaced by a law on large-scale privatisation, and the process of privatising banks and telecoms began.

By mid-1999 the private sector accounted for 75 per cent of GDP, and the book value of residual state ownership was only about $300 million, with its market value being even lower.[28]

One of the main tasks was to amend for some of the irregularities of the previous privatisation process. The National Property Fund was responsible for carrying out a review of companies whose initial privatisations involved irregularities, or whose owners failed to pay their full instalments to the Fund. For instance, the privatisation of the oil and gas enterprise, Nafta Gbely in 1996 was declared invalid and 46 per cent of its stake is to return to state hands.[29]

The Slovak Republic shares with its Czech counterpart the drawbacks of a weak financial sector. Under the Mečiar government banks had been encouraged to take on loans to enterprises, and by 1999 it was estimated that bad loans accounted for 33–44 per cent of total loans of the main banks.[30] At the end of 1999 the government transferred bad loans equivalent to 10 per cent of GDP to the Consolidation Agency and Consolidation Bank.[31] The three largest banks are

Vseobecna Uverova Banka (VUB), Slovenska Sporitelna (SLSP), and Izvesticna a Rozvojova Banka (IRB) which accounted for 44 per cent the assets of the banking sector in 1998 (down from 72 per cent in 1993).[32] In 2000 87 per cent of SLSP was bought by Erste Bank of Austria. A deal was reached with the Italian Intesa Bank in 2001 over VUB, and the Slovak government agreed to privatise IRB by the end of 2002.

The government introduced new bankruptcy legislation in 2000, but improvements in judicial performance are still required. Capital markets remain illiquid and fragmented, and in view of the continued weakness of the stock exchange, measures are necessary to protect minority shareholders' rights and set up an independent securities regulator.

Capacity to cope with competitive pressures and market forces within the Union

Assessment of whether an applicant country is 'able to cope with competitive pressures and market forces within the Community' is extremely difficult in practice. What is required is a comprehensive, sector-by-sector analysis of the present economic performance of that country and predictions of likely future developments in an enlarged market. As a result, analyses of how far the applicant countries will be able to meet competitive pressures in the EU tend to be piecemeal and incomplete.

An indication of the scale of the task involved is given in the analysis of the competitiveness of different countries carried out by the International Institute for Management Development in Lausanne. Each year 47 countries are ranked on the basis of numerous variables which take into account factors such as economic performance, research and development, and openness to the outside world. In 2000 290 variables were used.[33] Two-thirds of the data is taken from statistics, and one-third is based on interviews with business executives. One of the criticisms made of the approach is that it tends to identify competitiveness with current success.[34]

In the face of these difficulties, it is interesting to recall Krugman's attack (1996, pp. 3–23) on competitiveness as 'a largely meaningless concept' when applied to countries.[35] In the case of the Copenhagen criteria, what really seems to be at stake is the question of how many firms, or sectors will go out of business and how many lay-offs there will be when a country joins the EU, and this will clearly also depend on when accession takes place.

The future ability of Czech and Slovak industries to compete in an enlarged EU market will depend on developments in productivity, relative wages and exchange rates and so on. However, it is also true that a country will be better able to cope with competitive pressures (and *ceteris paribus* will require less further restructuring of its industry) the higher the level of economic integration achieved prior to accession.

Given the near impossibility of carrying out a complete assessment of competitiveness, the approach used here is to see how far present levels of integration can provide an indication of future capacity to cope in an enlarged market. In assessing the degree of economic integration (or integration of markets) achieved, trade (including outward processing trade or the de-localisation of production) and FDI will be taken into account.

Trade with the European Union

Any analysis of trade between the EU, and the Czech Republic and Slovakia respectively must take into account both the present level and structure of trade.

Prior to 1989 trade in the Eastern bloc was organised according to the international socialist division of labour, and trade with the West was kept to an unavoidable minimum.[36] The institutional framework for trade was the Council for Mutual Economic Assistance (CMEA). When the CMEA was formally wound up in 1991 the challenge of readjusting trade patterns was daunting. The question which immediately arose concerned the level of trade between the EU and the CEECs in the long run. In other words, what would be the 'normal' level of trade if Communism had not been introduced.

In addressing this question the most frequent approach adopted was that of gravity models which attempt to predict the level of bilateral trade flows on the basis of variables such as GNP, population, geographical distance, and, in some cases, preferential trading arrangements.[37] The results for the Czech Republic and Slovakia of a study of this type carried out by the EBRD are presented in table 6.2.

As is evident from table 6.2, since 1989 there has been a rapid redirection of CEEC trade away from other transition economies and towards the EU. However, the redirection of Czech and, in particular, Slovak trade towards the EU was less than predicted by the gravity model, and was less than in other CEECs such as Hungary or Poland (see table 6.2). This is largely to be explained by the split of Czechoslovakia in 1993, when former internal trade became international trade between the two countries, but it also reflects the Eastward-looking policy orientation of the Mečiar government.

Although the Czech Republic and Slovakia formed a customs union in January 1993, the Slovak share in Czech trade declined steadily from 18 per cent in 1993 to 9 per cent in 1998.[38] The dissolution of Czechoslovakia partly explains the 18 per cent increase in Czech trade with the EU in 1993. The existence of the customs union is sometimes advanced as an argument for simultaneous accession of the two countries to the EU. However, the process of eliminating tariffs on manufactures and harmonising trade concessions throughout Europe[39] reduces the economic consequences for the customs union if one country joins before the other.

Early studies found that the sectoral composition of CEEC trade was changing relatively slowly.[40] During the first few years of transition CEEC exports tended to remain relatively low in R&D and skill content, reflecting slow progress in building up an advanced industrial base. With the collapse of the

Table 6.2 Increase in the EU share of the total trade of the Czech Republic and Slovakia over the 1989–97 period (%)

	Total exports, 1989	*Actual share of EU in exports 1997*	*Predicted EU share of export trade, 1997*[a]	*Actual share of transition countries in exports, 1997*	*Predicted share of transition countries in exports, 1997*[a]	*Total imports 1989*	*Total imports 1997*
Czech Republic and Slovakia	18.2 (EC)[b] 4.6 (Austria) 6.6 (GDR)	61.0 (Cz. Rep.) 45.0 (SK)	72.0 (Cz. Rep.) 65.0 (SK)	22.0 (Cz. Rep.) 51.0 (SK)	0.07 (Cz. Rep.) 0.11 (SK)	17.8 (EC)[b] 5.5 (Austria) 7.8 (GDR)	62.4 (Cz. Rep.) 39.5 (SK)
Hungary	24.8 (EC)[b] 6.4 Austria 5.4 GDR	70.0	65.0	19.0	10.0	29.0 (EC)[b] 8.6 (Austria) 6.2 (GDR)	63.0
Poland	31.8 (EC)[b] 1.5 (EFTA)	71.0	73.0	22.0	0.09	34.2 (EC)[b] 3.8 (EFTA)	64.0

Notes: [a] The predicted trade levels were obtained from EBRD 1999 *Transition Report* which uses a gravity model relating bilateral trade flows to geographical distance, and the size of the economy of trading partners. According to the model, VTij (the bilateral volume of trade between two countries) is a function of Yi (the GDP of country i), Ni (the population of country i), and Dij (the geographical distance between countries i and j). See text for explanation.
[b] The statistics are for EC 12 in 1989 and EU 15 in 1997

Source: European Bank for Reconstruction and Development, Economist Intelligence Unit, and *Rocznik Statystyczny* (Poland).

CMEA, the CEECs were forced to sell products which would have been destined to Eastern markets in the West.

Subsequently, the countries most advanced in transition, and, in particular Hungary and the Czech Republic, succeeded in gradually moving to a larger share of higher technology products in exports.[41] The turnaround for these countries came in 1993/94 with the end of transitional recession and the beginning of positive economic growth. The exports were generally produced in firms which were either newly established or restructured, and firms which had not modernised often had problems in maintaining their share in foreign markets.

From table 6.3, which breaks trade down by major category, Czech exports in machinery and transport equipment and miscellaneous manufactured articles appear to have been performing best. Many of the firms and sectors with a positive performance of restructuring and exports in both the Czech Republic and Slovakia have either managed to attract FDI or have evolved special arrangements with foreign partners, such as outward processing trade.

Slovak export performance has been positive in the car industry, distribution, the food industry and electrical equipment where FDI has taken place,[42]

Table 6.3 The structure of foreign trade (% total imports or exports)

	Czech Republic			*Slovakia*		
	1993	*1995*	*1999*	*1993*	*1995*	*1999*
Imports by SITC						
(1+2) food and live animals, beverage and tobacco	7.3	6.3	5.4	8.8	8.0	6.2
2 crude materials, inedible	5.0	4.5	3.1	5.2	6.0	3.8
3 mineral fuels and lubricants	11.1	7.8	6.6	20.9	17.5	9.5
4 animal and vegetable products etc.	0.4	0.3	0.2	0.2	0.2	0.2
5 chemicals and related products	12.1	11.8	12.0	11.3	13.6	11.3
6 manufactured goods classified chiefly by material	15.9	20.3	20.6	15.1	17.8	18.3
7 machinery and transport equipment	36.1	37.1	40.4	29.3	28.9	37.7
8 misc. manufactured articles	11.7	11.9	11.7	9.0	8.0	12.9
9 goods not classified elsewhere	0.4	–	–	0.2	–	–
Exports by SITC						
(1+2) food and live animals, beverage and tobacco	7.8	5.6	3.6	6.4	5.9	3.5
2 crude materials, inedible	6.1	5.2	3.7	4.9	5.1	3.8
3 mineral fuels and lubricants	6.2	4.3	2.9	4.9	4.2	4.7
4 animal and vegetable products etc.	0.2	0.2	0.1	0.1	0.1	0.1
5 chemicals and related products	9.5	9.3	7.2	12.0	13.2	7.9
6 manufactured goods classified chiefly by material	29.9	32.2	25.5	38.8	40.4	27.5
7 machinery and transport equipment	27.6	30.4	43.2	19.4	18.8	39.4
8 misc. Manufactured articles	12.7	12.8	13.7	13.4	12.2	12.9
9 goods not elsewhere classified	–	–	–	–0.1	–	0.1

Source: *Statistical Yearbook of the Czech Republic* (*Statistickà Rocenka Ceské Republiki*), and *Statistickà Rocenka SR* and the EIU (Economist Intelligence Unit) for Slovakia.

while the Czech Republic has a similar experience for products such as automobiles, televisions and certain other telecommunications products.

Outward processing involves the international fragmentation of production, or carrying out different stages of the production process in different countries. Czech and Slovak exports to the EU associated with outward processing trade (OPT) have been growing faster than non-OPT exports.[43] This increase is largely to be explained by preferential treatment for OPT by the EU, in particular, in the Europe Agreements where tariffs were removed on OPT exports of clothing and textiles, but not on many categories of direct exports.

Traditionally OPT tends to be used in labour-intensive, and relatively low-skill sectors such as textiles and clothing, furniture and footwear. However, the Czech Republic and Slovakia have also been involved increasingly in OPT arrangements in higher-technology sectors such as telecommunications equipment, electrical machinery and auto parts. Geographical proximity to Austria and Germany has played an important role in facilitating these arrangements.

However, despite the increase in exports of more skilled, human capital-intensive, technology-intensive products, even in countries such as Hungary and the Czech Republic, a large share of exports remain in 'sensitive' sectors which tend to be intensive in unskilled labour. The sensitive sectors are generally defined as: agriculture, textiles, clothing, coal, footwear, steel and chemicals.[44] These are the sectors which tend to be characterised by overproduction at a world level, and the present EU members are committed to concerted efforts at reduction of capacity in some of these sectors such as steel and agriculture. Eichengreen and Kohl (1998) found that the share of chemicals, agriculture and other sensitive sectors still accounted for 20.6 per cent of Czech exports, and 23.4 per cent of Slovak exports in 1996.[45]

Foreign direct investment

FDI in the Czech Republic increased from $ 2.5 billion in 1998 to $4.9 billion in 1999 (see also table 6.4). It is expected to be in the order of $4–$5 billion in 2002.[46] Much of the investment boom in the Czech Republic since 1998 was due to late privatisation, but there was also a growing trend towards greenfield investment, in particular, in the automobile, electronics and electrical engineering sectors.[47] A significant share of FDI has been concentrated in a small number of very large investments including VW in Skoda Auto,[48] Philip Morris in the tobacco industry, and Matsushita, Philips, LG Electronics and Flextronics International in the electronics sector. At the same time, according to the OECD,[49] there was foreign participation in as many as 13,000 enterprises in the Czech Republic.

There have been positive spillover effects from FDI in the Czech Republic both for some domestic suppliers of components and in encouraging other FDI.[50] In 1999 CzechInvest found that among the larger manufacturing companies, foreign direct enterprises account for about 60 per cent of exports and added 19,000 jobs.[51]

Table 6.4 Foreign direct investment

	1992	*1995*	*1996*	*1997*	*1998*	*1999*	*2000 projection*	*Cumulative inflows, 1989–99*	*Cumulative inflows, 1989–98 per capita*	*FDI inflows per capita 1998*	*FDI inflows as per cent GDP 1998*
Czech Rep.	983	2,526	1,388	1,275	2,485	4,912	6,000	14,924	967	241	4.5%
Slovakia	100	202	251	177	508	701	1,500	2,111	326	94	2.5%

Source: EBRD Transition Report 1999 and Transition update, 2000.

FDI was attracted to the Czech Republic by the relatively good infrastructure and easy access to Germany and Austria; the skilled labour force, and the Czech tradition of mechanical engineering and technological research. The Klaus government (1992–97) had argued that these advantages, together with macro-economic stability and liberalisation, should be enough to attract foreign investors, but at that time there also seemed to be a preference for domestic rather than foreign ownership. This policy was reversed in April 1998 when the subsequent Czech government introduced a package of FDI incentives.

The cumulative total of FDI to Slovakia was only $2.1 billion by the end of 1999, but in 2000 FDI reached $1.5 billion (see table 6.4).

Under the Mečiar regime FDI was discouraged by the 'perceived lack of transparency, consistency and predictability in the implementation of investment related laws and regulations'[52] and by the apparent preference of the Slovak authorities for domestic ownership and control of enterprises. The slow progress in privatisation also meant few opportunities for foreign investors.

In contrast, the Dzuringa government has attempted to promote FDI with cuts in corporate taxes, special tax breaks for ten years for foreign investors, and measures to increase commercial transparency. These incentives were improved in 2001. The September 1999 privatisation law paved the way for sales of majority shares in Slovak Telecom and the three remaining large state-owned banks, and of a minority share in energy sector companies.[53]

Although overall FDI remains low, a few large investors have played a key role in transforming the Slovak economy, including Volkswagen (which accounted for 16 per cent of all exports in 2000), Siemens, and Tesco. US Steel bought into the steel group, VSZ, while 36 per cent of the Slovnaft refinery was sold to the Hungarian oil and gas company, MOL, in April 2000.[54] FDI deals in high-technology sectors have been relatively few in number, with Sony, Matsushita and On Semiconductors being the most significant.

Adherence to the objective of Economic and Monetary Union (EMU)

The applicant countries are obliged to endorse the ultimate objective of EMU, but this does not imply that they have to meet the Maastricht criteria at the time of accession.[55] It is essential to bear in mind that convergence criteria are not the same as accession criteria. Nonetheless, as Agenda 2000 points out,[56] the Maastricht convergence criteria should 'remain key points of reference for stability-oriented macroeconomic policies and must in time be fulfilled by the member states on a permanent basis'. The Maastricht criteria should not therefore be regarded as a short-run objective for the CEECs, but as a medium- to long-term goal.

The budget deficit has been growing, and the public debt in the Czech Republic rose to an estimated 20.1 per cent in 2001. However, if contingent liabilities such as the bad loans placed with the Consolidation Bank, and government liabilities are taken into account, according to the OECD public debt could be as high as 60 per cent of GDP.[57]

As the Czech experience suggests, problems of definition or specification may arise in applying the Maastricht criteria in transition economies.[58] The concept of public deficit in the Maastricht Treaty refers to central, regional and local government as well as social security funds, but in the Czech Republic the state budget excludes the operations of local authorities, and various extra-budgetary funds and off-budget agencies.[59] Moreover, proceeds from privatisation are included as current revenue (rather than the normal procedure of treating them as a capital transfer in national accounts).

The Czech government was due to increase transparency from 2000 with the presentation of a budget based on consolidated accounts. However, government statements suggested that new off-budget funds might be created, and experience shows that such funds are often subject to a less tight budgetary procedure (OECD 2000, p. 62). Moreover, further complications arise from the creation of a new regional level of government which began in 2000, though some time was expected to elapse before implementation was complete.

The budget deficit in Slovakia has been brought down to an estimated 3.8 per cent for 2001, but this fails to include bank restructuring, which amounts to another 1 per cent of GDP. Other contingent liabilities not covered by the budget include social funds such as those for pensions, health care and unemployment. Consolidated accounts of the government sector are due to be introduced with the creation of a new central treasury system.[60]

Satisfying the fiscal criteria (see table 6.5) on a sustainable basis could prove difficult in both countries. Although external discipline can play a useful role where fiscal deficits are too high, excessive concern for budgetary constraint may hinder transition. In common with other CEECs, the Czech Republic and Slovakia face pressure for additional government spending from a number of sources including improvements in infrastructure, and consolidation of bad debts. The task of taking on the *acquis* also calls for budgetary expenditure in areas such as the environment, increasing nuclear safety, and improvement in administrative and judicial capacity. The two countries also require fundamental reform of their pension and social security systems, health care, and education, and Slovakia has also embarked on a public investment project of housing construction.

Table 6.5 The fiscal criteria in the Czech Republic and Slovakia

	Government debt as % GDP			*Government surplus/deficit % GDP*				
	1997	*1998*	*1999*	*1996*	*1997*	*1998*	*1999*	*2000*
Czech Republic	13.0	13.4	15.0	−2.3	−2.3	−1.6	−3.8	−4.2
Slovakia	23.7	26.0	28.4	−1.9	−4.4	−5.8	−3.6	−6.7

Source: EBRD and Deutsche Bank Research, Euro Watch.

On the revenue side, tax reform is also necessary in both countries, with measures to improve tax collection, eliminate distortions[61] and rebalance the tax burden, with an increased role for VAT (value-added tax) and personal taxes on income. The Czech Republic and Slovakia are also likely to encounter difficulties in meeting the inflation criteria (see table 6.6). In general, inflation in transition countries is higher than in the EU. Price liberalisation in these countries is incomplete, in particular, in the housing and energy sectors. Economic transformation may also contribute to inflationary pressures in other ways. When the formerly closed and inefficient centrally planned economies were opened up to market forces a process of catching up with rapid gains in productivity occurred. If the productivity gains are faster in the traded than in the non-traded sector, this could generate inflation.[62]

Table 6.6 Inflation and long-term interest rates in the Czech Republic and Slovakia

	Inflation (average annual increase in CPI)							*Long-term interest rates*		
	1995	*1996*	*1997*	*1998*	*1999*	*2000*	*2001*	*1996*	*1997*	*1998*
Czech Republic	9.1	8.8	8.5	10.7	2.5	4.0	4.8	12.5	13.9	10.5
Slovakia	9.9	5.8	6.1	6.7	10.1	12.0	4.5	13.2	16.2	16.2

Source: EBRD 1999 Transition Report.

The National Bank of Slovakia was able to build a high level of credibility through its tough anti-inflation stance, and its success in developing a stable, transparent approach to policy,[63] and this has helped to keep inflation relatively low, though still far higher than the EU average. The Czech authorities kept monetary policy tight after the 1997 crisis, and in 1999 managed to undershoot the inflation target. However, as the Czech authorities pointed out, much of this undershooting was due to an exogenous fall in food, energy and tradable goods prices, and from 2000 inflation again began to rise.

The exchange rate criteria entails that a country should remain within the 'normal' band of the exchange rate mechanism (ERM) without tension and without initiating depreciation for two years. For the accession countries, unless they are allowed to join the ERM before they become EU members, this means that full participation in the third stage of EMU would have to wait for two years after joining the EU. Some CEECs have therefore argued in favour of joining the ERM prior to accession.

Participation in the ERM would entail automatic and unlimited intervention at the margin, though the ECB and Central Banks of participating countries could suspend intervention if it threatens price stability. Given that price stability is the primary objective of the European Central Bank (ECB), it is doubtful how far it would be prepared to take on intervention in favour of the currencies of the CEECs prior to their accession.

Attempting to peg the nominal exchange rate in a transition economy is a difficult task (see table 6.7), as the Czech experience illustrates.[64] Initially the magnitude of devaluation prevented the exchange rate from acting as an effective anchor. Subsequently, nominal currency stability and a higher rate of inflation than in OECD countries undermined the cushion which an undervalued exchange rate provided in the early years of transition. The real appreciation of the exchange rate was not matched by increases in productivity, and Czech firms began to lose competitiveness. The Czech Central Bank spent an estimated $2 billion in reserves in an attempt to maintain the fixed exchange rate system,[65] before switching to a managed float based on a target rate of 17–19.5 koruna per D-Mark in May 1997.

Table 6.7 Exchange rates in the Czech Republic and Slovakia

	Czech Republic					*Slovakia*				
Currency	Czech koruna					Slovakian koruna				
Current regime	Managed float, shadows Euro					Managed float, shadows DM				
Likely future arrangements	Managed float, shadow Euro					Switch to Euro shadow				
	1996	*1997*	*1998*	*1999*	*2000*	*1996*	*1997*	*1998*	*1999*	*2000*
Exchange rate annual average (per US $)	27.1	31.7	32.3	34.3	38.6	30.7	33.6	35.2	41.4	46.2

Source: EBRD and Financial Times Survey, *Slovakia*, of 4 July 2001, and Financial Times Survey, *The Czech Republic*, of 12 December 2001.

Subsequently the Czech exchange rate was subject to strong fluctuations, with sharp appreciation against the Deutschmark until November 1998, an equally sharp depreciation until March 1999, followed by a tendency to appreciate. The 1998 appreciation was probably due to the large interest-rate spread between the Czech and Deutschmark-denominated investments, while the subsequent depreciation reflects a narrowing of that spread and the repercussions of the Asian and Russian crises. The recovery from early 1999 can be explained by the improvement of the current account and speculative capital inflows associated with the privatisation process (OECD, 2000, p. 40).

Largely as a result of the credibility of the National Bank, Slovakia was able to maintain a fixed exchange rate regime from 1991 with a central rate that remained unchanged until 1998 apart from a 10 per cent devaluation in 1993.[66]

The high levels of fiscal and current account deficits, and uncertainty with regard to the outcome of the September 1998 election led to speculation against the koruna. The National Bank of Slovakia lost an estimated nearly $1 billion between August and October 1998 before deciding to abandon the fixed exchange rate regime and allowing the currency to float. The currency fell immediately by 10 per cent, but subsequently recovered and proved relatively stable.

Conclusions

From the discussion here it emerges that while substantial progress has been made in both the Czech and Slovak Republics, crucial tasks for a second phase of transition remain. Continued efforts have to be made in controlling inflation and maintaining fiscal discipline. The transformation of the financial system and the elimination of bad debts must remain high priorities. Though the transfer from state to private ownership has proceeded rapidly, further efforts are needed in order to ensure realisation of other objectives of privatisation, such as fairness and efficiency (which requires effective methods of corporate governance). The process of industrial restructuring is still far from complete in both countries, while choosing an effective exchange rate policy and social security reform remain challenges for the next few years. It therefore seems likely that the process of economic transition will continue even after EU accession.

Notes

1 The *acquis communautaire* is the body of EU legislation, practices, principles, and objectives accepted by the member states. It is composed of the Treaties; legislation enacted at the EU level and judgments of the European Court of Justice; Justice and Home Affairs; the Common Foreign and Security Policy and Treaties of the EU with third countries. The *acquis* has been accumulating over the years and now amounts to some 12,000 legislative acts.

2 Analysis of the political criteria and of progress in legal approximation are excluded from the present discussion. For analyses of progress in meeting the political criteria, see, for example, S. Senior-Nello and K. Smith, *The Consequences of Eastern Enlargement of the European Union in Stages* (Aldershot: Ashgate Publishers, 1998), H. Grabbe, and K. Hughes, *Enlarging the EU Eastwards*, Chatham House Paper (London: Royal Institute of International Affairs, 1998) or G. Avery and F. Cameron, *The Enlargement of the European Union*, (Sheffield: Sheffield Academic Press, 1998). The condition that enlargement should not slow the momentum of integration is also left out here, partly because most of the key decisions (on reform of EU institutions, and extension of the CAP (Common Agricultural Policy), Structural Funds and freedom of movement of labour to the new EU members) are being taken almost exclusively by the existing EU member states.

3 An analysis of progress in developing administrative and judicial capacity is beyond the present discussion, but is an area where both the Czech Republic and Slovakia have encountered difficulties.

4 Enhanced co-operation or flexibility allows for the possibility of some Member States proceeding more rapidly with deeper integration in certain areas.

5 EC Commission (1997). *Agenda 2000, COM (97) 2000 final*, 15 July 1997, Supplement to the Bulletin of the European Union 5/97, p. 40.

6 Though interpretation of the inimitable bureaucratic language of these documents is not always straightforward.

7 According to the World Bank's World Development Report (1999), in 1997 the GNP per capita was $9,680 in Slovenia and $5,200 in the Czech Republic.

8 OECD, *Economic Survey of the Slovak Republic* (Paris: OECD, 1999).

9 EC Commission, 1999 EC, *Regular Reports on Progress towards Accession*, http://europa.eu.int/comm/enlargement.

10 *Financial Times* (25 May 2000).
11 Unless otherwise stated, the statistics on privatisation are taken from the European Bank for Reconstruction and Development (various years).
12 *Financial Times Survey: The Czech Republic*, 12 December 2001.
13 The cross-ownership is partly the result of the restriction on the IPF's ownership to not more than 20 per cent of the shares of a company, and the requirement that the holding in any one company cannot exceed 10 per cent of the IPF's portfolio.
14 According to *The Economist* (19 April 1997), some 750,000 people or 7 per cent of the population suffered losses as a result of the activities of the investment privatisation funds.
15 As described, for instance in M. Uvalic and L. Vaughan-Whitehead, *Privatisation Surprises in Transition Economies: Employee-Ownership in Central and Eastern Europe* (Aldershot: E. Elgar 1997).
16 European Bank for Reconstruction and Development, *1997 Transition Report and Transition Update*, London.
17 As late as 1997 the NPF maintained a minority ownership of 47 per cent in Komercni Banka, 43 per cent of Ceska Sporitelna and 33 per cent in the Investicni a Postovni Banka (European Bank for Reconstruction and Development, *1997 Transition Report*, p. 147).
18 According to the EBRD *2000 Transition Update*, the share of non-performing loans in the total was still 30 per cent.
19 According to A. Bratowski, I. Grosfeld and I. Rostowski, *Investment Finance in De Novo Private Firms: Empirical Results from the Czech Republic, Hungary and Poland.* CASE-CEU Working Paper Series, No. 21 (Warsaw: Centre for Social and Economic Research, Central European University, October 1998), as reported in OECD, *Economic Survey of the Czech Republic* (Paris: OECD, 2000), the share of bank credit in the financing of new firms over the 1990–94 period was 20.7 per cent in the Czech Republic compared with 4.2 per cent in Hungary and 4.4 per cent in the Czech Republic.
20 In some cases, such as Skoda Plzen or Chemapol, the managers of unrestructured firms were even able to expand their activities.
21 Earlier measures include, for instance, the Czech and Slovak Ministries of Finance directly taking over loans amounting to 13.3 billion kcs from the Investicni a Postovni Banka in 1992. In 1994 the Czech government allocated 7 billion kcs for Agrobanka, Komercni Banka, and KOB to write off bad loans of state enterprises to be restituted to former owners.
22 To meet these difficulties, M. Rodlauer, 'The Experience with IMF-Supported Reform Programs in Central and Eastern Europe', *Journal of Comparative Economics* Vol. 20 (1995), 104, argues that an effective strategy to tackle the problem of bad debts should: strengthen enterprise discipline and discourage firms from taking on further bad loans; create a new banking philosophy whereby banks choose and monitor clients carefully; and evolve an overall framework for dealing with bad debts which includes bank recapitalisation through the state budget.
23 *Financial Times Survey: The Czech Republic*, 12 December 2001.
24 *Ibid.*
25 The Securities and Exchange Commission can make recommendations, but the sole authority to issue regulations remains with the Ministry of Finance. The vague juridical character of the Securities and Exchange Commission even leaves its ability to enforce legislation open to question (OECD, 2000, p. 104).
26 The White Paper makes reference to Articles 85, 86 and 90 of the Treaty of Rome relating to competition rules, and Article 92 concerning state aids. However, although taking on a ready-made legal system and avoiding a long process of trial and error may have advantages, it also runs the risk that the imported system may not always be tailored to the specific needs of the transitional economy (see A. Smith, P. Holmes, U. Sedelmeier, E. Smith,

H. Wallace, and R. Young, *The European Union and Central and Eastern Europe: Pre-Accession Strategies*, SEI Working Paper No. 15 (Brighton: Sussex European Institute, 1996) for a discussion of this point).

27 Opinion on Slovakia, Section 2.1.

28 EBRD 1999 Transition Report.

29 *Ibid.*

30 *Ibid.*

31 EBRD 2000 Transition Report.

32 EC Commission, 1999 Regular Report.

33 The results are published in the *World Competitiveness Yearbook*, IMD, Lausanne, website www.imd.ch/wcy.html.

34 Though it is curious to note that the Copenhagen criteria refer to 'ability to cope with competitive pressures' rather than competitiveness.

35 P. Krugman, *Pop Internationalism* (Cambridge, MA: MIT Press, 1996) criticises the analogy of countries competing with each other on the global marketplace like big corporations on a number of counts. Firstly, if a corporation is not competitive it will go out of business, but this is not the case for countries as they have have no well-defined bottom line. Criticising Laura D'Andrea Tyson's definition of competitiveness as 'ability to produce goods and services which meet the test of international competition while our citizens enjoy a standard of living which is rising and sustainable', P. Krugman argues that in a country with little external trade what is at stake here is essentially domestic productivity. Even in a country with trade such as the US, unlike a corporation a large share of output (90 per cent in the case of the US) is produced for domestic use. Moreover, when corporations compete, one person's gain is another person's loss, and, according to the principle of comparative advantage, this is not the case for countries.

36 For a more detailed discussion of these questions see S. M. Senior-Nello, *The New Europe: Changing Economic Relations between East and West,* (Hemel Hempstead: Harvester Wheatsheaf, 1991).

37 For an early survey of analyses of East–West trade based on gravity models see CEPR, *Is Bigger Better? The Economics of EC Enlargement,* Monitoring European Integration 3 (London: Centre for Economic Policy Research, 1992). A second type of analysis is based a historical approach. The best-known attempt to apply the historical approach is that of S. M. Collins and D. Rodrik, *Eastern Europe and the Soviet Union in the World Economy,* (Washington DC: Institute for International Economics, 1991) who use a 1928 League of Nations trade matrix for the Soviet Union and the CEECs, and evidence of how the trade of comparator countries in Western Europe has developed since to predict a long-run trade matrix for Eastern Europe. According to their estimates, 55 per cent of Czechoslovak imports, and 46 per cent of exports would be with the EC.

38 According to Czech national statistics.

39 This occurs through the pan-European cumulation system whic was established at the request of the 1993 Copenhagen Council, and includes the EU (15), the CEEC (10), and Malta, Cyprus, Turkey, Iceland, Norway and Switzerland. The agreement adopted the schedule for tariff reductions of the Europe Agreements which means that all tariff barriers on manufactures will be removed by 2001. The Agreement also entails harmonisation of rules of origin, so the parts and components produced in any country belonging to the European trading bloc are treated as domestic components.

40 Such as Z. Drábek, and A. Smith, *Trade Performance and Trade Policy in Central and Eastern Europe*, CEPR Discussion Paper No. 1182 (London: Centre for Economic Policy Research, London, 1995), EC Commission, 'The Economic Interpenetration between the European Community and Eastern Europe', *European Economy Reports and Studies,* No. 6 (1994) and R. Faini and R. Portes, *European Union Trade with Eastern Europe: Adjustment and Opportunities* (London: Centre for Economic Policy Research, 1995).

41 See, for example, World Bank, *Czech Republic: Toward EU Accession. Main Report* (Washington, DC: World Bank, 1999).

42 OECD, 1999, p. 107.

43 The share of OPT exports in total exports to the EU was 4.6 per cent for Czechoslovakia in 1988, and 11.4 per cent and 19.9 per cent for the Czech and Slovak Republics respectively in 1996: B. Eichengreen and R. Kohl, 'The External Sector: the State and Development in Eastern Europe', in J. Zysman, and A. Schwartz (eds), *Enlarging Europe: The Industrial Foundations of a New Political Reality.* Research Series No. 99 (Berkeley: University of California, 1998), pp. 169–201.

44 The inclusion of chemicals among the sensitive sectors is justified by the large share of EU anti-dumping measures in this sector, but it is not accepted by all authors. For instance in CEPR (1992) chemicals are not included in the list of sensitive sectors.

45 The importance of agriculture is relatively less in the Czech Republic (accounting for 3.3 per cent of GDP in 1998) and Slovakia (5.8 per cent of GDP) compared with an average of 8.6 per cent of GDP for the ten applicant CEEC countries in 1998.

46 According to Martin Jahn, the head of CzechInvest (the foreign investment promotion agency), as reported in the *Financial Times Survey: The Czech Republic*, 12 December 2001.

47 *Financial Times*, 25 May 2000.

48 Following the takeover of Skoda Auto by VW, in 1995 car production reached 200,000 units, almost half of which were exported to the EU. EC Commission (1997b) *Commission Opinion on the Czech Republic's Application for Membership of the European Union*, 15 July 1997, Supplement to the Bulletin of the European Union 14/97, p. 67. EC Commission (1997b) *Commission Opinion on the Slovak Republic's Application for Membership of the European Union,* 15 July 1997, Supplement to the Bulletin of the European Union 9/97.

49 OECD, *Economic Surveys 1995–1996: The Czech Republic* (Paris: OECD, 1996), p. 76.

50 For example, the decision by Philips to set up a $191 million picture tube plant was influenced by the presence of television assemblers there (*Financial Times*, 19 April 2000).

51 *Financial Times*, 28 October 1999.

52 OECD, 1999, p. 43.

53 In 2001 stakes of up to 49 per cent are expected to be sold in SPP and Transpetrol, the transporters of Russian gas and oil, and in *Slovenska Elektrarne* (*Financial* Times, 25 May 2000).

54 EBRD, Transition Update 2000, p. 76. Following an investigation into Mečiar's privatisation techniques, a 10 per cent stake in Slovnaft had been renationalised. MOL also acquired the right to increase its stake to above 50 per cent after 2 years.

55 The Maastricht Treaty spelt out five criteria: (1) successful candidates must have inflation rates no more than 1.5 per cent above the average of the three countries with the lowest inflation rate in the Community; (2) long-term interest rates should be no more that 2 per cent above the average of that of the three lowest inflation countries; (3) the exchange rate of the country should remain within the 'normal' band of the exchange rate mechanism (ERM) without tension and without initiating depreciation for two years; at the time of the Maastricht Treaty the 'normal' band referred to the margins of +/–2.25 per cent, but since August 1993, it is taken to refer to +/–15 per cent; (4) the public debt of the country must be less than 60 per cent of GDP; (5) the national budget deficit must be less than 3 per cent of GDP.

56 Section 3.3 of the Opinions.

57 As reported in *Financial Times Survey: The Czech Republic*, of 12 December 2001. According to a Czech government evaluation carried out in conjunction with the World Bank, if various off-budgetary institutions were included in the general government

accounts, the 1998 budget deficit would have been 3.5 percentage points higher than indicated by official statistics. The study suggests that in gross terms the hidden public liabilities of *Konsolidacni Banka, Ceska Financi,* the National Property Fund and various state loan guarantees amounted to 17 per cent of GDP.

58 One result of the application of the convergence criteria in the EU(15) has been a process of standardising definitions, though this is far from complete. For a discussion of this issue see Krenzler, H. and Senior-Nello, S. *The Implications of the Euro for Enlargement,* Robert Schuman Centre Policy Paper 99/3 (Florence: European University Institute, 1999).

59 OECD, 2000, p. 45. Extra-budgetary funds include the Road Fund and the Housing Fund.

60 OECD, 1999, p. 50. A further difficulty arises from the lack of official estimates of the budget situation prepared on the basis of an *accruals* system, i.e. taking into account revenues and expenditures deferred from one year to the next.

61 For instance, in the Czech Republic the tax system is biased in favour of self-employment (OECD, 2000, p. 19).

62 This phenomenon is called the Balassa–Harrod–Samuelson effect. When a small economy opens to international trade its export prices are set at the world level. If the country is on its production possibility frontier, increased productivity in traded goods leads to increased wages in the traded-goods sector. However, if wages are eqalised between the traded and non-traded goods sectors, and the non-traded goods sector has lower productivity, inflation will increase.

63 As described in OECD, 1999, p. 63.

64 Initially the koruna's exchange rate was based on a basket made up of the dollar and D-mark.

65 *Financial Times* (1 December 1997).

66 The regime involved targeting a currency basket in which the weight of the Deutschmark was 60 per cent and that of the dollar was 40 per cent, roughly reflecting the currency composition of trade.

Tibor Papp

7

Who is in, who is out?
Citizenship, nationhood, democracy and European integration in the Czech Republic and Slovakia

Introduction

On 5 December 1997, most daily newspapers in Slovakia reported the statement of European Parliament Deputy A. Oostlander regarding Slovakia's accession status to the European Union (EU): 'You either have to change your opinion, or change the government.'[1] According to Slovak Prime Minister Vladimír Mečiar, the statement constituted an unprecedented interference in the internal affairs of Slovakia, and Oostlander's behaviour was unprofessional, irresponsible and unfit for a member of the European Parliament. Mečiar said that the call for the dismissal of a democratically elected government contravened all accepted international norms, and called the affair another example of the double standards applied to Slovakia. Deputy Prime Minister Marián Húska was quick to contend that Slovakia is treated as a second-class state because it refused to become the vassal of rich and powerful western countries. A promise of vigilant protection of Slovak national interest concluded Húska's emotional statement.[2]

This exchange of opinions raises several questions. First, are EU methods used to evaluate applicants consistent, or arbitrary? Even though the EU evaluates with consistency economic and political conditions, some instances of arbitrariness would be difficult to dispute. Turkey, for instance, appears to be at least as well prepared for accession as Cyprus: yet while the former remains on the sidelines, the latter is a leading candidate for the next enlargement. Latvia and Lithuania could note that although Estonia's citizenship policies toward the Russian minority are more discriminatory then theirs, they have been told to wait while Estonia was invited to begin negotiations.[3]

Second, can the EU pressure toward a change of government resolve a country's democratic deficit? While one could agree that Mečiar is an unpleasant man to negotiate with it is hard to imagine that a change of government through means other than free and fair elections would lead to more democracy. It is also argued that democratisation takes place from the top down, when often despotic governments secure order and bring economic growth.[4] Moreover, transitional polities are sensitive to external interference, and given the strong correlation between democracy and economic growth,[5] attempts to destabilise growth promoting governments, could be counterproductive in the long run. The EU's bet on the Dzurinda government, for instance might have improved Slovakia's accession status, yet, populists like Vladimír Mečiar, or Robert Fico keep on winning the popular vote.[6] With little improvement in ethnic relations and a massive increase in unemployment, the chances of the EU preferred government in the next elections appear dismal.[7]

This leads to a third question: should the EU apply accession criteria consistently to all applicants?[8] It is true that some applicants are politically more stable, prosperous and ready for accession than others, and their institutions appear more compatible with the standards proposed by the EU.[9] Ironically, countries that are the least stable and prosperous, with institutions least compatible with those of the EU, are expected to make the most rapid and fundamental changes if they wish to be considered for accession. But can countries achieve and sustain political stability and economic growth through rapid and fundamental changes? I argue, contrary to the 'democratisation through incorporation and convergence' thesis,[10] that accession strategies are likely to vary and have different results in distinct polities, and evaluation criteria therefore should be adapted to individual countries, rather than applied across the board. The resulting approach, known as 'differentiated integration',[11] is therefore likely to benefit all parties involved.

Even if a temporary retreat from EU standards will not make countries more democratic in the short run, it is likely to increase the EU's influence over the nature of political (and economic) change in the long run by reducing uncertainty and transaction costs involved in the process.[12] This occurs because rapid and fundamental changes create, by definition, institutions that do not correspond with the pre-existing ones, and the subsequent social, political and economic interaction continues to take place through a set of informal, rather than through the new, super-imposed formal institutions.[13]

A comprehensive analysis of the EU's approach to the evaluation of new applicants would go beyond the scope of this chapter. Therefore, I shall focus on the cases of the Czech Republic and Slovakia, more specifically on their approximation policies (and the evaluation thereof) in the field of citizenship policy. A comparison of the two countries is feasible, because they have a common experience of communism, they shared the same state between 1918 and 1992, and because their chances for membership at the moment of the dissolution of Czechoslovakia in 1993 appeared roughly equal. In 1998, however, the Czech Republic was *in*, while Slovakia was *out* of the first round of accession negotiations.[14] Following the change of government in 1998 the chances of Slovakia improved, in spite of the fact that the new ruling coalition faces formidable obstacles in its efforts to comply with the accession criteria. In short, a comparison of the post-1993 developments in the two countries, reveals to what degree changes in their accession status result from inconsistencies in evaluation and accession strategies at the EU level, and to what degree from changes at the domestic level.

To keep the evaluation consistent, it seems profitable to focus on the politics of citizenship. First, on the conceptual level there is an implicit relationship between the concepts of citizenship, nationhood and democracy. Consequently, while the focus on citizenship policies makes the analytical and empirical work more manageable, it also remains relevant for the understanding of democratisation, and brings in the external dimension of the integration process.

A country's understanding of nationhood reveals a lot about the degree of tolerance one would exhibit toward the members of other nations. When the understanding of nationhood is derived from primordial and ethnic concepts, for instance, one is likely to experience less tolerance toward non-citizens and other nationals.[15] Moreover, a degree of democracy is reflected in the nature of relations between the state and the citizens. In other words, states approach differently consultations with citizens, and give distinct degrees of protection from arbitrary action.[16]

Finally, while Article 8 of the Treaty of European Union[17] revived the academic debate on changing understanding of citizenship in contemporary Western democracies, a surprisingly insignificant part of this debate focuses on post-communist countries.[18] This deficiency is disturbing mainly because Western paradigms rarely fit when applied in the countries of Central and Eastern Europe. Therefore, the academic community could gain useful theoretical insights from a systematic application of citizenship politics in the EU's evaluation of applicant countries.

Following a scholarly literature review on citizenship, I define the relevant concepts, and outline a theoretical framework in which relations between nationhood, citizenship, democracy and EU integration are analysed. I then compare the evaluations of the Czech Republic and Slovakia in 'Agenda 2000'. I argue that inconsistencies in evaluation are, at least in part, the result of two methodological problems: the absence of comprehensive definitions and analytical frameworks; and the EU's consequent ignorance of the domestic constraints of applicants. In part, however, inconsistencies can be traced directly to the lack of desire of EU leaders to sit down and negotiate with controversial political figures such as Vladimír Mečiar.[19] I conclude that the EU strategies of eastward enlargement hinge on a paradox where the EU demands the most substantial changes from the countries that are the least fit to carry them out; and thus that all involved parties could benefit from the revaluation of this approach.

Citizenship, nationhood, democracy and European integration: concepts and definitions

Two different currents of the scholarship on citizenship shall be considered in this chapter. The first treats the relationships between EU member-states, their citizens, and the Union.[20] Its arguments could be divided into three categories, where citizenship is understood respectively (1) as rights and obligations that establish an individual's membership of a nation-state; (2) as membership in any space outside of the nation-state where individual and collective rights can be legitimated; or (3) as rights and obligations that place the individual somewhere between the first two possibilities.

The second broad current of scholarship treats the relationship between citizenship and democracy. Two distinct approaches can be identified here. In the first approach, developed by T. H. Marshall, the extension of equal political, civil, and social rights to citizens led gradually to the destruction of old status-based hierarchies and ultimately to democracy.[21] Charles Tilly, on the other hand, disputes the progressive, linear, and evolutionary character of citizenship. Tilly argues that the democratic component of citizenship is, first, the result of a bargaining process between rulers and ruled which began in eighteenth-century western Europe; and, second, the consequence of the emulation of the 'Western model' by nation-states which were founded at a later point.[22]

I will review these arguments, and then I propose a framework for a relational definition of citizenship that incorporates nationhood and democracy. Finally, I will suggest a method for evaluation of the degree of democracy.

Citizenship, nationhood and European integration

Scholars who understand citizenship as a membership of a nation-state view European citizenship with scepticism.[23] Raymond Aron believed that European citizenship is impossible for structural reasons, because it would have to involve the transfer of political and legal powers from the national level, and such a transfer would require a sustained popular demand for European Federation.[24] Rogers Brubaker argues that citizenship is likely to remain a bastion of national sovereignty, because its definitions continue to reflect a deeply rooted understanding of nationhood.[25] Both views are supported by Charles Tilly. Tilly sees citizenship as one of the underlying organisational features of modern nation-states, and concludes that it is unlikely to shed its close relationship to nationhood, because the construction of new organisational relations entails substantial transaction costs.[26]

The second group of scholars dismisses the contemporary idea of citizenship as merely membership of a nation-state. Yasemin Soysal and David Jacobson point to the changing conventional characterisation of citizenship. They argue that international migration, supranational associations, and the nearly universal acceptance of basic human rights constitute an alternative space for legitimisation of individual and collective rights. From their point of view, citizenship of the union – a formal extension of rights to free movement of goods, services, capital and people – cannot be considered a major obstacle to European integration.[27]

The third strand of explanations agrees that the contemporary conception of citizenship in Europe has inched away from the conventional, national understanding. Yet these authors by no means share the optimism of Soysal and

Jacobson concerning the irrelevance of the conventional conception of citizenship for European integration. Some of them point to the rising fortunes of European nationalist parties at the ballot box, and suggest that many individuals wish neither to abandon national citizenship as traditionally understood, nor share its benefits with foreigners.[28] Hence, integrative pressures from the EU, some argue, actually contributed to the radicalisation of citizenship policies, and even threaten the well established inclusive and non-ethnic principles of national citizenship laws.[29] This view is supported by empirical research that points to a correlation between cycles of economic decline in the member states, with instances of rising resentment toward foreigners, and a declining support for European integration.[30] Finally, Baldwin-Edwards, Baubock and Meehan argue that the citizenship of the union has had little impact on the legalisation of migrant and guest workers of non-member states, it continues to limit the movement of unemployed and young people,[31] and has not yet provided the anticipated stimulus for the much desired harmonisation of voting and naturalisation laws of member states.[32]

At the same time, according to Meehan, the new citizenship is neither national nor cosmopolitan, but multiple in that 'identities, rights and obligations associated with citizenship are expressed through an increasingly complex configuration of common Community institutions, states, national and trans-national voluntary associations, regions and alliances of regions'.[33] Yet, the new rights and obligations in most cases predated the conception of European citizenship, making it a post hoc construction with spurious legitimacy and credibility. Those who attribute the relaxation of naturalisation laws in traditionally strict countries like Germany[34] or the trends toward a growing acceptance of dual citizenship by west European countries to the citizenship of Europe are therefore missing the point.[35] Fortunately, the consensus remains that the conventional understanding of citizenship as a membership of a nation-state endures, and thus the legitimisation of European citizenship remains problematic.

Citizenship, democracy and European integration

Investigating the emergence of citizenship rights in England, Marshall traced the formative period of civil rights to the eighteenth century, and the protection of the individual's freedom and property from the state. Then, the political rights of the nineteenth century enabled citizens to participate in the political process through elections. Finally, the social rights of a welfare state provided entitlements to social security. According to Marshall, citizenship 'is a status bestowed by those who are full members of a community. All who possess the status are equal with respect to the rights and duties with which the status is endowed'.[36] Citizenship, in Marshall's view, is thus linked to democracy in that equality in the application of rights and duties first helped to destroy the class hierarchy of medieval England, and then challenged the inequalities of twentieth-century capitalism.

Marshall's theory is criticised on several grounds. First, since the evolution of citizenship rights in England took place in relative isolation and in a culturally homogeneous society, his model requires modification when applied to states where these conditions are not met. Second, the teleological model according to which citizenship rights progressed from political, through civic, to social, assumes the culmination of this process in a full welfare state. Today, welfare states are under constant pressure from an increasing global competition. Third, citizenship rights in the former communist states have taken a reversed evolutionary trend: first came the social rights inherent in the socialist economic systems, then civil rights via the increasing challenge to authoritarian regimes from dissidents in the 1970s and 1980s, and finally the acquisition of political rights, in the case of CEE states after the 1989 revolutions.[37] In short, the relatively new states – for instance states that became independent in the aftermath of Soviet empire[38] – have neither the time, nor the need to go through a similar evolutionary process. They can emulate the Western model, and make adjustments that best fit their present demographic, cultural, social and economic conditions.

An alternative to Marshall's explanation was proposed by Tilly. According to Tilly, modern citizenship can be traced to the 1792 French constitution, which granted voting rights to wage-earning males who took an oath to defend the nation and constitution. In Tilly's interpretation, the expanding military activity of the revolutionary state increased the need for conscription and revenue, and forced state agents to strike bargains with the reluctant subjects. Thus, citizenship, defined as a 'tie entailing mutual rights and obligations between categorically defined persons and the state' was established through accords between the state and its subjects. The increasing demands of the state and the subsequent inclusion of further groups in the bargaining process made democracy possible.

This does not mean that all new states fit the same paradigm, nor that the bargaining was finished with the establishment of a welfare state. On the contrary. On the one hand, the availability of the Western model makes emulation not only possible but relatively easy. On the other hand, contemporary citizenship rights seem to hinge on the extent to which globalisation undermines the capacity of states to fulfil their commitments.[39] The increasing momentum of European integration, therefore, might weaken the bond between the nation-state and the citizens, but only if it can offer a viable alternative to the rights and benefits provided by contemporary nation-states. Since the process of integration involves significant costs to the member states, and the eastward enlargement will require additional resources in aid and low-interest loans, the bond established between the nation-state and its self-interested citizens will most likely remain a formidable obstacle to European integration.

Concepts and definitions: towards a new theoretical framework

In an effort to compromise between conventional and post-modern conceptions, Baldwin-Edwards, Baubock, Heater and Meehan treat citizenship as a bundle of rights and obligations which link an individual with society.[40]

Although the substitution of a 'society' for the 'nation-state' in this definition creates opportunities for unconventional conceptualisations of the link between citizenship and individuals, the definition fails to explain how, and by whom rights are guaranteed. The rights anchored in the citizenship of the union, for example, are conferred on every person holding the nationality of a member state, and are guaranteed by the agents of participating states rather than by EU enforcement mechanisms.[41]

More importantly, such a conceptualisation of citizenship does not establish a relationship between citizenship, nationhood and democracy, it does not incorporate all relevant components these concepts have in common, and it takes a procedural or substantial approach, rather than an appropriately relational one.[42] Building on the work of Charles Tilly, I propose therefore to begin with the following concepts:[43]

- *State:* an organisation controlling the means of coercion within a delimited territory and exercising a priority in some respects over all other organisations within the same territory.[44]
- *Polity:* the set of relations among the agents of the state and all major political actors within the delimited territory.
- *Rights:* enforceable claims, the reciprocal of obligations.
- *Citizenship:* rights and mutual obligations binding state agents and a category of persons defined by their legal attachment to the state.

Along these lines, *Nationhood* and citizenship are linked in that a state establishes a category of persons who by virtue of membership in a specific group acquire rights and obligations *vis-à-vis* the state.[45] Citizenship is considered *broad* insofar as it extends membership to persons living within the state's bounded territory, and *equal* insofar as its rights and mutual obligations apply to these persons.

Citizenship might vary along two dimensions: first, from *exclusive* to *inclusive*; and second, from *primordial* to *learned*.[46] Then the *primordial* and *exclusive* variety of citizenship could be egalitarian in that it is applied to all who fit the specific criteria of membership, yet by no means broad because it excludes all those who do not fit the criteria. *Primordial* and *inclusive* citizenship could then be considered broad but by no means egalitarian because of the underlying and enduring classification of citizens according to the established specific criteria. The *learned* and *exclusive* variety of citizenship could be considered as broad and egalitarian insofar as new candidates can assimilate to the existing culture. Finally, the *learned* and *inclusive* variety is broad and egalitarian in that the new candidates are willing to adhere to the existing norms and rules (see table 7.1).[47]

Any polity should then be considered *democratic* insofar as it establishes broad and equal citizenship; provides for binding and transparent consultation of citizens with respect to governmental personnel and policies; and guarantees the protection of citizens from arbitrary action of state agents.

Table 7.1 Varieties of citizenship

	Exclusive	*Inclusive*
Primordial	*Folk or ethnic model*: expression of an ethnically homogeneous society where citizenship is acquired by descent (Israel). I.	*Imperial model*: facilitates integration of different people under the domination of one national group (the Ottoman or British empire). II.
Learned	*Republican model*: citizenship is acquired by birthplace, and naturalisation by cultural assimilation (France). III.	*Multicultural model*: citizenship by birth, and naturalisation through adherence to norms and rules (Canada, Australia). IV.

Finally, for purposes of evaluation we might want to think of states as falling somewhere along four continua on a scale form 0 to 1, where:

1 citizenship can be: narrow (0) to broad (1)
2 citizenship can be: unequal (0) to equal (1)
3 consultation with citizens: none (0) to extensive (1)
4 protection from arbitrary action: none (0) to extensive (1)

A state then is a complete democracy when rated (1, 1, 1, 1), while a state rated (0, 0, 0, 0) is a complete tyranny. A state with (1, 1, 0, 0) rating is a populist dictatorship, and so on. For a better orientation, contemporary western democracies are likely to be rated somewhere in the neighbourhood of (0.80, 0.90, 0.75, 0.85).[48]

Citizenship in the West and the East

Differences between contemporary West European and CEE states, as well as among CEE states, should caution those who set EU accession standards. First, EU members are mature states with well-established bureaucracies and accepted institutional rules.[49] Their conceptions of citizenship evolved gradually, and reflect a deeply rooted understanding of nationhood.[50] Second, the capacity of EU member states is relatively high, in that they are able to structure inter and intra-state relations,[51] extract revenue, and maintain low levels of violent crime.[52] Consequently, Western states are well positioned to make changes required by the approximation clauses in the Treaty of European Union. Finally, the citizenship policies of EU states are to a large extent governed by the mutually accepted policies of harmonisation (convergence). Since harmonisation implies mutual concessions one might encounter political opposition toward further relaxation of citizenship laws in Britain and France, where these laws are relatively *inclusive* and are extended, with some qualifications, to legal immigrants who demonstrate the required degree of cultural adaptation.[53] On the other hand in Germany, where citizenship is relatively *exclusive* and derived from the principle of descent (*primordial)*, political opposition toward the relaxation of these laws appears less salient.[54] All this makes the Western states well positioned to make and implement changes required by the approximation clauses of the EU.

By contrast, CEE states are relatively less mature, institutionally less stable, and their paradigms of citizenship are often made to fit the contemporary demographic, political, cultural, social and international environment. In CEE states, the idea of citizenship is therefore seldom rooted in a fully developed understanding of nationhood. Moreover, the capacity of CEE states is usually low in that they are rarely able to design and implement strategies that structure inter and intra-state relations,[55] extract revenue, and maintain low levels of violent crime.[56]

There are, furthermore, significant differences among CEE states. A comparison between the Czech Republic and Slovakia suggests that the Czech state enjoys a more soundly established governmental and economic infrastructure and greater institutional stability than Slovakia. The Czech state inherited the infrastructure of the Czechoslovak state, and the Czech lands were the more industrially developed region of the federation. In addition, many of the 100,000 Slovaks who decided to stay in the Czech Republic after the 1993 break-up had been employed in the state bureaucracy. This benefits the Czech state, but deprives Slovakia of qualified bureaucratic personnel. Finally, the understanding of Czech nationhood evolved gradually throughout the nineteenth century, and was institutionalised during the inter-war Czechoslovak Republic; while Slovakia is currently engaged in the processes of state and nation-building.[57]

In short, the comparisons of CEE states with their Western counterparts, and of the Czech Republic and Slovakia reveal a paradox. The well-established and institutionally-stable Czech Republic is expected to make only gradual, incremental, and in the case of the EU members mutually convergent changes in their approximation policies; while new, currently nationalising, poorly established, and institutionally unstable Slovakia is required to make rapid and fundamental changes that converge towards artificially developed standards. Such changes could actually destabilise domestic institutions; and even if formally accepted by CEE countries, might not create conditions for politically sustainable changes. Therefore, if the aim of EU accession strategies is to develop stable institutions that guarantee democracy, the rule of law and the protection of human and minority rights, West European standards should serve as a point of orientation rather than as absolute requirements.

Citizenship in the Czech Republic and Slovakia

The evaluation of the two countries in Agenda 2000 clearly distinguishes their accession status. The Czech Republic, according to the report, has stable and properly functioning political institutions, carried out free and fair elections, allows the opposition to play a normal part in the operation of institutions, and therefore 'presents the characteristics of a democracy, with stable institutions guaranteeing the rule of law, human rights, and respect for and protection of minorities'.[58] At the same time, the report adds that the judiciary does not operate properly, and that the Czech citizenship law discriminates against the Roma.[59]

Slovakia was the only country among the ten CEE applicant that failed to fulfil the political criteria for accession. In the Commission's view, the institutional framework defined in the Slovak Constitution corresponds to that of a parliamentary democracy, but the degree of institutional stability is unsatisfactory.[60] In addition, the report expresses concerns about the independence of the judiciary, the government's use of the secret service, and the treatment of the Hungarian and Roma minorities. Agenda 2000 calls the elections held in Slovakia free and fair, but does not mention the citizenship law.

I will argue below that the reports are correct with respect to institutional stability, but are not fairly critical regarding the treatment of the Roma in the Czech Republic. Changes in the Czech Citizenship Law are not only long over due, but they also appear to be politically sustainable in that their implementation is unlikely to cause institutional instability. In Slovakia, however, changes made in citizenship and minority policy have already reached the politically sustainable limit, in that neither the present government nor its alternatives could make concessions to the Hungarian parties without risking the support of their constituencies. The most recent is the example of the public administration reform, where the Dzurinda government refused the Hungarian Coalition Party's (SMK) demand for an ethnically constituted region in the Komárno area. In this respect, the results of the post-Mečiar government in minority relations show little real improvement.[61]

The EU's insistence on more profound changes could therefore increase institutional instability, and even adversely affect democratisation. Once again, this suggests the advantages of country-specific, 'differentiated integration' and 'flexible standards', as opposed to the 'democratisation through incorporation' and 'set criteria for admission' approach to eastward enlargement. I am not suggesting that Slovakia is more democratic, nor that Slovakia rather than the Czech Republic should have been considered for the first round of accession negotiations by the EU. What I hope will emerge from this enquiry is that a rigorous, rather than arbitrary country-specific approach in which each applicant is evaluated in the context of pre-existing social, political and economic conditions (rather than being compared to a set of specific criteria) is beneficial for all parties concerned. For the applicant countries it brings a gradual and sustainable approximation of the EU set standards, while for the EU it delivers a reliable new member state.

The following comparison of the Czech Republic and Slovakia will reveal differences in the understanding of nationhood, the nature of citizenship, and the degree of institutional stability in the two countries. First, the Czech state is relatively mature and institutionally stable; while the Slovak state is in the making, and each major political and societal actor is struggling to design myopic institutional arrangements which grant immediate, rather than enduring benefits. Consequently, the institutional system of the Czech Republic facilitates bargaining and consensus, while politics in Slovakia resembles a zero-sum game where the gain of one party is automatically the loss of the other.

Second, nationhood in the Czech Republic has developed in response to state-seeking nationalism, while in Slovakia this development has a state-led character.[62] During the process of state-seeking nationalism, the Czechs developed a deeply rooted ethnic understanding of nationhood and a moderately (if occasionally more than moderately) ethnocentric conception of citizenship. Since in Slovakia nationhood and citizenship are evolving, both are being shaped by the bargaining process between domestic political actors and external third parties (the EU). Consequently, whether the Slovak conception of citizenship will acquire an exclusionary/ethnic, or inclusionary/civic character will depend upon the outcome of a bargaining process in which the EU could play a decisive role.

The Czech Republic

The Czech state is relatively mature, and the understanding of Czech nationhood is well established. The tradition of Czech statehood extends to the Czech Kingdom (Zeme Koruny České), while its institutional foundations can be traced in part to the inter-war Czechoslovakia, and in part to the Czechoslovak Federation.[63] The political rules of governance are well defined, anchored in the Czech constitution, and respected by the involved parties. At the same time, however, state capacity to collect revenue and control violent crime and corruption is relatively low when compared to the EU member states.[64]

The contemporary understanding of Czech nationhood evolved in response to the continuous presence of its strong and often assertive German neighbour. The Czech national revival had a state-seeking character, and its definition of Czech nationhood was ethnic, defined against the 'hereditary enemies of the Czechs', the Germans.[65] The primary work that framed the developing understanding of Czech nationhood was František Palacký's interpretation of Czech history, in which a systematic distinction was drawn between 'us', the Czechs and 'them', the Germans, and the historical misfortunes of the Czechs linked to the presence of the Germans.[66] Palacký had a profound influence on late nineteenth-century Czech national revivalists, artists and writers, who helped to authenticate his interpretation of the past.[67] The popular anti-German attitudes were exacerbated during the First World War, and peaked during the *Protektorat* and the subsequent expulsion of the Sudeten Germans in 1945.[68]

While the dominant understanding of Czech nationhood in 1918 was firmly ethnocentric, Czechoslovak President Tomáš G. Masaryk and his associates envisioned the new, multi-ethnic state built on liberal democratic principles. Hence, the citizenship and language laws of 1921 were relatively moderate, assimilations and inclusive.[69] During the discussion of the Language Law in 1921, parliamentary deputies argued that it would be intelligent to exceed the minimal requirements for protection of minorities stipulated by the Treaty of St German, in order to protect the Czech liberal-democratic image from complaints by German and Hungarian minorities.[70]

Nevertheless, twentieth-century Czech history supports Brubaker's argument that an ethnocentric understanding of nationhood, once developed, tends to endure. Despite the inter-war language and citizenship laws, there was no comprehensive strategy to include or assimilate the German and Hungarian minorities. On the contrary, ethnic claims in regions with a high concentration of Germans were routinely suppressed by force.[71] After the Second World War, democratic Czechoslovakia expelled nearly three million ethnic Germans, of whom (according to the Czech–German Historical Commission) some 18,000–30,000 perished in the process. Those Germans and Hungarians who remained in Czechoslovakia (communist after 1948) had no citizenship rights until 1952.

Today in Czech Republic, human rights organisations note ongoing discrimination of the Roma minority, racially motivated attacks on Asians and Africans, the pattern of government inaction against these trends, and the maintenance of a discriminatory citizenship law. Although problems with the Roma are by no means unique to the Czech Republic, the increasing number of racially motivated physical attacks is disturbing. Human rights organisations attribute this trend to the lenient treatment of perpetrators. According to the International Helsinki Federation (IHF), in 1994 there were 62 attacks on the Roma, in 1995 90, in 1996 157, and 233 in the first 11 months of 1997.[72] These numbers are significantly higher than in Slovakia, where in 1997 there were 19 such incidents, in 1998 21, in 1999 15 and in 2000 35 instances.[73]

Moreover, between 1990 and 1996, 17 Roma were killed in Czech Republic, and several hundred more were injured. But, of more than two hundred persons accused of these acts, fewer then one hundred were convicted.[74] The conviction rate for similar incidents in Slovakia, on the other hand, is around 80 per cent.[75] Racially motivated violence in the Czech Republic does not exclude foreigners from Asia, Africa, or the Middle East. The murder of a Sudanese student in Prague in November 1997 attracted attention to the problem of racial intolerance in Czech Republic, and a number of politicians took part in a public demonstration against racism and xenophobia.[76] A few months later the son of the Libyan ambassador was severely beaten by skinheads in the city of Brno.[77]

Another example of ethnic exclusion was occasioned by a July 1997 television programme that depicted gypsy immigrants living a prosperous life in Canada. The documentary sparked a massive exodus of Roma from the Czech Republic. Certain Czech politicians suggested that the documentary was the best thing the TV station has done this far, and the programme should be aired more often. The Major of Ostrava, Jana Lickova, even offered to pay $600 toward the air ticket of every Roma who decided to leave her city.[78]

Czech authorities began to deal with the problem systematically in 1995, in response to increasing criticism from the UNHCR, OSCE and the EU. In 1996 the parliament passed a resolution denouncing racism and xenophobia, and 120 new positions were created for specialists in the fight against racism and extremism.[79] Yet there was no significant improvement in the work of the judiciary. Cases of racially motivated acts were often characterised as 'personal fights', and light sentences sent the message that such crimes were not considered serious.[80] According to the director of Nadace Nová Škola, 'there is bias in the treatment of Roma in every sphere of life in the Czech Republic, from the top government officials all the way down to the owner of the village pub'.[81] In sum, while most anti-Roma activities are attributed to a small group of extremists and the far-right Czech Republican Party (CSR), Czech governments have done little, and the Czech public by its silence implicitly approves the present state of affairs.

The Citizenship Law of 1 January 1993 seems to fit the ethnocentric and exclusionary definition of Czech nationhood, and is criticised by international organisations such as the UNHCR, OSCE and the Council of Europe.[82] The law temporarily excluded from Czech citizenship all Slovaks who had permanent residence in the Czech Republic, it created a number of stateless people, and lends itself to discrimination against the Roma.[83] Article 18 granted Slovak citizens the opportunity to apply for Czech citizenship, provided that the applicant had resided for at least two years in the Czech Republic, had a certificate of exemption from Slovak citizenship, and had no criminal record for the past five years.

Thus arose a class of people who were ineligible for Slovak citizenship, failed to meet Czech requirements, and became stateless. Moreover, even individuals who were arrested but not persecuted were automatically disqualified from Czech citizenship.[84] Only on April 1996 was the law amended, and the Ministry of Interior empowered to waive the five-year clean-record requirement. Yet, the Roma were often given no information or were given misleading guidance regarding citizenship issues. Out of 255 surveyed Roma who were not granted Czech citizenship, 80 per cent were long-term residents, 50 per cent had clean criminal records, only 19 had been convicted of serious crimes and 26 of petty offences.[85]

The ethnocentric conception of Czech nationhood continues to shape the understanding of Czech citizenship. At the same time, the Czech state continues to maintain its liberal democratic character, and certain outstanding political figures have moderated the exclusionary character of Czech citizenship.[86] Given the liberal democratic tradition of Czech statehood, the relative stability of Czech institutions, and the general desire of Czechs to join the West, moderation of citizenship policy is the most viable option at this time. Therefore, there is no reason for the EU not to insist on implementation and enforcement of laws that facilitate the exercise of inclusionary and equal citizenship rights for the Roma. Such laws have to be implemented now, in order to provide a sufficient time for the society that has to adjust to the new, formal rules of interaction. A failure to moderate the Czech conception of citizenship today might lead to an increase in the resentment of Czechs against certain kinds of foreigners once the Czech Republic joins the EU.

Slovakia

Compared to the Czech Republic, Slovakia is a new and less stable state, inhabited by an ethnically more heterogeneous population, and engaged in an intense process of state and nation-building.[87] Activities aimed at the construction of Slovak nationhood are primarily state-led,[88] though the process of nation-building incorporates competing conceptions of Slovak nationhood. The understanding of Slovak nationhood remains therefore ambiguous, and the conception of Slovak citizenship is malleable and often inconsistent with governmental policies. Under these conditions, the EU's role in shaping the understanding of Slovak nationhood and the conception of citizenship could be significant, and the EU's influence is likely to increase with the flexibility of accession criteria. This does not mean that the Mečiar government should be rewarded for its democratic deficit, but an explicit recognition of its achievements in the sector of citizenship policy could be desirable for both Slovakia and the EU.

The contemporary Slovak state is being built on the ruins of the former federation, mainly because the Czech state inherited most of the federal state's infrastructure. Slovakia lacks the option of building a new state on a pre-existing paradigm of liberal democracy, and lacks able and moderate political figures such as Masaryk or Havel who could shape the democratic character of the new state. The new state is also relatively weak in its capacity to extract revenue, control violent crime and corruption, and structure internal relations.[89] All of this creates favourable conditions for institutional instability, which is reflected in incoherent decisions in domestic and foreign policies in general, and in citizenship policy in particular. More pressure from the EU, therefore appears counterproductive.

Contemporary efforts to construct and authenticate a credible conception of Slovak nationhood represent a range of interests. While the initial phase of the nineteenth-century Slovak national revival was similar to the Czech experience, the Slovak revivalists lacked a 'hereditary enemy' against whom to identify. The process of national revival was stifled after the 1848 revolution, and the Slovaks lacked scholars of Palacký's stature to frame Slovak history and their understanding of nationhood. Moreover, whereas in the Czech lands professional associations, artists and writers helped to disseminate and authenticate the sources of Czech nationhood in the nineteenth century, until the 1930s Slovakia lacked such groups of intellectuals.[90] Most urban centres in nineteenth-century Slovakia were inhabited by Hungarians and Germans. After the 1866 Ausgleich, the Slovak-speaking population of the monarchy was subjected to Magyarisation.[91] In 1918 the Slovaks were under Masaryk's doctrine of Czechoslovakysm effectively incorporated into a so-called Czechoslovak nation, and until the late 1930s the Slovak National Party (SNS) was unable to gain a significant electoral support.[92]

Efforts to create and authenticate new sources of national identification are controversial and short-lived. In Spring 1996, for instance, Milan Ďurica, a history professor at the University of Bologna, published a controversial book financed by PHARE. Ďurica's book, *Dejiny Slovenka a Slovákov* (*The History of Slovakia and the Slovak People*), which depicted the 1939 Slovak Republic as liberal, and the treatment of Jews during the war as lenient, was intended to serve as a supplementary high school history textbook. After criticisms from the Slovak Academy of Sciences, teachers' associations, Jewish organisations, and the EU, Mečiar was forced to make a public announcement regarding the removal of the work from schools.[93]

The revived Slovak National Party proposed projects that would allocate state funds for a travelling exhibition of 'Slovakia's Written Heritage', or would shift competencies over history, language and literature curricula from the Ministry of Education to Matica Slovenská (Slovak Publishing House).[94] Both initiatives were rejected under pressure from the media and teachers associations. Inflammatory speeches of Slovak nationalists about the role of Hungary in Slovak history are immediately publicly analysed and refuted.[95] In short, the construction and authentication of a consistent and uncontested conception of Slovak nationhood – whether ethnocentric or civic – appears unlikely in the near future.[96]

Inconsistencies of Slovak politics are further exacerbated by institutional instability. The rules of the game structuring the interaction of political actors are outlined in the constitution, but have not taken hold in the Slovak political life. The Mečiar government's programme after the 1994 elections, for instance, declared that 'party diversity is an attribute of democracy which the party (HZDS) supports'. Yet the same programme pointed out that 'diversity will not be allowed to lead to a permanent political crisis whether in open or hidden form'.[97] The latter conception of 'diversity' prevails in contemporary Slovak politics. It is reflected in the confrontation between the prime minister and the president, in the exclusion of opposition parties from parliamentary committees (including the controlling organ of the secret service), and the unconstitutional expulsion of unruly members of the governing coalition from parliament.[98] All this took place after the government memorandum accompanying the application of the Slovak Republic to the EU proclaimed: 'Developments in the Slovak Republic show that democratic institutions are firmly anchored and that despite various political changes the constitutional system is stabilised'.[99]

Inconsistencies in the construction of Slovak nationhood coupled with institutional instability are also noticeable in the domestic and foreign policies of the Slovak government. The 1993 constitution was written in the 'name of the Slovak nation', which provoked an outcry from the Hungarian and other minorities.[100] There was no change to the preamble in spite of the fact that Hungarians became after the 1998 elections members of the governing coalition, and demanded the change at the most recent constitutional reform in 2001.[101]

At the same time, the 1993 Citizenship Law has an inclusionary and civic character. The law permits any person who by 31 December 1992 was a citizen of the Czechoslovak Federation to claim Slovak citizenship, and permits dual citizenship.[102] In another instance, the governmental coalition passed a discriminatory language law – parts of which were ruled unconstitutional – at the same time Slovakia signed the Citizenship of the Union agreement.[103] The signing of the European Charter of Regional Languages in 2001 was not without controversies either. The Hungarian politicians once again repeated their threat to quit the coalition if the law does not correspond with the proposed wording.[104]

Efforts to establish favourable conditions for broad and equal citizenship are likely to face obstacles in new, multi-ethnic, and institutionally unstable states such as Slovakia. First, the state's inability to structure internal relations opens opportunities for political entrepreneurs to forward ambitious claims. Second, in such circumstances political entrepreneurs are likely to make claims on behalf of the respective ethnic constituencies.[105] Third, such claims, more often than not, will bear on the interests of other ethnic groups, and lead to ethnic discord and polarisation.

Today we can see already that a change of government made little difference concerning the degree of institutional stability, and for the EU, in order to maintain some degree of coherence and continuity in its accession policies, it is likely to remain counterproductive to reject one and prefer another government only because of personal reasons. Since neither the understanding of nationhood nor the conception of citizenship has yet attained clear contours, the EU strategies will play an important role in shaping the future of Slovakia. Therefore, if the EU desires to maintain its influence over Slovakia, it should not try to either isolate, or embrace it because of personal changes in government, should avoid statements and policies that can be exploited by Slovak nationalists who oppose integration,[106] and should set consistent and meaningful evaluation criteria.

In short, while the EU is in a position to set relatively high standards for integration in the Czech case, Slovakia, at least for the time being, should be held to less demanding standards. The relative stability of the Czech state makes higher standards of accession attainable without threatening the stability of institutions, while the EU's insistence on high standards in Slovakia might empower the nationalists. Flexible, yet coherent criteria and country-specific strategies of eastward enlargement seem therefore more appropriate.

Conclusion: citizenship, democracy and European integration in the Czech Republic and Slovakia

Using the scheme for evaluation of the degree of democracy proposed above, the Czech Republic and Slovakia could be evaluated as follows:

The Czech Republic

Citizenship: narrow to broad	0.5 (0.6 after 1999)
Citizenship: unequal to equal	0.3 (0.6 after 1999)
Consultation with citizens	0.8
Protection from arbitrary action	0.7

Slovakia

Citizenship: narrow to broad	0.8
Citizenship: unequal to equal	0.5 (0.6 after 1998)
Consultation with citizens	0.7
Protection from arbitrary action	0.3 (0.6 after 1998)

The Roma remain the only significant and problematic minority group in the Czech Republic. If one agrees with Ralf Dahrendorf that 'the true test of the strength of citizenship rights is heterogeneity',[107] the Roma minority is the true test of Czech citizenship. Until 1999 when, under EU pressure and an enduring criticism of Václav Havel, substantive changes were made in the judiciary system and a massive campaign against racism and xenophobia has been launched by NGOs, the Czechs barely managed to get a passing grade for their citizenship politics.

The high marks for consultation with the citizens and for protection of citizens from arbitrary action suggest a relatively high degree of institutional stability in the Czech Republic. Therefore a change toward more inclusive and egalitarian citizenship policy is likely to be politically and socially sustainable.[108] Thus there is no reason for the Czech government to further postpone the signing and ratification of more than thirty UN and EU documents concerning human rights.[109] Neither should Canada or Britain hesitate about the reinstatement of visa requirements for Czech citizens in case of another exodus of the Roma. The EU should push for a more inclusive and equal conception of citizenship in the Czech Republic now, since once the Czech Republic becomes a full member state, it might be too late to moderate the Czechs' ethnocentric understanding of nationhood.

Slovakia's citizenship laws are broad, yet there are problems concerning equality. Since the proportion of minorities in Slovakia is more than twice as great as in the Czech Republic, a higher grade for the degree of equality seems justified. In the area of consultation with citizens, all elections were ruled free and fair, and one should not blame Mečiar for the opposition's lacklustre performance. After the 1998 parliamentary elections, the new governing coalition had a chance to improve the international image of Slovakia, but it would be myopic to anticipate rapid and fundamental changes concerning institutional stability and state capacity. Privatisation in Slovakia still lacks transparency, and state property continues to be used to reward powerful individuals for party loyalty. Massive corruption scandals during the privatisation of the Slovak Telecom resulting in the dismissal of several ministers serve as a good example.[110] We see an improvement, however, concerning cases like the abduction of the president's son, unconstitutional expulsion of unruly deputies from the parliament, the sabotage of the May 1997 referendum, and other. The protection of citizens from arbitrary action in Slovakia was less inadequate before 1998 than it is today.

Since Slovakia rather than the Czech Republic is the true test of alternatives to the EU strategy of eastward enlargement, it seems reasonable to ask what should be done regarding its alleged democratic deficit. I propose to take as the point of departure Tilly's argument that citizenship is related to democracy in that it engenders an ongoing bargaining process between state agents and societal actors over rights and obligations.[111] If so, the assumption that a simple government change will repair Slovakia's democratic deficit remains no more than wishful thinking (especially in view of current support for former Prime Minister Mečiar). It can be improved only through incremental changes that decentralise political power, decrease uncertainties in the interaction of political and societal actors, and lead them to accept the rules of the game as the best possible option for all parties.[112] Only an electorate that is actively engaged in the bargaining process with state agents can accomplish such a systemic change. International isolation of Slovakia is also not desirable at this point, because external actors could play a decisive role in shaping Slovakia's transformation.[113] Harsh words like those of Mr Oostlander might strengthen popular support for the extreme nationalist and populist political parties.

In short, if the aim of EU accession strategies is to develop stable institutions that guarantee democracy, the rule of law and the protection of human and minority rights, west European standards should serve as a point of orientation rather than a template for impossibly demanding accession criteria. A little more should be demanded from the Czech Republic, and somewhat less from Slovakia, and both countries can join the union together.

Notes

1 *SME, Pravda, Národná Obroda, Slovenská Republika*, or *Nový Čas* of 5 December 1997.

2 'Slova Oostlandera sú pre HZDS vyjadreniami chorého, tútorského politikárenia', *SME* 6 December 1997.

3 J. Zielonka, 'Politics without Strategies: The EU Policies toward Central and Eastern Europe', in J. Zielonka (ed.), *Paradoxes of European Foreign Policy* (London: Kluwer, 1998) pp. 131–145. The Slovak government often complains about double standards regarding the state of democracy and their treatment of minorities in the country. Vice-Premier Tóthová argued that the Hungarian minority of Slovakia is not treated worse than the Russians of Estonia, yet Estonia is among the five Central and Eastern European countries that are likely to take part in the first round of accession talks to the EU. How to account for the acceptability of Cyprus remains a mystery. See also Z. Lukaš and S. Szomolányi, 'Slovakia', in W. Weidenfeld (ed.), *Central and Eastern Europe on the Way into the EU* (Bertelsman Foundation Publishers, 1996), 201–224. The authors claim that the simple replacement of the current political elite in Slovakia would greatly improve the political performance of the Slovak Republic. They fail to explain what led them to this belief.

4 D. A. Rustow, 'Transition to Democracy: Toward a Dynamic Model', *Comparative Politics* Vol. 2 (1970), 357; G. O'Donnell and P. Schmitter, *Transition from Authoritarian Rule: Tentative Conclusions about Uncertain Democracies* (Baltimore: Johns Hopkins University Press, 1996); M. Burton, R. Gunther and J. Higley, 'Elite Transformations and Democratic Regimes', in M. Burton *et al.* (eds), *Elites and Democratic Consolidation in Latin America and Southern Europe* (Cambridge: Cambridge University Press, 1992),

pp. 20–24; G. Di Palma, *To Craft Democracies: A Chapter on Democratic Transitions* (Berkeley: University of California Press, 1990), pp. 56–78.

5 S. Huntington, *Political Order in Changing Societies* (New Haven: Yale University Press, 1968); S. M. Lipset, K.-R. Seong, and J. Torres, 'A Comparative Analysis of the Social Requisites of Democracy', *International Social Science Journal* No. 136 (1993), 155–175; G. O'Donnell, *Modernization and Bureaucratic Authoritarianism: Studies in South American Politics* (Berkeley: Institute of International Studies, University of California, 1973).

6 For recent opinion polls see *Pravda* (17 March 2001), 2. According to MVK polling agency, Mečiar's HZDS would get 24 per cent of the vote and Fico's SMER 21 per cent, and the nearest from the coalition parties is Dzurinda's SDKU with 12 per cent, while the SOP dropped to 1.5 per cent.

7 See the National Labor Office statistics at www.nup.sk

8 J. M. Wiersma, the spokesperson of the European Parliament who visited Slovakia in October 1997, gave Slovakia 6–7 weeks to fulfil the criteria required for the country's inclusion in the accession talks. 'Slovensko ma 6–7 tý dnov na to, aby splnilo kritéria na zacatie rozhovorov o vstupe do EU', *SME*, 15 October 1997, 1. The components of the democratic deficit that turned Slovakia into a single CEE country that failed to fulfil the political criteria are: (1) lack of respect for the constitution; (2) disrespect for the rights of the opposition; (3) inappropriate use of the secret police by the government; and (4) mistreatment of minorities. 'Slovakia', *Agenda 2000*, Doc/97/8, Strasbourg/Brussels, 15 July 1997.

9 A. Przeworski, *Democracy and the Market* (Cambridge: Cambridge University Press, 1991), pp. 20–28; C. Tilly, 'The Emergence of Citizenship in France and Elsewhere', in C. Tilly (ed.), *Citizenship, Identity and Social History* (Cambridge: Cambridge University Press, 1996), pp. 223–236.

10 J. Pinder, 'The EC and Democracy in Central and Eastern Europe', in G. Pridham, E. Herring and G. Sandorf (eds), *Building Democracy? The International Dimension of Democratization in Eastern Europe* (London: Leicester University Press, 1994), pp. 119–144. See also the 'Introduction' by the authors of the edited volume, pp. 7–32.

11 H. Grabbe and K. Hughes, *Eastward Enlargement of the European Union* (London: Royal Institute on International Affairs, 1997), pp. 46–51. Differentiated integration would allow each country to be treated separately and would reward its efforts to approximate EU standards in proportion to difficulties arising from economic and institutional constraints. This approach is different from the multi-speed incorporation, according to which each country should approximate the developed standards although the approximation might not happen at the same pace.

12 See the literature on new institutional economics. For instance, D. North, *Institutions, Institutional Change and Economic Performance* (Cambridge: Cambridge University Press, 1991); J. Knight, *Institutions and Social Conflict* (Cambridge: Cambridge University Press, 1992); T. Eggertsson, *Economic Behavior and Institutions* (Cambridge: Cambridge University Press, 1990). All three authors agree that institutions – understood here as the formal and informal rules of the game – reduce uncertainty in day-to-day individual and group interaction.

13 See North, *Institutions, Institutional Change and Economic Performance*, especially Chapter 5 on informal institutions.

14 See for instance, D. Meth-Cohn, 'The New Wall', *Business Central Europe* (September 1997), 19–22. Slovakia is the single applicant which failed to fulfil political criteria for accession. This conclusion surprises many who are familiar with political conditions in Romania, Bulgaria and Cyprus.

15 R. Brubaker, *Citizenship and Nationhood in France and Germany* (Cambridge, MA: Harvard University Press, 1992).

16 For the classical study of citizenship and democratisation see T. H. Marshall, *Class,*

Citizenship and Social Development (Westport, CT: Greenwood Press, 1973). See also Tilly, 'The Emergence of Citizenship', pp. 224–236.

17 Article 8, The Treaty of European Union. For an extensive summary see P. Close *Citizenship, Europe and Change* (London: Macmillan, 1995), pp. 241–253.

18 A few of the rare exceptions are Z. Kavan, 'Democracy and Nationalism in Czechoslovakia', in B. Einhorn *et al.* (eds), *Citizenship and Democratic Control in Contemporary Europe* (Cheltenham, Edward Elgar, 1996), pp. 24–39; P. Korcelli, 'Current Issues Related to Migration and Citizenship: The Case of Poland', in Baubock (ed.), *From Aliens to Citizens*, Chapter 8.

19 A. Burges, 'Writing Off Slovakia to the East? Examining Charges of Bias in British Press Reporting on Slovakia, 1993–1994', *Nationalities Papers* Vol. 25, No. 4 (1997), 659–683.

20 M. Baldwin-Edwards, 'Citizenship of the Union: Rhetoric or Reality, Inclusion or Exclusion?', in Kososnen, Pekka and Madsen (eds), *Convergence or Divergence? Welfare States Facing European Integration* (Brussels, Commission of the EC, 1995); M. Baldwin-Edwards, *Third Country Nationals and Welfare Systems in the EU* (Florence: European University Institute, 1997); Brubaker, 'Conclusion', in *Citizenship and Nationhood*; D. Ceasarani and M. Fulbrook (eds), *Citizenship, Nationality and Migration in Europe* (London: Routledge, 1996); Einhorn *et al.* (eds), *Citizenship and Democratic Control in Contemporary Europe*; C. Joppke (ed.), *Challenge to the Nation-State: Immigration in Western Europe and the United States* (Oxford: Oxford University Press, 1998); Y. Soysal, *Limits of Citizenship: Migrants and Post-national Membership in Europe* (Chicago: University of Chicago Press, 1994); B. van Steenbergen (ed.), *The Condition of Citizenship* (London: Sage Publications, 1994), Chapters 2 and 3; A. Wendt, 'Collective Identity Formation and the International State', *American Political Science Review* Vol. 88 (1994), 384–398.

21 T. H. Marshall, *Citizenship and Social Class* (Cambridge, 1950).

22 Tilly, 'The Emergence of Citizenship'.

23 R. Brubaker, 'Introduction', in R. Brubaker (ed.), *Immigration and the Politics of Citizenship in Europe and North America* (Lanham: University Press of America, 1989), p. 3.

24 R. Aron, 'Is Multinational Citizenship Possible?', *Social Research* Vol. 41 No. 4 (1974), 638–656.

25 Brubaker, *Citizenship and Nationhood*, 3.

26 Tilly, 'The Emergence of Citizenship', pp. 1–17.

27 Y. Soysal, 'Changing Citizenship in Europe', in Ceasarani and Fulbrook (eds), *Citizenship, Nationality*, pp. 17–29. This view is supported by D. Jacobson, *Rights across Borders* (Baltimore: Johns Hopkins University Press, 1996).

28 Several British politicians expressed a desire to maintain the sovereign right to regulate immigration: *Guardian*, 14 March 1995, and 24 March 1995. Jean-Marie Le Pen and Philippe Villiers both ran on an anti-immigrant platform in the French presidential elections. Jorg Haider's *Freiheit Partei Oesterreichs* won over 22 per cent in the Austrian general elections. R. Mitten, 'Jorg Haider: The Anti-immigrant Petition and Immigration Policy in Austria', *Patterns of Prejudice*, Vol. 28, No. 2 (1994), 27–47; C. Muddle, 'One Against All, All Against One! A Portrait of the Vlaams Block', *Patterns of Prejudice* Vol. 29, No. 1 (1995), 5–28.

29 D. Cesarani, 'The Changing Character of Citizenship and Nationality in Britain', T. Kushner, 'The Spice of Life? Ethnic Difference, Politics and Culture in Modern Britain', and P. Weil, 'Nationalities and Citizenships: The Lessons of the French Experience for Germany and Europe', all in D. Ceasarani and M. Fulbrook (eds), Chapters 4, 5 and 8. See also A. Geddes, 'Immigrants and Ethnic Minorities and the EU's Democratic Deficit', *Journal of Common Market Studies* Vol. 33, No. 2 (1996), 197–217. Geddes argues that EU policies are one sided because they emphasise control of immigrants and asylum seekers, but do little in terms of immigrant rights or combating racism and xenophobia.

30 S. Panebianco, *European Citizenship and European Identity: from the Treaty of Maastricht to Public Opinion Attitudes* (University of Catania: December 1996), or www.fscpo.unict.it/vademec/jmwpo3.ht
31 M. Baldwin-Edwards, 'Citizenship of the Union', in R. Baubock (ed.), *From Aliens to Citizens*, 209–210.
32 Baldwin-Edwards, 'Citizenship of the Union', 6–7.
33 M. Baldwin-Edwards, 'The Emerging European Immigration Regime: Some Reflections on Implications for Southern Europe', *Journal of Common Market Studies* Vol. 35, No. 4 (1998), 495–519. Baldwin-Edwards argues that the resolutions of JHA governing migration are particularly incoherent because they allow substantial national variations.
34 In France, for instance, a draft law was proposed that would grant asylum not only to refugees who fear oppression from a state, but also to those whose life is threatened by non-state groups (Islamic fundamentalists in Algeria). Moreover, under the proposed law, citizenship is to be granted to children born on French territory to non-French parents: R. Graham, 'Delicate Balancing Acts', *Financial Times* (17 November 1997) 2.
35 D. Cinar, 'From Aliens to Citizens: A Comparative Analysis of Rules of Transition', in Baubock (ed.), *From Aliens to Citizens*, Chapter 3.
36 Marshall, *Class, Citizenship and Social Development*, 18.
37 These developments fit the countries of CEE, yet in China, one can speculate, civil rights might follow after the expansion of political rights. In either case, Marshall's model does not seem to fit.
38 The dissolution of the Soviet Union, Yugoslavia and Czechoslovakia created twenty-one new states.
39 Tilly, 'The Emergence of Citizenship', pp. 224–236.
40 For D. Heater, (*Citizenship. The Civic Ideal in World History, Politics and Education* (London: Longman, 1990)) citizenship could be associated with any territorial unit from a small town to the entire universe. For the purposes of my argument it is sufficient to limit this association as either being directed toward the nation-state or the EU. For Marshall, on the other hand, citizenship was attached not so much to territory, as to a variety of rights some possessed while others did not.
41 Seven rights are listed in the Citizenship of the Union. These are the rights: (1) to free movement; (2) of residence; (3) to vote and stand in local elections; (4) to vote and stand in EP elections; (5) to consular assistance in countries where one's member state is not represented; (6) to petition the EP; (7) to appeal to the Ombudsman. Yet, there is clearly no viable enforcement mechanism in place at the EU level that could compete with those of member states.
42 A substantive definition of democracy, for instance, describes outcomes such as equality or liberty. Its procedural definition examines processes such as free and fair lections, participation, and the like.
43 C. Tilly, 'The State of Nationalism', *Critical Review* Vol. 10, No. 3, 299–306. See also Tilly, 'The Emergence of Citizenship', 224–236.
44 With some modifications this is the definition originally developed by Max Weber and then reformulated by a number of contemporary social scientists: S. N. Eisenstadt, *The Political System of Empires* (New York: Free Press, 1969), p. 5; M. Mann, 'The Autonomous Power of The State', *Archives Europeénnes de Sociologie* 25 (1984), 187–188; G. Poggi, *The State: Its Nature, Development and Prospects* (Stanford: Stanford University Press, 1990), pp. 19–24; T. Skocpol, *State and Social Revolutions* (Cambridge: Cambridge University Press, 1979), p. 26; M. Weber, *Economy and Society* (New York: Bedminster Press, 1968), p. 64.
45 Tilly, 'The Emergence of Citizenship', pp. 231–232.
46 M. Baldwin-Edwards, 'Citizenship of the Union: Rhetoric or Reality, Inclusion or Exclusion?', in Kosonen *et al.* (eds), *Convergence or Divergence?*; Brubaker, *Citizenship and*

Nationhood; Tilly, 'Citizenship, Identity and Social History', in Tilly (ed.), *Citizenship*, pp. 9–10.

47 Derived from the concepts of *exclusivity* and *inclusivity* of citizenship, similar arguments were made by Brubaker, *Citizenship, Nationhood*, and L. Greenfeld, *Nationalism, Five Roads to Modernity* (Cambridge, MA: Harvard University Press, 1992). Brubaker, for instance, came up with the *civic (inclusive)* and *ethnic (exclusive)* ideal types of nationhood, while Greenfeld distinguished between *individualistic (exclusive)* and *collectivist (inclusive)* varieties.

48 Tilly, 'The Emergence of Citizenship', pp. 233–234.

49 From the literature which understands institutions in this sense, see D. North, *Institutions, Institutional Change and Economic Performance* (Cambridge: Cambridge University Press, 1990), pp. 3–5; J. Knight, *Institutions and Social Conflict* (Cambridge: Cambridge University Press, 1992), p. 4.

50 Brubaker, *Citizenship and Nationhood*, 3.

51 For state capacity see K. Barkey, and A. Parikh, 'Comparative Perspectives on State', *Annual Review of Sociology*, Vol. 17 (1991), 510–528.

52 There are several indicators commonly used to measure state capacity. I argue that the state's capacity is high to the extent its agents are able to collect revenue from their citizens and protect them from violent crime. J. M. Hobson, *The Wealth of States: A Comparative Sociology of International and Political Change* (Cambridge: Cambridge University Press, 1997).

53 Kushner, 'The Spice of Life?' and Weil, 'Nationality and Citizenship'.

54 The German Aliens Act of 1990 for the first time recognised the right of young foreigners who returned to their parents' country to re-immigrate to Germany.

55 This is particularly true about new multi-ethnic states such as Slovakia, where internal ethnic relations often spill over into the international realm and vice versa. Moreover, due to the fragility of political configuration in the Slovak party system, attempts to manipulate ethnic relations could destabilise the domestic political scene.

56 Both the Czech Republic and Slovakia have dismal records in revenue extraction and crime prevention. According to the Czech Ministry of Finances, Czech firms and entrepreneurs owe the state 63 billion CK from the year 1996. As far as crime prevention is concerned, only 45 per cent of all criminal cases committed in Slovakia in 1996 solved and successfully prosecuted. *Pravda*, 15 October 1997.

57 The nationalisation efforts of Slovakia are too numerous to list. Recent examples include diversion of large funds from Pro Slovakia, a government sponsored foundation on promotion of the Slovak culture, for projects like a travelling exhibition of allegedly Slovak ancient manuscripts that are enshrined in a wooden reconstruction of a church building from the times of the great Moravian empire; numerous publications that attempt to reconstruct some one thousand years of Slovak history (some written by historians, but most by story-tellers); and the effort by *Matica Slovenská* to take over the job of curriculum development for lower middle schools from the Ministry of Education.

58 In *Agenda 2000* institutions are understood as political actors (individuals or organisations) rather than the rules of the game based on sanctions and rewards. *Agenda 2000*, DOC 97/17, 15–6.

59 The report does not mention other forms of discrimination against the Roma.

60 In this passage it appears that the commission is using the term 'institutions' in both senses. On the one hand, the reference to an 'institutional framework', seems to imply the 'rules of the game' understanding; on the other hand, however, passages in the text suggesting 'integration' of institutions into political life, mean that the authors have in mind actors, rather than rules. This, I believe, creates inconsistencies and ambiguities in the report. *Agenda 2000*, DOC 97/20, A/1.3.

61 Public administration reform in Slovakia is one of the key requirements of the EU, and

to a large extent it hinges on the formation of new, economically sustainable regions. In spite of the fact that the Coalition of Hungarian Parties is a member of the ruling coalition, their partners refused to accept the creation of the Komárno region which would have had a majority of Hungarians. This by itself would not be surprising, but the ensuing political debate brought up arguments from the supposedly 'more democratic governing coalition' which were similar to the arguments of the Mečiar government. See *Pravda*, 3 April 2001.

62 Brubaker distinguished between French and German understandings of nationhood, where in France the state-led efforts resulted in an inclusionary and universalistic understanding of nationhood that in turn shaped the nature of French citizenship, while in Germany the state-seeking effort contributed to the evolution of a folk-centred, ethnic, and differentionalist conception of citizenship. Tilly generalises the same argument in that while state-seeking nationalism is more likely to result in an ethnic understanding of citizenship as opposed to the state-led variety, it is by no means rare to encounter the ethnic version of citizenship in the later case.

63 Here I not only mean the organisational structures, but also the objects and skilled administrative personnel that were employed in the state administration. Slovakia, in 1993, had to designate, renovate or even build, the places in which the state agencies could perform their functions. The best known example is the residence of the president, that was moved on several occasions from the Bratislava Castle, to the old town hall, and finally to the Grasalkowitch palace.

64 The Czech Finance Minister, Ivan Pilip, reported that in 1996 the state failed to collect 63 billion ($20 million) CK in taxes. According to Hobson, the collection of revenue in CEE states is between 50 and 60 per cent, in Russia only about 25–30 per cent, while in the EU countries it is 80–90 per cent. 'Daňové úniky v ČR', *Pravda*, 1 October 1997, p. 13. Crime rates, kept at relatively low levels under the communist regime, went up some 300 per cent between 1990 and 1992. Although in decline, the relative crime rate in the Czech Republic is still high. The Klaus government was forced to resign in November 1997, in the aftermath of a corruption scandal concerning the Civic Democratic Party (ODS).

65 J. Rak, *Bývalí Čechové* (Praha: Nakladatelstvi H&H, 1994), pp. 99–109.

66 The accuracy of Palacký'shistoriography is often challenged. Josef Pekar, for instance, argued that the Husites were first and foremost fighting to reform Catholicism, and that the nobility who fought at Bílá Hora were actually mostly German and, more than anything else, Catholic. J. Pekař, *O Smyslu Českých Dejin* (Rotterdam: Accord Publishing, 1977).

67 The works of Alois Jirásek that were inspired by Palacký's interpretation of Czech history became, and continue to be, assigned readings in Czech (formerly also in Czechoslovak) elementary and middle schools, and they provided popular themes for dramatisation and movies.

68 The idea of expulsion is attributed mostly to President Edvard Beneš, who lobbied the Allies for support during his exile in London. Nevertheless, the works of T. G. Masaryk, the 1922 constitution, the Czechoslovak doctrine and the institutional foundations of the interwar republic were motivated to a considerable degree by the desire to maintain and if needed also to defend the state vis-à-vis the vividly present German threat. T. G. Masaryk, *The Meaning of Czech History* (Chapel Hill: University of North Carolina Press, 1973); F. Peroutka, *Budováni Státu, III* (Praha: Lidove Noviny), pp. 1285–90; J. Pešková *et al.*, *Dejiny Zemí Koruny České, II* (Praha: Paseka, 1992), 168–170; L. Stehule, *Československý Stát v Mezinárodním Právu a Styku* (Praha: Laichter, 1919).

69 According to Pešková, the ethnic composition of the interwar republic was: Czech 51 per cent; German 23.4 per cent; Slovak 14.5 per cent; Magyar 6.2 per cent; Ruthenian, Ukrainian and Russian 3.8 per cent, and Polish and Jewish 1.1 per cent. Pešková, *Dejiny Zemí*, 168.

70 Peroutka, *Budování Státu*, 991.
71 *Ibid.*; Pešková, *Dejiny Zemí*, 186–191.
72 International Helsinki Foundation, *Annual Report, 1997: Human Right Developments in 1996* (Vienna: REMA-Print, 1997), 83–94.
73 *SME* (29 March 2001).
74 'Tisíce l udí demonštrovalo v Prahe proti rasizmu', *Pravda* (11 November 1997), 1.
75 *SME* (29 March 2001).
76 'Smrt vyburcovala verejnost', *Pravda* (11 November 1997). The article reported 10,000–15,000 protesters at the event.
77 *Reuters Electronic News Service* (4 February 1998).
78 J. Perlez, 'Boxed in Bias: Czech Gypsies Look to Canada', *The New York Times* (31 October 1997), 3.
79 International Helsinki Foundation, *Annual Report* (1997), 90.
80 'Czech Republic: Roma in the Czech Republic', *Human Rights Watch/Helsinki Newsletter*, Vol. 8, No. 11.
81 *Nadace Nová Škola* is a Prague human-rights NGO that has worked with Roma since 1992. Personal interview with director Laubeova, Prague, 18 July 1997.
82 UNHCR, Regional Bureau for Europe, Division of International Protection, *The Czech and Slovak Citizenship Laws and the Problem of Statelessness*, February 1996; Council of Europe, *Report of the Experts of the Council of Europe on the Citizenship Laws of the Czech Republic and Slovakia*, April 1996.
83 Nadace Nová Škola, for instance, reported that immigration officials routinely dismissed itizenship applications of Roma, even if they were long-term residents and had no criminal record. According to Baobock, on 30 June 1994 70,000 Roma were turned into stateless people in the Czech Republic, because they had not applied in time for citizenship of the new state. Rainer Baubock, *From Aliens*, 229.
84 UNHCR, Regional Bureau for Europe, Division of International Protection, *The Czech and Slovak Citizenship Laws and the Problem of Statelessness*, February 1996.
85 Tolerance Foundation, *From Exclusion to Expulsion: The Czech Republic's New Foreigners*, Section on Judicial Expulsion, Prague, November 1996.
86 Havel spoke out against the inaction of Czech leaders concerning the ongoing violence against Roma.
87 The statistics of Slovakia's ethnic composition are contested. According to the 1991 census the Slovaks constitute 85.69 per cent, Hungarians 10.76 per cent, Roma 1.44 per cent, Czechs 1.00 per cent, and the Moravia, Rusin, Ukrainians, German, Polish and others comprise the remaining 1.11 per cent. Other estimates put the Hungarians at 12 per cent and the Roma at 7 per cent of the population. See the *Materials of the Slovak Statistical Office* (Bratislava, 1993).
88 In the case of Slovakia one has to agree with Gellner who argues that it is the modern state that created the nation and not the other way around. E. Gellner, *Nations and Nationalism* (Ithaca: Cornell University Press, 1983).
89 On crime in Slovakia see I. Pivarči and E. Klotton, 'Štatistiky Kriminálnej činnosti na Slovensku, *Pravda* (15 October 1997). The statistics show that only 29 per cent of 97.684 criminal acts committed in 1996, were solved; 69 per cent of crime was identified as property crime and 11 per cent as violent crime. Moreover, some publicists suggested that there seems to be a close connection between state agencies (namely the secret service) and organised crime in Slovakia. L. Pittner, 'Predstavitelia podsvetia sa dostávajú do povedomia príslušníkov Policajného zboru ako spojenci moci', *SME* (20 October 1997), 4–5.
90 Professional associations in the Czech lands became important centres for the dissemination of nationalist ideology.
91 S. Cambel et al, *Dejiny Slovenska, III* (Bratislava: Veda, 1992), pp. 244–253.

92 The electoral support for the SNS never exceeded 6.9 per cent, and most Slovaks voted for a variety of Czechoslovak parties.
93 'Ďuricova príručka dejín nebude v školách', *SME* (2 July, 1997); D. Čaplovič, 'Politika a naše dejiny', *Pravda* (13 June 1997) 7; D. Kovác, 'Dnes by táto kniha nebola financovaná', *Forum* (12 June 1997) 2.
94 The exhibition *Napísane zostane: Najstaršie klenoty Slovenského písomníctva* displays texts in German, Latin, Russian and Greek from the eighth through the fifteenth century.
95 During the visit of Jean-Marie Le Pen to Slovakia, Ján Slota, the chair of SNS made a speech in which he depicted the Huns, allegedly the ancestors of contemporary Hungarians, as the 'misfortune of Europe'. He claimed that they pillaged, burned and illed during their conquest, and since the Slovaks survived the ordeal then, they will not be pushed around by the descendants of such barbarians today. Even Le Pen publicly distanced himself from Slota's opinions the following day, and all news papers (with the exception of the pro-SNS, *Slovenská Republika*) launched an attack on the speech.
96 Naturally, there are numerous examples like these, and my intention here is to present only an illustration of a two-way process in which various attempts to interpret and authenticate historical events are successfully challenged.
97 G. Mesežnikov, 'Domestic Political Developments and the Political Scene in the Slovak Republic', in M. Bútora and P. Hunčík (eds), *Global Report on Slovakia: Comprehensive Analyses from 1995, and Trends for 1996* (Bratislava: Sandor Marai Foundation, 1997), pp. 11–31.
98 Mesežnikov, 'Vnútropolitický vývoj a politická scéna', in M. Bútora (ed.), *Slovensko v Pohybe: Slovensko 1996* (Bratislava: Inštitút pre Verejné Otázky, 1997), pp. 15–36.
99 Cited in Mesežnikov, 'Domestic Political Developments', 14.
100 Ústava Slovenskej Republiky (Bratislava: Danubia Print, 1993). For a reaction, P. Huncik *Slovensko pre Slovákov* (Bratislava: Nadácia Sandora Máraiho, 1993).
101 Especially the left wing of the governing coalition, the Party of the Democratic Left (SDL) and the Party of Civic Understanding (SOP) opposed vehemently the change of preamble. The opposition the Slovak National Party (SNS) offered its support in parliament to the Slovak coalition parties in order to exclude the Hungarian influence from the decision-making process. See *Pravda* (10 January 2001).
102 'Zákon Národnej Rady Slovenskej Republiky o Štátnom Obcianstve', Part 1/sec. 3/sec. 1.
103 'Ochrana občana', *Pravda* (11 November 1997), 3.
104 See *Pravda* (21 January 2001).
105 On the relationship between the state's internal capacity and group formation see Hobson, *The Wealth of States;* J. Migdal, 'Strong States, Weak States: Power and Accommodation', in Wiener and Huntington (eds), *Understanding Political Development* (Prospect Heights: Waveland Press (1987).
106 Ján Slota of the SNS is against EU integration because, he argues, the single aim of Western countries is to rob Slovakia of its wealth.
107 R. Dahrendorf, 'The Changing Quality of Citizenship', in B. van Steenberger (ed.), *The Conditions of Citizenship* (London: Sage Publications, 1994), p. 17.
108 The marks in the last two areas are lower because of the undemocratic Press Law, inadequate legal framework for the economic transition, the prime minister's arrogance, and the lack of transparency in the privatisation process.
109 M. Kusý, '*Stav l'udských práv*', in Bútora (ed.), *Slovensko 1996*, 51.
110 The Minister of Post, Telecom and Transport, František Palacka stepped down when he was found guilty of misconduct during the privatisation of the Slovak Telecom, and the State secretary of the same resort, František Kurej, stepped down with him. The Ministers of Industry and Defence have met a similar fate for similar reasons. Most of them are sitting in the Parliament, referred to by the opposition as the 'depository of corrupt politicians'.

111 Tilly, 'The Evolution of Citizenship'. New institutional economists tend to conceptionalize democracy in a similar manner. See A. Przeworski, *Democracy and the Market* (Cambridge: MA, Cambridge University Press 1991).

112 Przeworski, 'Introduction', in *Democracy and the Market.*

113 Some scholars argue that only the total economic isolation of Slovakia from the EU states could develop sufficient pressure on the contemporary ruling coalition. It could be objected that the isolation of Slovakia might lead to an even greater institutional instability and eventually to an authoritarian regime. See I. Samson, 'Proclamations, Declarations and *Realpolitik* in Current Slovak Integration Policy', *Perspectives,* Nos 6–7 (1996), 51–9.

Petr Kopecky and Peter Učeň

8

Return to Europe?

Patterns of Euroscepticism among the Czech and Slovak political parties

Introduction

It is undoubtedly true that the issue of European integration has undergone a dramatic development in the Czech and Slovak Republics since the early 1990s. In both countries, it has changed from a relatively minor and consensual issue into one characterised by its clear presence within the structure of domestic political competition. In the aftermath of regime change Czechoslovak politics was marked by a widespread euphoria concerning the 'return to Europe'. The 1989 regime changes in Central Europe were commonly interpreted by domestic actors as a 'return to normality' that equalled 'return to Europe'.[1] This mood implicitly included an expectation of the return of the post-communist countries to the family of liberal democracies. European integration was perceived as a logical consequence of the 'return to normality'. Moreover, the integration was seen as automatic – a technical process rather than a political problem – and a matter of time. The post-communist countries were also assured by their western European counterparts of the desirability and viability of EU enlargement. Within this atmosphere – spiritually very favourable to integration – the Czech and Slovak Federal Republic officially launched its efforts, aiming at association with the EU in December 1990.

It was only in the domestic tensions concerning the form of a common state that the first instances of a more varied usage of integration-related arguments slowly started to emerge. In short, arguments over the necessity of formally reforming the Czech–Slovak relationship within the federation came out as soon as early 1990. They were commonly upheld by Slovak politicians and a considerable part of the population, and the relevancy of the issue was admitted by the Czech side as well. Yet, discord on this topic soon appeared. A non-negligible part of the Slovak elite subscribed to the 'concept of the sovereign nation as an equal partner in the common state'[2] – a somewhat blurred vision on which even Slovak politicians could not find consensus as to its possible organisational form. The most common were references to the federation with strong republics and the federal centre with relatively weak competence derived from and delegated by the republics. This was basically a confederation project contested and refused by Czech side.

The foreign policy implication of this way of conceptualising the future form of the state was first of all a demand to grant republics (i.e. Slovakia) certain foreign policy competence and powers despite the fact that foreign policy was always considered a federal matter. This was inevitably introduced by the concept of the 'sovereign nation' without direct reference to an independent state. A Slovak demand for a special Ministry of International Co-operation for the republic was also backed by arguments of preparation for European integration. However, the most paradoxical use of the integration argument by some Czech and Slovak politicians occurred during the period preceding the split of the Czechoslovak federation as well as within campaigns of ex post justifications of this event by the Slovak government. It took the form of slogans that tried to convince the public that separation was desirable for a better and more effective integration into Europe. As a typical argument within these campaigns, Žiak[3] quotes Jozef Moravčík (then federal foreign ministry) saying: 'We do not carry out the transformation of Slovakia into independent state with intention of isolation. On the contrary, we do it in order to contribute to the process of international co-operation as a sovereign unit.' Accordingly, prime minister Mečiar said in 1992: 'If we integrate ourselves through Czecho-Slovakia we will not build a system that would guarantee for Slovakia participation in negotiations as an equal partner; we will condemn ourselves to the role of a region and ethnic group.'[4] On the occasion of the first day of state independence he maintained that 'a creation of the state represents the chance for all its citizen to participate directly in European as well as global integration'.[5]

After the split this Europe-as-an-excuse-for-separation type argument, apart from being adopted by virtue of necessity, also took over the optimistic 'federal' mood concerning the case of integration. The Slovak establishment carried on assuming that the process of integration would continue at the same pace and in a non-problematic manner, as was the case for Czechoslovakia. Prime Minister Mečiar declared that 'Slovakia is condemned to be successful'[6] when referring to integration. An 'automatism of integration' attitude in the 1993–94 period was mainly based on the country's status as a successor to Czechoslovakia, its geographical position, fair economic performance, and a strategy of steady fulfilment of technical-administrative matters concerning integration such as, for example, the European questionnaire. In spite of certain declarations that deviated from official governmental statements about European integration as a primary goal of the country's foreign policy, there was no important political actor which directly rejected or disputed pro-European orientation. European integration was only gradually changing from a consensual issue into a subject of a serious political conflict. Similarly, the new Czech government, as well as a large part of the opposition, assumed that the newly emerged Czech Republic had a better chance of joining the EU without Slovakia (and other Visegrád partners). However, also there, and despite European integration remaining the official priority of the government, criticisms of EU and its policies and institutional arrangements slowly started to appear in the press and among the elites, signalling cracks in the hitherto commonly shared and almost unconditionally positive perspective on European integration.

The aim of this chapter is to provide an overview of stances on European integration among the Czech and Slovak parties and explore their patterns. In particular, we are interested in what Taggart[7] termed as Euroscepticism, that is, a relatively broad diversity of positions encompassing contingent, qualified, or outright opposition to the process of European integration. We shall show that while unqualified Euroenthusiasm was typical for 1989, the more varied usage and stances on European integration has been a corollary of intensified talks on enlargement towards the end of the 1990s. Our exploration of these strands of Euroscepticism will be confined to the elite level, and namely to the level of political parties, as we have detected them through the study of party programmes and documents, political speeches and various journal and newspaper articles. Since neither of the two countries has, at least until very recently, conducted a full public debate on the meaning and implications of European integration, and since popular support for the EU hovers around a lukewarm 46 per cent of approval in the Czech Republic and 58 per cent of approval in Slovakia,[8] we consider attitudes and stances of party elites as a good starting point of analysis of Euroscepticism. It is the elites who will form the discourse on integration and shape the preferences of citizens, and it is the elites who have been involved in the many diplomatic and political negotiations about Czech and Slovak accession to the EU.

The chapter is organised into three sections. In order to provide background information, the chapter begins with two sections analysing the foreign policy and geopolitical orientation-related stances of the main political parties in both countries, with a particular focus on EU related matters. For the Czech Republic, the analysis will include all major right-of-centre parties (Civic Democratic Party – ODS, Christian Democrats – KDU-ČSL, Freedom Union – US) which, until 1998, were part of the governing coalition(s). We will also include analysis of the opposition, both the Social Democrats (ČSSD – now the governing party), as well as the so-called extremist opposition – the Communist Party of Bohemia and Moravia (KSČM), and the Republicans (SPR-RSČ – after the 1998 elections an extra-parliamentary opposition). As far as Slovakia is concerned, the main stress will be put on positions of the Movement for Democratic Slovakia (HZDS). However, we also include analysis of HZDS' former coalition partners – the Slovak National Party (SNS) and the Slovak Workers Association (ZRS). The analysis of the former opposition parties (until 1998) includes: the Christian Democratic Movement (KDH); the Democratic Party (DS), whose stances were very much comparable with the stances of the now extinct liberal Democratic Union (DÚ) and the stances of the Slovak Democratic and Christian Union (SDKÚ); and the Party of Democratic Left (SDL´). The final section then provides a comparative analysis, exploring and generalising about the patterns of Euroscepticism across these two countries.

European stances among the Czech political parties

The ODS, and its leader Václav Klaus, have long been known as the most vocal critics of European Union related matters in the Czech Republic. During a meeting of the World Economic Forum in Davos in 1995, for example, Klaus engaged in a heated exchange with the EU commissioner Hans van der Broek concerning the Union's agricultural policies. Van den Broek insisted that the Central European candidates should adopt their agricultural sectors to EU standards. He was rebuffed by Klaus, who said that if anything needed to be changed, it was the agricultural policies of the EU. Angry commissioner retorted by stating that it was not the EU who wanted to get into the Czech Republic. This highly charged and publicised event should not, however, obscure the fact that ODS and its leader have been consistently in favour of the Czech Republic joining the EU. As the largest party in a right-of-centre coalition, which governed in the Czech Republic between 1992 and 1997, ODS held an essentially positive approach towards EU. It was under ODS leadership that the Czech Republic officially applied, in January 1996, for EU membership. Although governmental policy at that time assumed that the Czech Republic was better off in its attempt to join EU in a solo effort, rather than in a co-ordinated strategy with the other Visegrád countries, namely Poland and Hungary,[9] accession to EU (and NATO) represented the most important goal of foreign policy, from which the ODS never diverted.

Indeed, the party's perception is that the Czech Republic has already joined Europe, in both a practical sense (a democratic system was established) and a cultural sense (belonging to the sphere of western European values). Such are arguments which the ODS uses to justify its general pro-European orientation. Concerning the EU as a system, the declared desire to join is based on arguments typical of a liberal-conservative party. In particular, the ODS states that the EU is important as an instrument of peaceful co-operation in Europe, and that, economically, there is no alternative but for a small country like the Czech Republic to join the EU. The ODS sees the process of European integration primarily as a means to enlarge markets, and thus to further deepen economic co-operation between countries already engaged in a high level of financial, trade and labour exchanges. In a televised debate on BBC in March 1998, the ODS leader Klaus also stated that a small country like the Czech Republic should find it advantageous, if not essential, to join the European common currency (EMU).

That said, the economic arguments have for long been accompanied by a critical approach to several aspects of EU, again not dissimilar to critical approaches of several like-minded parties in western Europe. The ODS declared in its 1998 electoral manifesto that, once within the EU, it would actively support the expansion of all aspects of European free trade, including the extension of EU borders to incorporate new states (and thus markets). In that basic vision, the party differs little from (parts of) the British Conservative party, which has long been a source of inspiration for ODS, cultivated through a number of institutional and personal links. The EU bureaucracy – perceived as large and unaccountable – is clearly at the centre of ODS criticism of EU, as are the (perceived) complicated and over-grown EU legislation and generous social policies of several member states. Increased political integration is not welcomed by the ODS either. The party declares in its manifesto that the Czech Republic is a sovereign state, which should not get diluted in some sort of super state structure, erected without having deeper social, political and cultural roots. All these remarks are framed in the overall pro-EU position, which carefully balances often sharp criticisms. Nowhere is this more prominent than in Klaus's own writings which, for example, declare the EMU is the most important economical decision in Europe since the Second World War. It then analyses its pros and cons, and ends up with sceptical comments that EU-related matters are discussed in superficial and politically motivated ways, precluding much-needed critical and realistic analysis.[10] Indeed, while Klaus often laments the lack of knowledge of the EU among the Czech population, the enlightenment he offers is almost invariably a mix of positive and critical remarks.

Clearly then, while actively and openly supporting the accession of the Czech Republic to EU, ODS has developed a relatively cohesive, visible and critical position on European integration, which is consistent with its ideological orientation, and which represents so far the most elaborate statement on these matters among the former governing parties. The declared stances of the other two right-of-centre parties – KDU-ČSL and US – are in slight contrast to ODS. In fact, it is hard not to avoid the feeling that both parties developed their positions on EU primarily as an opposition to the sometimes sharp tongue of ODS, rather than from some form of party-wide or ideological discussion. The issue of EU has thus been framed, at least partly, in the terms appropriate for tactical and electoral purposes. Both parties appear firmly pro-European and pro-EU, almost unconditionally if compared to a critical approach of ODS, and implicitly against the stances of ODS. Moreover, their positions have never extended beyond short general declarations. For example, KDU-ČSL supports the full integration of the Czech Republic to European structures, as well as an (unspecified) active approach of the country within the EU. Also in general terms, the party states that the EU should be reformed in the way that it takes more into account voices of smaller states. And, similarly to the US, the KDU-ČSL supports EU enlargement as well as its deepening.

The Social Democrats (ČSSD) have an unambiguously positive attitude towards European integration too. Similarly to SDL´ in Slovakia (see below), the party grounds its strongly pro-EU attitude by subscribing to the European-wide project of the European socialists. It conceives the Union as a venue for the advancement of the modern social democratic project. Similarly to the two right-of-centre Czech parties, ČSSD frames its position as an opposition to the vision of Klaus and his ODS, and the party programme explicitly denies any negativism and arrogance towards EU (as exhibited by ODS). As a reference to ODS negative attitudes and previous foreign policies towards other candidate countries, ČSSD also supports a wider regional co-operation towards EU accession. In addition, the EU is viewed and desired by the party not merely as a free trade zone, but as a space for active participation in the creation of better economic, political, security, environmental, as well as cultural and human relationships – as a basis of a social market economy. The party explicitly and fully supports the Maastricht Treaty. Indeed, soon after ČSSD took over the government following the 1998 elections, it formulated and carried out an extensive programme of reforms and legislative acts to speed up the full adjustment of the Czech Republic in anticipation of the 2003 entry date to the EU.

From the two parties considered on the extremes of party political spectrum, the Communists (KSČM) are, perhaps surprisingly, the more vocal and comprehensive critics of EU. While the party embraced EU shortly after the regime change in 1989 (but always opposed NATO), its stances developed over time into a far more critical approach. Although the party is generally pro-European, in that it sees the need for the Czech Republic to join the EU, it wants the country to do so only on an equal basis, under the condition that it will be able to influence what is going on in Europe. In addition, KSČM is highly critical of current EU arrangements. The party conceives of the EU, and of the Maastricht Treaty in particular, as a tool of multinational capital in furthering exploitative policies in Europe. The integration processes are seen as dominated by, and protective of, primarily German interests – criticisms which had close parallels in the party's ferocious opposition to the Czech–German bilateral agreements on the settlement of property claims made by the organisations representing former Sudetenland inhabitants, expelled from Czechoslovakia at the end of the Second World War due to their commonly adjudged complicity with Nazi regime.

The KSČM is thus not against the Czech Republic joining EU, but prefers a cautious and incremental approach, opposing the alleged eagerness with which 'the Czech elites' push for enlargement. The elements of new left ideological agenda, sometimes uneasily cobbled together with elements of nationalism, are clearly apparent in the stance on EU matters. The explicit reference to 'return to Europe' means for KSČM advancing the project of self-management economies within European countries. It also means a thorough democratisation of EU institutional arrangements, curbing the influence of (a too large) bureaucracy and (too powerful) multinationals, as well as the introduction of a more balanced decision-making system, protecting the interests of smaller states. The new left agenda, embraced incrementally as KSČM underwent the process of ideological restructuring after 1989, and is also visible in the demands for a more participatory forms of democracy within the EU. The party rejects the existence of only formal representative democratic institutions and demands the introduction of direct forms of democracy. The party demands that the Maastricht Treaty should be re-negotiated accordingly. It should also be re-negotiated in a way which does not imply the elimination of national sovereignty (as now), but rather in a manner which provides for decisions to be based on a widespread agreement between the member states.

In many respects, therefore, KSČM comes out as far more critical of the EU than the ODS, and also as the party with by far the most open and elaborate position on the matters concerning European integration in the Czech Republic (see www.kscm.cz). In that, it is also more explicit than the Republicans (SPR-RSČ) – the party considered by many analysts and politicians on the extreme right of the political spectrum.[11] Owing to its nationalist, and fierce anti-German and anti-NATO propaganda (in many respects similar to KSČM), the Republicans perceive the EU in largely negative terms. The party appears as pro-European in the desired general geopolitical orientation of the Czech Republic, but at the same time it is more or less anti-EU. The (often implicit) critique of the EU has focused mainly on statements concerning the sell-out of Czech industry and property to Western companies (embraced by the Czech elites betraying the interests of the country). In the party's vision, the integration into the EU is supposed to only enhance such sell-outs, and reinforce the domination of the EU by the interests of multi-national capital (which also pervaded the Czech Republic). However, in comparison to KSČM, SPR-RSČ rarely goes beyond such general remarks, and its EU stances remain largely vague, unspecific and subject to frequent changes.

European stances among the Slovak political parties

The HZDS, in government until the 1998 elections, undoubtedly played a pivotal role in the difficult path towards EU membership that Slovakia undertook since its emergence as an independent state at the end of 1992. The doubts about its declared Europeanism stemmed from an uncertainty as to what geopolitical vision was actually adopted by the party. The HZDS and its leader Vladimír Mečiar have been accused from the early 1990s of attempting to combine the advantages of association with the European Union with the (mainly hypothesised) advantages of a kind of special relationship with Russia. Duleba[12] defines the rationale of the HZDS vision of the special relationship with Russia as taking place in two stages: the first stage (1990–91) was mainly an attempt to minimise economic losses caused by the collapse of the Council for Mutual Economic Assistance. The second (1992–93), and more important stage, was the development of a vision that Slovakia should become a bridge (mainly in economic terms) or a gateway country between the East and the West. An assumption of paramount importance in this vision was the idea that 'the closer the relations between Slovakia and Russia, the more important Slovakia would become for the West'.[13] This indicates an element of blackmail that was clearly present in Mečiar's strategy of pressure on the EU in order to make it overlook some of Slovakia's integration problems. Indeed, since the HZDS was the main governing party, its attitude towards the EU cannot be discussed without noting the lack of success of the government's integration policy, namely its unwillingness and failure to fulfil political criteria set up in Copenhagen.

The doubts concerning the HZDS Europeanism thus deepened in the Summer of 1997 when government behaviour was interpreted as further intensification of the isolationist traits of Slovakian governmental politics that took place as a response to the refusal of NATO to invite Slovakia for entry talks and to the publication of the evaluation of applicant states by the European Commission. These doubts were also intensified by the development of foreign policy stances among the then HZDS's coalition partners – the Slovak National Party (SNS) and the Slovak Workers Association (ZRS). During the tenure of Mečiar's government, these stances developed from a 'reserved integrationalism' to an 'undeclared isolationism', whereby the latter could take on a rather ferocious format, especially in declarations aimed at the domestic audience. For example, following Slovakia's exclusion from the first wave of EU enlargement in 1997, the SNS maintained that the impact of a decision was not to be dramatised. It stressed that the EU should have based its decision on economic criteria rather than something else. The party also did not conceal its negative stance as to what an adoption of minority treatment standards requested by EU would mean in the case of Slovakia, even though it did not, at that time, declare any official anti-European statements.

The ZRS – created before the 1994 elections and falling into oblivion following the 1998 elections – did not question pro-European passages of the governmental programme when the party joined Mečiar's government in 1994. However, when in 1996 one Slovakian journalist managed to obtain an original (never published) type-written draft version of the party programme, including a full support for the EU and NATO, the party leader Ján Lupták publicly declared this version of the document a result of a typing error! Furthermore, commenting on summer 1997 rejection of Slovakia by EU the party expressed its opinion that 'a natural development of a process of Slovakia's integration into the EU is more desirable than politics of dictate', and that Slovakia wants to enter the EU 'as an equal partner rather than an inferior republic'.[14] As reported by the press,[15] during the 1998 electoral campaign the ZRS leader Ján Lupták said that 'Slovakia can live without membership of the EU. The country has fertile soil and hard working hands. We do not want to import their surplus products. We will grow our own tomatoes, peppers, and red melons'.

Both the HZDS and SNS have nevertheless developed in a slightly different direction after they passed from incumbency to opposition in 1998. While the HZDS tries hard to present its pro-European face, SNS endorses more open Euroscepticism. Indeed, the nationalist and anti-European wing within the HZDS was notably muted after the 1998 elections and, for example, the party declared membership in EDU its official goal. HZDS also adopted critical stance towards its former coalition partner SNS, accusing the party of being xenophobic and anti-European. Indeed, SNS in opposition no longer masks its Euroscepticism, as it had done while the party was in government. For example, the SNS expert on issue of integration and vice-chair Jozef Prokeš in late 1998 compared the EU to a fire. He said integration was not desirable, but there was probably hardly any way to avoid it. He stressed the country should prepare for accession in the same way as a household should be ready for a fire; when it comes, it is easier to handle the ramifications. Also, while the SNS is now trying to distance itself from previously declared 'spiritual alliance' with parties such as the French Front National of Le Pen or the Serbian Radical Party of Vojislav Seselj, it also tries to establish connections with western national parties, such as Italian Alleanza Nazionale, allied in the 'Europe for the Nations' group of the European Parliament.

Nevertheless, EU-related stances are also marked by a large degree of instrumentality, particularly with respect to HZDS. Within its current campaign for 'European recognition', the party sometimes ostensibly displays Europeanism. For example, Mečiar published a book, in 2000, in which he claims to subscribe to a federal and rather centralised version of European integration. He claims not to be a supporter of the 'Europe of the regions' nor the 'Europe of the nations' but of the 'United States of Europe', with elected central government and parliament. In parliamentary debates, however, the HZDS (supported by the SNS) often play a negative role in the process of adoption of the *acquis communautaire* – the process which commits Slovakia to make its legislation compatible with that of EU. HZDS, in concert with the SNS, opposes legislative acts, labelling them as a betrayal of Slovak interest by the current ruling coalition. Both parties imply that adoption of the *acquis* would make the possibility of the 'extinction of Slovak statehood' much more probable. Indeed, the fact that a constitutional commitment to open the country to the EU is declared a nightmare by the current opposition, leads the present ruling coalition to accuse HZDS of cynical insincerity of its proclaimed Europeanism.

The parties of the new ruling coalition – the Slovak Democratic Coalition (SDK), SDL′, Party of the Hungarian Coalition (SMK; the pre-electoral merger of the three ethnic Hungarian parties in Slovakia) and the new Party of Civic Understanding (SOP) – were manifestly pro-European while in opposition[16] and remained so also as incumbents. They are 'pro-integrationist by default'. Foreign policy and European integration was an area where the new government achieved the most rapid success and recognition. Slovakia's international isolation was broken and the country entered into accession negotiations with the EU. (By the end of the year 2000 it concluded negotiations on ten chapters of the *acquis*.) Thus, European integration became one of the most important sources of legitimacy and proof of successful rule. It is little wonder that ruling parties have no incentives to undermine this legitimacy by a detailed discussion on the practical impact of accession on the country's economy and social sphere. The government strives for the fastest possible progress in accession, which is presented as the only chance for the country. This applies mainly to the parties allied in the SDK, but also to the two middle-sized ruling parties – the SOP and SMK.

The Christian Democrats (KDH), have, however, always been a slight exception. KDH stood firmly in the camp of pro-European forces in Slovakian politics during the Mečiar era. However, the party occasionally showed signs of what we call here a 'watchful Europeanism'. Being divided into two wings – one of them with opinions identical to the 'unconditional support' of the civic right – the party's dominant faction also includes proponents of a more careful attitude toward a complete opening of the country to the West. The reasons for the ambivalence of the Christian Democratic attitude, as best embodied in the opinions of KDH leader Ján Čarnogurský, are of a cultural and religious character. It includes a high sensitivity to Russian interests in East Central Europe. Further, it is tainted by a conservative fear of western values and way of life that, as sometimes interpreted by Čarnogurský himself, are not particularly suitable for the Slovak people. The above mentioned factors for example led to a rather lukewarm support of the KDH for Slovakia's integration into NATO.

However strong the conservative distrust of the West by the conservatives in the KDH may be, the party nevertheless wholeheartedly expressed its approval of the association with the EU. Čarnogurský[17] did not praise the EU as a politically efficient unit. Rather, he pointed out its economic success and based the argument about desirability to join EU on economic grounds. Although at times the KDH was suspected of sympathies for the idea of Slovakian neutrality, the logic of the 1995–97 developments within Slovakian politics caused a visionary element of the KDH's geopolitical conception to be muted in favour of a clear political pro-European choice. Contemporary KDH, after it lost its more modern and liberal components to SDKÚ, is clearly conservative Christian party, and perhaps the most Eurosceptic of all coalition parties. It does not deny its generally pro-European attitude, but its 'watchful Europeanism' is now evident and 'natural'. The party tends to use arguments similar to the Czech ODS. For example, party vice-chair Vladimír Palko declared in 1999 that EU was a project which 'deserves due recognition' but KDH did not perceive accession as a sort of entering paradise. Palko complained about the EU as being thoroughly socialist and believed that the struggle between left and right has to be fought within the EU (as well as in Slovakia) before accession becomes more attractive aim.

The Party of the Democratic Left (SDL') had an unambiguously positive attitude to European integration. As exemplified by the article by its ex-party leader,[18] the party denies any conceivable alternative to European integration. It considers the EU to be 'a really trustworthy political, economic and security alternative' as well as 'an important pre-condition for the stability of the central European region'. The party grounds its pro-European attitude by subscribing to the European-wide project of the European socialists, similar to the Czech ČSSD. It thus conceives the Union's attractiveness in terms of its suitability for the advancement of the modern socialist project. It appreciates the social progress and high level of social welfare achieved by the member states of the EU. Finally, the party believes that Slovakia's early integration will also mean the promotion of domestic social democratic interests. The SDL′ shares the vision of the European socialists and endorses the aim that the Union should become a social one. It also maintains that a high level of social and environmental safety in the EU should become the basis for a social market economy which, in turn, would help the union and its member states to cope with the problem of unemployment.

Nevertheless, the SDL′ too has undergone certain modification of its political stances. Since the leadership change in 1996, and especially after joining the government in 1998, its positions became characterised by more radical social rhetoric and by increasing involvement in clientelistic practices. Social radicalisation was caused by the ascendancy of a new dominant faction, which replaced the former leadership of moderate young politicians with strong social democratic leanings at the helm of the party. Uninhibited pro-Europeanism was one of the features of the 'social democratic face' the party was showing to the public under the leadership of Peter Weiss. Many believe its was not the true face of the party; the real one was a dormant mentality of 'old structures' which re-emerged with the ascent of a new leader, Jozef Migaš. Migaš and his faction brought the party to electoral success and to government with a claim of a more aggressive defence and promotion of leftist values, the interests of labour and a less submissive relationship with its centre-right coalition partners. Most importantly, the SDL′ inherited from the HZDS the role of promoter of the 'eastern vector of the Slovak foreign policy'. It is believed to have a direct connection with the above-mentioned clientelistic relationships because the SDL′ has evidently allied with certain economic interest groups in the (nuclear) energy sector which have either an interest in co-operation with, or direct ownership ties to, Russia. The SDL is perceived as the most anti-reform force of the current coalition and stands accused of undermining the country's integration chances. However, there has been no display of open Euroscepticism by the SDL′.

Patterns of Euroscepticism

In the previous sections we described the basic configuration of the main political parties' attitudes towards European integration. In the Czech Republic, these attitudes range from unconditional support for the Christian Democrats and the recently emerged Freedom Union, through the socially motivated endorsement of the Social Democrats, to the visibly critical stances of the ODS and of both parties considered on the extreme of the political spectrum (the KSČM and SPR-RSČ). In Slovakia, these attitudes range from unconditional support of the civic right in Slovakia, through the economically and socially motivated endorsement of the Christian democrats and the democratic left, to the traits of isolationism (more or less overt) of the HZDS, the SNS, and the now almost extinct ZRS. What do these positions tell us about Euroscepticism in the Czech and Slovak Republics?

Our first observation is that while the issue of European integration is no longer ignored by any major party in both countries, the discussion on the matter still tends to be, in general, quite shallow. The focus on policies in debates surrounding EU integration among the Western parties is certainly much less evident in the presentation of the problem in Czech and Slovak Republics, on the party level, as well as (if not even more), on the mass level. The reason obviously is that, apart from the abstract political-symbolic level, the European integration started to affect domestic politics in East Central Europe only in a relatively recent past: with the acceleration of accession talks, with the EU decision on first countries likely to join, and with the agreement on procedures for preparation and screening of prospective candidates.

However, it is also striking to see that if the stances of parties are compared between the two countries only, it is possible to identify even less direction and focus in Slovakia. Eurosceptic positions expressed by (some) Czech parties and politicians tend to be more of a practical and policy-oriented nature. For example, Klaus's critiques of the EU is most of all a critique of certain policies, for example of the CAP or the EU decision to boycott Austria following Haider's entry to the government. Such critiques are typically framed as a kind of smuggling socialism back to the Czech Republic through the back door (economy), or as a disregard to the principle of state sovereignty (the EU's human rights policies). Similarly, the KSČM engages in a relatively detailed discussion of the Maastricht Treaty in its party programme, warning the Czech voters on the danger of losing national sovereignty, and trumpeting its will to re-negotiate the whole treaty. Nothing like this ever occurred in Slovakia, certainly not until the 1998 elections. The view of European integration by Slovak eurosceptics took the form of a critique at a symbolic level mainly, and focused on disputing the value and impartiality of EU demarches and other official criticisms of misconduct of domestic politics under Mečiar's governments. Furthermore, both pro-Europeans and eurosceptics have been engaged in critical debates on the EU in the Czech Republic, while in Slovakia only eurosceptics took part in it. Those who are pro-European in Slovakia tended to pretend that potentially problematic aspects of the EU do not exist.

For example, in order to cope with this 'rain of reproaches', the previous Mečiar government adopted a set of defensive and justificatory arguments aimed at the domestic as well as the international audience. These arguments ranged from a simple denial of any of Slovakia's integration problems to direct accusations of the EU and the USA as forming a conspiracy against Slovakia. A basic list of themes employed by the former ruling coalition included the misinterpretation of the EU demarches as basically positive 'friendly warnings', or the accusation that both the EU and USA lacked vital information on which to base their judgements, thus over-estimating the problems of Slovak politics and disregarding the real state of democracy in the country. Furthermore, the ruling coalition also blamed western institutions for a biased attitude and use of double standards for applicant countries. The accusations of domestic opponents – press, the then opposition parties and the president – of disloyal behaviour and of damaging 'the image of Slovakia abroad' represented a crucial element of Mečiar's politics too. It is no wonder, then, that the issue of European integration overwhelmed the polarised coalition–opposition battle, and that this polarisation is at least partly responsible for the nature of the debate in Slovakia. Gradually, it became one of the focal points of the way opposition distanced itself from the policies of Mečiar's coalition. Opposition parties appealed to voters by stressing their 'European compatibility', and pointing out that their coming to power represented the only possibility of salvaging the country's damaged chances for accession to EU.

This suggests that the nature of party competition – i.e. the sharp political polarisation in Slovakia that is absent in the Czech Republic – can largely explain these differences, and we return to this issue shortly. However, it also appears that these differences are at least partly influenced by the stage of integration in which the two countries found themselves. While the Czech Republic has for long faced a set of 'adjustment demands' from the Commission, with all the implications for domestic policy-making, the domestic discussion on European integration in the long-excluded Slovakia centred mainly around abstract notions and the symbolic values of accession. This was certainly the case during the Mečiar era. In the meantime, of course, Slovakia has entered accession negotiations with EU too. And as we have demonstrated in the empirical sections of this chapter, the parties' stances on the EU too gradually became somewhat more elaborate and related to practical exigencies of accession process. Yet, because the polarisation of Slovak politics has not withered away, and because the now government parties continue to use Europe in largely the same symbolic way as when they did in opposition, the Slovak political scene still appears to lack interest in practice-orientated debate on the ramifications of accession.

Our second observation is that neither the Czech nor the Slovak Republic have had an unequivocal anti-EU party. Our analysis of party stances shows that Euroscepticism manifests itself in either the existence of anti-EU party factions, or in somehow qualified EU positions, i.e. pro-EU in principle, but opposing one or more aspects of the current EU arrangements. The factional pattern of Euroscepticism is more typical for the Slovak political discourse, while the pattern characterised by open and/or qualified Euroscepticism is more typical for the Czech Republic. The HZDS is a good example of factional Euroscepticism, which is more difficult to identify in the Czech Republic. The integration stance of the HZDS, which we characterised as 'undeclared isolationism', came out mainly from a faction of fierce anti-Europeans within the party. There was a certain division of roles between party politicians concerning the way of conveying messages about the EU to different audiences. Bound by the government programme, Mečiar and cabinet members hardly ever openly declared anti-European attitudes. However, isolationist speeches in front of mainly domestic audience were conveyed by a special group of party politicians not directly involved in government business. Similarly, in the post-1998 period, the HZDS adopted a very instrumental approach to EU, appearing pro-European in its official declarations, but also quite anti-European on the domestic political scene.

This leads us to several final observations, all linked to the relations between patterns of Euroscepticism and the position of parties in their respective national party systems. As we indicated above, the positioning of parties on EU issues partly depends on their position in national party systems. The pattern we can observe in both republics is that the opposition parties tended to define their stances as counter-positions to an identifiable incumbent opponent. This was most clearly exhibited in Slovakia, where parties like the KDH, but also the DÚ (whose many party elites were once in leadership of SNS), shifted from initially evolving Eurosceptic positions to a firm pro-European stance. As we also indicated above, this may well be peculiar to the polarised nature of political conflict in Slovakia. However, a similar pattern is also observable in the Czech Republic, where the ČSSD, in particular, explicitly defined its stances as a counter-position to ODS. Even more interestingly, both former coalition partners of the ODS – KDU-ČSL and the US (and the ODA before 1996) – made their positions juxtaposed against that of a perceived party rival: becoming strongly pro-EU meant to be strongly anti-Klaus and anti-ODS. Similarly, ODS became far more open in its critique of EU after losing elections in 1998, sometimes blaming the ČSSD government for uncritical and complacent attitudes in accession negotiations with EU.

This would obviously seem to suggest that Euroscepticism (or pro-Europeanism) is largely a matter of electoral politics and appeals, or of the dynamic of the government–opposition divide, rather than a matter of party identity. Thus understood, the party positions on European integration represent no more than a soft issue, which parties use instrumentally to establish a sense of difference with identifiable opponent. However, this would obscure the fact that the existing Euroscepticism of the ODS, and particularly of the KSCM, in the Czech Republic are actually in tune with the declared ideological principles of the parties involved. Equally importantly in Slovakia, Eurosceptic utterances of SNS, and also of the nationalist wing of HZDS, cannot be seen in isolation from both parties' focus on national identity. What can thus fluctuate is the accent on either pro-European or anti-European stances at certain periods in time, but we maintain that certain strands of Euroscepticism in both countries might very well be rooted in a broader sense of party identity.

In any case, it appears that Czech and Slovak cases support Taggart's[19] observation that Euroscepticism stems from a combination of party ideology *and* the relative position of parties in the political system. In fact, nowhere has this been more apparent than in the case of KSČM and SPR-RSČ in the Czech Republic, which closely resemble the status of protest parties. As Taggart observes: 'Euroscepticism as an ideological appendage to a more general systemic critique is the most pervasive form of party based Euroscepticism in Western Europe'; it is 'often symptomatic of the reaction of certain types of parties to the party systems in which they find themselves and to the prevailing model of the political party'.[20] In that sense, the Czech situation is more similar to Western Europe than the Slovak situation in that the Czech Republic does have true protest or extreme parties – i.e. parties perceived by the other established parties as non-democratic, anti-system, and without a coalition potential. And it is in this sense that locating the main sources of fierce, consistent and long-term Euroscepticism will be easier in the Czech Republic, providing, of course, that the relative position of these 'fringe' parties remains the same.

Conclusion

There cannot be any doubt that the issue of European integration has undergone dramatic changes in the Czech and Slovak Republics. It has moved from being a relatively consensual issue, framed in the essentially positive (and simplistic) term 'return to Europe', into an issue which has already become a feature of party competition. This chapter, focused on elite attitudes to European integration, underpins what was to be expected: although we find it difficult to locate a clearly anti-European party in the Czech and Slovak Republics, the analysis of party stances shows that positions on European integration have clearly become more pronounced and varied than in the period immediately following the collapse of communism. Euroscepticism – a broad diversity of positions encompassing contingent, qualified, or outright opposition to the process of European integration – is perhaps a still less focused, structured and informed set of positions than in Western Europe. However, the mere fact Czech and Slovak parties tend to be more articulate on the issue, and that the issue has become a part of political competition, justifies further scrutiny.

The different positions in which the two countries find themselves with respect to accession negotiations shapes patterns of Euroscepticism among their respective parties. We expect the existence of Euroscepticism as a critique of policies of conditionality of the EU to continue in the Czech Republic, with Slovakia, now fast catching up following the renewed accession talks after the fall of the Mečiar government, eventually exhibiting similar reactions to various exigencies of the enlargement process. However, given the (still) polarised nature of Slovak party politics, which forced the issue of European integration to become a divider between government and opposition, the 'abstract-symbolic' arguments over the EU in Slovakia will probably continue as the main frame of domestic debates for some time to come.

This chapter also supports earlier observations[21] that relate Euroscepticism to the shape of party competition. For example, the existence of a not too small element of populist/protest party phenomena (KSČM, SPR-RSČ) in the Czech Republic – noted for its absence in Slovakia – is a good predictor of Euroscepticism., because these parties use Euroscepticism as part of a wider critique of the system from which they feel excluded. Moreover, the mainstream parties sometimes employ Euroscepticism (or uncritical pro-Europeanism) strategically, in order to highlight a sense of difference with an identifiable (usually incumbent) opponent. Thus, a key question ahead of the projected 2003–5 accession date is whether the critics of integration want and will be able to find a sufficient political and electoral base to make the European issue an integral part of party identity, or perhaps even a new cleavage. A full answer to this question would obviously require a closer look at the correlation between party/elite-based attitudes to Europe, and the attitudes of party supporters. However, our preliminary analysis of party stances suggests that to characterise Euroscepticism in the Czech and Slovak Republics as merely a soft issue might obscure its deeper association with the values and ideologies of certain parties, and thus underestimate its potential to influence the nature of party competition.

Notes

1 K. Kumar, 'The 1989 Revolutions and the Idea of Europe', *Political Studies*, Vol. 40 (1992), 439–461.
2 D. Malová, 'Parliamentary Political Parties in Slovakia and the European Integration Process', paper prepared for the conference on 'The Role of Central European Parliaments in the Process of European Integration', Prague, September 1997.
3 M. Žiak, *Slovensko: od komunizmu kam?* (Bratislava: Archa, 1996), pp. 144–145.
4 M. Leško, 'Dejiny jednej premárnenej podpory', *SME* (27 June 1997).
5 *Ibid.*
6 *Ibid.*
7 P. Taggart, 'A Touchstone of Dissent: Euroscepticism in Contemporary Western European Party Systems', *European Journal of Political Research*, Vol. 33 (1998), 363–388.
8 *Applicant Countries Eurobarometer* (Brussels: European Commission, 2001), 5.
9 A. Černý, 'Prague's Reality Check', *Transitions* Vol. 5, No. 4 (1998), 52–55.
10 V. Klaus, *Obhajoba zapomenutých myšlenek* (Prague: Academia Praha, 1997) especially pp. 347–367.
11 V. Dvořáková, 'The Politics of Antipolitics? The Radical Right in the Czech Republic', paper presented at the conference on 'Liberalism, Social Democracy and Fascism in Central Europe', Sandbjerg, November 15–18 (1996); C. Mudde, 'The New Roots of Extremism: The ABCs of the rising right', *Transitions* Vol. 5, No. 7 (1998) 44–47.
12 A. Duleba, 'Pursuing an Eastern Agenda', *Transitions* Vol. 2, No. 19 (1996), 52–55.
13 *Ibid.*, at 52.
14 *SME* 17 July 1997.
15 For example, *SME* 21 September 1998.
16 F. Šebej, 'O čo ide v zahraničnej politike Slovenskej Republiky', *Domino Efekt* Vol. 3, No. 20 (1994).
17 J. Čarnogurský, 'Identita Európy', *Literárny týždenník* Vol. 8, No. 1 (1995).
18 P. Weiss, 'Integrácia – politické otázky a problémy, *Nové Slovo* No. 15 (1997).
19 Taggart, 'A Touchstone of Dissent'.
20 *Ibid.*, at pp. 372, 384.
21 *Ibid.*

PETER BUGGE

9

Czech perceptions of EU membership: Havel vs. Klaus

Introduction

The events of November 1989 launched the Czechs into a truly revolutionary transformation process. Within a few weeks the old order virtually collapsed, and the population and its new leaders had to act in a new social, political and economic order, at home as in the surrounding world. Since the 'velvet revolution' the Czechs have therefore witnessed an intensive struggle not only about political and economic power or control, but also about the broader interpretation of these events. One might call it a fight about a 'meta-narrative', about the formation of an authoritative discourse that can make sense of the enormous changes and justify political action.

A core task has been to reinterpret the nation's identity and role in the surrounding world to adjust to the challenges of 'globalisation' following the fall of communism. In the Czech case these narratives have focused on 'Europe' as a symbolic 'home' for the nation and on 'Europeanisation' as a label for the desired accommodation to the new environment. As then Prime Minister Václav Klaus expressed it in December 1993, 'the question of our position in Europe today and in the future is in fact the question of our national and state identity'.[1] In concrete terms, this 'Europe' has had its inescapable centre of gravity in the EU and since 1989 membership has been an official Czech (before 1993 Czechoslovak) desideratum. This has generated a need to present the EU as a reasonable incarnation of the European idea, but the concrete nature of the EU and its complex impact on Czech politics and society invites a discursive tension between European ideal and EU reality.

This is reflected in the discourses of Václav Havel and Václav Klaus. Undoubtedly these two men have been the public figures most consistently shaping public opinion since 1989.[2] Both have held high political offices throughout the period, both have very actively propagated their views at home and abroad, while at the same time they incarnate two different approaches to politics, two different views of the world, and as a consequence two different, yet representative, attempts at creating authoritative narratives about the Czechs and Europe/the EU. This chapter offers a close analysis of the two men's discourses on their own nation, Europe and the EU, discourses that given the prestige of their authors are likely to contribute significantly to the shaping or framing of the broader public perception of these issues.[3]

The political setting

Speeches and writings (and in a broader sense discourses) are not produced or received in a vacuum, so a brief introduction to Czech relations with the EU and to the political roles of Havel and Klaus is called for. For a start, one may divide the years since 1989 into three periods on the basis of both domestic and international events.

The fall of the communist regime brought many people from the former 'dissident' elites to power. Among them were Václav Havel as President and his friend Jiří Dienstbier as Foreign Minister, and in much these two men and their ideas shaped Czechoslovak foreign policy in the first phase, which lasted until 1992. Their most urgent concern, the liberation from Soviet hegemony and the dismantling of its institutions (the Warsaw Pact and the COMECON), was achieved by 1991. When formulating policy alternatives Czechoslovak leaders oscillated between 'utopian' calls for new all-European co-operative structures and a 'pragmatic' leaning towards membership of existing western organisations such as the EU and NATO.[4] Much emphasis was put on regional co-operation with Poland and Hungary in the so-called *Visegrád group*, and in 1991 the three negotiated a new kind of association agreement with the EC, the *Europe Agreement*, regulating relations between the EC and each state without, however, committing the EC to enlargement. Politically as well as economically, the agreement was not altogether satisfactory from a Czechoslovak perspective, and the outcome illustrated the limits of the euphoric belief of 1989–90 in a harmony of wills and interests in a new Europe without walls.

The first phase ended with the change of government after the elections in June 1992 and the succeeding division of Czechoslovakia. In the new Czech government with Václav Klaus as Prime Minister and Josef Zieleniec as Foreign Minister economists with a very different background from that of the 'old' dissident elites predominated, and the change of political course was pronounced. Vladimír Handl has compared the shift to a move from the doctrine of '*liberal institutionalism*' to that of '*realism*', expressed in an outright rejection of any Visegrád co-operation (except for intergovernmental agreements on trade) and in many a critical remark about the Maastricht Treaty and the EU.[5] The government believed that the Czech Republic could be better joining the EU quickly on its own hand, and it was very confident in its evaluation of the Czech performance, especially in the economic field which was considered crucial to EU accession. Thus Klaus could say that the Czech Republic was in no hurry to join the present EU while at the same time declaring that 'we will be ready to join the EU earlier than the EU will be ready to accept us'.[6]

At the concrete level of Czech–EU relations, results were, however, modest. After the split, a new Europe Agreement was negotiated which in some respects was even less favourable to the Czech Republic than its Czechoslovak predecessor, and although 1993 brought a breakthrough with the June Copenhagen summit's recognition of the perspective of an Eastern enlargement, there was still no timetable for membership, nor any specific guidelines for the preparation thereof. On the Czech side, government declarations gave a rather contradictory picture of calls for an early admission on the one hand and vocal Euro-scepticism on the other, and the net effect in practical politics was summarised by one critical observer as '*Euro-passivity*'.[7]

Only by 1995 did the Klaus government come to realise that the 'solitary' approach did not bring the expected results while the boasting might be counterproductive.[8] The government stepped up domestic preparations for membership, and on 23 January 1996 the Czech Republic as the last but one of the central and east European applicants (Slovenia came later) submitted its application for EU membership. Meanwhile even the EU began to act more consistently, leading to the White Paper of May 1995, which offered specific suggestions for how to prepare for participation at the inner market, and to the Madrid decision of December 1995 to initiate accession talks six months after the conclusion of the Intergovernmental Conference in Amsterdam in 1997.

By sheer coincidence the December 1997 decision to start negotiation talks with the Czech Republic and other applicant countries nearly coincided with the fall of the Klaus cabinet in November, and with these events the third phase may be said to have begun. A caretaker government led by Josef Tošovský took office, succeeded after early elections in June 1998 by a Social Democratic minority government headed by Miloš Zeman, which however has based its political survival on a controversial 'contract' with Klaus's now main opposition party, the Civic Democratic Party (ODS), a contract securing Klaus the post as Chair of the Chamber of Deputies in the Czech Parliament. In January 1998 Havel, now an active opponent of Klaus, had been elected President for a second five-year term.

With the initiation of enlargement negotiations in March 1998 Czech membership of the EU has increasingly become a question not of *if*, but of *when* and *on which conditions*. In opposition as in government the Social Democrats have been vocal supporters of the EU and of Czech membership, although the efficiency or consistency of their actual policies in this respect may be discussed. In opposition, Klaus has stepped up criticism of the EU, among other things suggesting in June 2000 an early Czech referendum on EU membership, before the conclusion of the accession talks.[9] Officially, Klaus and the ODS are still in favour of Czech membership, but the relative neglect of this issue during Klaus's reign and the later vocal hostility suggests at best an ambivalent stance, starkly contrasting President Havel's unequivocal support of Czech membership of NATO and the EU.

Václav Havel: making a home of Europe

In his 'dissident' writings Havel had shown only a marginal interest in foreign politics or issues of European identity, but after 1989 he soon possessed himself of the field, successfully using his office to become the representative voice of the Czech Republic abroad, and a key interpreter of the country's foreign policy interests at home. With his many years in office, he also incarnates the continuity of Czech post-communist policies, despite the split of Czechoslovakia in 1992 and various changes in government. The evolution of Havel's views on these issues will be traced in each of the three phases presented above.

The basic features of Havel's world outlook took shape from 1990 to 1992. Most importantly, he soon embraced the idea of European unity, albeit at first with rather hazy ideas about its institutional shape. In his long political essay from 1991, *Summer Meditations*, Havel spoke of the unique chance for Europe to become 'one big community, based on the principle of "unity in diversity"' and called the idea of a European confederation a step in the right direction.[10] Political unity was, according to Havel, not just politically advantageous, it followed logically from Europe's status as *one civilisation*, based on a shared culture to which the central and eastern European countries had contributed for centuries until they were brutally forced to depart from their natural path. Presented like this, the future integration of these countries into western European structures was turned into a 'homecoming' to where one had historically belonged.[11]

Havel also sought to delimit this civilisation and determine Europe's relations to the two super-powers. Havel presented himself as an admirer of the USA, but in 1990 he repeatedly demanded that Europe should 'at last be able to stand guard for itself' as a natural 'connecting link' between the superpowers.[12] In 1991, however, when Czechoslovakia began to turn towards NATO, Havel stressed how Europe was 'civilisationally deeply tied to the North American continent, her younger brother' and how these ties had to be preserved.[13] With regard to the USSR Havel often spoke of the necessity of helping the country, but he oscillated between presenting the USSR as a *partner* for, or a *member* of the European civilisational community. The idea of a Europe connecting the super-powers suggested partnership only, but Havel also said in 1990 that he saw no reason why 'some or all of the European nations within the present Soviet Union could not at the same time be members of a European confederation and of some eventual "post-Soviet" confederation.'[14] By 1992, by contrast, he spoke only of the need to create a 'system of unity in diversity not only on a pan-European and Atlantic scale but on a Euro-Asian scale as well',[15] vaguely implying a dichotomy between Europe and North America on the one hand and a post-Soviet 'Euro-Asian' entity on the other.

Meanwhile, Havel's reflections on how to achieve European unity underwent a significant change. In 1990 Havel flirted with a pan-European confederation based on the Council of Europe but in 1991 he effectively buried the idea, insisting that the EC must be the driving force and model for the integration of Europe as a whole.[16] From late 1990, Havel began to mention the perspective of Czechoslovakia joining the EC, from 1991 he emphasised the significance of membership, and in his 1992 new year's address he called the Europe Agreement the 'perhaps most important treaty in our post-war history, a treaty which really opens the door to the political and economic environment of democratic Europe'. [17] So, within two years the EC moved from the periphery to the centre of Havel's considerations about European unity.

Havel mostly spoke in a positive vein, convinced that goodwill and a harmony of interests would prevail. In the optimistic parts of his speeches Havel referred to 'Europe' rather than to 'the West', placing the Czechs in 'central Europe' or 'central and eastern Europe', never in 'eastern Europe' or 'the East'. In the early speeches 'the West' occurred only once, when Havel with a touch of criticism said: 'We have awakened, and now we must arouse those in the West who have slept through our awakening.'[18] This was soon to become a pattern: when Havel had to criticise he turned to the old confrontational terms of 'West' and 'East'.[19] In 1991 he described the problems of the 'post-communist countries' and their fight to join the 'advanced West' and blamed this West for its unnecessary caution based on old stereotypes. He also for the first time supplemented his appeals to the good will of 'democratic western Europe' with a horror scenario:

> I also think that it would be deeply unjust and that it might even have very pernicious consequences for the stability in all of Europe if the emergence of a European confederation in any way curbed the approximation of the new central and eastern European democracies to the European Community . . . An artificially delayed or hampered . . . economic reform in these countries could easily lead to great social and political instability, which in the end would necessarily destabilise all of Europe.[20]

So eventually Havel's discourse of a 'natural' new pan-European order crackled and collided with an older discourse of confrontation between an advanced West and a problematic East, in which a scepticism towards the intentions of 'the West' became patent. As Havel had problems offering *political* arguments for western European engagement in central and eastern Europe, he also resorted to appeals to a 'negative' western self-interest, threatening that a collapsing East would drag the West with it into the abyss.

Havel's political authority was probably somewhat reduced in his new office as Czech president since 1993, while simultaneously Václav Klaus strove hard to dominate the Czech political scene. But Havel remained a prolific commentator of international affairs and a central spokesman for his country, and five new facets of his thinking about Europe and the EU during these years deserve mentioning.

First, Havel now explicitly defined Russia as a 'Euro-Asian power' juxtaposed to a 'Euro-Atlantic' or 'Euro-American' civilisation.[21] Though often expressing his belief in the peaceful co-operation of different 'spheres of civilisation' within a larger global civilisation, Havel has been preoccupied with defining civilisational borders, and in particular with avoiding 'the existence of zones of states that are unsure of where they belong'.[22] Havel, however, uses double standards when determining the civilisational place of nations. With regard to Lithuania he said that 'everyone should enjoy the inalienable right to say for himself where he sees his deepest roots and where he considers himself to belong in terms of his cultural and historical links, his background and the values he may share with others'. [23] Russia, by contrast, was granted no such freedom of choice. When Havel said that 'Russia, for its part, is a huge Euro-Asian power with a great gravitational potential of its own; it has the right to maintain its own identity', this was only the right to maintain the 'Euro-Asian' identity that he had already meted out to it.[24] Since 1993 Havel has thus included America in and excluded Russia from 'his own' civilisation, with everything that follows in terms of recommendations for the political organisation of Europe.

Secondly, Havel vehemently rejected the principle of ethnically defined nation states and pointed at European integration as the best way to overcome the dangers of nationalism.[25] In his 1994 new year's address Havel warned the nation against seeing the new Czech state as 'the mere pinnacle of the nation's being'. He brought up Yugoslavia and juxtaposed a 'programmatically national' principle of statehood to one founded on the 'civic principle', linking the latter to civil society and European integration. Unification would not, he claimed, bring 'all European nations, ethnic groups, cultures and regions to merge into some amorphous pan-European sea, nor is it to create a kind of monstrous superstate'.[26] On the contrary, Havel insisted, the only good option for the Czech nation was to accept the spirit of a 'civic Europe', which in concrete terms also demanded the surrender of parts of the national sovereignty to the EU.[27]

Thirdly, Havel combined his critique of nationalism with an extended narrative on European history. Europe was not merely a civilisational and cultural entity, he claimed: 'Europe . . . has always been and still is in essence one single and indivisible political entity, though immensely diverse, multifaceted and intricately structured.'[28] He saw European history as one big attempt to shape this structure and define the relations between its parts. Hitherto, however, the result had mostly been orders built on, and consequently overthrown by, force, but according to Havel the driving idea behind the EU had been a 'magnanimous attempt' to give Europe an order based on democracy, peace and co-operation, which could now finally be extended to the whole continent. Accordingly, Havel interpreted all tensions in Europe after 1989 as a struggle between the democratic principle (the idea of the EU) and the anti-democratic principle of nationalism and authoritarianism.[29]

Fourthly, Havel was increasingly specific in his evaluation of the EU. Having embedded the EU as a key positive actor in a greater narrative of the European battle between good and evil, he kept measuring actual EU performance in this light. In his March 1994 speech to the European Parliament he praised the Maastricht Treaty as a great 'technical' achievement which however left him with a feeling of want. The EU did have an ethos, he was convinced, but it had become invisible behind the technicalities and petty arguments. To win over people, Havel said, the EU must 'impress upon millions of European souls an idea, a historical mission and a momentum. It must clearly articulate the values upon which it is founded and which it intends to defend and cultivate. It also must take care to create emblems and symbols, visible bearers of its significance',[30] in other words pursue a conscious identity politics resembling nation building. Havel also asked from the EU a clear commitment to enlargement, including a specific timetable for all of Europe not yet included, although he did acknowledge that enlargement could not happen overnight.[31]

Presented like this, obligations were stronger on the EU than on the applicant side in the sense that enlargement was justified by history and culture as such, by Europe's civilisational unity, *before* any specific political or economic criteria entered the game. Therefore Havel paid relatively little attention to what the Czechs had to live up to, although at home at times he stressed also the Czech obligation to prepare for EU membership legally and economically, and not least by cultivating 'Europeanness'[32]

Finally, Havel's scepticism towards Western Europe did not disappear. The threat to Europe came not only from nationalists, but also from 'the weakness and indifference on the part of the democrats',[33] he said in Holland in 1995, and in March 1996 he told the Czech Parliament that 'the danger of a Munich spirit is taking wings again over Europe'.[34] Havel kept warning that western European self-absorption and neglect of the other half of Europe would inevitably lead to the destabilisation of the whole continent, arguing (with frequent references to Yugoslavia) that time was working against the democrats.[35] In fact, the strong words can be seen as indications of the *weakness* of the Czech position *vis-à-vis* the EU and of Havel's difficulties with constructing a narrative capable of convincing western European decision-makers about the necessity of enlargement.

Even in the third phase new accents can be detected, probably reflecting the improved prospects of Czech membership since 1998. Havel has become increasingly positive in his evaluation of the EU as it is, and far more concrete. This is obvious if one compares his February 2000 address to the European Parliament with his 1994 address. Havel himself did so, noting with satisfaction that the EU was now doing what he had called for six years before, i.e. engaging in a process of self-reflection on the deeper significance of European integration.[36] But if in 1994 Havel had been highly critical of the Union's excessive focus on technicalities, he now excused the EU, arguing that only the dramatic events since 1989 had made necessary the explicit formulation of the values and goals that had been a self-evident premise ever since the beginnings of western European integration after the Second World War.[37]

Havel insisted that a speedy enlargement should remain the number one concern of the EU but now he also took direct part in the debate about the future institutional structure of the EU, suggesting a more openly federal arrangement with an EU constitution and a bicameral European Parliament with the second chamber composed of an equal number of representatives from all member states, elected indirectly by the national parliaments. This, he argued, would make the Commission a more purely executive body and lessen the need to use a national key in the appointment of its members.[38] Even in the field of security and defence Havel demanded a more vigorous EU, seeing in the NATO intervention in Kosovo a proof that Europe was still far too dependent on the USA when solving European problems, not only 'in its own territory, but also in the wider field within the range of its rays, that is, in the area that may one day belong to it'.[39]

So Havel has come to embrace the EU more and more unconditionally as the only suitable framework for the propagation and defence of a basic set of European values. More than before, he has also begun to stress the importance of the EU at home, engaging in a sharp polemic with Václav Klaus and the ODS about Czech national interests and identity. Membership, Havel insists, is a unique historical chance for the Czech Republic, since the norms and values of the EU ought to be shared also by the Czechs and since a healthy national life demands engagement in the surrounding world. To strengthen his argument Havel has repeatedly evoked T. G. Masaryk, the founding father of Czechoslovakia and a key historical authority, arguing that he too was in favour of European integration and of seeing the 'Czech question' in a global context.[40] Havel stresses that sovereignty and identity are not the same thing, and that surrendering parts of the country's sovereignty to a supranational body does not in any way threaten Czech national identity. Havel's conclusion seems to sum up nicely his present position: 'an open international environment and advanced democratic culture of our neighbours, friends and allies constitute the best ground for the advancement of our own uniqueness'.[41] For Havel, the more the Czechs engage in European integration, the more – or rather the better – they realise what is truly Czech.

Václav Klaus: the dilemmas of a 'Eurorealist'

In Václav Klaus's perception no such simple equation of harmony between the national and the European level exists, at least not as the latter has been defined by the EU. From the outset there has been an element of self-contradiction or paradox in his claims that the Czech Republic wants membership of the EU when held up against his outspoken criticism of the same EU, and while in his years as Prime Minister Klaus self-confidently tried to reconcile or overcome these contradictions, he has begun to speak of them as an onerous political dilemma. But first a look at his views from 1992 to 1997:

For a start Klaus insisted that 'Europe can never be enlarged (or narrowed) by anybody. Europe is Europe no matter which institutions emerge in it', and that 'the Czech lands have always been a part of Europe'.[42] Speaking to the Council of Europe in Strasbourg in January1995 he expressed his belief that Europe was 'more than the sum of its parts . . . and that Europe is very real' even if one cannot see or touch it.[43] Europe thus appears as a given entity, and unlike Havel Klaus has devoted little energy to defining its substance or borders.[44] Klaus has also spoken with sarcasm about a 'western Europe that likes to call itself Europe',[45] but when in Bavaria in 1993 he said that 'if we want to live in European contexts we must, after forty years of separation, Europeanise ourselves internally and also in our foreign politics'.[46] 'European' and 'Europeanise' clearly referred to western European norms for economic and political life. Similarly, in the statement that 'Europe should strive to contribute to the integration and inner stability of the countries of the former eastern bloc',[47] 'Europe' as an acting subject can hardly mean anything but western Europe or the EU. And so even Klaus, for all his justified opposition to it, has difficulties escaping the self-centred 'Euro-discourse' of the EU.

Like Havel, Klaus has a model for the interpretation of European history. Whereas in Havel's vision a dynamism arose from the struggle between the principles of force or co-operation, nationalism or civil society, Klaus finds the motor of development in the tension ('as old as Europe itself') between 'unifying, pan-European tendencies on the one hand and individualising, more national aspirations on the other'.[48] Klaus insisted that 'Europe in its very substance is a "multi-speed" continent' and that both division or fragmentation and forced unification were bad for Europe.[49] Still most of his warnings were spent on unification: When introducing the tension between unifying and individualising principles, he continued the list with oppositions of protectionism and free market, statism and liberalism, dogma and common sense, lies and truth, making it very clear that the adherents of a 'pan-European government, pan-European currency, pan-European standard for the shape and size of bottles of beer or wine, a common European citizenship, a common European social legislation and such things'[50] belonged on the side of the former.

Klaus's negative view of European unification was closely related to his view of the nation. Klaus persisted that 'the whole idea of Europe should not be based on a too simplistic repudiation of nationalism',[51] and warned against replacing legitimate national feelings with an 'artificial, bureaucratic supranationalism imposed from above'.[52] 'It is already clear now', he said at another occasion, 'that different Europeans will not seek their identity in a Europe totally without borders, but on the contrary with the help of them. It is borders or clear demarcations that give us a clear identity'.[53] Klaus was full of praise for the British conservatives, and he joined John Major in saying that the EC must remain a union of sovereign nation states.[54] He was convinced that the overwhelming majority of Europeans would accept European integration only if the nation-state remained the primary unit. The debate about integration could then focus on what and how much to transfer to the supra-national level, but not on the hierarchy of institutions as such.[55]

This allowed Klaus to identify the central political challenge for the Czechs in their relationship to Europe/the EU as follows: 'The Czech Republic is facing one important task: how to be European without at the same time dissolving in Europeanness like a lump of sugar in a cup of coffee'[56] or, with a metaphor that reveals a certain defensiveness in his perception of the Czech position *vis-à-vis* (western) Europe, present also in Havel's reasoning: 'The post-communist countries . . . face a double task today: finding their own identities and not losing them straightaway on their road to Europe.'[57]

Klaus has offered two rather conflicting interpretations of EC/EU integration history that share only their rejection of Maastricht. In his first account, he portrays the present version of integration as founded on ideological paradigms from the first two-thirds of the twentieth century, characterised by a distrust of a spontaneously working free market and a belief in size, unification, planning and state intervention. These paradigms gave birth to the Maastricht project, which however in Klaus's opinion increasingly appears as outdated, practically and theoretically. Therefore, Klaus predicts, the EU will change towards deregulation and economic openness, towards 'a belief in the market and not in the state'.[58] In this 'optimistic' scenario, Maastricht is the swan-song of an old EC philosophy, but Klaus also has another account which evaluates the 'original vision' of the EC far more positively, while seeing Maastricht as the first omen of something new and threatening:

> The original vision – prevention of a replay of the disastrous Second World War, to integrate Germany into Europe in a new way, to promote the values of freedom and democracy against the communist ideology, to promote welfare by removing trade barriers and by creating a common market – was more or less accepted by most Europeans. That vision has been quietly replaced by a more comprehensive vision – Europeanism, more co-ordination from a single place [etc.].[59]

This contradiction may reflect Klaus's unease about the future direction of the EU, but it also reveals an ambiguity in his evaluation of integration. The second account clearly recognises the *political* value of the EC/EU project, while elsewhere Klaus has denied it any value at all: 'the success of western Europe depended not on the institutions of the European Community, but on a free society, private ownership and a free market'.[60]

Klaus's answer to why at all he wants his country to join this kind of EU is held in very general terms: 'we do not want to be deprived of advantages stemming from membership in European institutions . . . [and] we share the same European values as our western neighbours', and so 'we are ready to participate in a reasonable European integration.'[61] The exact nature of these advantages remains unclear, but a 'reasonable' integration clearly refers to international co-operation based on economic liberalism. This reduction of the idea of the EC/EU to free trade and open markets allowed Klaus to declare his country ready for integration before the EU itself, and to ask the EU 'for a realistic timetable for the major moves toward integration and, above all, for a permanent, pragmatic scrutiny of the nature of this integration'.[62]

Klaus was also much in favour of a 'multi-speed' Europe since it facilitated Czech integration into the EU. 'Widening' rather than 'deepening' was his priority, since, as he put it, it was easier to get on a slow train than on an express train. His resistance to the Maastricht Treaty therefore seems based also on a fear that the concentration on 'internal affairs' might make the EU forget eastern Europe.[63] But like Havel, Klaus had difficulties offering concrete arguments for why the EU should enlarge, and he too resorted to moralistic appeals to the 'Europeanness' of western Europe and to its responsibility to 'heal the unorganic wound between the West and the East of this continent'.[64]

Klaus's basic views have changed little after his ousting as Prime Minister in late 1997, but in recent years the ambiguities and inner conflicts in his attitude to the EU have become even more pronounced. Klaus openly admitted in an interview in 1999 that there was no sensible alternative to the ongoing European integration process, even if he was deeply sceptical of its present form, and that this left him in a burdensome position.[65] Several factors have made Klaus's dilemma more pronounced. First, Czech membership has come closer and so too has the moment of clear-cut decision making. Secondly, the EU has not embraced the neo-liberal principles as envisaged by Klaus in the early 1990s; on the contrary Social Democrats dominate in most member states. And finally, Klaus has realised that he/the Czech Republic have very little leverage with EU policies, in short they have to accept the EU as it is.[66]

Klaus's attacks on the EU have become increasingly vehement: he accuses the integration process of being elitist, without popular support and in reality directed against the interests of the citizens of the member states. In particular, the sanctions against Austria upset Klaus, who saw them as proof that an 'international intellectual elite' had defined itself as the only true 'holders of truth, reason, and progress' and waged a war against the sovereign nation-state without hesitating to discard 'standard political mechanisms' to obtain its goals.[67] Since the mid-1990s Klaus had been an outspoken critic of the EMU from an economic point of view, but now he also stresses how the EMU will call forth a fiscal and political union, a United States of Europe, again without a proper prior discussion, and without a proper strong political leadership to even explain or defend the necessity of these steps.[68]

Mostly, Klaus has directed his wrath against the 'eurocrats' in Brussels. Each year in November the publishing of the Commission's annual reports on the Czech Republic's progress towards accession has provoked a broadside, as in 1998 when Klaus challenged not only the facts of the report, but also its overall legitimacy, arguing that 'civil servants have nothing to blame the governments of any state for'.[69] These attacks have evolved into a series of public quarrels with the Commissioner for Enlargement, Günter Verheugen, revealing both men as capable of astonishing verbal abuse.[70] In his 1998 article Klaus also accused the Brussels bureaucracy of conspiring against enlargement, a recurring motif revealing that Klaus is still at least as afraid of exclusion as he is of the EU. In Stockholm in December 2000 he even indirectly admitted a certain shared interest between the Commission and the applicant countries: 'The bigger the EU, the bigger the political role and prestige of EU bureaucracy. As a result of it Brussels is more in favour of enlargement than individual member countries.'[71] One can, however, hardly accuse Klaus of having tried to capitalise politically upon this insight.

For all this hostility, Klaus still insists that it is in the interest of the Czech Republic (and all applicant countries) to join the EU as soon as possible. Interestingly, he has offered more concrete arguments at home than abroad. In an interview in 1999 with the magazine *Prostor* Klaus stressed the economic gains, not so much from the structural funds as from an inflow of direct foreign investment following the Czech Republic's inclusion in the European economic space with its standard legal framework.[72] In Stockholm, by contrast, he said that it was difficult to calculate what would be most costly, entering or not entering, and offered only the 'no alternative' argument, the unwillingness to 'stay in a sort of vacuum'.[73] In a speech in London in January 2001 he drove this argument even further, claiming that 'unfortunately, membership or non-membership in EU has become a differentiating factor suggesting who is and who is not a "normal, standard (or standardized), mature, decent, obedient European" country.' And so, he said, the Czechs just had to bow their heads and join.[74]

Klaus's sarcasm is strong enough to undermine his surface message, as are many other of his political moves. In 2000 Klaus vehemently attacked the negotiation policy of the Social Democratic government, calling it an 'unconditional capitulation' to the EU and accusing it of being uncritical and self-humiliating in its adoration of Brussels as before them the Communists with regard to Moscow. He also complained in June 2000 about the prevailing 'Protectorate mentality' in the country (a hint at Czech subservience during the occupation), whereby he managed to associate the EU with both Nazism and Communism.[75] In June 2000 Klaus also suggested an early Czech referendum on the EU to be held before the conclusion of the negotiation talks, an idea sharply criticised by all other parties as a populist attempt to destabilise the negotiations. And in March 2000 Klaus surprised everyone with a very critical speech on T. G. Masaryk, whom he accused of being a socialist and an enemy of freely competing political parties, and of damaging national interests by wasting time on far too lofty visions of a new European and global order.[76] Czech politicians, it follows, should care only about the national interest.

Conclusion

Klaus's critique of Masaryk was unmistakably directed at Havel who has striven hard to bolster his own authority by styling himself as a natural heir to Masaryk's ideas and policies. But the incident also reveals the emphasis both men have put on offering authoritative interpretations of the 'meaning' of Czech national life, including its place in the world. Eventually, the perception of Europe and self can hardly be separated. The image of Europe often contains a self-portrait, and conversely the view of the nation influence the approach to its surroundings.

So, the divergent views on European integration offered by Havel and Klaus stem considerably from their sharp disagreement on the role of the nation-state. For Klaus the nation-state is the cornerstone of everything – sovereignty, identity, political and economic decision making. Europe, he claimed, was more than the sum of its parts, but his emphasis is on the parts, not on the whole, which is best served if not in any way institutionalised or unified. Therefore, the EU has come to serve as a main 'Other' in Klaus's discourse, the incarnation of everything the Czechs are not or should not be. For Havel, by contrast, the nation-state is not a value in itself; if anything, it is an obstacle to the realisation of the values that he associates with Europe as a whole. Havel dissociates identity from sovereignty and seeks to present Europe, and increasingly even the existing EU, as the natural 'home' for the Czechs. His 'Other' is internalised, it is the dark side of the Czech past and present: nationalism, xenophobia, materialism, self-sufficiency. If in Klaus's 'philosophy' of European history the task was to find an *equilibrium* between unification and fragmentation, best achieved in the nation-state, Havel's 'philosophy' demanded the *victory* of good over evil, of a Europe of democracy over a Europe of force. In that sense, Havel's vision is far more radical than that of Klaus.

But the discourses of the two also have many common features. Both insist on enlargement and for both, integration finds its primary justification in Europe's character as a civilisational entity. When appealing to the EU, both claim a Czech *historical right* to belong to the (Western) European community and both talk of a *historic chance* to overcome the 'unnatural' division of Europe (though without being very specific about the character of this chance, Havel's threats about the consequences of the opposite excepted). This line of reasoning may well express a fear that enlargement will cost the EU (as admitted by Klaus), and that a standard political or economic cost–benefit analysis is not enough to bring about the political will to enlarge in the member states. With regard to the Czech interest, the *lack of alternatives* argument has been curiously predominant, both with Havel who embraces the present EU, and with Klaus who deplores it. It seems that the fear of being excluded, present in both men's discourse, testifies to an acute awareness of the discrepancy between the proclaimed 'belonging' to Europe and the reality of an EU–Europe not quite recognising this.

Notes

1 Česká republika a myšlenka evropské integrace, speech at the reception of the Konrad Adenauer Prize, Prague, 21 December 1993, printed in V. Klaus, *Česká cesta* (Praha: Profile, 1994), pp. 149–154 (quotation p. 152). The popular slogan of 1989 of a '*return*

to Europe' is a fine example of this use of Europe as a metaphor. In the perspective of homecoming all the things that were to be introduced – from a new political system to new habits of everyday life – were familiarised and given historical credibility, and with its connotations of the prodigal son the slogan also contained a clear appeal to 'Europe' for acceptance.

2 The daily *Lidové noviny* brought an informal opinion poll in the Spring of 2001 on who had influenced Czech society most in the 1990s: Havel was in the first place and Klaus in second. Third, was not the prime minister since 1998, Miloš Zeman, but the charismatic owner of a private TV station, Vladimír Železný.

3 Needless to say any comprehensive account of Czech views must be supplemented with an analysis of other actors, including the political parties, the 'expert community', and the general public. See the contribution by Petr Kopecký and Peter Učeň on attitudes towards the EU among the Czech political parties. Expert views and perceptions of Europe and the EU in selected Czech media are analysed in P. Bugge, 'Home at Last? Czech Views of Joining the European Union', in N. Parker, and B. Armstrong (eds), *Margins in European Integration* (Basingstoke and London: Macmillan, 2000), pp. 214–225.

4 The 'Utopian' approach primarily involved security, as the dissolution of both NATO and the Warsaw Pact was initially envisaged and the CSCE presented as the nucleus of a new security system. But in May 1990 Havel acknowledged the vitality of NATO and in 1991 Czechoslovak leaders began to advocate membership for their country. In a similar spirit Havel suggested in May 1990 before the Council of Europe that this organisation could become 'the core around which a future European Confederation would crystallise.' V. Havel, *The Art of the Impossible: Speeches and Writings, 1990–1996* (New York and Toronto: Alfred A. Knopf, 1997), p. 42. This vision of the Council of Europe, rather than the EC, as the nucleus of a politically united Europe was brought up occasionally in 1990–1991. See J. Šedivý, From Dreaming to Realism – Czechoslovak Security Policy, *Perspectives* 4, Winter 1994/95, 61–71, and R. Břach, *Die Außenpolitik der Tschechoslowakei zur Zeit der 'Regierung der nationalen Verständigung'*, Schriftenreihe des Bundesinstituts für ostwissenschaftliche und internationale Studien, Köln, Band 22 (Baden-Baden: Nomos Verlagsgesellschaft, 1992).

5 V. Handl, 'Translating the Czech Vision of Europe into Foreign Policy: Historical Conditions and Current Approaches', in B. Lippert, and H. Schneider (eds), *Monitoring Association and Beyond: The European Union and the Visegrád States*, Europäische Schriften des Instituts für Europäische Politik; Bd. 74 (Bonn: Europa Union Verlag, 1995), pp. 130 ff, 133 ff; see also V. Handl, 'Tschechische Europapolitik: Profilsuche und Kursbestimmung', *Integration* Vol. 16, No. 3 (1993), 125–137, at pp. 129 ff; V. Cihlár and J. Hrich, 'Achievements of the Czech Republic on its Road to the European Union', in B. Lippert, and H. Schneider (eds), *Monitoring Association and Beyond: The European Union and the Visegrád States*, Europäische Schriften des Instituts für Europäische Politik, Band 74 (Bonn: Europa Union Verlag, 1995), p. 333. Václav Havel was elected Czech President shortly after the creation of the Czech Republic, but much of the foreign policy initiative passed over to the cabinet, although the Czech constitution reserves an important constitutional role for the president in foreign relations and forces the government and the president to co-ordinate their activities in this field. Handl, 'Translating the Czech Vision of Europe into Foreign Policy, p. 144 ff; A. Gerloch, *et. al.*, *Ústavní systém České republiky* (Praha: Prospektrum, 1994), p. 101 ff.

6 Klaus for *International Herald Tribune*, 1 February 1993, quoted from Handl, 'Translating the Czech Vision of Europe into Foreign Policy, p. 136, note 22; see also p. 134, and V. Leška, *et al.*, 'Česká republika a region střední Evropy', in V. Kotyk (ed.), *Česká zahraniční politika: Úvahy o prioritách* (Praha: Ústav mezinárodních vztahů, 1997), pp. 87–124, at p. 114.

7 J. Jakš, 'The Czech Republic on the Road to the European Union: Problems of the Mutual

Interaction of the Transformation and Integration Processes in the 1990s', *Perspectives* 3 Summer (1994), 141–149, at 148.

8 At one point European Commissioner Hans van den Broek had to tell Klaus that 'it is not the European Union which wants to join the Czech Republic'. Quoted from M. Rhodes, 'Post-Visegrád Cooperation in East Central Europe', *East European Quarterly* Vol. 33, No. 1 (March 1999), 51–67, at p. 67, note 41. From 1996 onwards, in particular,growing economic and domestic political problems also led to a moderation in tone. Also, the government ealised that the EU favoured enlargement in groups, which led to a renewed Czech interest in regional co-operation. See Rhodes, 'Post-Visegrád Cooperation in East Central Europe', Leška, *et al.*, 'Česká republika a region střední Evropy', p. 111.

9 See the debate in *Lidové noviny, Právo, Dnes* and other dailies on 5 June 2000 and in the following week. The fall of Klaus was accompanied by a split in his party leading to the departure of many more 'pro-European' politicians, including former foreign minister Josef Zieleniec. This may also have facilitated Klaus's taking a more radical stance.

10 V. Havel, *Letní přemítání* (Praha: Odeon, 1991) pp. 63, 67. In the same process, Havel downplayed the role of the nation-state, envisioning a Europe (including Czechoslovakia) in fifteen years' time where the EC had a strongly integrated political leadership, where borders had become a mere formality and where many competences were delegated to a supra-national or a regional level. i.e. a clearly federalist scenario. *Ibid.*, p. 87.

11 *Ibid.*, p. 64. See also Havel's speech at the reception of the Charlemagne Price, Aachen 9 May 1991; printed in V. Havel, *Vážení občané (projevy Červenec 1990 – Červenec 1992)* (Praha: Lidové noviny, 1992), pp. 77–80.

12 See Havel's speech to the US Congress in February 1990 and his May 1990 speech in Strasbourg; both in Havel, *The Art of the Impossible*, quotes from pp. 13 and 41.

13 Havel, *Letní přemítání*, p. 64; see also his Aachen speech of May 1991 (reference in note 11).

14 Quoted from Havel, *The Art of the Impossible*, p. 47. This wording might include both the Baltic nations and the Ukrainians or Russians, but in Aachen in 1991 Havel said that 'no future European order is thinkable without the European nations of the Soviet Union, which are an inseparable part of Europe, and without links to the great community of nations the Soviet Union is becoming today', implicitly suggesting that the Baltic nations are more genuinely 'European' than the Russians. Quoted from Havel, *Vážení občané*, p. 79.

15 From a speech at the CSCE Summit in Helsinki, printed in Havel, *Vážení občané*, pp. 194–197; quotation from p. 196.

16 Havel spelled this out at a conference in Prague June 1991 on European Confederation, attended also by President Mitterrand, an ardent spokesman of confederation as a supplement to a smaller, strongly integrated EC. Havel's speech is printed in Havel, *Vážení občané*, pp. 86–92.

17 Novoroční projev, 1 January 1992, printed in Havel, *Vážení občané*, pp. 133–140, quotation from pp. 137 ff.

18 Speech to the Polish *Sejm* and Senate, Warsaw 25 January 1990, printed in Havel (1990), pp. 39–46, quotation on p. 44.

19 T. G. Ash has discovered a similar 'semantic division of labour' in Havel's pre-1989 writings, T. G. Ash, *The Uses of Adversity: Essays on the Fate of Central Europe* (New York: Random House, 1989), pp. 183 ff.

20 Said at the Prague conference on European Confederation (see note 16), quotation in Havel, *Vážení občané*, p. 91. A similar use of the West–East dichotomy and the invocation of the threat of a spillover appeared in Havel's speech at the CSCE summit in July 1991 (see note 15).

21 Havel also used concepts such as 'European civilisation', 'the classical European west' or

even 'Western European' and 'Central Asian' spheres of civilisation. See the article 'The Co-Responsibility of the West', *Foreign Affairs* (22 December, 1993), printed in Havel, *The Art of the Impossible*, pp. 134–141.

22 Speech at a NATO conference in Warsaw, 21 June 1996, where Havel also juxtaposed the 'Euro-Atlantic region' and the 'Euro-Asian entity'. Printed in V. Havel, *Projevy a jiné texty z let 1992–1999 (Spisy 7)*, (Praha: Torst, 1999), pp. 609–615, quotation on p. 613.

23 Havel in Vilnius 17 April 1996, speech printed in V. Havel, *Projevy a jiné texty z let 1992–1999*, pp. 579–595, quotation on p. 591. On 1 July 1997 in Kiev, Havel declared with a mixture of objective and subjective arguments that 'Not only geographically, but also because of its whole past history and the values it now embraces with an ever greater emphasis, Ukraine is a thoroughly European nation.' Speech printed in V. Havel, Projevy a jiné texty z let 1992–1999, p. 690–698, quotation on p. 697.

24 From the Vilnius speech, quotation in Havel, *Projevy a jiné texty z let 1992–1999*, p. 593. In Kiev Havel mentioned how Ukraine finds itself in the 'gravitational fields' of 'the Euro-American world' and on the other hand 'the Russian Federation, which has always been and will remain a big Euro-Asian power' (*Ibid.*, p. 697).

25 At the CSCE Summit in Vienna, 8 October 1993 Havel said: 'The greatness of the idea of European integration on democratic foundations consists in its capacity to overcome the old Herderian idea of the nation-state as the highest expression of national life. Thus, European integration should – and must, if it is to succeed – enable all the nationalities to realise their national autonomy within the framework of a broad civil society created by the supranational community.' Printed in Havel, *The Art of the Impossible*, pp. 128–133, quotation on p. 130.

26 Novoroční projev 1 January 1994, printed in *Ibid.*, p. 150.

27 Speech to the European Parliament, 8 March 1994, printed in Havel, *Projevy a jiné texty z let 1992–1999*, pp. 219–230, on the issue of sovereignty see in particular p. 222.

28 Speech at the reception of the Charlemagne Prize, Aachen 15 May 1996. Printed in Havel, *Projevy a jiné texty z let 1992–1999*, pp. 596–608, quotation on p. 602.

29 Havel presented this interpretation both at home and abroad, most consistently perhaps in his speeches to the European Parliament in March 1994, and in Aachen in 1996 (see notes 27 and 28).

30 Reference as in note 27, quotation on p. 228. Ironically, the EC had especially since the mid-1980s invested a lot in this kind of 'identity politics', complete with flag, hymn and history books, with very poor results. See B. Boxhoorn, 'European Identity and the Process of European Unification: Compatible Notions?', in M. Wintle (ed.), *Culture and Identity in Europe* (Avebury: Aldershot, 1996), pp. 133–145 and A. D. Smith, 'National Identity and the Idea of European Unity, *International Affairs*, Vol. 28, No.1 (1992), 55–76.

31 Havel, *Projevy a jiné texty z let 1992–1999*, p. 224.

32 See Havel's 1995 New Year's Address, printed in Havel, *Projevy a jiné texty z let 1992–1999*, pp. 343–357, especially p. 354. In his speech to the Parliament on 9 December 1997 – during the government crisis that lead to the resignation of Klaus – Havel criticised the pride, provincialism and parochialism that had led his government to disrupt the Visegrád co-operation and neglect the task of explaining to the citizens the historic importance of membership of the EU and NATO. Speech printed in Havel, *Projevy a jiné texty z let 1992–1999*, pp. 733–753.

33 The 1995 Geuzenpenning, Vlaardingen, 13 March 1995, printed in Havel, *The Art of the Impossible*, pp. 188–192, quotation on p. 191.

34 '*Mnichovanské nebezpečí se opět nad Evropou vznáší*'. Speech printed in V. Havel, *Projevy a jiné texty z let 1992–1999*, pp. 560–578, quotation from p. 576. The reference is to the appeasement politics of the Munich conference in September 1938 where Britain and France for fear of a confrontation with Germany 'betrayed' Czechoslovakia, and the sentence contains an indirect critique of western passivity in former Yugoslavia.

35 In Aachen in 1996 Havel said with an explicit warning to the EU: 'unless democrats proceed in a timely manner to build the internal structure of Europe as a single political entity, others will start building it their way – and the democrats could be left with only their eyes to cry with. The demons that so fatally affected European history – most disastrously in the twentieth century! – are biding their time'. Reference as in note 28, quotation on p. 603.

36 Speech from the internet: www.hrad.cz/president/Havel/speeches/2000/1602_uk.html (as of April 2003). Havel does admit that he himself had not in earlier years speculated about his European identity and that he would even have found the question odd or pathetic.

37 *Ibid.* Havel now also showed far more understanding than before for the necessity of complex institutional and administrative procedures, denying that this in itself represented any 'democratic deficit'. See his article in the daily *Mladá fronta dnes*, 24 March 2001, *Identitu nám nikdo zvenčí nemůže vzít*, English version on the internet: www.hrad.cz/president/Havel/speeches/2001/2403_uk.html (as of April 2003).

38 Havel first aired these ideas in a speech to the French Senate in March 1999 (found at: www.hrad.cz/president/Havel/speeches/1999/0303_uk.html (as of April 2003), and repeated them in a more elaborate form in Strasbourg the following year (reference as in note 36).

39 From the Strasbourg speech (reference as in note 36). Havel suggests that the EU must become a 'human rights policeman' within the whole area defined as belonging to 'European civilisation'. Havel is not very explicit about how an independent EU as a strong actor in European security combines with a continued strong – and enlarging – NATO, another major concern of Havel's in the late 1990s.

40 See his speech on the Czech national holiday, 28 October 1998, printed in Havel, *Projevy a jiné texty z let 1992–1999*, pp. 812–815, and his speech in Hodonin, 6 March 2000, on the 150th anniversary of Masaryk's birth, printed in *Lidové noviny*, 7 March 2000, p. 11. Already in Olomouc, 7 March 1993, he had used Masaryk's authority in support of an activist stance in the Yugoslav crisis, speech printed in Havel, *Projevy a jiné texty z let 1992–1999*, pp. 65–70.

41 From a speech at the Prague Castle on the Czech national holiday, 28 October 2000, found at: www.hrad.cz/president/Havel/speches/2000/2810_uk.html (as of April 2003).

42 Evropa v perspektivě setkání v Davosu, *Lidové noviny* 7 February 1994, also in Klaus, *Česká cesta*, pp. 166–168, quotations from pp. 166 and 167.

43 'Europe: Our Visions and Our Strategies', speech delivered to the Council of Europe, Strasbourg, 30 January 1995, printed in V. Klaus, *Renaissance: The Rebirth of Liberty in the Heart of Europe* (Washington, D.C: Cato Institute, 1997), pp. 95–100, quotations from pp. 95 and 96.

44 Terminologically Klaus keeps to 'Europe', avoiding Havel's 'Euro-American civilisation' and using 'the West' only rarely (and then with 'western Europe' as a sub-category). Speaking in Bavaria in 1993 he once referred to 'western Christendom, which – together with eastern Christendom – became the foundation stone of European civilisation' (Změny v Praze a evropské souvislosti, 22 March 1993, printed in Klaus, *Česká cesta*, pp. 131–137, quotation on p. 131), whereas in one of his rare references to Russia Klaus placed the country outside Europe, though more for political than for historical or cultural reasons: 'Europe and the world should not close themselves before [Russia], they should not isolate it, although they on no account must offer it membership of such exclusive "clubs" as NATO or the European Union. Ten years is too little to realise a consistent transformation of such a country.' Deset let 'perestrojky', Lidové noviny 6 March 1995, p. 5.

45 V předvečer kodaňské schůzky, *Lidové noviny* 14 March 1993, also in V. Klaus, *Česká cesta*, pp. 147–148.

46 Reference as in note 44, quotation on p. 132.

47 From his March 1993 speech in Bavaria (see note 44), quotation from V. Klaus, *Česká cesta*, p. 137. Generally, Klaus is less afraid than Havel of the term eastern Europe, including also his own country.
48 Evropské zadrhele a maso, *Lidové noviny* 19 April 1993, printed in V. Klaus, *Česká cesta*, p. 53–54. Quoting T.G. Masaryk, Klaus here calls it a task for Europe to create harmony between the forces of centralisation and autonomy.
49 Vicerychlostní Evropa, *Lidové noviny* 19 September 1994, printed in V. Klaus, *Dopočítávání do jedné* (Praha: Management Press, 1995), pp. 136–138, quotation from p. 136.
50 Reference as in note 49. Quotation on pp. 53–54. Accordingly, Klaus warned against making Europe bigger only to be able to compete with the USA or with Japan, since 'we don't believe in size'.
51 From a speech in Prague, May 1994, printed in V. Klaus, *Renaissance*, pp. 105–108, quotation on p. 107.
52 From the Konrad Adenauer Foundation Prize acceptance speech, Prague, December 1993, printed in V. Klaus, *Renaissance*, pp. 119–125, quotation from p. 120.
53 Nerozpustit se v evropeismu, speech in Frankfurt 18 January 1993, printed in V. Klaus, *Česká cesta*, pp. 138–140, quotation on pp. 139–40. It is interesting to compare with Havel who, though adherent of a Europe where borders lose their importance, was equally eager to define such borders or demarcations, only *around* Europe rather than *within* it.
54 John Major o Evropě, *Lidové noviny*, 26 September 1993, printed in V. Klaus, *Česká cesta*, pp. 143–144. On 17 February 1996 Klaus wrote in *Lidové noviny*: 'It is our duty to give our country to our children at least in the shape in which we got it from our parents. Not a single square metre smaller, not a bit less sovereign. And no negative change in this direction may follow from the present Czech-German discussions, nor from today's at times somewhat simplified pan-European unionist plans.' ('Podivná demagogická aktivita ČSSD'). This was said when the Klaus government was exposed to populist attacks for selling out of Czech national interests to the Germans, but if his statement on sovereignty were to be taken literally, it openly contradicts the official policy of Klaus's own government, as well as the obligations accepted by it with the signing of the 'Europe agreement' with the EU.
55 Reference as in note 50. See especially pp. 136–137.
56 From Klaus's speech in Bavaria, 1993 (see note 44), quotation on p. 136.
57 From the Adenauer speech (see note 53), quotation on p. 125. Repeated in May 1994 in Prague (see note 52), quotation in Klaus, *Renaissance*, p. 106.
58 From the Adenauer speech (note 53), quotation on p. 123. Some of the most vehement attacks on the Maastricht 'spirit' are omitted in this English translation; compare with the Czech version in Klaus, *Česká cesta*, pp. 149–154, in particular p. 151.
59 From the Strasbourg speech January 1995 (see note 43), quotation on p. 99.
60 Evropa v perspektivě setkání v Davosu, *Lidové noviny*, 7 February 1994, printed in Klaus, *Česká cesta*, pp. 166–168, quotation on p. 166. Klaus repeatedly insists that European institutions are only means, not goals in their own right, and that as such they make sense only if they support free trade and a free market.
61 From the May 1994 speech (see note 52), quotations from p. 105, emphasis added.
62 From the Adenauer speech (note 53), quotation on p. 125.
63 'A deepening of the European Union without us is not and cannot be a victory for us.' Reference as in note 50, quotation from p. 138. In 1993, Klaus was very upset about the Maastricht Treaty's attempt to focus only on deepening at a time when the collapse of communism gave all of Europe a historic challenge and a historic chance. Therefore, he claimed, the post-communist countries were fully entitled to criticise the protectionism and lack of openness in the West. V předvečer kodaňské schůzky, *Lidové noviny* 14 June 1993, printed in Klaus, *Česká cesta*, pp. 147–148.

64 From the Bavaria speech (see note 44), quotation on p. 137.
65 Česká cesta do Evropy: přání nebo realita? Interview with Václav Klaus and Miloslav Vlk, in *Prostor* pp.43–44, 1999, pp. 43–50, see especially p. 43.
66 This already dawned upon Klaus in his last years in office. In a parliamentary debate on the Czech application for membership, February 1996 he proclaimed: 'we must say that we enter this organisation such as it is. I think that none of us takes it seriously that we could hand in an application and . . . trumpet forth in advance that we take half of it and not the other half, I think that everybody knows well that such a thing does not come into consideration'. Found at the home-page of the Czech Parliament: (www.psp.cz/eknih/1993ps/stenprot/039schuz/s039022.htm). This is a far cry from Klaus's lecturing the EU around 1993, but if in 1996 Klaus was ready to accept 'the whole menu' this idea has since then become increasingly unpalatable to him.
67 Klaus in a speech in Wachau, Austria, 23 June 2000. Found at Klaus's home-page: www.klaus.cz/klaus2/asp/clanek.asp?id=VQ0arfbPd1Og (as of April 2003). Klaus had been equally critical of the military intervention in Kosovo.
68 See the Wachau speech (note 67), and Klaus's speech in Stockholm, 13 September 2000, found at: www.klaus.cz/klaus2/asp/clanek.asp?id=gxyrBAuCozFV (as of April 2003). See also his article Bruselský komisař a česká referenda, *Večerník Praha*, 15 June 2000.
69 From an article in *Lidové noviny*, 5 November 1998.
70 The quarrel includes exchanges on Klaus's June 2000 call for an early Czech referendum on EU membership, on the Commissions annual report of November 2000, and again in June 2001 when Verheugen publicly accused Klaus of being a dangerous populist threatening the enlargement process.
71 Reference as in note 68. In an article of 16 November 2000 in the daily *Bohemia* (Důležitá nebo nedůležitá zpráva Evropské komise?) criticising Verheugen and the Commission's annual report, Klaus by contrast downplayed the political significance of the Commission, arguing that decision making ultimately rests with the member states who will allow enlargement only when they see an advantage in it (and Klaus has often stated that preserving all status quo is very advantageous for the member states). The logical conclusion of this line of reasoning is of course that if inter-governmentalism still characterises all major decision-making in the EU there is much less to fear in terms of loss of sovereignty etc. than otherwise argued by Klaus.
72 Reference as in note 65, see in particular p. 48. Klaus also stressed the short-terms risks in terms of growing unemployment and increasing competition pressure.
73 Reference as in note 68.
74 Speech at a seminar of British Euro-sceptics, Chatham House, London, 12 January 2001, found at: www.klaus.cz/klaus2/asp/clanek.asp?id=dlCkllrcOha9 (as of April 2003). In the same speech Klaus expressed his hope that 'the balance between intergovernmentalism and supranationalism will not be fundamentally shifted', suggesting again an understanding of EU decision making contradicting his general demonising of the Brussels bureaucracy and the alleged 'Maastricht unification'.
75 See his article of 16 November 2000 (reference as in note 71), and the summary of his statements in Czech television and on an ODS conference in *Právo*, 12 June 2000. One might point out that at the same time Klaus and his ODS guarantee this government's survival!
76 Masarykův obraz v dnešním Česku, speech at a conference celebrating Masaryk's 150th birthday, printed in *Lidové noviny*, 4 March 2000. The attack on Masaryk's European policies is all the more striking because Klaus himself in the early 1990s repeatedly drew on Masaryk's authority, quoting him in support of his own arguments on the correct balance between centralising and autonomist forces. See for instance his May 1994 speech in Prague, reference as in note 51.

Catherine Perron

10

Local political elites' perceptions of the EU

The EU integration process in the West remained for many years in the hands of a small governmental elite. This 'spirit of elite democracy'[1] is increasingly criticised in the West. A wider participation of the citizens in EU-related decision processes is required everywhere and especially in East Central European accession processes. In these countries this particular model of integration is not valid.

The main reason for this is that citizens are bound to play a major role in the ratification process. Public opinion has a great importance and therefore a Western-type, elite-driven strategy is not sustainable. Governments have a weak legitimacy in post-communist countries, which means that a wider range of people and political actors than governmental elites should be involved in the accession process for the prospect of EU accession to be successfully completed. As Ágh notes, because of the growing dissatisfaction of the population with national elites, a 'new deal' or social contract is needed if people are to vote for EU integration in a referendum. There is a need for a wide-scale and substantial debate on the EU at all levels.[2] Therefore I will examine in this chapter the position local politicians have towards the EU enlargement.

The first and maybe most important reason to study elites, is because they play a major role in the diffusion of information and knowledge about the EU towards citizen. They should articulate and shape the debate. The role of elites is particularly crucial during periods of institutionalisation of a new political system, times in which 'the functions of political leaders are more comprehensive than merely decision-making or the articulation of interests of the electorate [. . .] Leadership is also about the interpretation of the events, and the "management of meaning"'.[3]

The local political elite, holding an intermediary position between the citizen and the national elites could be of strategic importance in this 'new deal' with the population. They should be an important and very effective instrument in the promotion of a (positive) image of Europe and of European integration and in the diffusion of knowledge and opinions on this subject. Therefore their attitudes towards integration matter.

From a domestic point of view, it is of importance to observe if the Czech intermediary elites (local politicians) break with the dominant discourse over the EU which is mainly influenced by former Prime Minister Václav Klaus, who himself has a very critical attitude.[4] Do intermediary elites provide the citizen with a more differentiated view on the topic? Do their statements vary from the dominant discourse, or do they only reproduce it? To what extent are alternative visions of Europe, such as President Havel's for example, taken over by these intermediary elites? A good sign for the Czech integration process and for democracy in general would be if they were able to enrich the debate.

Further, local politicians will play a large role in establishing the Czech Republic's new regional administrations. These regions will benefit from EU financial support. Local elites will therefore become directly concerned with European matters.

We can also assume that local politics will increasingly become the breeding ground of the Czech national political elite, as in consolidated democracies. Today, by contrast to what has happened immediately after the revolution,[5] some experience with politics is required in order to enter the national political scene. Logically, local politicians who gained experience in running city councils are very likely to become tomorrow's national political elite. They will be in charge of the implementation of EU enlargement currently being negotiated. Some of them, moreover, might even be in national leadership roles, in the government or in parliament, by the time the Czech Republic enters the EU.

My data consist of a sample of 10–15 of the most influential local politicians inside the city councils of three different Czech cities: Plzen, Olomouc and Kladno.[6] There, I interviewed the mayor, deputy mayors, the heads of the political clubs and the most active people in the city council, selected by 'snowball effect'.[7] The scope of questions asked during the interviews was very broad and open-ended. Questions dealt with the political careers of the politicians, their experience with politics before and after 1989, and their views on Czech politics at the local and national levels. Even though they were not specifically about EU accession, this topic was nevertheless discussed.

This sample was not set up according to the national representation of the parties but rather, given the lesser importance of party membership at a local level, according to the most influential people in the city councils and party results in local elections.[8] The following, emphasises trends within this group of politicians as a whole, however I will point it out when substantial differences appear according to party lines.

This survey was conducted between March 1997 and March 1998. This was prior to the actual beginning of the negotiations, which will certainly affect the opinion of local politicians. Nevertheless it reveals the position that 'Europe' has in the Czech political debate, and helps us understand which images, representations and concepts of Europe were conveyed by the political elite. It is of major importance to the EU to be aware of patterns of behaviour, and attitudes of possible new members towards the Union. As Greek integration, which was in many ways done too rapidly, demonstrates, it is important to know the 'Euro-capacities and integration capacities' countries have. And this is not only true for economics but also for politics. It is important to know how well prepared citizens, and the political community as a whole are. Intermediary elites provide us with a good insight on this topic.

This study proceeds in four steps. First, I discuss the general question of the relevance of the enlargement debate of the Union to local elites. Second, I will look at how local political elites perceive and justify the Czech Republic's belonging to 'Europe'. Third, I look closely at the content of their image of the European Union. Finally, I examine local elites fears related to EU accession.

As we will see, local politicians have a surprisingly weak knowledge of the EU, its functioning and its goals. But more troubling is the low interest they show on the subject. This allows a vision of Europe, rooted in their pre-Second World War experience which is outdated, and a simplified and one-sided understanding of the European Union. All these elements lead us to the conclusion that intermediary elites are not yet prepared to take on the difficult task of preparing Czech citizens for EU accession. The responsibility of all this lies less with local politicians themselves than with national political actors (elites and parties) who failed in giving the issue of EU integration the importance and the attention it deserves, and with the EU itself who did not set as a priority the large involvement of populations in the accession process.

The relevance of the issue of integration to local politicians

It is important to note that the issue of the Eastern enlargement of the EU was very rarely raised spontaneously by local politicians during the interviews. This is, of course, partly due to the fact that this topic was not the primary theme of the interviews, but it remains a striking feature of the elites' attitude. Whereas other specific features of Czech foreign policy were often mentioned in their answers to various questions about today's most important issues in politics (as for example relations with Germany or with various Eastern neighbours) or in domestic politics (the model of economic development, the question of privatisation, the mode of local administration or decentralisation), this one was not. Two points – the very low level of the debate, and a feeling of not being concerned with this issue – are the main explanatory factors for this.

The first striking feature is the lack of information local politicians have about the process of EU accession. When the question about their opinion on entering the European Union was raised, the common first reaction was to state their lack of knowledge about this specific subject, and then to complain about the deficiency of information. Local politicians often did not feel entitled to state an opinion, given their position. European integration was still perceived as related to the domain of a few experts. This proves the enormous need for information on this subject in the Czech Republic. As the head of the foundation for assistance to local administration[9] puts it, 'it is high time to tell the city-administratives that entering the EU will affect them: not only do they have to get prepared to deal with Brussels in order to ask for Community aid, but they will also be affected by various legislative changes, and by whole set of new administrative documents to be used'.[10]

This low level of knowledge is partly due to the fact that local politicians have had no concrete experience with the EU till today. The information available about this issue still remains too abstract.[11] This insufficiency might be partially completed once negotiations have started. At the time when these interviews were realised, this was not yet the case.

Further, this can be analysed as a problem connected to the political parties that failed in making their members aware of the crucial importance of this issue.[12] Parties, in their role as provider of information failed. This confirms Ágh's statement that 'the parliamentary parties and even more, the interest organisations are rather weak in this respect. They may have some Euro-ideas, but certainly, they do not have yet, or only in a very limited way, their own Euro-policies, with experts, staffs, and mobilisation capacity on Euro-issues',[13] but it also points out that the question of EU accession is not yet considered as a major one in the parties themselves.

The content of local politicians' remarks, which have a very superficial and vague character confirm this little knowledge. Europe and the EU are always evoked in general terms, and arguments for or against it are mainly generic ones. More specific terms connected to current debates about EU enlargement and future development, such as the Maastricht or the Amsterdam treaty, the EMU, federal versus confederal Europe, subsidiarity, implementing the *acquis communautaire* etc. never appear, neither do statements about effects expected at a local or regional level. The debate is still very unfocused. Arguments tend to be less rational than emotional. Local elites' statements are closer in this respect to public opinion[14] as shown by opinion polls among which 'uncertainty and confusion are dominant',[15] than to governmental positions.

The vagueness of local politicians' statements about EU accession makes it impossible to reflect opinions about technical issues as well as the possible effects of the integration at a local level. Such questions are not yet clearly articulated in local politicians' minds. Still, an analysis of the perceptions linked to 'Europe' and the process of integration, and of such things as mental maps, frontiers, self-definition, and images of the 'other' already tells us a lot about their attitudes towards the subject.

If local politicians admit that they do know little about the European Union and the process of integration, they do also willingly admit that this is far from being a major concern to them. The following reaction to the question about EU enlargement is widespread: 'it's an opinion . . . I don't know . . . I must admit that I myself do not have an opinion on this. I don't feel concerned, it doesn't concern my daily life' (An ODS city council representative).

This general attitude also indicates a disconnection between local politics and national politics which is a more general feature in the Czech Republic.[16] Local politicians have an understanding of their role and function in today's Czech system which is particular. They tend to insist on the fact that local politics are not comparable to national politics, party politics playing a lesser role. Local elites claim to be less subject to political infighting than their national counterparts. They voice a strongly anti-ideological position, affirming that local politics is the place for efficient policies, practically, pragmatically and concretely oriented, whereas national politics is presented as the opposite. This difference between national and local politics is partly true, but insisting so much on it, is also a way to avoid certain problems. It is a manner of saying that local politicians have clean hands, specially in a time of political crisis, and of not feeling concerned about difficult issues like that of European integration, for example.

Most of the time local elites answered the question about their position towards the European integration with the assertion that they would only give a 'general feeling' because they are not interested in national politics. They obviously connect this topic with foreign politics which allows them to say that they do not feel the need to keep informed about its developments. EU integration is rarely perceived as a process that could affect every domain of politics, even at a local level.

The unpreparedness of Czech politicians, except for a very small part of its national elite has, as a consequence, that there is an information vacuum on this subject that has to be filled. This makes it easier for a dominant discourse like Václav Klaus's one, to get a hold on the issue in the whole country.

An indisputable feeling of belonging to Europe

Before taking into account the European Union in particular, it seems important to look at the perception the Czechs have of Europe in a more general sense. After the fall of the Berlin wall, Europe needed to be redefined. The main questions were: which were its frontiers and what was 'Europe' standing for? Where did the former Soviet bloc countries belong to?

We shall first examine the mental maps which are linked today with the notion of 'Europe' for Czech local politicians; in other words, questioning where 'East' and 'West' lie, what these terms mean geographically, what 'Europe' is used for and how it is connected to the EU. We will try to figure out, where the Czechs stand, and what their self-understanding as Europeans is.

The vision of Europe of Czech local politicians tends to be outdated. Their discourse is full of references to the pre-communist past, which are used to explain many patterns of behaviour of today's Czech citizen. Experiences from the first half of the twentieth century often serve as explanatory factors for today's developments. Historical-cultural arguments prevail in their analysis of European identity. Czech local politicians do not doubt at all that their country belongs to Europe, even though their understanding of this term is very vague. Their mental maps – and this is specially true for the right-wing parties – include Bohemia in the 'western civilisation'. Arguments for this are diverse (historical, geographical, cultural, religious), but Christianity is the main one provided to demonstrate this belonging. As one of them puts it, 'these traditional values [the European ones] mostly come from an ideological conviction, and this [. . .] in Europe, is without debate Christianity, which is the pillar of European civilisation' (an KDU-ČSL city council representative).

It is mostly used in a negative way, in order to set a frontier between 'western civilisation' and 'eastern'. It is possible to draw a definition of 'eastern civilisation' in which local elites discern a tendency to carry on despotic types of regimes, and be subject to Islam. There is an amalgam made between Asia (as an economic threat because of the concurrence of a cheap labour force and of Chinese and Vietnamese emigration to the Czech Republic) and Islamic countries of the far or nearer East, which threaten with terrorist destabilisation.[17]

The religious argument of Christianity is very much used and seems to be the most obvious one to local politicians to justify their western roots. It is interesting to note that they do not perceive at all the presence of large immigrant Muslim populations inside the EU countries. This specific argumentation is not always used in a very rational way. There is a striking need to keep a distance from what is considered to be 'East' and non-European, in order to prove the 'natural' belonging of the Czechs to 'Europe' (which is mainly understood as the 'West').

Here images of 'the other' are relevant. It is clear that to the majority of local politicians, Czechs belong traditionally to this Western civilisation which stands for modernity and development. In their mental maps, this Western world does not extend much further behind the Czech Republic. Everything East of Moravia is seen a as a potential threat. It is interesting to notice that there is a certain vacuum of perceptions which is clearly due to the end of the Cold War. Certain concepts, such as 'Asia' and 'Islam' remain very unclear.

Europe in these terms, is experienced as a community of common values and cultures that should be defended against other cultures and values. The very problematic coexistence with the Roma minority is used to point out the impossibility or at least the great difficulties of the coexistence of various cultures.

> I can't imagine how Europe, your Europe, western Europe could be in contact with these waves [of immigrants from the East]. You know very well – in France you fight against it – it is enough with these immigrants, these people who have different mentalities, who are different from us ! [. . .] As far as Roma are concerned [. . .] this is a nation or a group of citizens which is rooted in its own habits. They have a different way of life. Maybe they used to live in an honest and correct – or let's say bearable way [. . .] But they are parasites, they weren't able to form their own community [. . .] they basically await what society will give them. [. . .]Tzigans are not able to live in reserves like American Indians, they have to be among citizen. Yes, I have to say, they need to be parasitical. (An KDU-CSL city council representative).

This proves, in the eyes of local politicians, the necessity to unite with countries that share the same historical, traditional and cultural background. They see a connection between the Roma issue and the problem of Islam. The latter is seen as the symbol of a radically different culture. Hence unifying with western Europe is seen from a defensive point of view, as a way to protect oneself against foreign influences believed too different to be assimilated.

As far as mental maps and frontiers are concerned, an analysis of the vision of Slovakia is very enlightening. Especially in the right-wing and Christian-democratic parties (ODS, ODA, KDU-ČSL[18]). Slovakia is considered as being part of this 'Eastern' world, regardless of the importance of Catholicism in this country,[19] whereas Bohemia is clearly part of the 'West'. Slovakia is surprisingly often presented and resented as a threat. The statements made in relation to this former sister-nation are the incarnation of the local elites' perception of threats to the Czech Republic by 'the other'. The discourse becomes often very emotional and irrational.

Mečiar's Slovakia represents the country through which destabilisation could gain the Czech Republic, thus, a country towards which the Czechs shall take their distances. 'Where is it written that something won't infiltrate through Slovakia? It doesn't have to be an open intervention, it could be for example the invasion of these Ukrainian Mafias to such an extent that they undermine us completely, so that then there could be a civil war, and so on!' (an ODA city council representative).

Slovakia is often used as an example of bad political influence, of 'oriental despotism', of a regime with a contagious political instability linked to the leftist, state-controlled, Mafiosi orientation. The persistence of Mečiar's regime, is due to the 'oriental mentalities' of its citizens and the influence of Russia. 'I absolutely do not like the way the situation in Slovakia develops [. . .] I was very opposed to the separation, but later I convinced myself out of my own experience that these people got crazy, like Hitler made fools of people in Germany' (an independent city council representative). This is of course the most radical assertion about this neighbour, which is stated as such only by a few right-wing politicians, nevertheless these kind of thoughts are wildly shared – even though in a milder way – among ODS, ODA and KDU-ČSL members.

Hence 'Europe' is seen as a way of establishing a maximum distance from these threatening neighbours, and to eastern influences. It is a way of defending the cultural homogeneity and political stability against the rest of the world and especially against a potential destabilisation coming from the East. 'It's beyond doubt that European civilisation, a united Europe, is the future for us. As far as we are concerned here in Europe, we do not have any real natural barriers that would protect us in case of an invasion of the Genghis Khan hordes. It is evident that if masses of Islam or Chinese invade, this will be a tragedy for us. It doesn't have to be direct, it can filter through unhappy Russia' (A KDU-ČSL city council representative).

This fear of destabilisation can be interpreted as one more sign of the feeling of uprooting the Czechs have after forty years of communist experience and the perception of the fragility of recent changes and the process of democratisation. This vision of Europe, attached to the past, which stresses the historic community, creates and nourishes the myth of tradition, and thereby provides the Czechs with an element of continuity, and the illusion of stability. It is linked to the perception the Czechs have of their own historical development as a continuity broken by the communist takeover in 1948. The communist period is analysed as an unhappy deviation of their 'natural' destiny, of which Western Europe is an example. Local politicians hold Western Europe for the image of what the Czech Republics development would have been, if there had been no communist takeover. The vision of the transformation process is the one of a rectifying revolution, of the return to what ought to be. 'The Czech mentality is very close to the German one, I would even say to the Bavarian one. We are also beer-brewers, we do not let ourselves destabilise easily, we are bound to the ground [. . .] but the difference between our people and the Bavarians is that they have grounds, whereas we do not have these grounds, we are uprooted. And we need to go back to this [. . .] in order to return to this traditional, classical direction, which Western democracies have' (A KDU-ČSL city council representative).

This is also a way to imply that the communist regime was imposed from the outside, thus exterior to Czech society. By avoiding asking about its roots in Czech history and society it permits one not to feel responsible for it. Because no critical analysis of the past is required, general amnesia is legitimated, which might have negative effects on the construction of democracy.

The idea of a 'return' to Europe and the image of the communist period which derives from it: a long deviation of some forty years, is also connected to the feeling that it is almost not necessary to explain why the Czechs should be part of the European Union. Local politicians' statements sense that they have always been part of Western Europe and that it was only an external coup in 1948 that separated them from the community of Western European states. Therefore they do not really see themselves as newcomers to the community of Western European states but more as lost sons[20] who after a long absence – historical deviation – return to their family. Implicitly, this means that integration is somehow a right.

The vision of Europe, of the EU, consists in one of a well functioning world made of prosperity, stability, democracy and security. This perception of a stable, functioning Europe is connected with the sense of continuity. Western Europe is perceived as a place of tradition, where nation-states have not been deeply affected by historical ruptures. This somehow idealistic vision[21] of a continuous, harmonious development in the West stands as an indicator of the depth of the trauma of the communist takeover in the Czech territories. The brutality of the shock still affects Czech society. Deep feelings of alienation and of uprooting are implicitly contained in these statements about Western development.

It is obvious that the European Union is linked to the image of the 'West' in general – that means the US included – in local politicians' assertions. This ambiguity has not yet completely disappeared. Their affirmations show that they want to join the West, that means benefiting from the above-mentioned factors (peace, democracy, security and well-being). However as the procedure of joining the EU started quite soon after the revolutions, people had little time to get familiar with the EU (at that time the EC) which was itself in the midst of a very rapid and profound transformation process,[22] realising what 'Europe' meant, beyond prosperity and stability, discovering that it is more complex than simply a club of prosperous countries trading with one another.

So far, it is possible to affirm that there is a clear feeling of belonging to 'Europe', meaning to the community of Western nations. This feeling is correlated to the fact that there doesn't appear to be an alternative to European integration. No other solution seems available to local politicians in a world which has become much more complex. The Union is the only way a small country such as the Czech Republic can resist 'globalisation' and defend itself against the wider world. There is no way the Czech Republic could remain alone in the new world order. 'About entering the Union there is no discussion. It is basically an inevitable necessity to join, because of economics and more generally because a society of the size of the Czech Republic cannot exist in the vacuum' (a KSČM city council representative).

The world became more complex with the disappearance of the Soviet empire and the end of the Cold War, but it is important to take into account that the Eastern European nations, being somehow protected against foreign influences and cut off from the outside world by the iron curtain, have not only been deprived of a clear-cut world order but they have also have had to face lots of aspects of the world that were unknown to them. They needed to get familiar with challenges that the Western countries were already facing for a longer period of time, and thus were more familiar with, like immigration for example.

It partly explains why local elites mostly provide us with defensive arguments when they advocate European unification. Unifying appears as a way of resisting new threats as, for example, the growing Asian 'empire'. The United States are quoted in this respect as the model for such a unification, which is realised in order to avoid a loss of influence in the world. There is a strong perception of the diminishing power of Europe after the Second World War among local elites. The only way they see to re-establish its influence in the world – especially after forty years of division during which it was dominated by the two superpowers – is to unify. Hence, it is mostly the outside world that pushes Europe towards unification, more than any internal necessity. 'Europe played a leading role in the world some centuries ago, and then it lost it in less than fifty years. Not only economically, I think also technologically and in general [. . .] Yes, Europe suddenly lost its influence on what happened in the world [. . .] In Asia you have China and Russia. India with its milliard of people means something. And what is Europe? [. . .] The world pushes Europe together' (an ODS city council representative).

. . . but uncertainties related to the Europe to be integrated

If for the reasons stated above, the wish to join 'Europe' is very widely shared by Czech local political elites, the meaning of that word remains ambiguous. As we have seen before, the Czechs have a strong feeling of belonging to the Western community of nations. They estimate that they share values and traditions with Western countries. This perception is the product of a vision inherited from the past, which is widely influenced by historic-cultural and religious arguments. When it comes to today's meaning of Europe, to the Western European structures to integrate such as the EU or NATO, things tend to become more complex and less evident.

In order to figure out how the Czech local political elite discerns EU integration, it is important to take into account that the current enlargement process is double: it means joining both the EU and NATO. Both issues are closely linked together in peoples mind. This connection expresses a lot about their expectations. Both integrations are expected to help securing the transition process and providing domestic stability from an economic as well as a political point of view. As we have just seen, the feeling of the necessity to join Europe is intimately connected with fears and threats. It is a way of defence against possible attempts at destabilisation from the outside.

Europe has no clear or single meaning for local politicians. Asked what they think about European integration they often respond about NATO first. Both issues are very closely linked in their minds. The desired reintegration in to Western Europe (the 'return to Europe') is concomitant with the necessity of also integrating Western structures. Non-Soviet Europe has changed over the years, it is no longer as it was in pre-war Europe. Therefore, returning to Europe means integrating the structures that have been created on the other side of the iron curtain. Therefore 'Europe' is today equal to the EU plus NATO.

Opinions about the necessity or not of joining NATO are much clearer and more assured than those about joining the EU in local politicians' statements. This is, first, due to the fact that the issue of NATO enlargement was a current political debate at the time. The ratification procedures were going on. The discussion was more advanced, thus better structured. Moreover, security arguments are in general easier to understand (specially among Czechs due to their experience of 1938, 1948 and 1968). Integrating into NATO seemed less costly, easier to fulfil and as promising as EU-integration, because in both cases most of the expected benefits are linked to stability. NATO membership is seen as an 'anti-38 insurance', obliging the West to feel responsible this time for the fate of small Central European nations – namely the Czech one. The latent fear for Russia due to the traumatic experience of forty years of soviet rule is the most obvious reason for this. 'I do not stop fearing Russia and integration into NATO-structures is the only way to be a part of a whole [. . .] that defends its members. Therefore into NATO, that's without debate for me. The sooner the better' (an independent city-council representative). The presence of Americans in the Atlantic Alliance is crucial in this respect. Czechs having painfully experimented with European alliances before, place great store in the transatlantic aspect of this defence alliance.

Among right-wing parties there is a consensus on this issue. Their statements on this topic contain much less ambiguity than on that of EU accession. Differences between left and right tend to be clear cut. Members of ODS, ODA, KDU-ČSL are indubitably favourable to NATO membership. While members of ČSSD[23] are mostly favourable too, their positions simply differ from right-wing parties in the call for a referendum. As far as representatives of the communist party, KSČM,[24] are concerned they are clearly opposed. 'Joining NATO is not acceptable for me for two reasons; one is that I think that there is no threat . . . there is no clear enemy against which it would be necessary to be protected, in such a way. And, second, other forms of security co-operation exist in Europe. Entering NATO will cost us the hell of a lot of money [. . .] which is not understandable for people today' (a KSČM city council representative).

For right-wing politicians on the contrary, it is very important to prevent a new foreign takeover from happening again. It is crucial to shield the Czech Republic by any means from the Russian sphere of influence, and NATO seems to be the surest way to do so. Here, the so-called Czech 'Munich complex' plays a very important role. Not only do most of the local politicians refer to the traumatic experience of 1938, when Czechoslovakia was abandoned by its allies, but 1948 and 1968 are also mentioned as painful recollections of Western non-intervention. Their experience with great powers' decision processes could be qualified as 'over us, without us'.[25] NATO, through the presence of the Americans, provides an insurance against a new 'Munich' and prevents the Czech Republic from being too dependent upon European powers such as Russia, Germany, France or Great Britain. The feeling of being a 'small nation' subject to great powers, especially since Czechoslovak separation, plays a significant role. 'I am in favour of NATO. I will tell you why. I am for joining NATO because I have a pretty recent experience of the threats of communism, which is still according to me, too powerful in Russia. Because we are a small country, we need an older brother. We do not have the choice, that's why we need NATO. If we would remain neutral, they would all fight for us, but the communists more than the West!' (an ODS city council representative).

Czechs want to counterbalance the loss of influence that was a consequence of the division of Czechoslovakia by tightening ties to Western structures. Having gained distance from the East, they want to benefit from the fact that the greatest part of their borders are now with Member States of the EU.

However, the threats Czech local politicians perceive today are less linked to a Russian military intervention than to the influence of such organisations as Mafias or clandestine immigrants, for example. 'I fear Islamic fundamentalism, I'm afraid of it because it is really powerful and unnoticed. I'm afraid of religious sects. But this Islamic fundamentalism is a great mass that has a systematic approach, and I have information that says that they infiltrate here, these nets already exist' (an ODA city council representative). The protection expected is more global than that of simple military protection.

The difference between the attitude of right and left-wing politicians derives from the different perceptions of Russia and of the threats connected to it. Left-wing, and especially communist, politicians favour a neutral position in the nineteenth-century tradition, whereas the right-wing politicians consider Beneš's foreign policy – trying to make out of Czechoslovakia a bridge between the East and the West – as a complete failure. Communists, on the contrary, consider the right-wing politicians' attempt to establish the clearest possible break with the East, and their efforts to give their country a single orientation towards the West as an error. They advocate good relations with Russia and their Eastern neighbours. Their arguments consist in saying that the Czechs, despite all the changes that occurred since 1989, are still much closer in political and economic terms to their Eastern neighbours, than to the West, and that it is in their interest not to break all the ties with them, since they are equal partners. If right-wing party members tend to see the Czechs clearly as a part of the western world, Communists, and to a lesser extent social democrats, are more nuanced. They tend to argue that NATO has lost its *raison d'être* in the post-Cold War world and that it should have been dismantled in the same way as the Warsaw pact was. As one of them put it, 'when the Warsaw pact was dismantled I think NATO should also have been dismantled. That's my personal opinion [. . .], if nobody threatens you, you don't need to defend yourself' (a ČSSD city council representative).

As the attitude towards NATO enlargement shows, Czech local politicians favour a solution where America is included. When it comes to the model of political and social organisation they aim for, one can again see a clear Anglo-Saxon influence: Great Britain and the US appear to local politicians to be better adapted models for post-communist countries, and more precisely to the breaking with communist habits, which is still one of their main goals. The persistence of legacies from the communist period, like the reliance on the state to solve problems and the lack of personal initiative, are still seen by local elites as entrenched behaviour patterns of citizens. They, who have mobilised themselves, who try to change things through personal involvement, deplore the inertia of their fellow citizens. They denounce as 'apathy' the legacies of the communist system which took care of all aspects of life. Breaking with this is a major goal and therefore only liberal models, based on the individual as a driving force, such as those of British or the Americans can be efficient.

> In this respect I must say that this orientation [. . .] towards the US is more adapted than the European one, because this European civilisation is more based on consensus and collectivism than the American one. In the end I have the feeling that Europe is not really resistant to these temptations, to these dangers. I mean to corruption, to speak frankly, because this corporate State is very much rooted in Europe [. . .] I think this represents somehow a danger for us, these post-Bolshevik Mafiosi structures are still alive here, they could penetrate them and overrule the economy (an ODS city council representative).

Other Western European models, such as German federalism, the Scandinavian welfare state, of the Spanish transition to democracy are never mentioned as possible examples to follow. Germany is only mentioned in order to measure the Czech Republic's advancement in the reform process. It is always the United States which is quoted for its political system. Even in the field of local politics, the US serves as an example. In the Anglo-Saxon model, local politicians discern an insurance against tendencies towards corporatism, the constitution of monopolies and oligarchies, things which are perceived, as we will later see, as dangers connected with the EU. 'I think that the Anglo-Saxon system is more immune to this [the rise of a new post-Bolshevik oligarchy]. This is why there has been attempts on the ODS side and namely on Klaus's side to sustain this Anglo-Saxon model and somehow to push aside the European one' (an ODS city council representative).

The fears connected with EU enlargement

Local politicians express worries about EU accession, which are of two different kinds: in the first place their fears are related to the functioning of the EU as such, whereas the second sort of worries are connected with their relation to the EU, and to a feeling of non-preparedness.

Even though Czech local politicians recognise the need for unifying Europe in the actual world context, they consider European integration more as a utopia than as a realisable project. In this respect, they often draw a parallel between communism as a form of shaping the world by an active will, and the EU and its projects for the future in creating a supranational entity with its own rules. Both experiences derive in their eyes from the same voluntary approach of transforming the world, an approach towards which they are very sceptical. In an ideal world the realisation of a Union of European countries would seem possible to them, just as communism might have been, but not in the real world with all its imperfections and jealousies.

> I think that this EU is somehow a utopia. I'm an economist, I'm not an expert on this. But it is a utopia and it reminds me a little of socialism. It would be perfect if everything would work the way it had to work, if people would be responsible, but I think it will be terribly difficult to establish a way of functioning among individual states, so that all of them could get advantages from it [. . .] I think that the idea of it is almost the same as the idea of socialism, or let's say communism: of course it is wonderful but it is based on something that is not realistic'. (an ODA city-council representative)

In the critiques of the EU two points are mentioned in particular, first the renunciation to the nation-state, second the corporate and bureaucratic aspect of the union.

As far as the question of the nation-state is concerned, there is a widespread fear of a loss of sovereignty. This is similar to other Western European countries, but it is also connected to the previous communist experience in which the struggle for democracy meant a struggle against Soviet hegemony and therefore was mingled with a struggle for national sovereignty. The nation-state remains the major reference point for the new democrats, even at the local level. They encounter great difficulties in supporting the aims of European integration and the need for a supranational unit. In this regard, Klaus's views on what Europe ought to be, and his belief in the nation-state[26] is much closer to their own views as Havel's call for a supra-national entity.[27] To most local politicians no significant European identity exists yet, and therefore it is not possible for them to relate sufficiently to Europe. The nation-state remains the primary point of reference for the citizen.

It is interesting to observe here, that while criticising further integration, the movement initiated by the Single Act of 1986 and the Maastricht treaty, the latter are never mentioned, neither is the EMU. The statements remain vague; nevertheless, this critique is one of the Maastricht project and the deepening of the Union, which one can find, in a more elaborated and argumentative way, in Václav Klaus's discourses.

The second source of critism of the EU derives from the very strong liberalism of Czech local politicians. They attack the over-regulation of the EU. 'Into NATO for sure, but into the EU it is a little more on the opposite, because I think a reasonable euroscepticism is healthy, is not really out of place. I fear a little these socialist structures, these big administrations in Strasbourg or elsewhere. I fear somehow that a kind of supra-national socialist state could emerge again' (an ODS city-council representative). Local politicians like to describe Brussels as an enormous interventionist bureaucracy that interferes in state-internal affairs. Hence the EU is often compared with an attenuated form of socialism that would endanger the newly introduced reforms. Europe is seen as being based on a collectivist tradition. One has to remember here the very negative connotations of both words: 'socialist' and 'collectivist' in post-communist elites' mouths. These terms stand for what is today considered as a forty-years-long failure.

There is an obvious concurrence in the political agendas of the EU and the post-communist countries. The priority Czech politicians have set is de-etatisation. Their first preoccupation was to disengage the state from all domains where public intervention was not absolutely necessary. Today they refuse to replace one bureaucracy (the Soviet-type one) by another (the European one), and see in Brussels a return to a form of over-regulation and acute interventionism they have just rejected. They also quote the lack of transparency and democracy of Brussels decisions, which is certainly not a theme particular to them.

One more reason they doubt the whole project is the diversity of interests among European nations. While the interests that link these nations together in the North Atlantic Treaty are clear to Czechs, those that bring European nations together in the EU seem more diffuse, thus less evident and more unstable to them. They often argue about the existence of too big differences between individual members of the Union, and wonder, for example, what can hold together countries like Greece and Germany.

Reservations about EU-integration derive from a second source of worries which are connected to a feeling of unpreparedness and weakness. There is general agreement on the fact that the entire process of joining the EU has gone too fast since the revolution, that there is still a lot to do, in internal and foreign politics before being ready to integrate with a Union of Western states. The process of implementing democracy and a market economy is still perceived as very fragile, needing more time to be stabilised. Things are not yet institutionalised enough to resist the shock of integration.

From an economic point of view, there is a latent fear of being abused by stronger partners imposing their interests, trying to get rid of competitors who would be too powerful to be resisted by the weak Czech economy. 'Look we are not strong enough economically to be considered as equal partners [. . .] we are still beginners, we are still learning, by ourselves, and these supranational companies are so powerful that we cannot resist them yet' (an ODS city council representative). Often agriculture is cited as an example of unfair treatment. Whereas the Czechs have opened their trade barriers, the EU has not, and therefore it creates unfair and disloyal competition for Czech agriculture which is no longer subsidised. Here again, they plead for a really free market, without such assistance.

But this feeling of unpreparedness does not only concern economic matters, it also applies to democracy. Local politicians worry that the shock of integration could destabilise a country not yet politically consolidated, that needs more time to adjust. The citizens are not seen as ready to bear such a shock, and they perceive the lack of a national elite, capable of dealing with EU representatives.

One of their major grievances against the EU, is the feeling that they are not treated like equal partners. There is a Czech 'inferiority complex' that expresses itself in the need to be recognised by the West, for their achievements and great pride in their transformation, especially in economics, a topic on which the Czechs tend to be very sensitive. There is a widespread complaint that Western experts do not understand the Czech situation, but at the same time, local politicians have the feeling that their radically different situation cannot fully be appreciated by the West. They express the belief that Western solutions do not apply to Eastern or Czech problems, for these are unique.

As far as communists are concerned, their arguments against the Union are less directed against its principles than connected to this feeling of integration being a premature process. They favour the enforcement of relations between Eastern and Western Nations and their citizens, but at the same time they know that the Czech Republic does not have the means to enter the Union today. In this regard, they share the recognition of other local politicians that there is a serious risk of being treated as the poor relation.

> Into the EU as soon as we are up to it. Look, there are states in Europe who disparage us, like the poorer ones, because our economy is not completed, and is stagnating, and because they will have to pay for us. Are we really ready for this? [. . .] We are not ready and I think that before [integration], we should put together this republic, repair and arrange our economy, stabilise the political situation [. . .] and then, I would be ready for a co-operation with other countries and maybe become an equal member of the EU, why not? (a KSCM city council representative)

This feeling that newly integrated central European nations would experience unequal treatment inside the Union is often mentioned. Local politicians worry that once they are members of the Union, everything will be dictated to them without their being able to influence decisions. This fear of powerlessness reinforces that one of being overruled and losing sovereignty. As an answer to this, communist politicians are the only ones to mention the possibility of acquiring tighter links with other Central European countries. Such co-operation is never mentioned by other party members as a possible response to one's own weakness.

Another point on which right and left differ is the question about whether or not it is necessary to hold a referendum on the question of EU enlargement.[28] This issue is only raised by social democrats and communists, among whom the trauma of the Czechoslovak separation has had the most impact. They want to avoid such a process happening again, in which a few government elites and parliamentarians decide crucial questions without consulting the citizens. They argue that this time, on a major issue such as EU-integration, they want a referendum, seen as a more democratic procedure.

> EU integration is a painful question. I tell you frankly, on this issue there should be a referendum. Categorically, that's what I ask for. But unfortunately there are people who want to avoid such a referendum like the devil a crucifix ! On fundamental questions about the existence of State and Nation, the State and the Nation should decide on their own, and not a handful of MP's [. . .] Our State fell apart thanks to an agreement between Mister Klaus and Mister Mečiar, and thanks to a sort of parliamentary decision, in which they overruled. They did not ask the nation, because it was opposed to this !' (a CSSD city council representative).

Mentioning the issue of referendum is also often a way of getting round the actual question of integration for these local politicians. They concentrate on this side issue, and thus do not give any opinion on the actual content of the accession process, about which they often have little knowledge and only a vague opinion.

To summarise, on can say that the idea that elites can be divided into two camps, one of the 'modernisers' which are for Europe, and one of 'traditionalists' which are sceptical towards the integration, does not apply here. Support and dismissal of Europe are much more diffuse, incoherent and complex.

There is a great convergence in the approaches towards enlargement among local politicians of all parties The need to enter the Union is not a matter of discussion, it is a certainty, but how and when to enter are both questionable. Members of the ODS tend to have a more aggressive and more self-assured discourse, than their fellow politicians, but in the end one finds the same hesitations, fears and questions among social democrats. The only motive that distinguishes left-wing from right-wing politicians is their lesser insistence on the critiques towards the functioning of the EU. Social democrats are not opposed to the continental welfare-state model. Even the communists share most of the fears and expectations of the other politicians. Their positions tend to diverge clearly on the question of NATO enlargement, but not really on that of EU integration.

At a local level, it is therefore possible to affirm that communists do not show any opposition in principle to entering the EU, they simply express doubts and warnings, which are less virulent than those expressed by ODS members! Communists use their position to stress the fact that a clearer and more in-depth debate about this very important issue is necessary. While defending these positions as an opposition party, they might contribute to improve the debate, forcing everyone to state clearly the advantages and disadvantages of enlargement.

Local communists politicians are the most obvious example of the existing gap between local elites, views and what parties claim are their foreign policy goals. Local politicians from other parties tend to be closer to the discourse of individual leaders, such as Václav Klaus for example, who has very critical position towards the European Union as portrayed by right-wing local elites. It is interesting to observe that the general scepticism towards EU integration, which is strongest among right-wing party members, neither reflects the general party line of the ODS, ODA or KDU-ČSL who all have as a primary foreign policy goal entry to the Union, nor voters' opinion, which tend to follow these party lines: those most favourable to the EU are to be found among ODS and ODA voters:[29] at the time of interviews 84 per cent of ODS sympathisers favoured integration, whereas 79 per cent of US sympathisers, 74 per cent of ODA sympathisers, 69 per cent of KDU-ČSL sympathisers, 59 per cent of ČSSD sympathisers and only 34 per cent of KSČM sympathisers[30] did.

Conclusion

Czechs believe that Europe is a 'necessary evil'. EU integration is promoted by parties and government as their main goal of foreign policy but it has only weak support inside the parties at a local level. The process of integrating with the EU remains a national elite-driven process. This is what Ágh calls the 'basic paradox of Europeanisation'.[31] Whereas this process should have moved from a very small governmental elite to a much wider popular debate, this has not occurred in Central and Eastern European countries. The attitudes of Czech local politicians illustrates this. There has been no 'serious treatment of Euro-issues' among political actors, like parties, until recently. This decisive shift will hopefully begin with negotiations.

Attila Ágh is right when he says that there has been a 'lack of recognition of the task [Europeanization] itself'. And that the political elites of these countries

> have been unable to see and understand the realities of the 'new Europe' [. . .] Europeanization has not yet become a real policy issue, although it should be the fundamental one, high on the agenda for public policy in these countries. Instead, there are [. . .] abstract ideological approaches [. . .] or at the most extremely pragmatic, actions in the field of the economy with reductionist simplistic views that only the economy matters, in the most restricted sense of export or import quotas.[32]

For Czech intermediary elites, European integration is a very complex and unsettled matter. There is a widely shared pessimism among local politicians towards the Czech Republic's integration prospects. At best, local politicians expect to join in the distant future. This would provide enough time to wait and see whether the EU undergoes a Yugoslav-like disintegration. Indeed, Yugoslavia was often contrasted with the EU as an example of a failed union. Distrust toward the European project is common. In the abstract it is a good idea, but local politicians doubt that it could really work.

There is a proportionally inverted relationship between local politicians' will to enter NATO and their will to enter the EU. The impression prevails among right-wing politicians that NATO-integration can adequately address the various problems of the Czech Republic and will cost less than integration into the EU. NATO, they feel, will not only provide security but will also guarantee political and economical stability. Furthermore, NATO is widely perceived as an insurance against a possible return of socialist ideas, and thus also functions as a political safeguard.

In the end, the attitudes of Czech local elites are very ambivalent. They are as divided between the dream of being part of the Union, and an unclear and negative perception of the costs and benefits of integration. They wish to be recognised by the Western world as an equal partner. Yet the whole process through which Europe builds up is highly suspicious to Czech local politicians. Above all, they perceive the EU as opposing the new post-communist ideology of liberalism and deregulation so dear to them.

These trends parallel similar findings by Zdenka Mansfeldová, who found that Czech citizens have moved from enthusiastic support for 'joining the EU as soon as possible', to a more circumspect attitude of 'joining under certain conditions'.[33] Explanations for this are fears and a feeling of insecurity. These shifts are due less to the fact that local elites have discovered what the EU is about, than to the lack of knowledge and debate on the contribution of EU integration to Czech development.

The intermediary elites' position is extremely ambiguous. While wishing to join the club, local politicians have the clear feeling that it might be too early to do so, and that it would be wiser to arrange things at home first, in order to be fully considered a member. If there is one thing they know for sure, it is that the transformation process will be long and painful – particularly in changing the habits and mentalities inherited from the former regime. Meanwhile, while they feel themselves to be European, they remain careful and sceptical.

Local politicians' statements show that there are few different points of view, and that they still need to learn a lot about the EU. This sparse knowledge, which is moreover under the influence of a dominant discourse: that of Václav Klaus and of the ODS – as in many other fields such as economics – prevents alternative visions from asserting themselves. The very strong influence of Klaus's vision of Europe shows the hold he had over foreign policy and the ability he had to mobilise political discourse on certain issues. However, his hold on Czech politics has diminished, since his party encountered great difficulties and he resigned from office in November 1997.

This one-sided discourse is a more general feature of Czech democracy, which sometimes tends to lack tolerance towards divergent opinions and may correlate to a strong longing for stability and the fear of destabilisation by leftist influences. This sometimes makes it difficult for local politicians to handle such notions as 'opposition', 'diversity', or the idea of a political 'alternative'. The fact that the discourse of local politicians is neither elaborate nor autonomous reflects the more general problems of a lack of pluralism and of the recreation of an independent local elite.

For these reasons, the EU should encourage different forms of dialogue. It should not limit itself to talks at a government or a top administrative level. It should also promote forms of association at low levels, between societies and local entities. By encouraging contacts among a diversified sample of representatives, it could also foster the emergence of a broader spectrum of opinions and knowledge.

Notes

1 A. Ágh, 'Democratic Deficit in the EU and the ECE accession process', *Budapest papers on Democratic Transition* (1998), No. 222.
2 A. Ágh, 'The Role of the ECE Parliaments in the Pre-accession Strategy', paper presented at the Prague conference on the 'Role of Parliaments in European Integration' (12–13 September 1997), p. 12.
3 A. Offerdal, D. Hanšpách, A. Kowalczyk and J. Patocka, 'The New Local Elites', in Harald Baldersheim *et al.*, *Local Democracy and the Process of Transformation in Eastern Europe* (Boulder, CO: Westview Press, 1996), p. 106
4 See A. Cerný, 'Prague's Reality Check', *Transition*, vol. 5, No. 4 (1998), 53.
5 During the first elections after the revolution, this was not the case, because the process of democratisation entailed a complete change of elite. Even local politicians had to leave and thus could not serve as replacements for national politicians. Hence, the national political elite was composed of people with little previous political experience beyond their participation in the velvet revolution and occasional role in underground or dissident movements.
6 These three cities are major Czech cities, which differ in their geographical position, history, population and economic orientation. They were selected to present the broadest spectrum of opinions possible given the resources at my disposal.
7 The 'snowball method' consists of asking the politicians I interviewed to recommend further people they would consider as important or influential, and thus selecting the people to meet based on the recommendations of local fellow politicians.

8 Therefore there are fewer CSSD members, as well as fewer Republicans than at a national level.
9 Foundation for assistance to local administration.
10 Interview with Marie Bednárová, 12 December 1997, in Prague.
11 Newspapers are the most important providers of information on this topic for local politicians as well as for the rest of the citizens.
12 It is to note that given the very weak number of 'Independents' elected in city councils of big Czech cities, with very few exceptions all the local politicians interviewed were members of one of the most important Czech parties (ODA, ODS, KDU-CSL, CSSD, KSCM).
13 Ágh, 'The Role of the ECE Parliaments', p. 15.
14 As shown in the IVVM poll done on 1–8 September 1997, only 8 per cent of the people asked state they are deeply interested in the EU, whereas 38 per cent state they are only interested from time to time, 33 per cent have few interest, nd 21 per cent no interest at all.
15 L. Neumayer, 'La vision de l'intégration de Vaclav Klaus'. *La nouvelle alternative* No. 49 (March 1998) p. 25.
16 Not only was there a disconnection between the national and the local political scene in the elite recruitment until recently, but the issues discussed at a local and a national level also differ very much.
17 One has to remember that the interviews were conducted more than three years before the terrorist attacks of 11 September 2001 on the World Trade Center in New York.
18 ODS stands for Civic Democratic Party, ODA for Civic Democratic Alliance and KDU-CSL for Christian Democratic Union–Czech People's Party.
19 And this, even though religion is much more important in Slovak national self-definition than in the Czech one!
20 See A. Hudala. Der Beitritt der tschechischen Republik zur EU. Eine Fallstudie zu den Auswirkungen der EU-Osterweiterung auf die finalité politique des Europäischen Integrationsprozesses (Münster, Hamburg, London: Ed. coll. *Osteuropa* (1996), p. 119.
21 Spain, Greece and Portugal are not perceived as having gone through major changes since the Second World War.
22 As Ágh puts it, 'EU integration has progressed at a tremendous speed for Central Europeans and it is still going on as they try to cope with the problems of their own transition process; thus their relative backwardness continues to increase as well.' In: A. Agh, 'The Europeanization of ECE Polities and the Emergence of the new ECE Democratic Parliaments', in A. Ágh (ed.) *The First Steps: The Emergence of East-Central European Parliaments* (Budapest: Hungarian Centre of Democracy Studies Foundation, 1994), p. 10.
23 CSSD stands for Czech Social-Democratic Party.
24 KSCM stands for Communist party of Bohemia and Moravia.
25 V. Hampl; 'Tschechische Europapolitik: Profilsuche und Kursbestimmung', *Integration*, No. 3 (July 1993) 125.
26 For both see Václav Klaus's statements in *The Economist*, 19 September 1994 in an article alled 'So Far, So Good'.
27 As Václav Havel says: 'the greatness of the idea of European integration on democratic foundations consists in its capacity to overcome the old Herderian idea of the nation-state as the highest expression of national life. Thus, European integration – should – and must, if it is to succeed – enable all the nationalities to realise their national autonomy within the framework of a broad civil society created by the supranational community'. Speech delivered at the Council of Europe, in Vienna, 8 October 1993. In V. Havel, *The Art of the Impossible* (New York and Toronto: Knopf, 1997), p. 130.
28 At the time no decision had been made on this issue by Brussels.
29 See: Z. Mansfeldová, 'Public Opinion to EU Membership in the Czech Republic and the Role of Political Elites', *Budapest Papers on Democratic Transition*, No. 216 (1997) 4–6.

30 IVVM, K názorum na vstup do EU, 30 January– 3 February 1998.
31 Ágh, 'The Role of the ECE Parliaments', pp. 22–25.
32 Ágh (ed.), *The First Steps: The Emergence of ECE Parliaments* p. 10.
33 Z. Mansfeldová, 'Public Opinion to EU Membership in the Czech Republic and the Role of Political Elites', *Budapest Papers on Democratic Transition*, No. 216 (1997), 2–3.

Anne Bazin

11

Germany and the enlargement of the European Union to the Czech Republic

The collapse of the communist system in Eastern Europe in 1989 coincides with the end of the partition of Europe, as well as that of Germany. Symbolically, these events are identified with the fall of the Berlin Wall, which reveals the close tie between the collapse of communism in Eastern Europe and German unification. The events of 1989 and the unification of Germany has permitted the reappearance in new terms of the German Question in Central Europe.

The period since 1989 has seen the return of Germany to the centre of Europe. For the first time in its history, Germany seems able to reconcile its geography with its political orientation and has revealed itself a force for stabilisation and integration at the heart of the continent. Its economic success is an example to all. With its geographic proximity and the pre-existence of cultural links, Germany is the most familiar among the Western models and its economic power within the European Union is yet another element of attraction. Germany for years has been perceived by Central Europe as the route to modernisation, as well as a privileged means of access to the West.[1]

The Czech Republic has for centuries had complex relations with its Germanic neighbour. As President Havel recently pointed out:

> Our relationship to Germany and the Germans has always been more than merely one of the many themes of our diplomacy. It has been a part of our destiny, even a part of our identity. Germany has been our inspiration as well as our pain; a source of understandable traumas, of many prejudices and misconceptions, as well as of standards to which we turn; some regard Germany as our greatest hope, others as our greatest peril.[2]

Czech–German relations can not today be approached only from a bilateral perspective but have to be considered on the European level as well. It is precisely the interaction between the European and the bilateral dimensions which creates the dynamics for the evolution of relations since 1989. On the bilateral level, relations are characterised by a structural asymmetry[3] which explains the way the relations are perceived on each side. On the European level, relations coincide with the 'return in Europe' of the Czech Republic which has, as its final objective, integration of the state into the European Union (and NATO), on one hand, and the European anchorage of German foreign policy on the other. The introduction of the European factor into bilateral relations opens new perspectives: it changes the way some questions are considered, especially because a regional (central European) approach helps to stand back from certain issues. It also changes the nature of some problems (for instance, the 'right to return' claimed by the Sudeten German will be solved the day the Czech Republic will become a member of the European Union. According to the liberty of residence and travel, Germans as well as any other European citizens will be allowed to settle in the Czech Republic[4]). It can also create some confusion: for instance, the cross-border co-operation between Germany and the Czech Republic or Poland within the Euroregions looks like 'classic' bilateral border co-operation (except for its financing) when it is in fact a European-level programme.

The question is to determine whether the 'Europeanisation' of bilateral relations brings the right answers to old issues which are affecting their evolution: the disputes inherited from the past (Sudeten German claims/Nazi victims compensation) and the imbalance between the two countries. The analysis of the evolution of relations since 1989 suggests a negative answer to the first question and a positive one to the second. Integration into the European Union could be seen as a central European answer to the recurring problem of this part of Europe: the consequences and the constraints imposed through the centuries by its geographical position between Germany and Russia.

In the issue of the enlargement, Germany is at once seen as one of the most important sources of support for Central European countries as they move west toward the European Union. It is also the beachhead (together with Austria) of the Union, as it reaches east. In its will to succeed in its 'return to Europe', the Czech Republic chooses to concentrate on close co-operation with Germany which, at the same time, defines itself as the best supporter of the CEEC on their way into the European Union. This specific quality given to relations with Germany soon becomes their main dimension, when the European 'aim' seems more precise and at the same time more difficult to reach. Germany, as a 'vehicle of integration' the CEEC count on, is also one which can set conditions for enlargement.

Relations between the Czech Republic and Germany is a large subject and here the focus will be on the enlargement issue itself: first the different layers of co-operation between the Czech Republic and Germany within the European context (national and regional) must be examined in order to identify the various vehicles for *rapprochement* with the European Union. This co-operation has a major impact on Czech perception of the European Union. The way in which the Czech Republic considers its integration into the European Union and the way it regards its relations with Germany leads to an analysis of the stakes involved in integration for the Czech Republic. In the last few decades, 'Europe' has been the key word of (West-) German foreign policy. German support for enlargement can be seen within this framework. Nevertheless it seems legitimate to question the convergence of German 'national interest', which is the subject of so much discussion among academics and politicians, and the interests of the rest of Europe as well as Central Europe. The intention here is to examine some of the stakes involved for Germany in enlargement, as well as to attempt to determine whether the Czech Republic represents a specific case for Germany. Finally, as the next enlargement of the European Union will modify relationships within the region, it is necessary to consider the impact of integration of the Czech Republic from a multilateral perspective.

Co-operation between the Czech Republic and Germany within the context of European Union

The European dimension of German–Czech co-operation is characterised by a complex interdependence. In Germany more than in the Czech Republic (and the difference is interesting in itself), the private actors on the economic and cultural level, as well as non-state actors, the *Länder*, the Euroregions and various other institutions play an essential role in relations with the neighbouring countries and within the European context.[5]

At the national level: economical, cultural and political co-operation

It is usually in economic terms that co-operation between Germany and the Central Eastern European Countries is discussed. Economic integration of the CEEC is understood to be the first step in a full and complete integration into the European Union (EU). The other member states do not show the same interest in enlargement nor do they seek to develop the same type of economic relations with the region as does Germany, which appears today to be the most dynamic and enterprising partner of the CEEC. Today Germany accounts for more than half of the commerce between the EU and the CEEC (all twelve candidates)[6] and that share has grown since 1989.[7] Germany has historically been a more dominant actor in the affairs of Central Europe than has the West. *Osthandel* was one of the two pillars, with *Ostpolitik* (on the political and ideological level) of the FRG's influence in Eastern Europe during the last few decades. In 1989 the German model of a *Wirtschaftswunder* was one of the most cherished hopes for all the countries of Eastern Europe.[8]

As for the Czechs, the European Union is their main economic partner. At the heart of the Union, Germany holds by far the most important position with more than half of the economic exchanges.[9] Germany is itself the main trading partner of the Czech Republic.[10] This German dominance concerns not only commercial exchange but also investments.[11] As with trade, the direct foreign investment data reinforces the picture and raises the question of an unevenness in the European Union – CEE integration, where Germany is playing a particularly important role. This becomes all the more clear if we consider that the other large member states like France or the United Kingdom are playing a very much smaller one. In spite of the importance of these investments for the CEEC they represent only a small portion of total German foreign investment, about 10 per cent as far as direct investment is concerned. But while this investment may seem limited on the German side, it reveals the profound and long-term engagement of Germany with the CEEC in commerce, co-operation and financial aid. It also represents, as does the relocation of German enterprises towards Central Europe, an opportunity to take advantage in the short term of lower operating costs than in Germany. Investment is, above all, a means of being present in the new and expanding markets which is in the medium- and long-term economic interest of Germany.[12] The question here is not whether this situation is more to Germany's or to Central Europe's advantage. What is interesting about these intense economic relations besides their visibility and 'social effect' is that they are for Germany an undeniable means of gaining direct and indirect influence on the development of the region and will eventually lead to the enunciation of new economic rules.

The economic presence of Germany in Central Europe, far more visible and more often discussed, is echoed by an intense cultural co-operation. 'Foreign cultural policy is, next to the cultivation of political and economic relations, an integral component of foreign policy.'[13] Bonn's cultural policy is officially part of a more general policy with regard to Central Europe.[14] The change is startling in this region where after four decades of communist rule, during which Germany (West Germany that is) was presented as a menace to these countries; and the memory of German occupation during the Second World War (in Bohemia–Moravia, but also in Poland) is associated with German political and cultural domination and is still considered a menace to the culture of the nation.

It is without doubt in the linguistic domain that German cultural policy is most active.[15] Language instruction is perceived as a long-term investment with positive economic and political dividends. Demand for German language instruction is strong in this part of Europe, even if English has made great progress and is today in direct competition with German. Of the approximately 20 million people worldwide who are learning German, more than 13 million of them are from Eastern Europe.[16] The German Ministry of Foreign Affairs spends more than 150 million DM in grants on the language programme alone, which is to say a budget four times as large as, for example, France's entire cultural – and not just linguistic – development programme in the region.[17] It is still too early to judge the results of this language policy,[18] but today more than 60 per cent of the population claims a desire to learn German[19] which remains the foreign language most used in the Czech Republic ahead of English.[20] This aspiration towards and interest in German culture is directly linked to the idea that it also represents an initiation into German-style prosperity. From this point of view, cultural and foreign policy can be seen as the third pillar of German foreign policy.

This dynamic German cultural, and not only linguistic, programme is born of two essential elements in today's Czech Republic: a geographic proximity to

Germany and Austria. Both are German speaking and both represent the path towards the West; and centuries of coexistence between the Germanic and Czech populations in Bohemia–Moravia. Without entering into the details of the relations between the Germanic world and Central Europe in the past centuries it must be understood just how important those relations are in cultural terms. The presence of a German population created a 'symbiosis'[21] among the populations in Central Europe and brings to them all, even after the disappearance of that German population (expelled or fled at the end of the war) a better understanding and knowledge of each other and their 'social codes'. On the other hand, the presence of a residual German minority (estimated at about 50,000 people) in the Czech Republic today plays no mediating role in this direction. Several reasons can be proposed to explain this, among them the fact that the German minority has been 'czechized' during the communist decades (the new generation is often not fluent in German, especially when they come from a mixed family) or that, from the Czech point of view, they are often assimilated to the Sudetendeutsche Landsmannschaft (Association of the expellees from Czechoslovakia) to which some of them in fact belong.

In the official framework of international treaties it can be seen that Germany explicitly supports the integration of the Czech Republic into the European Union. Thus in the treaty of good neighbourhood and co-operation between the CSFR and the FRG (renewed in the same terms with the CR after partition), signed 27 February 1992, Germany undertakes to 'uphold the efforts of the CSFR in view of satisfying the conditions for their total integration into the European Community' (article 10, paragraph 2). Similarly during negotiations of the Association Agreements with the European Community in 1991 and 1993 Germany was one of CEEC's most fervent supporters (even if, as may seem paradoxical, the negotiations with some German partners on certain economic points were especially long and difficult). The issue of integration in the European Union is on the agenda of every meeting between Czech and German politicians, whether it is to reaffirm a common political will or to discuss a specific file. Because of the proximity and also German political will to integrate its eastern neighbours in the European Union, these meetings are more frequent than those with the political leaders of the other member-states. This imposes Germany as the privileged interlocutor for the Czech Republic on the European scene.

Thus, German political foundations (all represented in the CR[22]) broadcast, for example, a German conception (and understanding) of European construction. Their goal is, for the most part, to promote democracy as well as to improve bilateral relations. A European dimension is clearly evident in this co-operative activity. Within the framework of conferences and seminars directed at elected officials or other actors on the Czech political scene, German politicians, of various political points of view (national political figures as well as union and local officials), are invited to come and speak and create a dialogue to cement relationships at all levels. It is not a matter of influence in the sense of imposing conditions, but the simple fact of being familiar with the German vision serves as a reference point for Czech political leaders, in acts of opposition or appropriation of these same concepts. The political foundations are a means of co-operation typically German which is used on a scale far beyond that of any other European nation.[23]

At the regional level, direct contact with the European Union[24]

Co-operation at the regional level within the European framework is in some respects simpler and clearer than the relations so far discussed. For the Czech Republic it represents a concrete contact with the European Union and allows for a different view of Germany and the Union in the border regions than in the rest of the country. The co-operation within the framework of the PHARE programme, for instance, fosters contacts at the local level between various German and Czech actors and works towards a wider diffusion of the rules and regulations of the European Union within the Czech Republic by way of Germany.

The fall of communism in Eastern Europe in 1989 and especially the opening up of the western Czechoslovakian borders has had a direct effect on the border regions in north, west and south Bohemia. These regions have become places of privileged contact with Germany. This evolution is all the more remarkable as the iron curtain had impeded all transborder relations for decades. More than an inter-state border, the Czech–German frontier is a boundary between the European Union and the Central European candidates for integration. Since 1989 the development of transborder activity with Germany in particular and the European Union in general has allowed the border regions to emerge as new actors on the Czech internal scene. Today, they play a specific role in the Czech debate not only on Czech–German relations (which will not be developed here) but also on European integration.

The opening of the western boundaries of Czechoslovakia in 1989 allowed the classical phenomenon typical of border regions to appear, especially along Bohemia's western border with Bavaria: the rapid reappearance of transborder commuting; the relocation of German plants to Bohemia and the associated threat of unemployment (on the German side[25]); the explosion of local businesses, but also of criminal activities and illegal business. The wide gap in the standard of living between the Czech Republic and Germany (especially Bavaria) plays a key role in developing cross-border activity.[26] To measure the upheaval this has meant for the border regions one must keep in mind that these areas (especially west Bohemia) had been left underdeveloped by the communist regime for decades, mainly for strategic and security reasons.

Today, the Czech–German border has become the European Union's border. Cross-border co-operation between the two countries represents for the Czech economy a direct contact with European Union rules: the exporting of products to Germany means exporting of products to the European Union, with all the norms, rules and regulations which that entails. Moreover, illegal immigration from countries, most notably from those to the east of the Czech Republic and Poland, is illegal immigration into the European Union itself. The threat of destabilisation, or at least the fear of instability, arriving from the east is often used in Germany as an argument for enlargement. In fact, one of the main pre-occupations of Germany since the early 1990s has been to extend the European Union's zone of stability to the East, so that the eastern boundaries of Germany would not coincide with those of the European Union or NATO.[27] The border regions are therefore not only geographically but also politically and economically concerned with this evolution.

Parallel to the development of informal transborder relations with Germany there exists a more institutionalised co-operation, especially with the financial and political support of the European Union. The European Commission considers that 'interregional and multinational co-operation as a means of promoting political stability and economic ties is especially important for the success of the pre-membership strategy'. The analysis of the cross-border co-operation programme (CRO-CO) within the PHARE programme, and more especially the German–Czech Euroregions part in that programme brings up essential questions in the debate on the European issue in the Czech Republic.[28]

The five Czech–German Euroregions were created on German initiatives starting in 1991: Egrensis, Nisa/Neiße, Labe/Elbe, Krusné Hory/Erzgebirge, Sumava/Böhmer Wald. They cover approximately the entire Czech–German border. Since their creation, they have been part of the Czech European policy. Cross-border co-operation is mentioned in the Association Agreement between the Czech Republic and the European Union signed in 1991. The aim of the Euroregions is to promote transborder co-operation in such different areas as the development of infrastructure and transportation, protection of the environment, support for small businesses, socio-cultural exchanges or, more generally the amelioration of the standard of living in those regions. If the difficulties differ from those encountered in Western Europe over the course of years, the goal remains the same: promoting understanding, stimulating economic development and finally reinforcing the process of European integration.

Even if it is obviously too early to draw any definitive conclusions, the success of the Euroregions projects appeared for a while (mid-1990s) compromised on the Czech side and the impact on the populations very limited (compared to Poland, for instance[29]). An analysis of the debates on the Czech–German Euroregions, from within and from without, illuminates several problems related to the topic of this chapter. Within the Czech Republic, the development of the Euroregions has revealed the weakness of the regional structures of the country. While, at the local level, the German interlocutors, whether from the *Länder* or from smaller communities, have real political power and enjoy financial autonomy, the Czech counterparts are difficult to identify and, above all, have no financial or political weight. More than the simple and direct heritage of imperial, and then communist, centralism, this situation is also the result of the policies conducted by the Klaus government after 1992. In fact, the national committee of regions was abolished in the fall 1990, as a symbol of one of the structures which had been in the hands of the old communist system, and no law on a new regional structure had been adopted until 3 November 1997. This especially long delay has had as a first consequence the creation of a gap between administrative levels of the state and the districts. And the law is only a first tentative step, almost symbolic, in the sense that it does not define the prerogatives of the new regions (in particular, neither their finances nor their power of taxation).

This brief description of a problem which might be considered as only an internal Czech Republic issue is more than just that. The obstacle to the development of the Euroregions was in the logic of the Czech politics which sees decentralisation as a threat to a state in the process of democratisation and national reconstruction. Prime Minister Klaus, constantly evoking Czech national identity in his European speeches shows (1993) how this central/regional issue must be considered from an international perspective:

> The hidden significance of the Euroregions is different. We must act very carefully and make a distinction between friendship, partnership, co-operation in cross-border projects and an attempt to undermine the identity of our State . . . We want to enter Europe as the Czech Republic. I do not believe that we want to enter Europe as the Euroregion Nisa, Labe or Sumava . . . Some mayors think that they can be in Europe sooner this way. I don't think so. I see that as a threat to the identity of our State.

This leads to the international (German, in fact) as well as the European dimensions of the issue of the Euroregions in the Czech Republic. Czech reactions were an illustration of a wider debate on European integration, on the future shape of the European Union, and the evolution of relations with Germany within that framework.

The Euroregions as seen from the rest of Europe are above all German–Czech, but for the Germans, as well as for the Czechs, they are part of their European policy. The Czech debate on the Euroregions has emerged in the following difficult context: German predominance within the European Union (so perceived in Prague) and the slow and difficult road to normal bilateral relations with Germany. It is especially in reaction to a German (and Bavarian) conception of the 'Europe of regions' that Klaus's words have to be understood, a Europe which would dissolve the Czech state and sense of identity. The Czech debate on Euroregions also shows that the German issue is at the core of Czech concern over Europe. It would be illusory to try to separate the two issues.

Some opponents of the Czech–German Euroregions within the Czech Republic do not hesitate to claim in a provocative manner that they are an instrument promoted by Germany to finance its economic development in Central Europe. The geographical delimitation of the Euroregions is not always easy, mainly for historical reasons, and is directly linked to the German issue in the Czech territories. There are, for instance, some similarities between a map of the Czech–German Euroregions today and a map of the Sudeten German territories before 1945.[30] Others prefer to justify their opposition to the financing of the Euroregions by explaining these regions are already favoured by the proximity of Germany and that it would make more sense to support the development of those regions located in the eastern part of the Czech Republic. There is no need to give more weight to these arguments than they deserve, but they do show how the German issue remains a constant in the European debate within the Czech Republic.

The questions raised by the creation of the Euroregions in the Czech Republic are linked to another phenomenon, that of the Europeanisation of relations at once among the member states and those between the member-states and the candidate countries. The Czech political hesitation concerning the Euroregions must be considered in a wider context: that of Czech policy toward the European Union and the integration process. The Czech–German relations have since 1989 been more and more integrated within a European framework: on the political level because these relations were considered in the Czech Republic as a means towards integration, and seen in Germany as a step towards enlargement; and on the economic level because the relations were determinate by the situation of the two countries, one belonging to the European Union and the other being a applicant country dealing with its post-communist transition.

A return to Europe through Germany[31] at the beginning of the 1990s[32]

In order to consider how the Czech Republic envisions its relations with Germany within the European Union, one has to look first at what integration means for the Czechs (to the public as well as to the political actors)[33] in order to identify their expectations and their fears *vis-à-vis* the European Union. An interesting way to consider integration into the European Union is to analyse how the process of rapprochement with the European Union is occurring at the same time as a separation from a difficult past.

One of the slogans of the 'velvet revolution' in Czechoslovakia in the Autumn of 1989 was: the 'return to Europe' which became a priority of Czechoslovakian foreign policy. During the first stage of political transition, Europe (used in a positive and general sense) represented a consensus in terms of foreign policy. It offered at the same time a successful model, an aim during an uncertain period, and a way to radically reject that previous geopolitical entity, the Soviet Union. The new Czechoslovakian politicians, of whom an important part were former dissidents (like Václav Havel, President of Czechoslovakia; Jirí Dienstbier, Foreign Minister; Petr Pithart, Czech Prime Minister etc.) introduced a new policy which was in many respects influenced by the debates held clandestinely before 1989, particularly on the German issue and on Europe.[34] The reunification of Germany was seen as the prerequisite to the reunification of Europe itself. Since at least the nineteenth century the German issue could not be separated from the European issue and the debate in the 1980s (not limited to Czechoslovakia, but involving intellectuals from all of Central Europe) brought it to the forefront once again.

Aware of the special place of Germany in Europe, the new Czech politicians were convinced that it was of greater importance to develop privileged relations with Germany on their way to European integration. In its first two years the new Czechoslovakia tried to develop and improve relations with its German neighbour, as a main partner and supporter of integration into European institutions. The unevoquial and unreserved support given by the Czechoslovak state from the very beginning to Germany's unification could be seen as part of this policy, as well as other symbolic gestures; for instance, the first presidential trip made by Václav Havel was to Germany, East and West, Berlin and Munich, symbolic cities for Germany as well as for all Europe. Changes in Czech foreign policy toward the European Union as well as Germany occurred with the change of government after the elections of June 1992. Václav Klaus became prime minister and Josef Zieleniec replaced Dienstbier as the minister of foreign affairs.

To be able to understand Czech policy toward the European Union today and how the German question interacts with this process, it is necessary to bear in mind some of the official and non-official arguments used by the Czech government when discussing the European integration process,[35] as well as the way in which the process is perceived in Prague.

In Prague[36] it is not considered necessary to justify why the Czech Republic is an applicant to enter the Union because it considers that it has always been part of Europe. The Czech territories were excluded from the rest of Europe by the take-over of the communist regime in 1948, which means, implicitly, by the former Soviet Union. This idea is well enunciated by the Czech writer in exile Milan Kundera in 1985, when he defines the fate of Central Europe in the 1980s to the 'kidnapped Occident'.[37] From this perspective, the fall of communism in 1989 is seen as the opportunity to 'return to Europe' after decades of totalitarism. The sense of belonging to Western Europe is reinforced by the conviction of and the affirmation by the Czech people of sharing the same values (in tacit opposition to the East), as proclaims Foreign Minister Zieleniec in an interview for *Lidová Demokracie* in 1994: 'The nations with which we feel tied and with whom we share the values of civilisation and a way of life are part of the European Union and NATO. Our place is in those institutions'.[38]

Security is another main argument in favour of the integration into the western institutions. The fact that the European Community has accomplished one of its main aims, maintaining peace on the continent among the member-states for decades is seen a great success and attraction for Central European countries. A former Czech minister of the economy Vladimir Dlouhy even considered that 'the idea of guaranteeing a durable peace on the continent is the basic and common stone for the European integration'.[39] The European Union is therefore also perceived as a way to contain and even control Germany or, to be more politically correct, a way to transform and put into perspective the geopolitical imbalance of the European scene from which the smaller states suffer, which is one of the preoccupations of the small European neighbours of Germany, as J. Zieleniec explains:

> I consider the integration of the Czech Republic into the European Union as an historic chance. Go and look at Denmark, the Netherlands, Belgium or Luxembourg, all these countries also have a troubled past and a troubled history of their relations with Germany. Those countries also consider the integration process as a chance for small nations.[40]

Although political relations with Europe and the process of integration has progressed in the last years, these elements have remained a constant in the discourse on Europe and do differentiate the Czech Republic from its Central European neighbours.

The Europeanisation of Czech–German relations

In 1989 bilateral Czech–German relations reach an entirely new context: democracy and the stated mutual desire for normalisation. Even if these relations could legitimately be considered by the political leaders of both the Czech Republic and Germany as being better than they have been in many years, they were not actually normalised until the signature of the joint Declaration of Reconciliation in January 1997 and the late 1990s. The 'German Question' in the Czech Republic as it has reappeared under a new light since 1989 may be defined in two ways: the gestation of a common heritage (the Sudeten German question in particular) and the imbalance – demographic, geographic, economic and political – between Germany and the Czech Republic. Beyond the initially and essentially bilateral nature of the question, it is its implications and the challenges it poses for Europe which are of interest here.

The German population of Czechoslovakia, established on the border territory (and in the main cities) since the middle ages, represents up to a third of the entire population of Bohemia at the start of the First Republic of Czechoslovakia.[41] The war, Nazi occupation and the final expulsion of nearly the entire German population from Czechoslovakia in 1945–47[42] profoundly disturbs relations between the Czechs and the Germans and the last brings no solution to the German question in Czechoslovakia as some had hoped it would.

The great majority of the Sudeten Germans, when they were expelled from Czechoslovakia, settled in Bavaria where they play a political and economical role of the first order. They are represented by the Sudetendeutsche Landsmannschaft (SL), a radical lobbying group. At the end of 1989 the SL presented the Czechoslovakian government a list of its demands, for the most part already established in their constituting charter of 1950: the right of return (Heimatrecht); indemnification for damages sustained during the expulsion; return of goods and property confiscated by presidential decrees in 1945 as well as the abrogation of those decrees. The traditional support of the Sudeten German for the CSU of Bavaria, a partner of the CDU at the heart of the government of Helmut Kohl, gives them the means of applying political pressure on the federal government and permits the SL to directly affect bilateral relations between the German and the Czech governments.

The radicalisation of this question in the early 1990s has led the representatives of the German Sudetenland to try to give a European dimension to their demands:[43] they have threatened to slow down the process of Czech integration into the European Union as long as the Sudeten question is not resolved;[44] as explained in 1994 the Bavarian Minister Edmund Stoiber: 'the only road to Brussels leads through Munich';[45] they intend to use politic pressure not just on the Bavarian CSU and its representatives in the federal and European parliaments but they even hope to be supported by Austria in this project.[46] Even if this menace seems to bear little weight in regard to the unswaying support of the German federal government for the integration of the Czech Republic into the European Union, it has been repeated several times in public and has been widely broadcast by the Czech media. The publicity surrounding the Sudeten questions, brought up by certain European parliamentarians –defenders of and spokesmen for the SL's demands in European institutions like the European Parliament– has been perceived in the Czech Republic as an attack on the rather positive image the country enjoys abroad and on the European scene. Nevertheless, the signature in January 1997 after 18 months of difficult negotiations of a Declaration of Reconciliation between Germany and the Czech Republic has officially permitted closure of the question at least on political and legal levels.[47] Without putting an end to the Sudeten German demands, it partly contributes to a certain 'marginalisation' of the radical trends of the SL in the debate.

Beyond this, a solution to the Sudeten German question also represents a foreign and European affairs goal, even if symbolic, for the German government on the eve of enlargement. After reunification, as Germany has strived to develop good, friendly relations with its neighbours, especially to the East, this problem was underestimated at first by the German government. The evolution of the Sudeten question embarrasses the German government precisely when it has to convince its eastern as well as its western partners of its goodwill with regard to the enlargement which it supports so eagerly. This question is also linked to the indemnification of the Czech victims of Nazism,[48] and appears to be the last stumbling block to normalisation of relations with Central Europe, and its resolution will allow Germany to turn the page on the Second World War.

The imbalance of power between the Czech Republic and Germany, not only in economic terms but also in terms of geopolitics and demography constitutes the other side of the German question which is of interest here. This inequality has been accentuated by the reunification of Germany on the one side and the partition of Czechoslovakia on the other. Today Germany is by a wide margin the largest economic partner of the Czech Republic and its economic might is considered by the Czechs as a key factor in their bilateral relations.[49] The rapid development of the German economic presence in the Czech Republic is particularly visible in as much as before 1989 it had been practically nil and very discreet. In this geopolitical context, integration into the European Union is perceived by the Czechs as a means to reduce German predominance in the Czech Republic by diluting it with the rest of Europe.

The European Union as a solution to the 'German problem'

Approaching the problematic of Czech–German relations from this angle points out their European dimension or even their 'Europeanisation'. The Czechs see their rapport with their German neighbour evolving into an increasingly 'triangular' relationship. The former Czech minister of Foreign Affairs, Josef Zieleniec, speaks of 'an integrated Europe where essential events are not played out on a bilateral level but multilaterally . . . and when we say that the principal goal of Czech foreign policy is integration into the European Union, we see several levels, one of which is our relationship with our great neighbour Germany'.[50] This evolution is a consequence of the Europeanisation of relations between member states and non-members and most especially with the candidate states. The prospect of integration, in effect, leads the candidate states to closer economic, judicial and social ties to the European Union. Attempting to consider these relationships as strictly bilateral no longer makes sense. The Czech population's perceptions of European integration are an illustration of the 'triangularisation' of the Czech–German relations and the intermingling of concerns over Germany and Europe. The Czech population perceives that the role and position of Germany in Europe and in the world is transformed by the fact that Germany belongs to the European Union and NATO.[51]

As far as the past is concerned, Germany would like to turn the page on the Second World War and establish relations with its Central European neighbours along new lines. On the Czech side, the Sudeten German issue embarrasses the government in that it has been a latent menace to all political discussions between the two states. Not only does the dispute threaten to tarnish the image of the Czech Republic, but it puts it in a more uncomfortable position *vis-à-vis* Western Europe than its Central European counterparts. Finally, it is a question of political will on both parts to regard to past points of contention and stumbling blocks, not bilaterally, but from a European perspective, as they pursue the process of integration and bring it to term. This leads necessarily to a redefinition of problems which no longer have the same meaning as they did in the past, and which can no longer be put in the same terms. These words of Wolfgang Schäuble, president of the CDU-CSU parliamentary group in the *Bundestag* are illustrative of this evolution:

> Being a member of the European Union also signifies a commitment on the fundamental liberties of the people of Europe. Amongst them is the freedom of movement and residence for the citizens of the member states, but also for Germans. Why should not the German people go and live and work in Silesia or in Bohemia?[52]

The Sudeten question thus changes perspective and the demand for a right of return no longer makes sense in this new context. Even if it would be too simple to speak of a 'solution', such an evolution nevertheless marks an important change. The problem is diffused and thereby relativised. Whether as referee, such as the European Justice Court, or as a third party, the European Union is a more and more effective interlocutor, when on the bilateral level no solutions can be found.[53]

Germany as an argument in the Czech debate on European integration

Even if there exists today a consensus at the heart of the Czech political leadership to support European integration (extremist parties are not under discussion here) there are a few voices raised, notably from within the former right-wing majority, to put into question the process of integration.[54]

A political philosopher close to Prime Minister Václav Klaus, Václav Belohradsky is an intellectual with influence at the heart of the ODS, even if he is not representative of party. His argument against a '*European* State' backed by Germany is of interest in as much as it expresses a certain current active in the Czech Republic.[55] As ardent opponent of the Maastricht Treaty which, according to Belohradsky, fixes 'as an objective of the European Union a progressive transformation of its institutions into a super-state called Europe', he denounces the European Union as being nothing more 'than one solution to the German question: by constructing a homogenous European State, Germany and the other European States evade the problems involved in a powerful national State of Germany within Europe'. He goes so far as to describe the European commitment of Germany as 'two faced German patriotism' which serves only as rhetoric to disguise the fact that Germany, now once again a 'normal nation State', is defending its own national interests. Belohradsky denounces the pre-eminence of Germany at the heart of the European Union (and the use of the traditional theme of the centrality of Germany on the European continent) which he presents as a threat to European construction, preferring to turn towards the United States and the 'Atlantism and Americanism which is the European road which leads to modern democracy'.

Without taking up the most critical and explicitly anti-German themes of his advisor and in a more politic and pragmatic register, the ex-Prime Minister Václav Klaus often refers more or less implicitly to Germany in his discourse on European construction. A central element in Klaus's approach to Europe is the question of identity. The manner in which European construction currently evolves presents a threat to the Czech identity in process of recomposition. The Central European States found themselves dragged into the Soviet empire only shortly after the collapse of three other empires (Austrian, Ottoman and Russian) and they find themselves today confronted by a difficult problem, 'that of finding their identity and not losing it on the road which leads to Europe'.[56] Klaus does not hesitate to stress the fact that: 'We [the Czechs] wish to become part of [advanced Europe] as a sovereign political entity, as the Czech Republic, which will neither be lost nor dissolved in Europe, and which has something to offer to the entity it will join.'[57] Klaus denounces the peril of a lack of a European identity today on which to build a unified Europe.

He then takes a clear and repeated position on the nature and the form of the European Union into which the Czech Republic would like to be integrated without ever putting into question this eventual integration. Klaus thus contributes towards defining the Czech Republic's position on the European Union in opposition to the other candidate states (see memoranda) in as much as he places it squarely in the centre of the internal discussion of the European Union on its future evolution: a federation of states, a confederation or a giant marketplace.

> We share the European values as our occidental neighbours and, just like them, we believe in the significance, the importance and positive influence of the process of European integration . . . The questions which we raise rather concern the form of European integration . . . If I say that we are resolved to join in a reasonable European integration, I do not say that we are in favour of an absolute and unconditional unification of Europe.[58]

Only the nation-state can provide an identity as a point of reference to its citizens. This statement implies that current European integration rests on strong nation states[59] and does not coincide with the concept of a stronger integration such as defended by federal Germany. The denunciation of a 'Europe of regions', upheld notably by Bavaria, fits this pattern as well.

On the economic level, the perception of the Czech public is also revealing both of the 'centrality' and permanence of the German issue in the European debate and of the ambiguity in their expectations, as well as those of other Central European candidates, in regard to Germany. When considering Germany's relations with its neighbours and especially with its eastern neighbours, German interests appear to be the main issue. A large majority (68 per cent to 32 per cent) believe that Germany hopes to create a political and economic dependence for Central European countries towards Germany, and 54 per cent to 33 per cent that it is in Germany's best interest to 'have a strong European Union to guarantee the prosperity of the weakest and smallest'. The Czech population is aware that if Germany appears to be a great supporter of their entry into European Union or NATO, it is because it is in Germany's own interests in that part of Europe. This factor is directly related to the question of the power and responsibility Germany wields in the Union as well as in the whole of Europe.

An ambivalence appears when, on one side, 53 per cent to 47 per cent, affirm that they would prefer Germany not to take more responsibility in the development of Europe, and on the other side, 44 per cent to 29 per cent, still consider Germany as the main supporter and guarantor of the integration of Central European Countries into the European Union and NATO.[60] Almost all believe that an economic rapprochement between the two countries would contribute favourably to bilateral relations and a large majority feel that entering the European Union and NATO would have the same effect. The image of Germany as a motor for European prosperity, stability and security is challenged by the image of Germany as a developing world power, with its own ambitions and interests. Furthermore, the power of Germany at the heart of the European Union and its dominant presence on the European economic scene have played and continue to play a double role: providing an element of attraction and a model of prosperity for an economy in transition but also an element of unease for the Czech Republic with its future level of political, social and economic independence uncertain in such a European Union.

German policy in Central Europe: a support for enlargement?

The collapse of communism in Eastern Europe was perceived in Germany as a step towards the reunification, which remained the main priority for months. Once reunified, Germany again occupied the centre of the European continent. Until then unambiguous, the FRG's commitment to Western institutions, EEC and NATO, although reaffirmed, changed in nature. Germany had to find a compromise between pursuing and deepening its engagement in the West, and especially within the European Union, and the restoration of co-operation with Central Europe which had been interrupted by decades of Nazi and communist totalitarism. A refusal to commit to go forward in Central Europe would destabilise and even compromise the process of transition in the region, while an overactive co-operative policy would be misinterpreted by Germany's Western counterparts. These allies were, in fact, ready to denounce the shift of German interests to the east and even to reawaken the myth of a *Mitteleuropa* under German influence.[61] At the same time it was recognised that Germany, since its reunification and the end of the Cold War, could and indeed had to play a more active role in foreign policy.

The question of the role Germany plays in Central Europe is posed in terms of the 'new responsibility' of a unified Germany because of its 'objective' potential power and its geopolitical situation[62] and leads back to 'classical' debates about: German power,[63] national interests, a hegemonic 'temptation' or the consequences of a central position in the middle of Europe.[64] Since 1990 and reunification, Germany seems more disposed to evoke its national interest.[65] Working on this issue, the political commentator Hans-Peter Schwarz defines Germany as a '*Nationalstaat*', the '*Zentralmacht Europas*' and '*europäische Großmacht*'.[66] According to Schwarz, Germany, because of its geographic position, its economic capacity, its cultural influence as well as its dynamism, has to play the role due to a central power, that is, a regional leadership acting as a mediator and stabiliser within the framework of the European Union. Above all, Germany has to normalise and contain its power to avoid reaching a hegemonic situation. Actually, the debate about 'German power' leads to the question of the use of this power.[67] In the last few decades, the European policy of the German government has been marked by the will to go beyond a national policy which might awaken fears among its partners. Germany legitimises its foreign policy in Europe by arguing that it acts not in its own interest but in the interest of the European Union and for greater stability on the continent. In this perspective, European integration is seen as a long-term solution to two leitmotifs of German policy: stability and security in Europe.[68]

The American political scientist S. Reich, in an article titled 'Should Europe fear the Germans or not?' recognises the structural power of Germany in its capacity to set agendas and limit the choices of its counterparts.[69] He defines this as a situation of 'hegesy', something like a potential hegemony. For Reich, Germany can not accept a situation of power because of its traumatic 'collective memory'. This realist approach (not the only one) does not bring enough light to bear on the importance of the interdependence which characterise German relations with the rest of Europe. The numerous non-state or substate actors (the *Länder*, private businesses as well as the *Bundesbank* and the Constitutional Court) are all independent of the central government and leave the state neither coherent nor dominant.[70] The risk (if any) would on the contrary come rather from the weakness of the state which would no longer be able to manage its citizens or subnational entities. In other terms German power is also beneficial to other European countries and any Western reservation finally would derive from a less active German involvement in Central Europe.[71]

The German government tends to structure its internal as well as external politics using the European integration framework. More than just an argument, Europe appears as a real ideology as is illustrated by the title of T. Garton Ash's book on Germany and Europe, '*In Europe's Name*'. During the last forty or so years, FRG's European policy has been subject to constraints: its geopolitical situation and Germany's reliance upon Western allies where even Brandt's Ostpolitik depended on the consent of the superpowers. In the context of European integration seen as a way of reducing the diplomatic disadvantages of a semi-sovereign West Germany, the 'Europeanisation' of Germany may therefore be seen as both an objective and an achievement of Bonn's European policy.[72] Today that Germany has recovered its sovereignty and seems more and more ready to behave as a 'normal' country; it remains to be seen to what extent European interests still coincide with those of Germany.

The new German Ostpolitik *after 1989*

The new German *Ostpolitik* after 1989 could be defined by a double objective: (1) the return to 'normality' which could be achieved through unification and reconciliation with the eastern neighbours; in others words, to close the chapter on the Second World War and become a 'normal' country; (2) the security issue: the geographic position of Germany, in the eastern part of the European Union, means that its oriental border coincides with that of the European Union (as well as Austria's since its integration in 1995). It is the border between the stability and internal prosperity of the European Union and the economic difficulties and potential instability of Central and Eastern Europe. The migratory pressure on German borders (generally originates from countries located further to the east), the fear of an influx of economic immigrants and the consequences of the ensuing political instability is taking hold seriously in Germany.[73] The financial and technical support that Germany provides to its eastern neighbours is linked to this stability issue. Considering these two priorities of German foreign policy *vis à vis* the East, the integration of these CEC in the European institutions (European Union and NATO) looks like part of the answer. The 'consequences of the instability' for Germany appear in several arguments in favour of the European Union's enlargement.[74] It would then mean that European enlargement coincides to a certain extent with German interests. A clear illustration of this can be read in the CDU-CSU's document the 'Lamers–Schäuble report' which was made public in September 1994. It is devoted to the future evolution of the European Union and sheds an interesting light on German foreign policy priorities:

> It is of particular interest to Germany that Europe not be exposed to centrifugal forces . . . It would be the first to suffer directly from the consequences of instability in the East. The only solution to prevent the return of the unstable pre-war situation which confined Germany in an uncomfortable position between East and West, is to integrate German Central and Eastern European neighbours in the post-war West European system. [The CDU-CSU report recalls that] if European integration does not evolve towards enlargement, Germany could, under security constraints be forced or incited to re-establish alone and by traditional means stability in Eastern Europe, which would be beyond its strength and would bring about the erosion of cohesion within the European Union.[75]

The main objective of enlargement is to insure that Germany is surrounded by 'order and stability'. It will once again find a centrality within a new context which breaks with a hundred and fifty years of German prevarication '*between Western and Russian overtures; between "Locarno" and "Rappallo"*'. In a sense, this *Mittellage* could contribute to recreating a natural order in a Europe conceived as a culturally homogenous socio-economic entity which covers the entire continent and which the Iron curtain had but temporarily divided.[76]

German constraints on enlargement

Germany and the Czech Republic signed a declaration of reconciliation in 1997 in which the two countries declared that they would not burden their relations with political and legal issues from the past. Several problems inherited mainly from the Second World War and immediately after have, in fact, seriously hampered bilateral relations since the beginning of the 1990s, when a favourable international context should have led to their rapid normalisation. Despite the declaration, the European Parliament voted in 1999 a resolution concerning the 'progress of the Czech Republic on the road to integration' in which the Parliament 'asked the Czech government [. . .] to abrogate the laws and decrees dating from the years 1945 and 1946 concerning the expulsion of ethnic groups from the former Czechoslovakia'.[77] A few days later (19 May 1999), the Austrian

Parliament (*Nationarat*) voted a similar resolution concerning the incompatibility between the European juridical order and the expulsion decrees from immediately after the war in the former Czechoslovakia and Yugoslavia (actually Slovenia). For the first time, a bilateral issue (the abolition / validity of the Beneš decrees) has discussed on the European level and used as an argument (and a condition) on the enlargement process to the Czech Republic. Moreover, the Austrian Chancelor, Wolfgang Schüssel, who had used a moderate tone during his first months at the head of the government and notably refused to establish a link between the two issues, changed his discourse in 2001: at the Sudeten German congress, he declared that it was for him 'very obvious that it would be necessary, before the entry of the Czech Republic into the EU that the Benes decrees at last belong to the past, because they are contrary to European juridical values'.[78] Despite the diplomatic formulation, he took a step that he had until then avoided: linking the two issues and it can today be envisaged that Austria use its voice at the European Council to block or slow down the enlargement of the EU.[79] A further hardening of Austrian position in the beginning of 2002 accentuated this fear in the Czech Republic.[80]

In Germany in the spring of 1998 there began a series of debates at the Bundestag, initiated by the parliamentary group CDU/CSU to draw the governments's attention to the demands of the *Vertriebene* and to establish a link between the integration of the Czech Republic into the EU and the abrogation of the Benes decrees.[81] The Bavarian minister-president Edmund Stoiber had been using the same argument in several of his declarations on the enlargement of the EU.[82] His political weight in Bavaria, within the CSU, and at the federal level since Helmut Kohl's departure in 1998, but above all since January 2002 when he became the CDU/CSU candidate to the chancellery for the parliamentary elections (September 2002)[83] gives to his words a political dimension which goes beyond the Sudeten issue in itself.

These attempts to put the expulsion issue on the European agenda should be viewed from three different angles. From the point of view of German domestic politics, they are part of a balancing process between the CDU and CSU which began after the electoral defeat in 1998. Stoiber's nomination to the candidacy at the beginning of 2002 confirmed this evolution. On the Austrian political scene however, Haider's breakthrough has only reinforced existing tendencies: during the 1990s the former minister of foreign affairs Alois Mock (ÖVP) had already backed the Sudeten associations in their demands, and Haider has long since expressed himself on this theme.

But it is above all at the European level that this new Austro-Bavarian activism is most troubling and the resolutions voted in different parliaments coincide with the start of an internal debate in Germany and Austria on enlargement. If the threats have not had an immediate political effect on negotiations between the Czech Republic and the Union and have been partly alleviated by European mediation, they have had a negative impact in the Czech Republic.[84] Today, only 38 per cent of Germans and 35 per cent of Austrians support European enlargement (among the EU 15 only the French are more reluctant, with 34 per cent).[85] These resolutions have had a negative impact on the Czech Republic where public opinion is not definitely convinced about integration into the European Union (about half of the Czechs support enlargement today). If integration had to be conditioned by the resolution of a bilateral issue which is recognised by both governments as insoluble (on the political and legal level), Czech opinion may decide to reconsider its European future.[86] After the signature of the common declaration in 1997, it was clearly Czech public opinion that the Sudeten issue would no longer be a political problem between the two countries. The Sudeten issue was also seen (perhaps too much so) as only a bileral dispute between the Czechs and the Germans and one which should not be evoked at the European level at risk of damaging the international image of the Czech Republic. Linking the two issues would also play into the sovereignists' hands in the Czech Republic: that bilateral issues might be negotiated at the European level provides an easy argument to the sovereignists who denounce the interference of the European 'super-state' in domestic affairs. It also reinforces the nationalist argument some politicians use (the communists for instance but also V. Klaus and part of the ODS) to denounce a Europe 'under German influence', that is a Europe in which Germany can impose its own interests in the name of the interests of Europe.

On a strictly European level, one should also stress the recent declaration of the German Chancellor Schroeder (as well as the Austrian Schlüssel) concerning the free movement of workers.[87] Both have asked the European Union to impose a seven-year delay on the future members in order to protect their own labour market. This condition has then been officially debated within a European meeting a few months later. It is considered by the applicants as a severe restriction upon their membership and a way of postponing their full integration. But more than that, it also gives the impression to the candidates that Germany is imposing its own interests upon the rest of the Union and therefore reinforces the Central European fear of entering a Union where Germany would be too strong.

That neighbouring Germany, who by virtue of its weight and geopolitical position within the EU is unavoidable, has moved from supporter and main advocate of the candidate countries to a difficult partner who imposes conditions and constraints, is a hypothesis which can now no longer be overlooked in Central Europe. This change poses a problem for certain candidates and in particular for the Czech Republic which has perhaps relied too heavily upon a single country within the Union. The change in Germany's attitude shows how much is at stake in the next enlargement, not only for the candidate countries but also for the members of the Union themselves.

A key actor and active supporter of enlargement, Germany is an important element in the future evolution of the European Union, inasmuch as this enlargement will move the centre of the Union toward the east. United Germany is also aware of the fears of its western European partners concerning its political or economic involvement in Central Europe. This is one reason it sees its foreign policy interests best served if it operates within a multilateral and integrated policy context.

Germany and the Czech Republic in a broader Europe

When in 1989, the Western European position was to suggest to the CEEC that they make it their common goal to succeed in their transition and join the West, the three Central European Countries concerned, Poland, Czechoslovakia and Hungary, clearly expressed their ambition to go it alone, each down their proper road (the so-called differentiation competition). If the short-term objective was to integrate western European institutions and thereby recover their position on the European political scene, the European Union was perceived as the ultimate goal. The Czech policy of the 'return to Europe' was, at least in the first years, marked by the determination to differentiate itself from its Central European neighbours. In the debates held before the division of Czechoslovakia, one of the arguments for separation which was supposed to positively influence the Czech people (who were not in favour of the separation of the two republics) was that it would speed integration into the European Union; and move the country's centre of gravity west like an artificial simulation to bring the Czech Republic closer to the centre of Europe and the European Union. Economic arguments were then quoted to prove such allegations. This policy of every man for himself risked reinforcing not only the already existing centrifugal tendencies, but also strategies of 'clientelism' towards the western countries which were supposed to help integration: Germany and Austria for Hungary, and Germany and Great Britain for the Czech Republic, for instance.[88]

The publication of the Lamers–Schäuble's report (Summer 1994) is a factor – one of the most visible – which allows Czech policy to evolve *vis-à-vis* its Central European neighbours, especially Poland, in the direction of a rapprochement. It is recognised and officially accepted in Prague that Poland, for Germany as well as for the rest of Europe, has a strategic role and position because of its size, its geographic position between the European Union and Russia, and its recent history. Even though the Czech economic transition is presented by the Czech government as being more advanced than that of Poland, the strategic issue, especially that of security, gives Poland a privileged position in the enlargement (of the European Union and NATO). After few years of 'competition', a co-operation between the two states has been recognised as being an advantage for both. One can note a change in the Czech political discourse toward Poland during the year of 1994, which has provoked, among other things a renewed intensive contact at the political level. But this rapprochement is not associated with any organisation or institution for Central European co-operation. Czechoslovakia, and later the Czech Republic, has during Klaus's era strongly resisted the triangle of Visegrád, which it considered a Western invention, an institution imposed from outside or a waiting room for the CEEC on the road to European Union: 'We managed to resist the recommendations of some of our western friends to create in Central and Eastern Europe a special subregional institution because it would separate us from Europe instead of leading us to it.'[89] After the signature of the association agreements, Visegrád is no longer seen as worthwhile. The lukewarm attempt at interregional organisation and the lack of a policy of co-operation within Central Europe shows that the Czechs choose to privilege their East–West relations, seen as more 'useful' on the way towards the European Union.[90]

The development of German policy toward Eastern Europe moves in the same direction. Since 1989 Germany has privileged the re-establishment of bilateral relations with its eastern neighbours but each in parallel, that is, without introducing any official differentiation between them and according to the global policy evoked earlier. The treaties of good neighbourhood and friendship from 1991–92 were coached in the same terms both with Poland and Czechoslovakia (then with the Czech Republic and Slovakia).

Nevertheless, some general tendencies at the European level lead to doubts as to whether the Czech Republic is going to find in integration what it is longing for. For instance, the creation of the Weimar triangle in 1994, where Germany, Poland and France meet together, could be seen as an important or at least a highly symbolic stage of the recomposition of the European continent. Even if it is only a forum for discussion, the simple fact of its existence confirms the will of these three countries to think together about the future of Europe. This development is important for the Czech Republic. The meetings of the Weimar triangle were not especially followed by Czech public opinion, but the Weimar triangle reaffirms the dichotomy between large and small nations in Europe and extends it to Central Europe. By including France in the process of co-operation in the region, this initiative not only gains a measure of transparency but also helps build confidence *vis-à-vis* the two most relevant countries in the 'enlargement game'.

Conclusion

Even if the debate on the nature and shape of a post-enlargement European Union will not be addressed here, some reflections on the subject are appropriate. The integration of some Central European countries will obviously contribute to alter the balance within the European Union (which has already changed after the previous enlargement). Whether it is matter of a shift in the European Union's centre of gravity towards the East, a shift of Germany towards the new centre of the European Union or a redistribution of power and centres of interest in Europe, this enlargement is going to transform the European Union. In 1989, with the euphoria of the 'return to Europe' which at last appeared possible and even inevitable, support for German reunification was seen more than ever as the last step to the unification of all Europe, with

Germany as the main and inescapable partner of the Czech Republic. Only a few years later, this perception has evolved. It is in reaction to a Germany which has become a European and Central European power that the Czech Republic considers its integration into the European Union and NATO as a means of finding a necessary counterbalance. There appears to be a paradox in the relations of the Czech Republic with the European Union, which can be summed up in this way: even as the Czech Republic hopes to find in integration into the European Union a means to counterbalance Germany's power, especially its economic power, and transform bilateral relations into multilateral relations, it dreads the idea that the European Union could become in effect a 'German Europe'.

For the Czech Republic, integration into the European Union is not only a 'return to Europe'. It is also a process of distancing itself from its past. Being able to integrate the European Union means being able to envision a different and more open future within a multilateral framework, after having pulled a veil over a complex past (communist and before). In this regard the Czech relations to Germany are revealing and illustrative of a complex process within the Czech Republic. The Czech–German rapprochement process initiated in 1989, for which the declaration of reconciliation from 1997 was a key step, has an important European dimension, which is the idea that the old disputes could be overcome by a common will to take part in European unification.

There exists today a direct link between the German question and the future configuration of Central Europe and of Europe as a whole. For many years, one of the main dilemmas of German foreign policy had been to find a compromise between *Ostpolitik,* that is the rapprochement with East Germany as a means to open up the East, and *Europapolitik,* the allegiance to the European Community and more generally to the West. Now, for the first time since the war, there is a chance to reconcile the two. And this is also the wish of Germany's Eastern neighbours.[91]

Since 1999 however, Germany and Austria have used enlargement and the European label as a negotiating device in their bilateral relations with the Czech Republic. This poses a question about the nature of the current enlargement and therefore concerns all of Europe. The way in which the Sudeten question has been brought into the European debate by some pressure groups in Germany and in Austria reveals in effect an inversion of the philosophy of European construction: the associations of expelled Germans and a part of the German and Austrian political classes require that the solution of bilateral differences be the condition of Czech (and Slovak) integration into the European Union. On the contrary, since the 1950s, the very idea of European integration rests on the shared will to construct a common future. It is the participation in this common project which is meant in time to alleviate tensions and create conditions for dialogue and reconciliation. The instrumentalisation and corruption of European construction which has been seen in the last few years has taken on greater importance since the beginning of 2002 and puts into question the way in which the next enlargement will take place. Finally, it is the successful enlargement of the EU which is at stake. The hope for future enlargement is that it will do for post-Cold War relations between Germany and its Eastern neighbours what European construction succeeded in doing for relations between Germany and its Western neighbours after the Second World War.

Notes

1 Timothy Garton Ash affirms that 'the contemporary model of the German democracy is arguably the most relevant of all . . . because it is a model built on the rubble of a totalitarian dictatorship and very deliberately designed to prevent the return of [such] a dictatorship. It is, one might say; a Western system built on Central European experience': in 'Eastern Europe: après le déluge, nous', *The New York Review of Books*, 16 August 1990, 59.

2 V. Havel, 'Czechs and Germans on the Way to a Good Neighbourhood', address by the President of the Czech Republic, Charles University, Prague, 17 February 1995.

3 A demographic asymmetry: 82 millions inhabitants in Germany vs. 10.3 million in the Czech Republic (after the loss of 5 millions Slovaks from the time of Czechoslovakia); a geographic asymmetry: 78,000 sq km for the Czech Republic and 357,000 sq km for unified Germany (Bavaria itself covers 70,500 sq km and has a population of 12 million); political asymmetry: Germany has been a stable democracy since 1949 (at least in the West) while the Czech Republic is still in the transition process; economic asymmetry: Germany is a G7 member and the richest country in Europe while the Czech Republic is working on the transformation of its economy into a maret economy; an asymmetry in terms of weight in international relations: Germany plays a decisive role in the European unification process, it is one of the pillars of NATO in Europe and after reunification has recovered its voice on the international scene. The Czech Republic, on the contrary, has difficulties in gaining visibility next to Poland, which is considered a strategic partner for the Western countries.

4 Actually, this is not absolutely true, because the Sudetendeutsche Landsmannschaft (the Sudeten German lobby in Bavaria) considers the 'right to return' not only as the chance of settling in the Czech Republic. It also claims the recognition of the right of a minority of Germans who would decide to go back there (schools, newspapers, bilingual administration etc.).

5 Here we will prefer an approach in terms of 'governance'. See S. Bulmer, *New Institutionalism, the Single Market and EU Governance* (Olso, ARENA Working paper 25/1997); G. Marks, 'Structural Policy and Multilevel Governance in the Europe Centrale', in A. Cafruny and G. Rosenthal (eds), *The State of the European Community*, 2: *The Maastricht Debates and Beyond* (Boulder, CO: Lynne Rienner, 1993); B. Kohler-Koch, 'Catching Up with Changes: The Transformation of Governance in the European Union', *Journal of European Policy*, Vol. 3, No. 3 (1996), 359–380; J. Richardson (ed.), *European Union: Power and Policy-Making* (London: Routledge, 1996); M. Pollack, 'New Institutionalism and EU Governance: The Promise and Limits of Institutionalist Analysis', *Governance* Vol. 9, No. 4 (1996), 429–458; L. Hooghe (ed.), *Cohesion Policy and European Integration: Building Multi-level Governance* (Oxford: Oxford University Press, 1996); A. Moravcsik, *Why the European Community Strengthens the State: Domestic Politics and International Cooperation* (Harvard Center for European Studies, Working Paper No. 52, 1994).

6 Germany was in 1995 the chief commercial partner for imports and exports between the member states of the European Union and the 12 CEEC (total $112 billion); 52 per cent for Germany, 17 per cent for Italy, 8 per cent for France. In 1995 German investments in the CEEC represented 19 per cent of total foreign investments (ahead of the USA and Austria, 14 per cent): *Business Week*, 3 February 1997, 14–17.

7 The CEE's share of total extra-EU trade in 1994 for Germany: exports to CEE = 10 per cent (Italy = 7.83 per cent); imports from CEE = 10.85 per cent (Italy = 7 per cent). Germany's share of CEE trade (per cent of total EU-12 exports to CEE-6): in 1989 = 42 per cent (Italy = 18 per cent) and in 1994 = 57 per cent (Italy = 13.5 per cent). H. Grabbe and K. Hughes, *Eastward Enlargement of the European Union* (London: The Royal Institute of International Affairs), pp. 28–29.

8 F. Westerman, 'Germany's Economic Power in Europe' in A. S. Markovits and S. Reich (eds), *The German Predicament: Memory and Power in the New Europe* (Ithaca: Cornell University Press, 1997), pp. 150–182.

9 Imports from the EU to the CR in 1997 = 531,357 Million Kc of whom 227,490 million Kc for Germany. Exports from the CR to the EU in 1997 = 430,489 million Kc of whom 257,312 million Kc for Germany. Source: German Embassy in Prague, 1998.

10 With 34 per cent of its importation and 38 per cent of its exportations (in 1998), ahead of Slovakia (with 13.2 per cent). German Embassy in Prague, 1998. In 2000, the chief partner for Germany among the CEEC has been for the first time the Czech Republic.

11 Direct investments in CR are in 1997 about $1.3 billion, of which 0.391 was from Germany (30 per cent). Source: German Embassy in Prague, 1998. Since 1990, the share of Germany in foreign investments in the Czech Republic is about 29 per cent (in total). Source: Czech ministry of industry and trade, 2000.

12 Some suggest that Central Europe could be for Germany what Mexico is to the USA. See, for instance, H. Rudolph, 'German Maquiladora? Foreign Workers in the Process of Regional Economic Restructuring', *Innovation: The European Journal of Social Sciences*, Vol. 7, No. 1 (1994), 137–150.

13 *Auswärtige Kulturpolitik, Almanach der Bundesregierung 1993/1994* (Bonn: Presse- und Informationsamt der Bundesregierung, 1994), pp. 149–151.

14 C. Höfig, 'Foreign Cultural Policy', in A. S. Markovits and S. Reich (eds), *The German Predicament: Memory and Power in the New Europe* (Ithaca: Cornell University Press, 1998), pp. 183–202.

15 It is mainly through the Goethe institutes that the German language programme is run.

16 C. Höfig, 'Foreign Cultural Policy', p. 198.

17 J. P. Goujeon, *Où va l'Allemagne?* (Paris: Flammarion, 1997), pp. 271–272.

18 In 1996, there were about 737,000 students and pupils studying German in the Czech Republic according to the German embassy in Prague.

19 I. Gabal, Friedrich Naumann-Stiftung, *Einstellung der tschechischen Gesellschaft zu Deutschland* (Prague, 1995).

20 *Eubarometer*, No. 7 (1997): 23 per cent of the population claims to speak German, (in Hungary, only 10 per cent of the population and 13 per cent in Poland).

21 Antje Vollmer, in a lecture at the Carolinum at the Charles University, in Prague, 5 October 1995.

22 Konrad Adenauer-Stiftung (CDU); Friedrich Naumann-Stiftung (FDP); Friedrich Ebert-Stiftung (SPD); Hans Seidel-Stiftung (CSU); Heinrich Böll-Stiftung (Grünen).

23 To take a very recent example, the Friedrich-Ebert and the Heinrich Böll Foundations financed an ambitious conference titled: 'The European revolution 1989 and the future of Europe' which took place at Prague Castle and brought together intellectuals from Central Europe and Germany.

24 See A. Bazin, 'Les Régions frontalières tchèques: différenciation interne et enjeux européens', *Revue d'Etudes Comparatives Est-Ouest* Vol. 29, No. 4 (1998), 229–255.

25 The high salaries in Germany attract German investors to the Czech Republic, whereas the Czech workforce seeks jobs in Germany. Nevertheless, it is today admitted that in Bavaria, for instance, the opening of the boundaries has had a globally positive effect on the economy of that Land.

26 In the early 1990s, the difference in the standard of living between Bohemia and Bavaria was 1 to 7.

27 Volker Ruhe, the German Ministry of Defence explained in a speech in May 1995: 'It is one of the vital interests of Germany that the frontier between stability and instability, between poverty and wealth, that the boundaries of NATO and the European Union do not coincide with the oriental frontiers of Germany. We want one day to ee these borders as permeable as the French–German border is today.' Speech delivered in Bonn, at the Deutsche Atlantische Gesellschaft, on 16 May 1995.
28 The CRO-CO Fund is the result of a resolution of the European Parliament, voted in 1993, which creates a special fund for Central and Eastern European Countries to help them to develop cross-border co-operation with the European Union's countries. CRO-CO is financed by a part of the PHARE programme. Up until that time, European funds dedicated to the cross-border co-operation within the INTERREG programme could only be granted to member states. The PHARE programme for the Czech Republic is 330 million ECU for the 1995–99 period, of this 47 per cent is assigned to cross-border co-operation. The CBC programme is divided as follows for the same period: with Germany: 75 million ECU; with Austria: 15 million ECU; with other associated countries: 72 million ECU.
29 See G. Lepesant, *Géopolitique des frontières orientales de l'Allemagne* (Paris: L'Harmattan, 1998).
30 In the case of the Euroregion Egrensis, its borders are more or less the same as those of the former historic province of the Egerland, a land which was independent until the seventeenth century and belonged t a Bavarian family.
31 See the title of an article published in the Czech daily *Lidové Noviny*, 19 December 1994, by Martin Danes: 'Do Evropy Pres Nemecko' ['To Europe through Germany'].
32 This study will be limited to the end of the Klaus era for reasons of sources and coherence. The first period of the social-democrat government are not enough to allow relevant analyses about the way the CSSD deals with the European issue. Nevertheless, integration into the European Union is presented today as the main objective of Czech foreign policy. The political programme of the CSSD for the legislative elections in June 1998 closely followed the current 'philosophy' of European integration, with for instance reference to the Maastricht treaty.
33 See chapter 9 by Peter Bugge in this volume.
34 Since the division of the continent was described as being contrary to its nature, it had to disappear in the short term. It is in this perspective that the debate was held to search for a new structure in a unified continent. Within the international context of the 1980s, the intellectuals in Central Europe approached the German issue from a global perspective. Dissident movements like *Charta 77* in Czechoslovakia considered the resolution of the German question as a key to getting beyond the partition of Europe. See M. Schulze-Wessel, 'Die Mitte liegt westwärts, Mitteleuropa in tschechischer Diskussion', *Bohemia* Vol. 29 (1988), 325–344.
35 See A. Hudalla, *Der Beitritt der Tschechischen Republik zur Europäischen Union, eine Fallstudie zu den Auswirkungen der EU-Osterweiterung auf die Finalité politique des europäischen Integrationsprozesses* (Hamburg: LIT, 1996).
36 Again, this was only until the end of the Klaus era, but the consequences can still be seen today.
37 M. Kundera, 'L'Occident kidnappé, ou la tragédie de l'Europe centrale', *Le Débat*, 27 (1983) 4–22.
38 *Lidová Demokracie*, 27 April 1994.
39 *Mlada Fronta Dnes*, 1 July 1995.
40 *Telegraf*, 9 May 1996.
41 In 1921, the German population represented 23 per cent of the Czechoslovak population (which is more than the Slovak population) and 33 per cent of the population in Bohemia. V. Mamatey, R. Luža (ed.), *La République tchécoslovaque 1918–1938* (Paris:

Librairie du Regard, 1987) p. 40. The term 'Sudeten German' first appears in the 1920s. It was first used to identify the Germans living in the border regions, and later all the German population living in Czechoslovakia.

42 The expulsion of the Sudeten Germans from Czechoslovakia in 1945–47 was enacted according to the decrees of the Czechoslovak president Edvard Beneš, and then the Potsdam Agreements (article XIII). This expulsion needs to be considered in a wider context: the flight and massive expulsion of the German population living in Central Europe (12 million people) and especially in Poland at the end of the war.

43 The SL is, among other, supported by the Pan-European Movement, led by Otto von Habsburg.

44 See, in particular, the repeated talks of Franz Neubauer, spokesman of the Sudeten Germans.

45 *FAZ*, 24 May 1994.

46 The former Austrian Foreign Minister, Alois Mock, delivered a speech to this end during the Sudeten German annual meeting at the Pentecost 1994, in Nuremberg. So did the current Chancelor, W. Schüssel, in 2001. And interviews with SL representatives in Munich in 1995 and 1997.

47 See A. Bazin, 'Tchèques et Allemands sur la voie d'une difficile réconciliation?', *Relations Internationales et Stratégiques* Vol. 26 (1997), 154–164.

48 In fact, the Czech Republic was the last country to be compensated by Germany for the Nazi occupation during the war.

49 See the sociological study about the border region: V. Houzvicka (ed.), *Reflexe sudetonemecké otazky a postoje obyvatelstva ceskeho pohranici k Nemecku*, [reflections on the German Sudeten issue and on the attitude of the inhabitants of the Czech border regions towards Germany] (Usti nad Labem, Sociologicky Ustav Akademie Ved Ceské Republiky Vyskumny Tym Pohranici, 1997). In a national survey conducted in Spring 1996, nearly half of those questioned considered the German economy a potential menace for the Czech Republic (study held by FACTUM agency in March 1996, 'Image from Germany': '*Does Germany represent an economic threat for our country?*': 48.8 per cent said yes and 43 per cent no). Or that it had a negative effect on the economy in the Czech Republic (poll IVVM, 2–7 February 1996, to the question 'How do you estimate German influence on the Czech economy?', 48 per cent answered 'rather unfavourable or very unfavourable', against only 39 per cent rather favourable (30 per cent) and very favourable (9 per cent).

50 *Respekt*, 4 January 1993.

51 In a sociological survey, 56 per cent of those interviewed, to 33 per cent who disagree, feel that because of Germany's integration into the European Union and NATO, there is no danger from that country. Despite the fact that the study shows that Germany is nonetheless still considered a potential threat, that response reassuringly coincides with the opinion (70 per cent for to 16 per cent against) that integration of the Czech Republic into the European Union; NATO is a way to improve current Czech–German relations. Integration into the European Union; NATO is seen as a means of destroying the fear of Germany in Czech society that is perceived (and presented) as one answer, even perhaps the best answer to the German problem today. Gabal, *Einstellung der tschechischen Gesellschaft zu Deutschland.*

52 Lecture at the *Bundestag*, 1 June 1995.

53 See for instance the resolution of the Temelin issue thanks to the mediation of the European Commission (Günther Verheugen).

54 See also chapter 9 by Peter Bugge in this volume.

55 V. Belohradsky, 'Proti Statu Evropa' ['Against the State-Europe'], *Literarni Noviny* Vols 51–52 (1996), 1–4. See also Jan Zahradil at the ODS Congress in October 2001 or any contribution by Klaus on the European Union.

56 V. Klaus, 'Evropa a My', ['Europe and us'] in *Lidové Noviny*, 18 May 1994.
57 V. Klaus, speech delivered for the reception of the Adenauer Prize, 21 December 1993
58 Klaus, 'Evropa a My'.
59 As a defender of liberalism and a supporter of the European policy held by England, Klaus saw in the European integration the creation of a large common market.
60 Sixty-two per cent of the people interviewed (to 32 per cent) think that 'Germany aspires to economic and political hegemony in Europe.' I. Gabal, *Einstellung der Tschechischen Gesellschaft zu Deutschland*: 54 per cent of the people interviewed were in favour of the greater engagement of German companies in Czech industry (against 40 per cent).
61 Starck, H., 'Les Dilemmes *mitteleuropéens* de l'Allemagne', *L'Autre Europe* (1996), 34–35.
62 S. Lemasson, 'L'Allemagne, l'Europe et la question de la Mitteleuropa', in F. Bafoil (ed.), *Les Stratégies allemandes en Europe centrale et orientale, une géopolitique des investissements directs* (Paris: L'Harmattan, 1997).
63 The definitions are numerous: is Germany a soft power, a 'regional power' (Elisabeth Pond, 'Germany Finds Its Niche as a Regional Power', *The Washington Quarterly*, Vol. 19, No. 1 (1996), 25–44), a 'world power inspite of itself' (C. Hacke, *Weltmacht wider Willen. Die deutsche Außenpolitik der Bundesrepublik Deutschland* (Stuttgart: Klett-Cotta, 1988), a 'new great power' (G. Schöllgen, *Die Macht in der Mitte Europas: Stationen deutscher Aussenpolitik von Friedrich dem Grossen bis zur Gegenwart* (Munich: C. H. Beck, 1992), p. 169.
64 See for instance A.-M. Le Gloannec (ed.), *L'Allemagne après la guerre froide: la vainqueur entravé* (Brussels: Complexe, 1993); D. Verheyen, *The German Question: A Cultural, Historical, and Geopolitical Exploration* (Boulder, CO: Westview Press, 1991); P. B. Stares (ed.), *The New Germany and the New Europe* (Washington, DC: The Brookings Institution, 1992).
65 H.-P. Schwarz, 'Germany's National and European Interests', *Daedalus* Vol. 123, No. 2 (1994), 81–106 and 'Germany's National and European Interests', in A. Baring (ed.), *Germany's New Position in Europe: Problems and Perspectives* (Oxford: Berg, 1994), pp. 107–130.
66 H.-P. Schwarz *Die Zentralmacht Europas: Deustchlands Rückkehr auf die Weltbühne* (Berlin: Siedler, 1994).
67 Cf. H. Arnold, *Deutschland Größe. Deutsche Außenpolitik zwischen Macht und Mangel?* (Munich: Piper, 1995) ou H. Müller, *Macht und Ohnmacht. Deutsche Außenpolitik vor dem Ende?* (Frankfurt/Main: Alfred Herrhausen Gesellschaft für internationalen Dialog, 1998).
68 Schwarz, 'Germany's National and European Interests'.
69 See A. Markovits and S. Reich, 'Should Europe Fear the Germans?', *German Politics and Society*, Vol. 23 (1991), 1–20 or the answer to this article from B. N. Golberger, 'Why Europe Should not Fear the Germans', *German Politics*, Vol. 2, No. 2 (1993), 288–310.
70 Golberger, 'Why Europe Should not Fear the Germans'.
71 See S. Bulmer and W. Paterson, 'Germany in the European Union: Gentle Giant or Emergent Leader?' *International Affairs* Vol. 72, No. 1 (1996), 9–32.
72 Bulmer and Paterson, 'Germany in the European Union'.
73 See the bilateral agreements between Germany and its Central European neighbours. For instance, in 1994 Germany signed two treaties with the Czech Republic and with Poland, according to which these states promise under certain circumstances to take back illegal emigrants who have been arrested in Germany, whatever their nationality, as soon as they enter Germany from these two countries (in the Czech case, this agreement comes along with financial aid from Germany of 60 million DM). This policy, to which is added other bilateral agreements (on foreign workers in Bavaria, for instance) contributes to the transformation step by step of the Czech–German border into an internal European Union border.

74 M. Jopp, 'Germany and EU Enlargement', in K. Kaiser and M. Brüning (eds), *East-Central Europe and the EU: Problems of Integration* (Bonn, Institut für Europäische Integrationsforschug e.V., 1996), pp. 107–120.

75 CDU-CSU Fraktion des Deutschen Bundestages, Überlegungen zur europäischen Politik (Lamers–Schäuble Bericht), 1 September 1994.

76 C. Deubner, 'L'Europe idéale de l'Allemagne', *Revue d'Etudes Comparatives Est-Ouest*, 4 (1996) 202. The question concerning the place of Germany in Europe refers to an abundant literature about the idea of 'centre'. Different definitions of a *Mitteleuropa* compete: *Zentraleuropa, Zwischeneuropa, Mittellage,* all of which attempt to explain how this position affects the role Germany is playing or should play in Europe. See J. Droz, *L'Europe centrale, évolution historique de l'idée de 'Mitteleuropa'* (Paris: Payot, 1960); K. Schlögel, *Die Mitte liegt ostwärts. Die Deutschen, der verlorene Osten und Mitteleuropa* (Berlin: Siedler, 1986); M. Stürmer, 'Die Deutschen in Europa', *Europa Archiv* Vol. 24 (1989), 721–732; A. Baring, *Deutschland, Was nun?* (Berlin: Siedler, 1990); P. Katzenstein (ed.), *Mitteleuropa, Between Europe and Germany* (Oxford: Berghahn Books, 1997).

77 COM (98) 0708-C4-0111/99, voted on 15 April 1999 at the European Parliament. See also COM (2000) 703-C5-0603/2000–1997/2180(COS), A5-0255/2001, voted on 5 September 2001 at the European Parliament (point 41 on the Beneš-decrees and points 42–44 on the Temelin nuclear plan).

78 Wolfgang Schüssel, speech at the congress of the Sudetendeutsche Landsmannschaft, 2 June 2001 in Augsburg.

79 Austria also tried to block the European integration of the Czech Republic because of the Temelin nuclear power plant, which it wants closed (Austria has been a nuclear-free country since the end of the 1970s).

80 Cf. the interview with Wolfgang Schüssel in *Der Standard*, 2 March 2002.

81 Among others:

29 May 1998: '*Vertriebene, Aussiedler und deutsche Minderheiten sind eine Brücke zwischen den Deutschen und ihren östlihen Nachbarn*'. The resolution was voted. The polish Parliament (Sejm) protested against this resolution in an official declaration denouncing 'the ambiguity' of the text.

29 June 1999 (non-voted): the text approved the resolutions voted at the European Parliament and at the Austrian Nationalrat a few weeks earlier. It had been introduced by Harmut Koschyk (CSU), Christian Schmidt (CSU), Karl Lamers (CDU), Wolfgang Schäuble (CDU), Peter Hintze (CDU), Michael Glos (CSU) and the CDU/CSU group at the *Bundestag.*

9 June 2000 (non-voted): asked for the recognition of the injustices committed against the Germans during the expulsion. It was introduced by Harmut Koschyk (CSU), Karl Lamers (CDU), Günter Nooke (CDU) and Katherina Reiche (CDU).

82 See his speeches at the Sudeten German Congress in Nurnberg, 11 June 2000, or in Augsburg, 4 June 2001: 'The decrees are no longer a problem that concerns only the Sudeten Germans. They have become a European Problem, a European wound. It seems impossible to me that the people and the nations from Europe could tolerate decrees or laws which are incompatible with international law, which legitimise injustice and which are discriminatory.' The abrogation of the Benes decrees has been mentioned in the CSU political programme (Stoiber is president of the CSU) since the mid-1990s.

83 The abrogation of the 'expulsion decrees' is mentioned in candidate Stoiber's political programme.

84 The European Commission, by way of the Commissionar of Enlargement, the German SPD Günther Verheugen, or of its spokesperson has often reaffirmed that there is no intention of linking bilateral disputes (the expulsion issue or the Temelin nuclea plant issue) with the integration of the Czech Republic in the EU.

85 *Eurobarometre*, 52 (2000).

86 A. Bazin and Rupnik, 'La Réconciliation tchéco-allemande, une longue route semée d'obstacles', *Politique Etrangère*, 2 (2001).
87 17 February 2001.
88 F. de La Serre, C. Lequesne and J. Rupnik, *L'Union Européenne: ouverture à l'Est?* (Paris: PUF, 1994), p. 120.
89 Klaus, 'Evropy a My'.
90 The signing in December 1992 of the Central European Free Trade Agreement (CEFTA) nevertheless marks the success of economic co-operation in the region, even if the level of exchange is lower than it was in 1989.
91 J. Rupnik, 'East-Central Europe: The Pivotal Role of Germany', lecture at the Council of Europe conference on 'Redefining the Borders in Europe', Leeuwarden, 20–22 April 1993.

Emil J. Kirchner

12

Cross-border co-operation between Germany and the Czech Republic

Introduction

Three contextual aspects can be considered as crucial to cross-border co-operation in Europe. These are the interactions between the two local or regional entities on either side of the dividing border, the inter-state or inter-governmental relations in which the respective regions are situated, and the European Union's role and contribution. Although cross-border co-operation has been investigated at each level,[1] the linkage between the three levels has been neglected. Studies of the individual aspects and contributions to cross-border co-operation are necessary elements in the collection of data but not sufficient for providing a comprehensive view on the motives, nature and direction of cross-border co-operation. A more holistic approach is in order which links meso-level issues with macro concerns of European integration and which is concerned with the interaction dynamic of the local/regional, national and European Union level.

In the Central and Eastern European context, cross-border co-operation has been associated with the erosion of barriers, pathways to European integration, the rebuilding of economies and the shaping of administrative and political cultures, the furthering of cultural exchange and improvement of relations between people. Cross border co-operation has also been linked to the principle of 'subsidiarity in that it is deemed 'closer to the people' than traditional, national forms'.[2]

To provide a greater understanding of the motives, nature and direction of cross-border co-operation requires examination of the activities and contributions made by each level (local/regional, state and European Union), and analysis of the interaction and influences among the three levels. This will be the aim here. Three theoretical endeavours appear relevant in this respect. Karl Deutsch's's[3] transactionalist approach relies primarily on local/regional or voluntary initiatives, i.e. communication and interaction from the bottom up. Neo-realist or liberal intergovernmentalism stresses the state-to-state motives and control in cross-border co-operation. The multi-level governance approach assumes a certain degree of self-reliance by the respective local or regional entities on both sides of the border, and links this with the process of European Union decision-making. The constructivist approach[4] can be seen as complementing the efforts of the multilevel governance (by placing emphasis on the process of Europeanisation in cross-border co-operation) and transactionalism (by focusing on the formation of regional identity in the cross-border setting).[5] A brief consideration of these approaches will help to illustrate their relevance for the study of cross-border co-operation.

For Deutsch[6] the essential background conditions of successful integration are the unbroken links of social communication across the mutual boundaries of the territories to be integrated, the relatively high geographic and social mobility of persons, and the multiplicity of the scope and the flows of mutual communications and transactions. Only in this way (rather than through temporary economic prosperity, or constitutional settlements) did Deutsch expect the goal of social integration could be attained. He considered integration to be the attainment, within a territory, of a 'sense of community' and of institutions and practices strong enough and widespread enough to assure, for a long time, dependable expectations of 'peaceful change' among its population. Among the indicators used by Deutsch for measuring the degree of integration attained are trade, mail flows, student exchanges, intermarriages, and joint art festivals, music concerts and sports events between peoples of Europe.

Concerning the motives for cross-border co-operation, Eike Schamp[7] has noted that the initial steps toward cross-border co-operation usually stem from the search for solutions to local problems and that local and regional initiatives most often begin such co-operation, rather than state, national, or international co-operation. The establishment of Euroregions (to be examined below) along the German eastern border with the Czech Republic can be viewed as spontaneous interaction in line with the transactionalist assumptions of Karl Deutsch, i.e. they reflect a bottom-up approach.

This approach can be contrasted with the state-centric approach which sees cross-border co-operation as state-inspired (bilateral treaties), state-sponsored (institutions and networks) and state-controlled (competencies and finance of the respective local or regional entities on each side of the border). The inter-state motives are seen as political, security and economic interests. The political ones are linked with the aim to create peaceful relations between Germany and the Czech Republic, including the settlement of minority problems, e.g. property claims. The security ones are associated with German aims to create a *cordon sanitaire* in the region or to extend zones of peace, stability and democracy eastward. The economic ones relate to access to each other's markets. In addition, it is assumed that Czechs perceive cross-border co-operation as a vehicle for improving relations with Germany, which could act as a stimulus to their European Union applications.

In this state centric approach, cross-border co-operation is seen as a means of overcoming Cold War suspicions and mistrust between Germany and its neighbours. Regional development projects help to bridge the rather large socio-economic gap between Germany and the Czech Republic (which might address the concerns some Germans have about migration from the east, and the social problems arising from economic strains, such as criminality and problems policing border crossings).[8]

Rejecting the state-centric concern with existing asymmetries of power or hegemony and the emphasis on state-bargaining and interest coalitions, the multi-level approach seeks to link different levels of decision-making and to give due recognition to the role of sub-national actors and international/regional institutions. According to Marks[9] a two-sided simultaneous process can be observed in Europe: a decentralisation of decision-making to sub-national levels of government, and a centralisation of new powers at the supra-national level. As European Union legislation is more effectively implemented at a grass-roots level, the European Union is increasingly concerned with the way in which sub-national governments operate. Subsequently, regions are no longer seen as subordinate features of central government, but rather deemed to have duties and allegiances with the supranational structures of the European Union. This increasingly strong relationship between the European Union and the sub-national governments is seen to undermine the role of national governments as the main political players in the European Union.

Multi-level governance concern with regional government also touches on issues of subsidiarity and democracy. The European Union depends on the region's closeness to the citizens in terms of legitimacy. As cross-border co-operation promotes the participation of citizens and social partners as well as politicians, in programmes, projects and decision-making, a similar link to subsidiarity, democracy and legitimacy can be made.[10] Districts and regions can also be assumed to have duties and allegiances to the structure of cross-border co-operation.

The forging of shared norms, values and identities is a concern of constructivist scholars, whose work can be deemed as complementary to the multi-level governance. They are interested in identity formation in cross-border regions.

The forging of shared norms, values and identities can be observed in two ways. Firstly, it can be observed within a discreet region. Scholars such as Deutsch,[11] and Adler and Barnett[12] identify regional awareness with shared principles, collectively held norms and common understandings, rather than on the expediency or contemporary conjunction of short-term interests. But they differ in their emphasis on quantitative and qualitative indicators to achieve and sustain regional awareness. Adler and Barnett[13] add a qualitative aspect to the process by which both interests and identities are created and evolve. They agree with Deutsch that interests and identities are shaped by particular histories and cultures, but expand on these by introducing, socialisation and discourse mechanisms, such as the use of language, the influence of material incentives, and interaction with other states. Furthermore, as Adler[14] points out, emancipation and ability of social and sub-national actors to introduce innovations, help transform or even constitute new collective understanding, which in turn shape the identities and interests.

Secondly, the forging of shared norms, values and identities can be part of a Europeanisation process (extension of European Union goals, values and decision-making procedures to, for example, post-communist European countries).[15] Compliance with the *aquis* gives the Commission (and the European Union) the ability to construct a 'social reality' and 'consciousness', and to build blocks of ideational as well as material' elements.[16] In line with this development, Schimmelfennig[17] argues that whereas the initial period of European Union–Central and Eastern Europe relations can be explained by the theory of liberal inter-governmentalism, constructivism can best explain the post-1998 period. However, as Mendelson[18] points out there is a need to specify when and how (positive or negative norm formation) transnational and domestic factors interact.

In the following, an attempt will be made to relate these theoretical approaches to developments in cross-border co-operation between Germany and the Czech Republic, as recorded in existing studies on the subject. Before engaging in this task, attention will first turn to the background conditions which have affected cross-border relations between Germany and the Czech Republic. We will then proceed to an examination of the three contextual arenas of cross-border co-operation (local, inter-state and European Union) and finish with an assessment of cross-border co-operation generally.

Background conditions on cross-border regions

There were many shared features in the relationship between Germany and the Czech Republic before 1945. They had always been influenced by each other in religion (Christianity), literature, music, 'Volkskultur', architecture and economic traditions.[19] The German language was reasonably widespread in the former Czechoslovakia until the Second World War,[20] and was the language of the educated classes in both these countries. However, the experience of the Nazi regime and the developments after 1945 undermined cultural and linguistic ties. The expulsion and flight of the German population at the end of the Second World War from Czech regions and the near re-population of those areas by the Czechoslovak government respectively with people from other parts of their territories into these border regions significantly affected inter-state relations and cross-border co-operation.[21] The effect of these policies was reinforced by centralised forms of government (communists regimes in East Germany and Czechoslovakia) with a corresponding drop in local autonomous actions and little encouragement for cross-border contacts.[22] In addition, the impenetrable iron curtain prevented contact with West Germany and resulted in the division of Europe into two fundamentally different economic and social systems, a period from which all three countries are only now beginning to recover.

All three states now work with similar systems, e.g. capitalism and liberal democracy. The mutual and multi-dimensional substance of reconciliation presupposes a democratic context.[23] There are also attempts to rekindle former links, e.g. between Bohemia and Saxony.[24]

However, there are still obstacles to overcome, such as old hatreds and mutual suspicion and language barriers (almost three-quarters of the population does not speak or understand the language of their neighbour[25]). Differences in administrative structures and gaps in the transportation and communication infrastructures present further hindrances to cross-border co-operation.[26]

Furthermore, the relationship between Germany and the Czech Republic is more complicated and carries more psychological effects than that with Poland. The older generation still associates terms like fascism and brutality with Germany, and their scepticism increases with Germany's current economic and political power. About 50,000 self-identified Germans live in the Czech lands.[27]

The extent to which these new circumstances can contribute to higher levels of social interaction and in turn create and sustain a sense of community among the cross-border regions depends in part on local/regional structures, and on governmental and European Union initiatives. We will first examine the local/regional context.

The local/regional dimension

The role of Euroregions in cross-border co-operation

Euroregions are organised forms of cross-border co-operation or 'institutionalised form(s) of co-operation between units of territorial administration or regional organisations of two or more states'.[28] They have been variously described as voluntary bodies – without a direct political mandate – and as advisory bodies.[29] Hence, they do not represent a new layer of government, since their decisions are not binding on any territory or group. Rather, they are a voluntary amalgamation of municipalities, towns and districts, which aim to promote trust and mutual co-operation and to stimulate trans-border developments in the areas of infrastructure, economy, environment, culture, leisure and other social spheres.[30] Their activities carry across the European, national, regional, and local levels (vertically) on both sides of the border as well across national borders (horizontally). According to Yoder[31] Euroregions often act as clearinghouses for various private and public organisations on both sides of the border.

Euroregions are not a constituent part of the European Union, nor are they indeed dependent on it. They exist within the context of the European Convention on cross-border co-operation between municipalities and regional administrative bodies, signed in Madrid 21 May 1980. In a wider context, they can be considered as laboratories of European integration.[32] Over forty Euroregions exist across Europe.[33]

They are long term, equipped with administrative, technical, and financial resources, and they have their own internal resolutions. The membership of Euroregions is rather fluid, the borders are largely arbitrary and depend on the will of particular interest groups or political-administrative options.[34]

Euroregions provide an important link or hinge between formal or institutionalised (top–down) forms of regional integration and informal or social integration (bottom–up) forms of regional integration. In one sense they represent a top–down approach, with an associated positive influence on the social interaction of diverse regional groups. In another sense, they act as a channel for a bottom–up orientation, helping to reinforce social integration (facilitating social transactions, cultural networks, information flows, and hence promoting trust between regional and local elites, and fostering a sense of regional identity). Overall the question is how and whether Euroregions reinforce organisational and social cohesiveness in cross-border regional settings, and whether they enable trust-generating activities in the form of transboundary civil society.[35]

Four Euroregions were established along the East German border with the Czech Republic between 1991 and 1995. These are Neisse–Nisa–Nysa, Labe, Erzgebirge/Krusnohori, Egrenis, Bayerischer Wald/Boehmerwald.[36]

Euroregions help to establish both institutional and cultural bridges. Institutional bridges bring together parallel organisations or administrative offices on both sides of the border to address common issues, such as vocational training, youth violence, provision of services to the handicapped, AIDS awareness and care for AIDS patients, services for the homeless, environmental clean-up, and ways to co-operate in cases of natural disasters. The cultural bridges include events, visits, and exhibits aimed at fostering mutual understanding of the neighbour's language, religion, and customs and, in doing so, help to overcome mutual suspicion and prejudice.[37]

Among the activities sponsored are: (1) cross-border children support/protection, e.g. issues of drugs, children without any parents, prostitution, youth criminality, and the mistreatment of children and young people; (2) cultural activities, e.g. sports festivals in winter and summer, common choral, dancing and music events, theatre exchanges, joint fairs, and joint film productions (e.g. five years Euro-region Erzgebirge), 1998; (3) joint newspapers, and common publications e.g. on social work, environment or the region; (4) artistic workshop days for young people and holiday camps; and (5) infrastructure projects, like the ferry across the Elbe.

Such efforts may help to create new, common interests. Whether this is the case, however, requires a move beyond a purely quantitative 'Deutschian' approach and measuring the qualitative aspects of 'transactions' which are taking place across the border. For example, the proliferation of institutions and networks in a cross-border region may not result in greater governance.[38] The fragmentation of municipalities in the Czech Republic raises questions about whether the local level is the appropriate level for cross-border co-operation projects. In the absence of regional self-government, and even a regional public policy of the central government, a number of regional development agencies (RDA) have been formed in the Czech Republic, but they lack financial independence and have to rely to a large extent on central government support.[39]

In an interview survey in 1998–99,[40] senior managers involved in cross-border co-operation identified the main problems for cross-border co-operation as:

1 language barriers;
2 different legislation;
3 incongruity of the three national parts (communal, regional and state);
4 different priorities and degree of interest in cross-border co-operation; and
5 inadequate professional institutional capacity for cross-border co-operation (at both communal and regional levels; partly because of limited municipal and districts budgets, and the related implication of raising the required matching funds when applying, for example, to the PHARE cross-border co-operation programme.

The negative implications of these findings are also reflected in a survey among mayors of Czech and German municipalities that are situated in the border area.[41]

The overwhelming majority of German mayors does not consider Euroregions to be a very effective instrument for regional development, whereas Czech mayors are much more positive about the usefulness of Euroregions. The majority of both the German and the Czech mayors thinks that Euroregions have a very low impact, or no impact at all, on the decisions of local councils. The survey results suggest that Euroregions are not very accountable to local councils.[42]

Knowledge among the Czech population in the border regions about Euroregions is mixed. An opinion survey in North Bohemia[43] indicated that 50 per cent knew about the existence of the Euro-region Labe-Elbe, but the other four Euroregions were not very well known.[44]

The same survey also found that 25 per cent of the respondents considered Euroregions as an instrument to solve peripheral problems which are characteristic of border areas; another 20 per cent saw them as improving contacts and relations with the population on the other side of the border; a further 17 per cent perceived Euroregions to be an outcome of the necessity for the Czech local and regional public administration to co-operate in order to manage scarce resources.

However 16 per cent saw Euroregions as an indicator of foreign political and economic expansion in the Czech Republic; and 10 per cent criticised the Euroregions for offering an artificial institutional framework for the pursuit of particular interests of some powerful stakeholders.

The results show that the activities of the Euroregions are not very well known to the population. One possible explanation is that these activities have not yielded visible outcomes.[45] (This lack of awareness, which may have implications for democratic accountability, will be taken up below.)

What becomes apparent is that Euroregions are associated more with the solution of specific problems of border areas than with the forging of common identities. The citizens living in this area perceive, firstly, the need to overcome language and communication barriers between the three countries with the appropriate instruments. They also see the need to remove hostile images and clichés and to build trust and municipal acceptance. At the municipal level, there is the necessity to be informed about land use planning and certain infrastructures of the 'other side', which function as common resources.

How do these perceptions relate to state-to-state or government-to-government efforts for bilateral co-operation?

Regional interstate–state co-operation

A number of bilateral treaties have been introduced since 1990, which, together with European Union financial assistance, have promoted cross-border co-operation. The starting point was the German–Czechoslovakia Treaty of Good Neighbourly Relations and Peaceful Co-operation, February 1992, which was subsequently followed up with separate treaties after the split between the Czech Republic and Slovakia. However, the treaty with the Czech Republic was not realised until 1996; largely because of claims by the Sudeten–German expellee organisation for lost property in the Czech Republic. It got reactivated in January 1997 with the German–Czech Declaration signed by Kohl and Havel. All these called for or made provisions for co-operation between regions and other local authorities, especially in the border regions. The treaties provided for regular consultations, economic and financial co-operation, an intensification of cultural exchange, co-operation in the field of environmental protection and guarantee of minority rights.[46]

Of a complementary nature are the: (1) the Czechoslovakia *Schulbuchkommission*, established in the 1960s; however, the latter had to stop its activities soon after 1968, but it was renewed in 1988; (2) bilateral Commission of Historians (Germany–Czechoslovakia), established in 1990; and (3) two Institutes of East-Central European Studies at the Universities in Leipzig and Marburg

However, reconciliation in German–Czech relations has not come easy. A breakthrough was finally achieved in 1996 with a declaration of reconciliation, which committed both sides to the establishment of a future fund, jointly administered, to finance projects of shared interest, such as youth meetings, care for the elderly, care for monuments and cemeteries, promotion of minorities, joint scientific and environmental projects. Such efforts are to benefit primarily victims of National Socialism in recognition of Germany's special burden and responsibility. The Germans agreed to contribute 140 million DM and the Czechs 20–25 million DM to the Fund over a four-year period.[47]

In August 2000, a foundation: Remembrance, Responsibility and the Future, was established, endowed with a 10 billion DM fund: one-half from industry and one-half from government. The green light for this fund was finally given in May 2001. The foundation will supplement existing restitution arrangements with humanitarian assistance, bringing help to former forced labourers and other Nazi victims quickly and unbureaucratically.

Reconciliation means restoring friendship, harmony, or communion. Applied to states, it incorporates a societal as well as a quest to generate a reservoir of mutual trust supportive of warm, friendly relations.[48] Official declarations of friendship between state leaders alone cannot create a climate of confidence and trust between societies. Government-to-government relations can, however, contribute to reconciliation by transforming the tone and range of official contacts, so that conflicts can be gradually discussed, and shared interests nurtured without suspicion. It is essential that treaties and statements by government leaders are translated into concrete structures or practices which facilitate contacts and understandings among the populations of the three countries in question.

A wide range of bilateral contacts and exchanges, both formal and informal, have taken place between Germany and the Czech Republic, of which only the most salient will be mentioned here.

Much effort has gone into a schooling and cultural dialogue, with co-ordination offices for youth and school exchanges, e.g. the German–Czech youth and school co-operation, supported by their respective ministries of culture. The latter has co-ordination centres in Regensburg and Pilsen. In 1996, there were youth exchanges going in both directions and totalling 6,000.[49] There are also 200 Bavarian–Czech partnership schools which promote exchanges. In addition, a German–Czech speaking grammar school in Saxony was established for pupils from both countries.

These exchanges are complemented by schoolteacher and university lecturer exchanges. They also benefit from the Czech Library for German language publications. The objective of these is to promote German literature in the Czech Republic. These initiatives are sponsored by the German Bosch Foundation, which supports similar initiatives in France and the United States.

Yet in spite of these dense levels of school exchanges, embedded in a wide range of social and cultural interactions, there are still some reservations among the respective populations, some of which arise because of current economic inequalities between Germans and Czechs, others relate to problems over different administrative and legal structures, whilst a third category is nourished on the issue of minority questions and property rights. The latter is a particularly thorny aspect in German–Czech relations.

Many Czechs continue to regard the German minority as a bridgehead rather than a bridge.[50] At the end of 1998 a hefty Czech majority still considered the deportation justified.[51] German governments, including that of Schröder, consider the expulsion an injustice and are critical of the Beneš decrees.

What hampers cross-border co-operation is different administrative and legal structures (*Länder* versus state administrations). Working groups take on a kind of auxiliary structure, which are supposed to compensate for missing administrative structures. But working groups do not have a strong resource base, which makes them very weak. Often, the members of the working groups also lack the adequate competencies. As a consequence, the working group rather resembles in many cases an informal social circle of enthusiasts than a team of experts.[52]

As any funding from the PHARE cross-border co-operation programme and from the German Regional Fund is based on the principle of co-financing, the municipal associations have to agree on some financial scheme as far as their own contributions are concerned. Since the investment needs of Czech municipalities are huge, PHARE cross-border co-operation-funded projects are sometimes perceived rather as a local investment resource than as a tool of cross-border co-operation.[53] There is a strong financial dependence on central government by Czech local and regional authorities.

Overall, there is a sense of frustration on the German part with regard to finding equivalent administrative counterparts in the Czech Republic. Jutta Seidel of the State Chancellery of the Free State of Saxony, speaking about her experience in organising transfrontier co-operation between Saxony and Poland and Saxony and the Czech Republic, emphasised the initial difficulties which had to be overcome and which resulted from administrative centralisation in the Czech and Polish Republics. According to Seidel it took years to create trust and willingness in Warsaw and Prague to allow their western border regions a degree of planning autonomy which would allow them to negotiate directly with their German counterparts.[54]

Another problem affecting German–Czech relations relates to prostitution, drug trafficking and passport forgery, e.g. passports issued under false names by the Czech authorities, or passports sold to potential illegal migrants. There is also illegal trade in arms and weaponry and smuggling of nuclear substances across the border, which is being seized by the German police, together with the growing phenomenon of organised human trafficking.

Some of these problems relate to European Union enlargement and require European Union-wide solutions

The European Union context

The European Union accession process and membership may well accelerate opportunities for forging bilateral connections and for defusing bilateral tensions. But it may also have some negative connections. As Vladimir Handle explains, lack of European Union engagement by the former Czech Prime Minister Klaus also influenced Czech–German relations. As he suggests, it made it impossible to exploit the historically unprecedented parallel nature of strategic interests in Czech and German European policy and to explore its limits. Moreover, it impeded a settlement of the issues arising from their tragic past.[55] (It is fair to assume that this also affected the progress of cross-border co-operation between Germany and the Czech Republic. A reverse correlation, occurred in the mid-1990s when the Sudeten Germans, of which a majority resettled in Bavaria, where it has support from the Christian Social Union, linked their property claims and their 'right to a homeland' (the abolition of the so-called 'Benes decrees' of 1945) with a condition for Czech European Union membership.[56]

Europeanization, which accompanies the European Union accession process, is viewed by Börzel and Risse[57] as the emergence of new rules, norms, practices, and structures of meaning to which member states are exposed and which they have to incorporate into their domestic structures. This transformation process would involve their regions and by extension cross-border regions between member states and applicants.

The Commission is interested in promoting regional policy and this includes cross-border regions, to have links with the regions, as one of the ways to be in touch with the public, and to promote European Union enlargement and integration. This opens direct links for Czech district or regional authorities with the European Commission, which in turn, especially after membership has been achieved, can assume great importance both in terms of their own right and in terms of relations with the Czech central authorities. If such a development were to take place, sociological institutionalism suggests that institutions which frequently interact, are exposed to each other or are located in a similar environment, and over time develop similarities in formal organisational structures, principles of resource allocation, practices, meaning structures, and reform patterns.[58] Whether the institutional interaction would proceed harmoniously along trilateral lines or would favour European Commission relations with cross-border regions at the expense of relations between cross-border regions and their respective central governments, remains to be seen. For the time being there seem to be no indications that such a process is in the making. Rather, contacts, as far as they exist between German–Czech cross-border regions and the European Commission, seem to be very tenuous and, to the extent to which they exist, primarily connected with European Union regional policy.

European Union regional development policy was created to diminish regional economic disparities within countries and throughout Europe. The European Union financial assistance for the respective Euroregions comes via the INTERREG II and the PHARE–cross-border co-operation programmes and represents a main source of financial aid for the Euroregions. Between 1994 and 1997, INTERREG funds provided over 2.5 billion euros to the German border regions in the east. On the other side of the border, European Union funding is also available in the form of the PHARE cross-border co-operation programme. The PHARE programme for Czech Republic provided 493 million euros between 1990 and 1997

However, knowledge about the PHARE and the INTERREG programmes is low in Czech regions near the German border: an opinion survey of mayors of municipalities in north Bohemia indicated that 80 per cent to 90 per cent knew nothing about either of the two programmes.[59] A similar lack of awareness by local politicians in the Czech Republic about European integration is noted by Perron.[60] She detected a lack of information by local politicians about the process of European Union accession; which was connected with 'a very low level of debate, and a feeling of not being concerned with this issue'. In her opinion 'there is a widely shared pessimism among local politicians towards Czech Republic integration prospects.[61] Whilst this situation has probably changed since the research was conducted in 1997/98, it raises a number of questions about causes and consequences. The cause for the low level of awareness, as Perron[62] suggests, can be found in the failure of political parties to make their members aware of the crucial importance of this issue.

The consequences of insufficient knowledge by local and regional elites relate at least to two issues. One concerns the 'democratic function' these elites are expected to play. By holding an intermediary position between the citizens and the national government, they can be considered as an important and effective instrument in the promotion of a (positive) image of Europe and of European integration.[63] There are indications that regional elites generally and cross-border authorities in particular fail to perform the role as 'opinion makers' or information providers, and thus a 'democratic function', with regard to European integration issues.[64] However, part of the reason for this is that regional governments, or more specifically district and municipal authorities in the Czech Republic, do not have policy-making ability.[65]

The second issue concern the role and importance of social interaction in cross-border co-operation and European integration; an aspect which will now be developed.

Public attitudes and cross-border co-operation

Deutsch[66] linked the behavioural component to the 'social learning' which mutual transactions provide for, i.e. the learning process under which the people who actually transcend the borders of their country get involved. Deutsch's insistence on the behavioural component was motivated by the lack of any dependable opinion polls which could show whether people act (behavioural component of support) the way they talk (attitudinal component of support). Hence, Deutsch tried to measure the support of European integration based not on what people 'say', that is, the attitudinal component of support, but mostly on what people 'do'. However, some transactions, e.g. competitive sport between countries, can augment conflict rather than simply help create or reinforce a sense of community. Difficulties of this sort made Deutsch concede that what to measure and what to infer from the collected data of transactionalism remain deeply problematic.[67]

For Karl Deutsch[68] the more one nation state (region) interacts with another, the more relevant they are to each other, and as the intensity of communications increases, so will the sense of common identity. Whenever it is the case that a population shares values, preferences, lifestyles, common memories, aspirations, loyalties and identifications, it is also the case that people within this population communicate with one another (i.e. transact) frequently, rapidly, clearly, and effectively, in a balanced manner, over a multiple range of social, economic, cultural and political concerns.

The Deutschian perspective of considering the 'community formation' and regional integration to be synonymous is criticised by Donald Puchala[69] who argues that although the transaction flows may describe various dimensions of regional integration, enabling us to make some evaluations of the progress of integration in various fields, transaction flows do not cause integration. They are, rather, a reflection of it. Puchala, in other words, challenges the predictive ability of transaction flows, arguing that these indices are not legitimised to measure the attitudes and perceptions underlying human behaviour. As neo-realists suggest, violent conflict has often occurred within highly integrated communities, sharing values and beliefs.

Rather than relying solely on quantitative measures on transactions and interactions of people across borders, it is important to provide qualitative assessments. This will be done with the help of a number of available opinion surveys. These involve (for the moment) attitudes of Czechs towards Germany and Germans, based on a series of empirical sociological surveys conducted since 1990. The last available survey is of October 1999.[70]

The survey also indicates that conflicts of Czech–German coexistence are still latent in attitudes today and form the background to current Czech–German relations. As a matter of fact whereas in 1993, 40 per cent of the respondents indicated that the past was an obstacle for co-operation, in the latest survey this rose to 70 per cent. Around 50 per cent felt that the common Czech–German declaration of 1997 would not solve the problem of the past. Equally two-thirds were of the opinion that the Sudeten Germans heavily affect Czech–German relations, and the same number considered the expulsion of Germans from Bohemia after the Second World War as correct, and supported the maintenance of the Beneš decrees. Moreover, the percentage of respondents who felt that the apology expressed by Václav Havel about the Sudeten Germans was sufficient for a solution of this problem rose from 24 per cent in 1991 to 46 per cent. Also 60 per cent declared that one needed always to be vigilant about Germany.

However, on a number of other issues, the perception of Germany is more positive. A majority of the respondents does not feel threatened by Germany, but rather sees Germany as a desirable economic and political partner, from which one can learn something, and as the main guarantor of European Union enlargement. Equally, almost two-thirds felt that German motivations for the latter were 'stability consideration' (to establish a zone of stability) rather than territorial gains. Germany holds first place among those countries with which the Czech Republic wishes to co-operate. The survey indicates that people under thirty and university graduates have a more positive attitude towards Germany.

The survey revealed that contacts with Germany occur mostly at the level of family relatives or friends. Another important category is based on work and business contacts with German firms. About 40 per cent of all inhabitants in the Czech border region go to Germany at least once a year. The intensity of contacts is greatest for what are identified as 'bearers' of the establishment of civic collaboration and cross-border community on the Czech–German border. A total of 72 per cent of those actively involved met their German partners at least once a month, and 29 per cent did so on a daily basis. Surprisingly 43 per cent of these activists indicated that they met on Czech territory, or in both countries (39 per cent). Germany as a place of meeting was only stated by 10 per cent of the respondents. Young and highly educated people comprise this group. They also manifest a higher level of tolerance towards Germans.

Zich[71] characterises the mutual interaction between Czechs and Germans as 'interpersonal', i.e. one off, or conducted for pragmatic purposes. In the majority of cases they are not repeated by the same actors and so do not create conditions for more links and recognition. The nature of cross-border co-operation is rather spontaneous with a prevailing organisational character. They can be associated with the concept of *Gesellschaft* (based on calculation and external considerations) rather than with the concept of *Gemeinschaft* (based on shared values and interests).

There is a degree of personal contact between the political, cultural and economic elites of both Germany and the Czech Republic. However, there is not a 'common identity', since the prejudices dating back to the Cold War years are still an important issue. That makes the old enmities still influential, though latent, through individual and institutional contacts. There is thus a long way to go before shared values and a common sense of identity seem to emerge.

However, there are also sufficient indicators that a fundamental shift in cross-border relations between Germany and the Czech Republic is taking place which bodes well for future cross-border co-operation.

Conclusion

Having examined cross-border co-operation between Germany and the Czech Republic from three contexts – local–regional interaction (bottom–up), inter-state or inter-governmental relations – and European Union relations, a number of conclusions can be drawn.

Firstly, dual changes in the border regions between Germany and the Czech Republic have taken place and are taking place. In part this is due to the opening of the border to Europe and to Germany; the East German *Länder* and the Czech western regions are no longer peripheral. In the case of the Czech border regions with Germany there is an expectation of economic social benefits, not only for the regions in question but also for the whole of the Czech Republic.

However, in the East German regions, there is a considerable exodus, in line with a 'go west' mentality.

Secondly, although it appears that many actors have good cross-border relations, these remain particular and often are not co-ordinated with other actors in a concerted effort to achieve collaboration. For example, economics are often divorced from cultural events –although their impact upon one another may be greater than assumed.[72]

Thirdly, cross-border co-operation between Germany and the Czech Republic as an authoritative agency has low visibility. Therefore the perception of its effectiveness is low. This perception is exacerbated by the fact that many of the cross-border co-operation programmes propagate highly inspiring aims, when emphasis on more practical aspects would perhaps be more appropriate, e.g. a concentration on border transparency and fluency, language barriers, informal meetings, concrete rules for mutual support. Another factor which hampers effectiveness is the disparity in administrative structures. Whereas on the German side there are strong autonomous regional (*Länder)* governments and well developed district and municipal structures, the Czech side has no regional counterparts and has by and large 'weak' district and municipal structures, which have to rely heavily on central government funding and fall therefore to a considerable extent under central government control.

Fourthly, it is difficult to overcome the prejudices and worries that have existed for years. The past conflicts of Czech–German coexistence are still latent in attitudes today and form the background to current Czech–German relations. This is particularly true of older people whose personal experience of the Nazi era has done much to shape their attitudes. The Sudeten Germans question, which is particularly prominent in Bavaria,[73] constantly draws Czech–German relations back into the past, attracting too great a share of interest. 'The concentration on the Sudeten problem means placing an undue emphasis on conflict and lack of understanding. Czech–German relations are wider-ranging than this and are not limited only to the Sudeten question.'[74] However, according to Houzvicka[75] Czechs apparently distinguish between relations with Germany (its culture, economy, political system) and the problem of the Sudeten Germans expelled from the former Czechoslovakia. He finds that two types of attitudes are becoming more and embedded: a positive view on Germany, and a rejection of the demands of the Sudetendeutsche Landsmannschaft. This would suggest that the past can be shaken off to some extent, and more contemporary images be passed onto the youth.

Fifthly, there are encouraging signs that the saliency of past German–Czech relations is gradually giving way to practical issues or concerns. The perceived economic inequality by the Czechs *vis-à-vis* their German counterparts is seen in Czech public opinion surveys in the border region with Germany as the most important element in relations with Germany; being approximately twice as important in the minds of people living in the border areas as is the weight of the historical memory of the conflicts between the Czech Republic and Germany in modern times.[76] Germany is perceived as a country with which it is worth all-round co-operation, but also which requires relatively strong vigilance. On the German side, practical issues of organised crime and the anticipated free movement of labour (which would come about through Czech European Union accession)[77] begin to outweigh concerns over claims to property rights by German expellees from the former Czechoslovakia.

Pragmatic reasons seem to prevail on both sides of the border as to the benefits of co-operation. On the Czech side they relate to economic benefits and European Union membership and on the German side to markets (exports) and the creation of stable regions. Both the Czech and the German sides emphasise collaboration on many practical problems, e.g. environment, transport, economic development, tourism, erosion of barriers, etc.

Sixth, in spite of evidence that cross-border co-operation between Germany and the Czech Republic has contributed to the furthering of cultural exchange and the improvement of relations between people, it has not been able to establish civic cross-border relations. The respective Euroregions have helped to intensify contacts between the border regions. However, it is difficult to isolate their contribution to a sustained and durable sense of a 'community feeling' based on mutual responsiveness, trust and high levels of what might be called 'cognitive interdependence'.[78] The present situation could, rather, be characterised as a parallel co-existence of two significantly different national specifics (differentiating economically, socially, in the lifestyle, by own culture etc.) influenced substantially by the presence and activity of other ethnic groups.[79] It will take time before either Euroregions or cross-border co-operation can be recognised as true pathways of European integration, in the sense of the social, cultural and political aspects. The forging of shared norms, values and identities in the border region is still in a fragile state. Though good progress is being made in this respect at the youth level, with well-developed exchange programmes in operation and the introduction of 'common history books' in schools.

Seventh, as shown in this study, examining different contexts (local/regional, inter-state and European Union level) enables a broader analysis of cross-border co-operation and helps to provide a better understanding as to how each level contributes, either positively or negatively, towards cross-border co-operation. This should make it possible to explore linkages, or overlapping influences, as for example, between the Czech attitude towards the European Union and its relationship with Germany. However, more work is necessary to promote such a holistic approach (between bottom–up and top–down research aspects) and to establish flows of influences between different levels or to determine saliency of a given level over others. A holistic approach of combining bottom–up and top–down research aspects, should also link more effectively quantitative (number and type of economic and social exchanges across the border) and qualitative sources (assessment on norm, value and identity sharing). This might enable a better understanding of how the bottom–up and top–down processes interact with each other and whether both processes contribute to an increased co-operation, mutual trust, a sense of community and common identity both within the regions involved and for European Union integration generally.

Notes

The author would like to acknowledge financial assistance provided by the British Academy (APN8434).

1 K. Eckart and H. Kowalke (eds), *Die Euroregionen im Ostens Deutschlands* (Berlin: Dunker and Humblot, 1997); G. Gruber, H. Lamping, W. Lutz and E. W. Schamp, *Neue grenzüberschreitende Regionen im östlichen Mitteleuropa* (Frankfurt: Institut für Wirtschafts- und Sozialgeographie der Johann Wolfgang Goethe Universität, 1994); V. Houzvicka, 'Euroregions as Factors of Social Change within the Czech–German Borderland', in J. Musil and W. Strubelt (eds), *Räumliche Auswirkung des Transformationsprozesses in Deutschland und bei den östlichen Nachbarn* (Opladen: Leske and Budrich, 1997), pp. 185–194; M. Jerabek, 'Tschechische Grenzgebiete und die grenzüberschreitende Zusammenarbeit mit der BRD', in *Planerische Zusammenarbeit und Raumentwicklungen in tschechischen, slowakischen und deutschen Grenzregionen* (Akademie für Raumforschung und Landesplanung, 1996), p. 231; A. Kennard, 'The German–Polish Border as a Model for East–West European Regional Integration: Transborder Co-operation on the Oder–Niesse Line', *German Politics* Vol. 4, No. 1 (1995), 141–149; E. J. Kirchner, *Transnational Border Cooperation Between Germany and the Czech Republic: Implications for Decentralization and European Integration* (EUI Working Paper RSC 98/50, 1998); E. J. Kirchner (ed.), *Decentralization and Transition in the Visegrád: Poland, Hungary, the Czech Republic and Slovakia* (Basingstoke: Macmillan, 1999); R. Kraemer, *Das Land Brandenburg und seine auswärtigen Beziehungen: Zur internationalen Vernetzung eines deutschen Bundeslandes* (Potsdam: Brandenburgische Landeszentrale für politische Bildung, 1995); M. Wolters, 'Euroregions along the German Border', in U. Bullmann (ed.), *Die Politik der dritten Eben: Regionen im Europa der Union* (Baden-Baden: Nomos Verlagsgesellschaft (1994), pp. 407–418; J. A. Yoder, 'Institutional and Cultural Bridges: An Assessment of the Euroregions', paper presented at the American Political Science Association Annual Meeting, 31 August–3 September 2000, Washington, DC (2000); F. Zich, *Euroregions along the Czech/German and Czech/Austrian Borders*, Institute of Sociology, Academy of Sciences of the Czech Republic, Prague (1993).

2 E. J. Kirchner, 'Subsidarity', in P. Clarke and J. Foweraker (eds), *Encyclopedia of Democratic Thought* (London: Routledge, 2001), pp. 687–691.

3 K. Deutsch, *Nationalism and Social Communication*, second edn (Cambridge, MA: MIT Press, 1966).

4 T. A. Börzel, 'Private Actors on the Rise? The Role of Non-state Actors in compliance with International Institutions', paper presented at the Annual Convention of American Political Science Association (Washington, DC, 1–3 September 2000); J. T. Checkel, 'The Constructivist Turn in International Relations Theory', *World Politics* Vol. 50, No. 2 (1998), 324–348; J. T. Checkel, 'Social Construction and Integration', *Journal of European Public Policy* Vol. 6, No. 4 (1999), 545–560; T. Risse, 'Let's Argue: Communicative Action in International Relations', *International Organization* Vol. 54, No. 1 (2000), 1–39.

5 E. Adler and M. Barnett (eds), *Security Communities* (Cambridge: Cambridge University Press, 1998).

6 Deutsch, *Nationalism and Social Communication.*

7 E. W. Schamp, 'Die Bildung neuer grenzüberschreitender Regionen im östlichen Mitteleuropa –eine Einführung', in G. Gruber *et al.* (eds), *Neue grenzüberschreitende Regionen im östlichen Mitteleuropa*, pp. 4–5.

8 Yoder, 'Institutional and Cultural Bridges', p. 4.

9 G. Marks, 'Structural Policy and Multilevel Governance in the EC', in A. W. Cafruny and G. G. Rosenthal (eds), *The State of the European Community: The Maastricht Debates and Beyond* (Boulder, CO: Lynne Rienner Publishers, 1993), pp. 391–410.

10 Yoder, 'Institutional and Cultural Bridges', p. 2.

11 K. Deutsch, *Nationalism and Social Communication; an Inquiry into the Foundations of Nationality* (New York: Technology Press and Wiley, 1953).

12 Adler and Barnett (eds), *Security Communities.*

13 *Ibid.*

14 E. Adler, 'Seizing the idle Ground: Constructivism in World Politics', *European Journal of International Relations* Vol. 3, No. 3 (1997), 319–363.

15 K. M. Fierke and A. Wiener, 'Constructing Institutional Interests: NATO and EU Enlargement', *Journal of European Public Policy* Vol. 6, No. 5 (1999), 722.

16 J. G. Ruggie, 'Constructing the World Polity: Essays on International Institutionalisation', *Pacific Review* Vol. 11, No. 4 (1998), 582–584.

17 F. Schimmelfennig, 'The Community Trap: Liberal Norms, Rhetorical Action and the Eastern Enlargement of the European Union', *International Organization* Vol. 55, No. 1 (2001).

18 S. Mendelson, 'Revealing the Power and Constraints of Norms and Networks: Democracy, Human Rights, and Russia', paper delivered at the 2000 Annual Meeting of the American Political Science Association, August–September 2000.

19 D. D. Laitin, *Culture and National Identity: The 'East' and European Integration*, EUI Working Paper RSC 2000/3.

20 F. Seibt, 'Tschechen, Slowaken und Deutsche: Chronic eines vielschichtigen Verhältnisses', *Zeitschrift zur politischen Bildung*, 4/98, 1998).

21 Jerabek, 'Tschechische Grenzgebiete', p. 43.

22 K. Eckart, *The European Regions at the EU-Border in East Germany*, discussion paper in German Studies, IGS98/4 (Institute of German Studies, University of Birmingham 1998).

23 A. L. Phillips, 'Politics of Reconciliation, Revisited: Germany and East-Central Europe', paper delivered at the 2000 annual meeting of the American Political Science Association, August–September 2000.

24 Formerly some of the regions, like Bohemia and Saxony, were part of an expanded economic and cultural area.

25 Reported in Entwicklungs-und Handlungskonzept Viadrina 2000, edited by the Euroregion Pro Europa Viadrine Mittlere Oder e.V. and the Organisation of Polish Communities of the Pro Europe Viadrina (Frankfurt/Oder and Gorzow, 1999), p. 25.

26 Yoder, 'Institutional and Cultural Bridges', p. 1.

27 CIA *World Factbook* (1995) 113.

28 T. Kaczmarek and T. Stryjakiewicz, 'Die Formen der sozialen und wirtschaftlichen Aktivitat im deutsch-polnischen Grenzgebiet', in K. Eckart and H. Kowalke (eds), *Die Euroregionen im Ostens Deutschlands* (Berlin: Dunker and Humblot, 1997), pp. 29–48.

29 H. Kowalke, 'Die neuen Euroregionen an der östlichen Aussengrenze der Europäischen Union', in Eckart and Kowalke (eds), *Die Euroregionen im Osten Deutschlands*, pp. 13–28.

30 Kennard, 'The German–Polish Border', p. 145.

31 Yoder, 'Institutional and Cultural Bridges', p. 3.

32 M. Kessler, 'Laboratory for European Integration: The Euroregions', *Inter Nationes*, Basis-Info, 14/1999/European Integration (1999) 14; L. Roch, 'Grenzüberschreitende Regionentwicklung-Basis europäischer Integration?', *Welt Trends*, 22/1999 (1999), 44–62.

33 Yoder, 'Institutional and Cultural Bridges', p. 1.

34 Kaczmarek and Stryjakiewicz, 'Die Formen der sozialen', p. 32.

35 J. W. Scott, 'Planning Co-operation and Transboundary Regionalism: Implementing Policies for European border regions in the German–Polish Context', *Environment and Planning C: Government and Policy* Vol. 16 (1998), 619–620.
36 2 and 3 involve Germany and Poland, 5 and 6 Germany and the Czech Republic; 1 comprises Germany, Poland and since 1997 Sweden; 4 involves Germany, Poland and the Czech Republic; and 8 involves Germany, the Czech Republic and Austria.
37 Yoder, 'Institutional and Cultural Bridges', p. 2.
38 Mendelson, *Revealing the Power and Constraints of Norms.*
39 M. Jerabek, T. Sliwa, O. Vidláková and G. Watterott, 'Administrative Co-operation in the Euroregion Neisse–Nisa–Nysa', in K. König and E. Löffler (eds), *Accountability Management in Intergovernmental Partnerships*, proceedings of an Expert Meeting at the OECD in Paris 3–4 September 1998, p. 207.
40 This survey involved managers of Euroregions and personnel involved in cross-border co-operation. For further details see Jerabek *et al.*, 'Administrative Co-operation', p. 214.
41 *Ibid.*
42 *Ibid.*
43 *Ibid.*
44 *Ibid.*
45 *Ibid.*
46 R. Stuth, 'Wettbewerb um Macht und Einfluss in Zentralasien', *Internationale Politik* Vol. 58, No. 3 (1998), 27.
47 A. Rossbach, 'Deutsch-Tschechische Erklärung, Deutsch-Tschechischer Zukunftsfonds, Deutsch-Tschechisches Gesprächsforum', *Zeitschrift zur politischen Bildung* 4/98 (1998), 76.
48 Phillips, 'Politics of Reconciliation', p. 2.
49 M. Corsa, 'Deutsch-tschechische Zusammenarbeit im Jugendbereich–Kreativ–Bunt–Informativ–Kritisch', *Zeitschrift zur politischen Bildung*, 4/98 (1998).
50 Phillips, 'Politics of Reconciliation'. p. 11.
51 *Der Spiegel*, Vol. 33 (1998), 117.
52 Jerabek *et al.*, 'Administrtive Co-operation', p. 202.
53 *Ibid.*
54 E. Bort, *Illegal Migration and Cross-Border Crime: Challenges at the Eastern Frontier of the European Union*, EUI Working Paper, RSC 2000/9 (2000) 19.
55 V. Handl, *Czech Integration Policy: End of Dichotomy?*, EUI Working Paper, RSC 2001/15 (2001) 63.
56 J. Rupnik, *The Implications of the Czecho-Slovak Divorce for the EU Enlargement*, RSC 2000/66 (2000) 27.
57 T. A. Börzel and T. Risse, *When Europe Hits Home: Europeanization and Domestic Change*, EUI Working Paper, RSC 2000/56 (2000) 10.
58 J. W. Meyer and B. Rowan, 'Institutional Organizations: Formal Structure as Myth and Ceremony', in W. W. Powell and P. J. DiMaggio (eds), *The New Institutionalism in Organizational Analysis* (Chicago and London: University of Chicago Press, 1991), pp. 41–62; P. J. Di Maggio and W. W. Powell, 'The Iron Cage Revisited: Institutional Isomorphism and Collective Rationality in Organizational Fields', in W. W. Powell and P. J. Di Maggio (eds), *The New Institutionalism in Organisational Analysis* (London: University of Chicago Press, 1991), pp. 63–82; J. W. Scott and J. W. Meyer, *Institutional Environments and Organizations: Structural Complexity and Individualism* (London: Sage Publications, 1994).
59 Rupnik, *The Implications of the Czecho-Slovak Divorce.*
60 C. Perron, *Views of Czech Local Politicians of European Integration*, EUI Working Paper, RSC 2000/39 (2000) 4. See also Perron's chapter 10 in this volume.
61 Perron, *Views of Czech Local Publications of European Integration*, p. 22.

62 *Ibid.*, p. 5.
63 *Ibid.*, p. 1.
64 Jerabek *et al.*, 'Administrative Co-operation', p. 211.
65 C. M. Dudek, *Can the European Union Influence the Functioning of Regional Government?*, EUI Working Paper, RSC 2000/49 (2000) 5.
66 Deutsch, *Nationalism and Social Communication*, p. 190.
67 A. Hurrell, 'Explaining the resurgence of Regionalism in World Politics', *Review of International Studies* Vol. 21, No. 4 (1995), 335.
68 Deutsch, *Nationalism and Social Communication.*
69 D. Puchala, 'International transactions and Regional Integration', *International Organization* Vol. 24 (1970), 732–763.
70 These surveys on the attitudes of the Czechs towards Germany, have been conducted since 1996 by the Institute of Sociology of the Czech Academy of Sciences, in V. Houzvicka, *Die Sudetendeutsche Frage und Beziehungen der Tschechen zu Deutschland*, Institute for International Relations, Prague (2000); V. Houzvicka, 'Germany as a Factor of Differentiation in Czech Society', *Czech Sociological Review* Vol. 6, No. 2 (1998), 219–240.
71 F. Zich, *Cross-border Contact of Czech Republic citizens and the Development of Czech Republic Citizens and Development of Czech–German Civic Relations*, Institute of Sociology, Academy of Sciences of the Czech Republic, Prague (2000).
72 J. Grix and V. Knowles, 'The Euroregion: A Social Capital Maximiser? The Case of the German–Polish Pro Europa Viadrina', unpublished paper, Institute of German Studies, University of Birmingham (2001).
73 As a large proportion of Sudeten Deutsche expelled from Czechoslovak territory after 1945 resettled in neighbouring Bavaria on the German side, where the Christian Social Union (CSU) has been the ruling party and a coalition partner of the Christian Democratic Union (CDU).
74 J. Rupnik, 'Dule itou zkouškou jsou v dy druhé volby', *Lidové noviny* Vol. 5, No. 5 (1995), 8.
75 V. Houzvicka, 'Germany and Entering NATO as a Differentiating Factor of Czech Society', *Germany and the East Central Europe since 1990*, Results of a research grant project of the Ministry of Foreign Affairs of the Czech Republic, Prague (1999).
76 Houzvicka, 'Germany as a Factor of Differentiation'.
77 An EU-wide opinion poll by Eurostat revealed that only 3 per cent of Germans were in favour of the free movement of the labour force from the Eastern neighbour candidate countries. See Eurostat survey of March 1998, quoted by Jacques Rupnik, 'The Implications')
78 Hurrell, 'Explaining the Resurgence', p. 352.
79 Zich, 'Cross-border Contact'.

Chronologies

Chronology of the Slovak Republic's accession to the EU

19 December 1988	The European Community and the Czechoslovak Socialist Republic sign the Trade and Co-operation Agreement.
1 April 1989	The four-year Trade Agreement on Industrial Products enters into force.
7 May 1990	The Agreement on Trade in Industrial Products is replaced by the Agreement on Business and Economic Cooperation.
16 December 1991	The European Agreement on the Association of the Slovak Federal Republic to the EC (the Association Agreement) is signed. Due to the break-up of Czechoslovakia the Agreement can neither be ratified nor enter into force.
4 October 1993	A separate Association Agreement between the EC and Slovakia is signed.
1 February 1995	The Association Agreement enters into force.
3 May 1995	The White Paper on the Preparation of the Associated Countries of Central and East Europe for the Integration into the Single Market is published.
27 January 1995	Slovakia officially applies for EU membership at the Cannes summit.
28–30 November 1996	A joint session of Resolution of the European Parliament on the need to respect human rights and democracy in Slovakia.
12–13 December 1997	The Luxembourg summit confirms the Commission's recommendation to start entrance discussions with six applicants only, Slovakia not included.
30 March 1998	Slovakia opens negotiations and turns in the country's National Programme for the Adoption of the Acquis.
4 November 1998	First Regular Report on Slovakia's Progress Towards Accession.
11–12 December 1998	The Council of Europe does not recommend direct negotiations on joining the Union with any of the second group candidate countries. However, it assesses positively the changes in Slovakia which took place after the parliamentary elections.
13 October 1999	Second Regular Report on Slovakia acknowledges substantial progress in many respects, moving Slovakia to the first group of candidates in practice.
10 December 1999	The Helsinki summit accepts Slovakia as a candidate for EU membership.

15 February 2000	Official negotiations on Slovakia's accession start in Brussels.
28 March 2000	Slovak position documents on the first chapters of the *acquis* are submitted in Brussels, practical negotiations start.
8 November 2000	Third Regular Report on Slovakia's Progress Towards Accession.
13 November 2001	Fourth Regular Report on Slovakia's Progress Towards Accession.
14–15 December 2001	The Laeken summit endorses EU enlargement as irreversible. Providing Slovakia finalises accession negotiations by the end of 2002, the country would take part in the 2004 European Parliament elections.
11 June 2002	26 out of 30 chapters of the European *acquis* are provisionally closed.
12–13 December 2002	The accession negotiations successfully accomplished at the Copenhagen Summit.

Chronology of the Czech Republic's accession to the EU

19 December 1988	The European Community and the Czechoslovak Socialist Republic begin to strengthen their links and establish diplomatic relations; Trade and Co-operation Agreement is signed.
1 April 1989	The four-year Trade Agreement on Industrial Products enters into force.
7 May 1990	Agreement on Trade and Commercial and Economic Co-operation is signed.
16 December 1991	The Association Agreement ('Europe Agreement') between the European Communities and the Czech and Slovak Federal Republic is signed.
1 March 1992	The trade provisions of the Europe Agreement enter into force by means of an Interim Agreement.
21–23 June 1992	The Lisbon European Council summit issues the first express statement of support for the effort of Central and East European (CEE) countries to prepare for accession.
4 October 1993	A separate Europe Agreement between the EC and the Czech Republic is signed after the split-up of Czechoslovakia.
21–22 June 1993	The Copenhagen European Council summit endorses eventual membership of CEE states as a goal; membership criteria are established, PHARE assistance reoriented and accelerated market access to the EU provided.
9–10 December 1994	The Essen European Council defines a pre-accession strategy to prepare candidate countries for EU membership.
1 February 1995	Czech Republic's Europe Agreement enters into force.
23 January 1996	The Czech Republic officially applies for membership in the EU.
16 July 1997	Agenda 2000 is adopted.

16 July 1997	The European Commission issues its (positive) opinion on the Czech Republic's application for membership.
12–13 December 1997	The Luxembourg European Council decides on an enhanced pre-accession strategy for all ten candidate countries but endorses the Commission's recommendation for early accession negotiations with the Czech Republic, Estonia, Hungary, Poland, Slovenia and Cyprus (the 'Luxembourg Six').
31 March 1998	Negotiations between the Czech Republic and the EU are opened.
4 November 1998	First Regular Report on the Czech Republic's Progress towards Accession.
13 October 1999	Second Regular Report on the Czech Republic's Progress towards Accession.
31 May 2000	Updated National Programme for the Preparation on the Czech Republic for membership in the European Union is approved.
8 November 2000	Third Regular Report on the Czech Republic's Progress towards Accession.
13 November 2001	Fourth Regular Report on the Czech Republic's Progress towards Accession is accompanied by the Commission's 'Strategic Document' confirming the enlargement 'roadmap'.
14–15 December 2001	The Laeken summit names the Czech Republic as one of the candidate countries that are to join in the 2004 European Parliament elections provided they finalise negotiation by December 2002.
28 February 2002	Czech delegates take part in the opening of the Convention on the Future of Europe in Brussels and in the ensuing discussions on institutional reform.
1 July 2002	25 out of 30 chapters of the EC *acquis* are provisionally closed.
12–13 December 2002	The accession negotiations successfully accomplished at the Copenhagen Summit.

Select bibliography

Ágh, A. (ed.), *The First Steps: The Emergence of ECE Parliaments* (Budapest: Hungarian Centre for Democracy Studies Foundation, 1994).

Ágh, A. 'The Europeanization of ECE Polities and the Emergence of the New ECE Democratic Parliaments', in A. Ágh (ed.) *The First Steps: The Emergence of East-Central European Parliaments* (Budapest: Hungarian Centre of Democracy Studies Foundation, 1994).

Ágh, A. 'The role of the ECE Parliaments in the Pre-accession Strategy'. Paper presented at the Prague conference on the 'Role of Parliaments in European Integration' (12–13 September 1997).

Ágh, A. 'Democratic Deficit in the EU and the ECE Accession Process', *Budapest Papers on Democratic Transition* No. 222 (1998).

Arnold, C. H. *Deutschland Größe. Deutsche Außenpolitik zwischen Macht und Mangel?* (Munich: Piper, 1995).

Aron, R. 'Is Multinational Citizenship Possible?', *Social Research*, Vol. 41, No. 4 (1974), 638–656.

Ash, T. G. *The Uses of Adversity: Essays on the Fate of Central Europe* (New York: Random House, 1989).

Avery, G. and Cameron, F. *The Enlargement of the European Union* (Sheffield: Sheffield Academic Press, 1998).

Baldwin-Edwards, M. 'Citizenship of the Union: Rhetoric or Reality, Inclusion or Exclusion?', in Kososnen, Pekka and Madsen (eds), *Convergence or Divergence?*

Baldwin-Edwards, M. 'The Emerging European Immigration Regime: Some Reflections on Implications for Southern Europe', *Journal of Common Market Studies*, Vol. 35, No. 4 (1998), 495–519.

Baldwin-Edwards, M. *Third Country Nationals and Welfare Systems in the EU* (Florence: European University Institute, 1997).

Baring, A. *Deutschland, Was nun?* (Berlin: Siedler, 1990).

Barkey and Parikh, 'Comparative Perspectives on State', *Annual Review of Sociology*, Vol. 17 (1991), 510–528.

Batt, J. 'Czechoslovakia', in S. Whitefield (ed.), *The New Institutional Architecture of Eastern Europe* (New York: St Martin's Press, 1993).

Bazin, A. 'Tchèques et Allemands sur la voie d'une difficile réconciliation?', *Relations Internationales et Stratégiques*, Vol. 26 (1997), 154–164.

Bazin, A. 'Les Régions frontalières tchèques: différenciation interne et enjeux européens', *Revue d'Etudes Comparatives Est–Ouest*, Vol. 29, No. 4 (1998), 229–255.

Bazin, A. and Rupnik, J. 'La Réconciliation tchéco-allemande, une longue route semée d'obstacles', *Politique Etrangère*, Vol. 2 (2001).

Bilčík, V., Bruncko, M., Duleba, A., Lukáč, P. and Samson, I. 'Foreign and Defence Policy of the Slovak Republic', in G. Mesežnikov, M. Kollár and T. Nicholson (eds), *Slovakia 2000* (Bratislava, 2000), pp. 233–296.

Bort, E. *Illegal Migration and Cross-border Crime: Challenges at the Eastern Frontier of the European Union*, EUI Working Paper, RSC 2000/9 (2000).

Börzel, T. A. 'Private Actors on the Rise? The Role of Non-State Actors in Compliance with International Institutions', paper presented at the Annual Convention of American Political Science Association (Washington, DC, 1–3 September 2000).

Boxhoorn, B. 'European Identity and the Process of European Unification: Compatible Notions?', in M. Wintle (ed.), *Culture and Identity in Europe* (Avebury: Aldershot, 1996), pp. 133–145.

Börzel, T. A. and Risse, T. *When Europe Hits Home: Europeanization and Domestic Change*, EUI Working Paper, RSC 2000/56 (2000).

Bratowski, A., Grosfeld, I. and Rostowski, I. *Investment Finance in De Novo Private Firms: Empirical Results from the Czech Republic, Hungary and Poland.* CASE-CEU Working Paper Series, No. 21 (Warsaw: Centre for Social and Economic Research, Central European University, October 1998).

Brubaker, R. (ed.), *Immigration and the Politics of Citizenship in Europe and North America* (Lanham: University Press of America 1989).

Brubaker, R. *Citizenship and Nationhood in France and Germany* (Cambridge, MA: Harvard University Press, 1992).

Bugge, P. 'Home at Last? Czech Views of Joining the European Union', in N. Parker, and B. Armstrong (eds), *Margins in European Integration* (Basingstoke and London: Macmillan, 2000), pp. 214–225.

Bulmer, S. *New institutionalism, the Single Market and EU Governance* (Olso, Arena Working paper 25/1997).

Bulmer, S. and Paterson, W. 'Germany in the European Union: Gentle Giant or Emergent Leader?' *International Affairs*, Vol. 72, No. 1 (1996) 9–32.

Burges, A. 'Writing Off Slovakia to the East? Examining Charges of Bias in British Press Reporting on Slovakia, 1993–1994', *Nationalities Papers*, Vol. 25, No. 4 (1997) 659–683.

Burton, M., Gunther, R. and Higley, J. 'Elite Transformations and Democratic Regimes', in M. Burton and R. Gunther (eds), *Elites and Democratic Consolidation in Latin America and Southern Europe* (Cambridge: Cambridge University Press, 1992) 20–24.

Bútora, M. and Bútorová, Z. 'Slovakia: The Identity Challenges of the Newly Born State,' *Social Research*, Vol. 60 Winter (1993), 705–736.

Bútorová, Z. (ed.), *Democracy and Discontent in Slovakia: A Public Opinion Profile of a Country in Transition* (Bratislava: Institute for Public Affairs, 1997, 1998).

Bútorová, Z. 'Public Opinion', in M. Bútora (ed.), *Slovakia 1997: A Global Report on the State of Society* (Bratislava: Institute for Public Affairs, 1998).

Brach, R. *Die Außenpolitik der Tschechoslowakei zur Zeit der 'Regierung der nationalen Verständigung'*, Schriftenreihe des Bundesinstituts für ostwissenschaftliche und internationale Studien, Köln, Band 22 (Baden-Baden: Nomos Verlagsgesellschaft, 1992).

Carnogurský, J. 'Identita Európy', *Literárny týzdenník*, Vol. 8, No. 1 (1995).

Ceasarani, D. and Fulbrook, M. (eds), *Citizenship, Nationality and Migration in Europe* (London: Routledge, 1996).

Cerný, A. 'Prague's Reality Check', *Transitions*, Vol. 5, No. 4 (1998), 52–55.

Chmel, R. 'Introduction,' in R. Chmel (ed.), *Slovenská otázka v 20. storočí* [*The Slovak Question in the 20th Century*] (Bratislava: Kalligram, 1997).

Christiansen, T. and Jørgensen, K. E. 'Transnational Governance "Above" and "Below" the State: The Changing Nature of Borders in the New Europe,' *Regional and Federative Studies*, Vol. 10 (2000).

Cihlár, V. and Hrich, J. 'Achievements of the Czech Republic on its Road to the European Union', in B. Lippert, and H. Schneider (eds), *Monitoring Association and Beyond: The European Union and the Visegrád States*, Europäische Schriften des Instituts für Europäische Politik; Band 74 (Bonn: Europa Union Verlag, 1995).

Cinar, D. 'From Aliens to Citizens: A Comparative Analysis of Rules of Transition', in R. Baubock (ed.), *From Aliens to Citizens*, Chapter 3.

Close, P. *Citizenship, Europe and Change* (London: Macmillan 1995).

Collins, S. M. and Rodrik, D. *Eastern Europe and the Soviet Union in the World Economy* (Washington, DC: Institute for International Economics, 1991).

Corsa, M. 'Deutsch-tschechische Zusammenarbeit im Jugendbereich–Kreativ–Bunt–Informativ–Kritisch', *Zeitschrift zur politischen Bildung*, 4/98 (1998).

Cottey, A. *East-Central Europe after the Cold War: Poland, the Czech Republic, Slovakia and Hungary in Search of Security* (Basingstoke: Macmillan, 1995), Chapter 5.

Dahrendorf, R. 'The Changing Quality of Citizenship', in B. van Steenberger (ed.), *The Conditions of Citizenship* (London: Sage Publications, 1994).

De La Serre, A., Lequesne, C. and Rupnik, J. *L'Union Européenne: ouverture à l'Est?* (Paris: PUF, 1994).

De Witte, B. 'Politics Versus Law in the EU's Approach to Ethnic Minorities,' in J. Zielonka (ed.) *Europe Unbound* (London: Routledge, 2002), pp. 137–160.

Deubner, A. 'L'Europe idéale de l'Allemagne', *Revue d'Etudes Comparatives Est-Ouest*, 4 (1996).

Deutsch, K. *Nationalism and Social Communication: An Inquiry into the Foundations of Nationality* (New York: Technology Press and Wiley, 1953).

Deutsch, K. *et al. Political Community and the North Atlantic Area* (New York: Greenwood Press, 1957), pp. 117–161.

Di Maggio, P. J. and Powell, W. W. 'The Iron Cage Revisited: Institutional Isomorphism and Collective Rationality in Organizational Fields', in W. W. Powell and P. J. Di Maggio (eds), *The New Institutionalism in Organisational Analysis* (London: University of Chicago Press 1991), pp. 63–82.

Di Palma, G. *To Craft Democracies: A Chapter on Democratic Transitions* (Berkeley: University of California Press, 1990), 56–78.

Diamond, L. 'Is the Third Wave Over?', *Journal of Democracy*, 7 (July 1996), 20–37.

Drábek, Z. and Smith, A. *Trade Performance and Trade Policy in Central and Eastern Europe.* CEPR Discussion Paper No. 1182 (London: Centre for Economic Policy Research, London, 1995).

Droz, J. *L'Europe centrale, évolution historique de l'idée de 'Mitteleuropa'* (Paris: Payot, 1960).

Dudek, C. M. *Can the European Union Influence the Functioning of Regional Government?*, EUI Working Paper, RSC 2000/49 (2000).

Dulaba, A. 'Zahranicno-politicka orientacia a vnutorna politika SR', in S. Szomolanyi (ed.), *Slovensko: problémy konsolidacie demokracie* (Bratislava: Slovenske zdruzenie pre politické vedy, 1997), pp. 187–203.

Duleba, A. 'Democratic Consolidation and the Conflict over Slovak International Alignment', in S. Szomolányi and J. A. Gould (eds), *Slovakia: Problems of Democratic Consolidation* (Bratislava: Slovak Political Science Association, 1997).

Duleba, A. 'Pursuing an Eastern Agenda', *Transitions*, Vol. 2, No. 19 (1996), 52–55.

Dvoráková, V. 'The Politics of Antipolitics? The Radical Right in the Czech Republic', paper presented at the conference on 'Liberalism, Social Democracy and Fascism in Central Europe', Sandbjerg, November 15–18 (1996).

EC Commission, 'The Economic Interpenetration between the European Community and Eastern Europe', *European Economy Reports and Studies*, No. 6 (1994).

EC Commission (1997) *Commission Opinion on the Czech Republic's Application for Membership of the European Union*, 15 July 1997. Supplement to the Bulletin of the European Union 14/97.

EC Commission (1997) *Commission Opinion on the Slovak Republic's Application for Membership of the European Union*, 15 July 1997. Supplement to the Bulletin of the European Union 9/97.

EC Commission, *Enlargement Strategy Report 2000*, Brussels, 2000.

Eckart, K. *The European Regions at the EU Border in East Germany*, discussion paper in German Studies, IGS98/4 (Institute of German Studies, University of Birmingham (1998).

Eckart, K. and Kowalke, H. (eds), *Die Euroregionen im Ostens Deutschlands* (Berlin: Dunker and Humblot, 1997).

Eggertsson, T. *Economic Behavior and Institutions* (Cambridge: Cambridge University Press, 1990).

Eichengreen, B. and Kohl, R. *The External Sector, the State and Development in Eastern Europe*, in J. Zysman, and A. Schwartz (eds), *Enlarging Europe: The Industrial Foundations of a New Political Reality*. Research Series No. 99 (Berkeley: University of California, 1998), pp. 169–201.

Einhorn, B., Kaldor, M. and Kavan, Z. (eds), *Citizenship and Democratic Control in Contemporary Europe* (Cheltenham: Edward Elgar, 1996).

Eisenstadt, S. N. *The Political System of Empires* (New York: The Free Press, 1969).

Faini, R. and Portes, R. *European Union Trade with Eastern Europe: Adjustment and Opportunities* (London: Centre for Economic Policy Research, 1995).

Fiala, P. and Mikš, F. *Úvahy o české politické krizi* (Brno: CDK, 1998).

Fierke, K. M. and Wiener, A. 'Constructing Institutional Interests: NATO and EU Enlargement', *Journal of European Public Policy*, Vol. 6, No. 5 (1999).

Fisher, S. 'Slovakia: The First Year of Independence', *RFE-RL Research Report*, Vol. 3, No. 1 (7 January 1994), 87–91.

Gabal, I. Friedrich-Naumann-Stiftung, *Einstellung der tschechischen Gesellschaft zu Deutschland* (Prague, 1995).

Garton Ash, T. *In Europe's Name* (London, 1994).

Geddes, A. 'Immigrants and Ethnic Minorities and the EU's Democratic Deficit', *Journal of Common Market Studies*, Vol. 33, No. 2 (1996), 197–217.

Gellner, E. *Nations and Nationalism* (Ithaca: Cornell University Press, 1983).

Gerloch, A. *et al.*, *Ústavní systém české republiky* (Praha: Prospektrum, 1994).

Golan, G. *Reform Rule in Czechoslovakia. The Dubček Era* (Cambridge: Cambridge University Press, 1973).

Golberger, A. N. 'Why Europe Should Not Fear the Germans', *German Politics*, Vol. 2, No. 2 (1993), 288–310.

Goujeon, J. P. *Où va l'Allemagne?* (Paris: Flammarion, 1997), pp. 271–272.

Grabbe, H. and Hughes, K. *Eastward Enlargement of the European Union* (London: Royal Institute of International Affairs, 1997).

Grabbe, H. and Hughes, K. *Enlarging the EU Eastwards*, Chatham House Paper (London: Royal Institute of International Affairs, 1998).

Greenfeld, L. *Nationalism, Five Roads to Modernity* (Cambridge, MA: Harvard University Press, 1992).

Gruber, G., Lamping, H., Lutz, W. and Schamp, E. W. *Neue grenzüberschreitende Regionen im östlichen Mitteleuropa* (Frankfurt: Institut für Wirtschafts- und Sozialgeographie der Johann Wolfgang Goethe Universität, 1994).

Hacke, A. *Weltmacht wider Willen. Die deutsche Außenpolitik der Bundesrepublik Deutschland* (Stuttgart: Klett-Cotta, 1988).

Haggard, S. and Kaufman, R. R. *The Political Economy of Democratic Transitions* (Princeton: Princeton University Press, 1995).

Handl, V. 'Tschechische Europapolitik: Profilsuche und Kursbestimmung', *Integration* 16, 3 (1993) 125–137.

Handl, V. 'Translating the Czech Vision of Europe into Foreign Policy: Historical Conditions and Current Approaches', in B. Lippert, and H. Schneider (eds), *Monitoring Association and Beyond: The European Union and the Visegrád States*, Europäische Schriften des Instituts für Europäische Politik; Bd. 74 (Bonn: Europa Union Verlag, 1995).

Handl, V. *Czech Integration Policy: End of Dichotomy?*, EUI Working Paper, RSC 2001/15 (2001).

Havel, V. *Letní přemítání* (Praha: Odeon, 1991).

Havel, V. *The Art of the Impossible: Speeches and Writings, 1990–1996* (New York and Toronto: Alfred A. Knopf, 1997).

Heater, D. *Citizenship: The Civic Ideal in World History, Politics and Education* (London: Longman, 1990).

Hobson, J. M. *The Wealth of States: A Comparative Sociology of International and Political Change* (Cambridge: Cambridge University Press, 1997).

Höfig, C. 'Foreign Cultural Policy', in A. S. Markovits and S. Reich (eds), *The German Predicament*, pp. 183–202.

Hooghe, L. (ed.), *Cohesion Policy and European Integration: Building Multi-level Governance* (Oxford: Oxford University Press, 1996).

Houzvicka, V. (ed.), *Reflexe sudetonemecké otazky a postoje obyvatelstva ceskeho pohranici k Nemecku*, [*Reflections on the German Sudeten Issue and on the Attitude of the Inhabitants of the Czech Border Regions towards Germany*] (Usti nad Labem, Sociologicky Ustav Akademie Ved Ceské Republiky Vyskumny Tym Pohranici, 1997).

Houzvicka, V. 'Euroregions as Factors of social Change within the Czech–German Borderland', in J. Musil and W. Strubelt (eds), *Räumliche Auswirkung des Transformationsprozesses in Deutschland und bei den östlichen Nachbarn* (Opladen: Leske and Budrich, 1997), pp. 185–194.

Houzvicka, V. 'Germany as a Factor of Differentiation in Czech Society', *Czech Sociological Review*, Vol. 6, No. 2 (1998) 219–240.

Houzvicka, V. 'Germany and Entering NATO as a Differentiating Factor of Czech Society', *Germany and the East Central Europe since 1990*. Results of a research grant project of the Ministry of Foreign Affairs of the Czech Republic, Prague (1999).

Houzvicka, V. *Die Sudetendeutsche Frage und Beziehungen der Tschechen zu Deutschland*, Institute for International Relations, Prague (2000).

Hrib, S. 'Being left behind', *Transitions* (April 1998), p. 57.

Hronec, B. 'Slovak Dilemmas with Identity and Nationality: The Controversy among

Slovak Intellectuals in the First Half of the 19th Century', in C. W. Lowney (ed.), *Identities* (Vienna: IWM, 1998).

Hudala, A. *Der Beitritt der tschechischen Republik zur EU. Eine Fallstudie zu den Auswirkungen der EU-Osterweiterung auf die finalité politique des Europäischen Integrationsprozesses* (Münster, Hamburg, and London: Ed. coll. Osteuropa 1996).

Huntington, S. *Political Order in Changing Societies* (New Haven: Yale University Press, 1968).

Huntington, S. P. 'Twenty Years: The Future of the Third Wave,' *Journal of Democracy* Vol. 8, October (1997).

Hurrell, A. 'Explaining the resurgence of regionalism in World Politics', *Review of International Studies,* Vol. 21, No. 4 (1995).

Innes, A. 'The Breakup of Czechoslovakia: The Impact of Party Development on the Separation of the State', *East European Politics and Societies,* Vol. 11, No. 3 (1997).

Innes, A. *Czechoslovakia: The Short Goodbye* (New Haven: Yale University Press, 2001).

Jacobson, D. *Rights across Borders* (Baltimore: Johns Hopkins University Press, 1996).

Jakš, J. 'The Czech Republic on the Road to the European Union: Problems of the Mutual Interaction of the Transformation and Integration Processes in the 1990s', *Perspectives* Vol. 3, Summer (1994).

Jerabek, M. 'Tschechische Grenzgebiete und die grenzüberschreitende Zusammenarbeit mit der BRD', *Planerische Zusammenarbeit und Raumentwicklungen in tschechischen, slowakischen und deutschen Grenzregionen* (Akademie für Raumforschung und Landesplanung, 1996), 231.

Jerabek, M., Sliwa, T., Vidláková, O. and Watterott, G. 'Administrative Co-operation in the Euroregion Neisse–Nisa–Nysa', in K. König and E. Löffler (eds), *Accountability Management in Intergovernmental Partnerships,* Proceedings of an Expert Meeting at the OECD in Paris 3–4 September 1998.

Jopp, M. 'Germany and EU Enlargement', in K. Kaiser, and M. Brüning (eds), *East-Central Europe and the EU: Problems of Integration* (Bonn, Institut für Europäische Integrationsforschung e.V., 1996), pp. 107–120.

Joppke, C. (ed.), *Challenge to the Nation-State: Immigration in Western Europe and the United States* (Oxford: Oxford University Press, 1998).

Kaczmarek, T. and Stryjakiewicz, T. 'Die Formen der sozialen und wirtschaftlichen Aktivitat im deutsch-polnischen Grenzgebiet', in K. Eckart and H. Kowalke (eds), *Die Euroregionen im Ostens Deutschlands* (Berlin: Dunker and Humblot, 1997), pp. 29–48.

Katzenstein, P. (ed.), *Mitteleuropa, Between Europe and Germany* (Oxford: Berghahn Books, 1997).

Kavan, Z. 'Democracy and Nationalism in Czechoslovakia', in Einhorn, Kaldor and Kavan (eds) *Citizenship and Democratic Control in Contemporary Europe,* 24–39.

Kennard, A. 'The German–Polish Border as a Model for East–West European Regional Integration: Transborder Co-operation on the Oder–Niesse Line', *German Politics,* Vol. 4, No. 1 (1995), 141–149.

Kessler, M. 'Laboratory for European Integration: The Euroregions', *Inter Nationes,* Basis-Info, 14/1999/European Integration (1999), 14.

Kettle, S. 'Of Money and Morality', *Transition* (15 March 1995) 37.

Kirchner, E. J. *Transnational Border Cooperation between Germany and the Czech Republic: Implications for Decentralization and European Integration* (EUI Working Paper RSC 98/50, 1998).

Kirchner, E. J. (ed.), *Decentralization and Transition in the Visegrád: Poland, Hungary, the Czech Republic and Slovakia* (Basingstoke: Macmillan Press, 1999).

Kirchner, E. J. 'Subsidarity', in P. Clarke and J. Foweraker (eds), *Encyclopedia of Democratic Thought* (London: Routledge, 2001), pp. 687–691.

Klaus, V. *Obhajoba zapomenutych myslenek* (Prague: Academia Praha, 1997)

Klaus, V. *Renaissance: The Rebirth of Liberty in the Heart of Europe* (Washington, D.C: Cato Institute, 1997).

Knight, J. *Institutions and Social Conflict* (Cambridge: Cambridge University Press, 1992).

Kohler-Koch, B. 'Catching up with Changes: the Transformation of Governance in the European Union', *Journal of European Policy*, Vol. 3, No. 3 (1996), 359–380.

Korcelli, P. 'Current Issues Related to Migration and Citizenship: The Case of Poland', in Baubock (ed.), *From Aliens to Citizens*, Chapter 8.

Kowalke, H. 'Die neuen Euroregionen an der östlichen Aussengrenze der Europäischen Union', in *Die Euroregionen im Osten Deutschlands* (1997), 13–28.

Kraemer, R. *Das Land Brandenburg und seine auswärtigen Beziehungen: Zur internationalen Vernetzung eines deutschen Bundeslandes* (Potsdam: Brandenburgische Landeszentrale für politische Bildung, 1995).

Kraus, M. 'Returning to Europe, Separately', in M. Kraus and R. D. Liebowitz (eds), *Russia and Eastern Europe after Communism* (Boulder, CO: Westview Press, 1996).

Kraus, M. and Stanger, A. (eds), *Irreconciliable Differences, Explaining Czechoslovakia's Dissolution* (Boulder: Rowman & Littlefield Publishers, 2000).

Krenzler, H.-G. and Senior-Nello, S. M. *The Implications of the Euro for Enlargement*, Robert Schuman Centre Policy Paper 99/3 (Florence: European University Institute, 1999).

Krivý, V. 'Mestá a obce vo volbách. Ako volili?' ('Towns and Villages in the Elections: How Did They Vote?'), Domino-fórum (Bratislava, 2, 1998).

Krivý, V. 'Volici' (Voters), *Domino-fórum* (Bratislava, 2, 1998), 7–9.

Krugman, P. *Pop Internationalism* (Cambridge, MA: MIT Press, 1996).

Kuehnl, K. 'The Czech Republic is an Integral Part of European Civilisation', in W. Nicoll and R. Schoenberg (eds), *Europe beyond 2000: The Enlargement of the European Union towards the East* (London: Whurr, 1998).

Kumar, K. 'The 1989 Revolutions and the Idea of Europe', *Political Studies*, 40 (1992), 439–461.

Kundera, M. 'L'Occident kidnappé, ou la tragédie de l'Europe centrale', *Le Débat*, 27 (1983), 4–22.

Kusy, M. 'Slovaks Are More . . .', in J. Jensen and F. Miszlivetz (eds), *East Central Europe: Paradoxes and Perspectives* (Szombathely: Savana University Press, 1998), pp. 53–76.

Laitin, D. D. *Culture and National Identity: The 'East' and European Integration*, EUI Working Paper RSC 2000/3.

Le Gloannec, A.-M. (ed.), *L'Allemagne après la guerre froide; la vainqueur entravé* (Brussels: Complexe, 1993).

Lemasson, S. 'L'Allemagne, l'Europe et la question de la Mitteleuropa', in F. Bafoil (ed.), *Les stratégies allemandes en Europe centrale et orientale, une géopolitique des investissements directs* (Paris: L'Harmattan, 1997).

Lepesant, G. *Géopolitique des frontières orientales de l'Allemagne* (Paris: L'Harmattan, 1998).

Leška, V. *et al*, 'Česká republika a region střední Evropy', in V. Kotyk (ed.), *Česká zahraniční politika: Úvahy o prioritách* (Praha Ústav mezinárodních vztahů, 1997).

Lijphart, A. *Democracy in Plural Societies: A Comparative Exploration* (New Haven: Yale University Press, 1977).

Lijphart, A. *Democracies: Patterns of Majoritarian and Consensus Government in Twenty-One Countries* (New Haven: Yale University Press, 1984).

Linz, J. and Stepan, A. in *Problems of Democratic Transitions and Consolidations* (Baltimore: Johns Hopkins University Press, 1996).

Lippert, B. 'Shaping and Evaluating the Europe Agreements: The Community Side', in B. Lippert and H. Schneider (eds), *Monitoring Association and Beyond: The European Union and the Visegrád States* (Bonn: Europa Union Verlag, 1995).

Lipset, S. M., Seong, K.-R and Torres, J. 'A Comparative Analysis of the Social Requisites of Democracy', *International Social Science Journal*, No. 136 (1993) 155–75.

Liptak, L. 'Niektore historické aspekty slovensej otazky', in R. Chmel (ed.), *Slovenska otazka v 20. storoci* (Bratislava: Kalligram).

Lukaš, Z. and Szomolanyi, S. 'Slovakia', in W. Weidenfeld (ed.), *Central and Eastern Europe on the Way into the EU* (Bratislava: Bertelsman Foundation Publishers, 1996) 201–224.

Machonin, P. *Socio-economic Changes in the Czech Republic. With an Appendix Concerning the 1996 Elections Results*, Working Paper 96:10, 1996 (Institute of Sociology, Academy of Sciences of the Czech Republic).

Machonin, P. *et al., Strategie sociální transformace českă společnosti* (Brno: Nakadatelství Doplněk, 1996).

Malová, D. and Rybár, M. 'The Troubled Institutionalization of Parliamentary Democracy in Slovakia', *Politicka misao. Croatian Political Science Review*, Vol. 37, No. 2 (2000), 99–115.

Mann, M. 'The Autonomous Power of The State', *Archives Europeénnes de Sociologie*, Vol. 25 (1984), 187–188.

Mansfeldová, Z. 'Public Opinion to EU Membership in the Czech Republic and the Role of Political Elites', *Budapest Papers on Democratic Transition* No. 216 (1997).

Markovits, A. and Reich, S. 'Should Europe Fear the Germans?', *German Politics and Society*, Vol. 23 (1991), 1–20.

Marks, G. 'Structural Policy and Multilevel Governance in the EC', in A. W. Cafruny and G. G. Rosenthal (eds), *The State of the European Community: The Maastricht Debates and Beyond* (Boulder: Lynne Rienner Publishers, 1993), pp. 391–410.

Marshall, T. H. *Class, Citizenship and Social Development* (Westport, CT: Greenwood Press, 1973).

Marušiak, J., Alner, J., Lukác, P., Chmel, R., Samson, I. and Duleba, A. 'The Foreign Policy and National Security of the Slovak Republic', in G. Mesežnikov, M. Ivantyšyn and T. Nicholson (eds), *Slovakia 1998–1999* (1999), pp. 167–196.

Masaryk, T. G. *The Meaning of Czech History* (Chapel Hill: University of North Carolina Press, 1973).

Mendelson, S. *Revealing the Power and Constraints of Norms and Networks: Democracy, Human Rights, and Russia*, paper delivered at the 2000 annual meeting of the American Political Science Association, August –September 2000.

Mesežnikov, G. 'Domestic Political Developments and the Political Scene in the Slovak Republic', in M. Butora and P. Huncik (eds), *Global Report on Slovakia: Comprehensive Analyses from 1995, and Trends for 1996* (Bratislava: Sandor Marai Foundation, 1997), 11–31.

Mesežnikov, G. 'Vnútropolitický vývoj a politická scéna', in M. Butora (ed.), *Slovensko v Pohybe: Slovensko 1996* (Bratislava: Institute pre Verejne Otázky, 1997) 15–36.

Mesežnikov, G. 'Vláda "velkej koalície"' ('Government of the "Grand Coalition"'), *Mosty* (Bratislava, 7, 1998), 8.

Meth-Cohn, D. 'The New Wall', *Business Central Europe* (September 1997), 19–22.

Meyer, J. W. and Rowan, B. 'Institutional Organizations: Formal Structure as Myth and Ceremony', in W. W. Powell and P. J. DiMaggio (eds), *The New Institutionalism in Organizational Analysis* (Chicago and London: University of Chicago Press, 1991), pp. 41–62.

Migdal, J. 'Strong States, Weak States: Power and Accommodation', in Wiener and Huntington (eds), *Understanding Political Development* (Prospect Heights: Waveland Press (1987).

Milward, A. *The European Rescue of the Nation-State* (London: Routledge, 1992).

Mitten, R. 'Jorg Haider: The Anti-immigrant Petition and Immigration Policy in Austria', *Patterns of Prejudice*, Vol. 28, No. 2 (1994), 27–47.

Moravcsik, A. *Why the European Community Strengthens the State: Domestic Politics and International Cooperation* (Harvard Center for European Studies, Working Paper No. 52, 1994).

Moravcsik, A. *The Choice for Europe: Social Purpose and State Power from Messina to Maastricht* (Ithaca: Cornell University Press, 1998).

Mudde, C. 'One Against All, All Against One! A Portrait of the Vlaams Block', *Patterns of Prejudice*, Vol. 29, No. 1 (1995), 5–28.

Mudde, C. 'The New Roots of Extremism: The ABCs of the Rising Right', *Transitions*, Vol. 5, No. 7 (1998), 44–47.

Müller, H. *Macht und Ohnmacht. Deutsche Außenpolitik vor dem Ende?* (Frankfurt/Main: Alfred Herrhausen Gesellschaft für internationalen Dialog, 1998). *Názory. Informacný bulletin* (*Opinions. Information Bulletin*), 8 (Bratislava: Public Opinion Research Institute, Statistical Office of the Slovak Republic, 1997, No. 1).

Neumayer, L. 'La vision de l'intégration de Vaclav Klaus', *La nouvelle alternative* No. 49 March (1998).

North, D. *Institutions, Institutional Change and Economic Performance* (Cambridge: Cambridge University Press, 1991).

Novák, M. 'Is There One Best "Model of Democracy"'? Efficiency and Representativeness: 'Theoretical Revolution' or Democratic Dilemma?', *Czech Sociological Review* Vol. 5, No. 2 (1997).

O'Donnell, G. *Modernization and Bureaucratic Authoritarianism: Studies in South American Politics* (Berkeley, Institute of International Studies, University of California, 1973).

O'Donnell, G. and Schmitter, P. *Transition from Authoritarian Rule: Tentative Conclusions about Uncertain Democracies* (Baltimore: Johns Hopkins University Press, 1996).

OECD, *Economic Survey of the Czech Republic* (Paris: OECD, all years).

Offerdal, A., Hanšpách, D., Kowalczyk, A. and Patocka, J. 'The New Local Elites', in Harald Baldersheim *et al.* (eds), *Local Democracy and the Process of Transformation in Eastern Europe* (Boulder: CO: Westview Press, 1996).

Orenstein, 'Václav Klaus: Revolutionary and Parliamentarian', *East European Constitutional Review*, Winter (1998), 53–55.

Panebianco, S. 'European Citizenship and European Identity: From the Treaty of Maastricht to Public Opinion Attitudes' (University of Catania: December 1996).

Parlamentné volby '98. Výskum pre International Republican Institute [Parliamentary Elections '98: Survey for the International Republican Institute] (Bratislava: FOCUS, 1998).

Patocka, J. *L'idée de l'Europe en Bohême* (Grenoble: Jerôme Millon, 1991).
Pehe, J. 'Krize politiky a politika krize. Ohlédnutí za odcházejícím rokem 1997', *Nová Přitomnost*, December (1997).
Peroutka, F. *Budováni Státu, III* (Praha: Lidove Noviny), 1,285–90.
Perron, C. *Views of Czech Local Politicians of European Integration*, EUI Working Paper, RSC 2000/39 (2000).
Peskova, J. *et al, Dejiny Zemi Koruny Ceské, II* (Praha: Paseka, 1992), 168–170.
Phillips, A. L. 'Politics of Reconciliation, revisited: Germany and East-Central Europe', paper delivered at the 2000 annual meeting of the American Political Science Association, August –September 2000.
Pinder, J. 'The EC and Democracy in Central and Eastern Europe', in G. Pridham, E. Herring and G. Sandorf (eds), *Building Democracy? The International Dimension of Democratization in Eastern Europe* (London: Leicester University Press, 1994), 119–44.
Poggi, G. *The State: Its Nature, Development and Prospects* (Stanford: Stanford University Press, 1990).
Pollack, M. 'New Institutionalism and EU Governance: The Promise and Limits of Institutionalist Analysis', *Governance*, Vol. 9, No. 4 (1996), 429–458.
Pridham, G. 'Complying with the European Union's Democratic Conditionality: Transnational Party Linkages and Regime Change in Slovakia, 1993–1998', *Europe–Asia Studies*, Vol. 51, No. 7 (1999).
Pridham, G. 'Rethinking Regime Change Theory and the International Dimension of Democratisation: Ten Years after in East-Central Europe,' in G. Pridham and A. Ágh (eds), *Prospects for Democratic Consolidation in East-Central Europe* (Manchester and New York: Manchester University Press, 2002), pp. 72–73.
Przeworski, A. *Democracy and the Market*, (Cambridge: Cambridge University Press, 1991).
Puchala, D. 'International transactions and Regional Integration', *International Organization*, Vol. 24 (1970), 732–763.
Putnam, R. 'Diplomacy and Domestic Politics: the Logic of Two-level Games,' *International Organization*, Vol. 42 (1988), pp. 427–460.
Regular Reports from the Commission on the Czech Republic's Progress towards Accession 1998, 1999, 2000, 2001, European Commission, Brussels.
Rhodes, M. 'Post-Visegrád Cooperation in East Central Europe', *East European Quarterly*, Vol. 33, No. 1 (1999), 51–67.
Richardson, J. (ed.), *European Union: Power and Policy-Making* (London: Routledge, 1996).
Risse, T. 'Let's Argue. Communicative Action in International Relations', *International Organization*, Vol. 54, No. 1 (2000), 1–39.
Roch, L. 'Grenzüberschreitende Regionentwicklung-Basis europäischer Integration?', *Welt Trends*, 22/1999 (1999), 44–62.
Rodlauer, M. 'The Experience with IMF-Supported Reform Programs in Central and Eastern Europe', *Journal of Comparative Economics*, Vol. 20 (1995).
Rossbach, A. 'Deutsch-Tschechische Erklärung, Deutsch-Tschechischer Zukunftsfonds, Deutsch-Tschechisches Gesprächsforum', *Zeitschrift zur politischen Bildung*, 4/98 (1998).
Rudolph, H. 'German Maquiladora? Foreign Workers in the Process of Regional Economic Restructuring', *Innovation: The European Journal of Social Sciences*, Vol. 7, No. 1 (1994), 137–150.

Ruggie, J. G. 'Constructing the World Polity: Essays on International Institutionalisation', *Pacific Review*, Vol. 11, No. 4 (1998), 582–584.

Rupnik, J. (ed.), *Le déchirement des nations* (Paris: Seuil, 1995).

Rupnik, J. (ed.), *Regards communs sur l'Europe* (Prague: CEFRES, 1998).

Rupnik, J. 'Eastern Europe: The International Context', in M. F. Plattner and A. Smolar (eds), *Globalization, Power and Democracy* (Baltimore: Johns Hopkins University Press, 2000), pp. 57–70.

Rupnik, J. *The Implications of the Czecho–Slovak Divorce for the EU Enlargement*, RSC 2000/66 (2000).

Rupnik, J. and Bazin, A. 'La difficile réconciliation tchéco-allemande', *Politique Etrangère* (2/2001), pp. 353–370.

Rustow, D. A. 'Transition to Democracy: Toward a Dynamic Model', *Comparative Politics*, Vol. 2 (1970).

Samson, I. 'Proclamations, Declarations and *Realpolitik* in Current Slovak Integration Policy', *Perspectives*, Nos 6–7, (1996) 51–59.

Saxonberg, S. 'The Fall: Czechoslovakia, East Germany, Hungary and Poland in a Comparative Perspective' (doctoral dissertation, Uppsala University, 1997).

Saxonberg, S. 'Nesnášenliví Čestí studenti. Ekonomistí liberálové, intelektuální dogmatici', *Nová Pritomnost* (August, 1998).

Sayer, D. *The Coasts of Bohemia: A Czech History* (Princeton, NJ: Princeton University Press, 1998).

Schamp, E. W. 'Die Bildung neuer grenzüberschreitender Regionen im östlichen Mitteleuropa –eine Einführung', in G. Gruber, H. Lamping, W. Lutz and E. W. Schamp (eds), *Neue grenzüberschreitende Regionen im östlichen Mitteleuropa* (Institut für Wirtschafts- und Sozialgeographie der Johann Wolfgang Goethe Universität, 1–18, 1994), pp. 4–5.

Schimmelfennig, F. 'The Community Trap: Liberal Norms, Rhetorical Action and the Eastern Enlargement of the European Union', *International Organization*, Vol. 55, No. 1 (2001).

Schlögel, K. *Die Mitte liegt ostwärts: Die Deutschen, der verlorene Osten und Mitteleuropa* (Berlin: Siedler, 1986).

Schmitter, P. 'The Influence of the International Context upon the Choice of National Institutions and Policies in Neo-democracies', in L. Whitehead (ed.), *The International Dimensions of Democratization, Europe and the Americas* (Oxford: Oxford University Press, 1996).

Schöllgen, G. *Die Macht in der Mitte Europas: Stationen deutscher Aussenpolitik von Friedrich dem Grossen bis zur Gegenwart* (Munich: C. H. Beck, 1992).

Schulze-Wessel, M. 'Die Mitte liegt westwärts, Mitteleuropa in tschechischer Diskussion', *Bohemia*, Vol. 29 (1988), 325–344.

Schwarz, H.-P. *Die Zentralmacht Europas: Deustchlands Rückkehr auf die Weltbühne* (Berlin: Siedler, 1994).

Schwarz, H.-P. 'Germany's National and European Interests', in A. Baring (ed.), *Germany's New Position in Europe: Problems and Perspectives* (Oxford: Berg, 1994), pp. 107–130.

Scott, J. W. 'Planning Co-operation and Transboundary Regionalism: Implementing Policies for European Border Regions in the German–Polish context', *Environment and Planning C: Government and Policy*, Vol. 16 (1998), 619–620.

Scott, J. W. and Meyer, J. W. *Institutional Environments and Organizations: Structural Complexity and Individualism* (London: Sage Publications, 1994).

Šebej, F. 'O co ide v zahranicnej politike Slovenskej Republiky', *Domino Efekt*, Vol. 3, No. 20 (1994).

Seibt, F. 'Tschechen, Slowaken und Deutsche: Chronic eines vielschichtigen Verhältnisses', *Zeitschrift zur politischen Bildung*, 4/98, (1998).

Senior-Nello, S. M. *The New Europe: Changing Economic Relations between East and West* (Hemel Hempstead: Harvester Wheatsheaf, 1991).

Senior-Nello, S. and Smith, K. *The Consequences of Eastern Enlargement of the European Union in Stages*, (Aldershot: Ashgate Publishers, 1998).

Shattuck, J. and Atwood, J. B. 'Defending Democracy: Why Democrats Trump Autocrats,' *Foreign Affairs*, Vol. 77 (March–April 1998), 167–170.

Skalnik-Leff, C. *National Conflict in Czechoslovakia: The Making and Remaking of a State, 1918–1987* (Princeton: Princeton University Press, 1988).

Skocpol, T. *State and Social Revolutions* (Cambridge: Cambridge University Press, 1979).

Smith, A., Holmes, P., Sedelmeier, U., Smith, E., Wallace, H. and Young, R. *The European Union and Central and Eastern Europe: Pre-Accession Strategies.* SEI Working Paper No. 15. (Brighton: Sussex European Institute, 1996).

Smith, A. D. 'National Identity and the Idea of European Unity', *International Affairs*, Vol. 28, No.1 (1992), 55–76.

Smith, K. E. 'The Use of Political Conditionality in the EU's Relations with Third Countries: How Effective?', *European Foreign Affairs Review*, Vol. 3 (1998), 253–274.

Soysal, Y. 'Changing Citizenship in Europe', in Ceasarani and Fulbrook (eds.), *Citizenship, Nationality*, 17–29.

Soysal, Y. *Limits of Citizenship. Migrants and Post-national Membership in Europe* (Chicago: University of Chicago Press, 1994).

Stares, A. P. B. (ed.), *The New Germany and the New Europe* (Washington, DC: The Brookings Institution, 1992).

Stehule, L. *Ceskoslovensky Stát v Mezinárodnim Právu a Styku* (Praha: Laichter, 1919).

Stürmer, M. 'Die Deutschen in Europa', *Europa Archiv*, Vol. 24 (1989) 721–732.

Stuth, R. 'Wettbewerb um Macht und Einfluss in Zentralasien', *Internationale Politik*, Vol. 58, No. 3 (1998).

Šútovec, M. 'Kam povedú tie dialnice?' ['Where Do Those Express Highways Lead?'], *Domino-fórum* (Bratislava, 1, 1997).

Szomolányi, S. 'Identifying Slovakia's Emerging Regime,' in S. Szomolányi, J. Gould (eds), *Slovakia: Problems of Democratic Consolidation and the Struggle for the Rules of the Game* (Bratislava: Slovak Political Science Association and Friedrich Ebert Foundation, 1997).

Taggart, P. 'A Touchstone of Dissent: Euroscepticism in Contemporary Western European Party Systems,' *European Journal of Political Research*, Vol.33 (1998), 363–388.

Tilly, C. 'The Emergence of Citizenship in France and Elsewhere', in C. Tilly (ed.), *Citizenship, Identity and Social History* (Cambridge: Cambridge University Press, 1996) 223–36.

Tilly, C. 'The State of Nationalism', *Critical Review*, Vol. 10, No. 3, 299–306.

Turnovec, F. 'Votes, Seats and Power: 1996 Parliamentary Election in the Czech Republic', *Communist and Post-Communist Studies*, Vol. 30, No. 3 (1997).

Vachudova, M. A. 'The Czech Republic: The Unexpected Force of Institutional Constraints', in A. Pravda and J. Zielonka (eds), *Democratic Consolidation in Eastern Europe* (Oxford: Oxford University Press, 2001).

Van Steenbergen, B. (ed.), *The Condition of Citizenship* (London, Sage Publications, 1994).

Verheyen, A. *The German Question: A Cultural, Historical, and Geopolitical Exploration* (Boulder, CO: Westview Press, 1991).

Vlachová, K. 'Czech Political Parties and Their Voters', *Czech Sociological Review*, Vol. 5, No. 1 (1997).

Wallace, H. 'Enlarging the European Union: Reflections on the Challenge of Analysis,' *Journal of European Public Policy* (forthcoming).

Weber, M. *Economy and Society* (New York: Bedminster Press, 1968).

Weiss, P. 'Integrácia: politické otázky a problémy', *Nové Slovo* No. 15 (1997).

Wendt, A. 'Collective Identity Formation and the International State', *American Political Science Review*, Vol. 88 (1994), 384–398.

Westerman, F. 'Germany's Economic Power in Europe', in A. S. Markovits and S. Reich (eds), *The German Predicament: Memory and Power in the New Europe* (Ithaca: Cornell University Press, 1997), pp. 150–182.

Wienert, H. and Slater, J. *East–West Technology Transfer: The Trade and Economic Aspects* (Paris: OECD, 1986), pp. 223–225.

Wightman, G. 'The Development of the Party System and the Break-up of Czechoslovakia', in G. Wightman (ed.), *Party Formation in East-Central Europe* (Aldershot: Edward Elgar, 1995), pp. 79–106.

Wolchik, S. *Czechoslovakia in Transition: Politics,Economics and Society* (London: Pinter, 1991), pp. 86–195.

Wolters, M. 'Euroregions along the German Border', in U. Bullmann (ed.), *Die Politik der dritten Eben. Regionen im Europa der Union* (Baden-Baden: Nomos Verlagsgesellschaft 1994), pp. 407–418.

World Bank, *Czech Republic: Toward EU Accession. Main Report* (Washington, DC: The World Bank, 1999).

Yoder, J. A. 'Institutional and Cultural Bridges: An Assessment of the Euroregions', paper presented at the American Political Science Association Annual Meeting, 31 August –September 2000, Washington, DC (2000).

Zahradil, J. *Manifest ceskeho eurorealismu* (Prague: ODS, April 2001).

Zajac, P. *Sen o krajine* [*A Dream about a Country*] (Bratislava: Kalligram, 1996).

Zakaria, F. 'The Rise of Illiberal Democracy,' *Foreign Affairs*, Vol. 76 (November–December 1997), 22–23.

Žiak, M. *Slovensko: od komunizmu kam?* (Bratislava: Archa, 1996), 144–5.

Zich, F. *Euroregions along the Czech/German and Czech/Austrian Borders*, Institute of Sociology, Academy of Sciences of the Czech Republic, Prague (1993).

Zich, F. *Cross-border Contact of Czech Republic Citizens and Development of Czech–German Civic Relations*, Institute of Sociology, Academy of Sciences of the Czech Republic, Prague (2000).

Zielonka, J. 'Politics without Strategies: The EU Policies toward Central and Eastern Europe', in J. Zielonka (ed.), *Paradoxes of European Foreign Policy*, (London: Kluwer, 1998), 131–145.

Zielonka, J. 'Ambiguity as a Remedy for the EU's Eastward Enlargement', *Cambridge Review of International Affairs*, Vol. 12 Summer/Fall (1998), 14–29.

Zielonka, J. *Explaining Euro-paralysis* (London: Macmillan, 1998).

Zielonka, J. (ed) *Europe Unbound* (London: Routledge, 2002).

Index

Adler, Emanuel 252
Agenda 2000 *see under* European Union
Ágh, Attila 199, 215
AIDS 255
Alliance of the New Citizens (ANO) 65, 67
Aron, Raymond 141
Atlanticism 233
Austria 2, 31, 38, 76, 80, 125, 129, 175, 221, 240, 242
  support for EU enlargement 39, 238

Baldwin-Edwards, Martin 142, 143
Barnett, Michael 252
Baubock, Rainer 142, 143
Bavaria 188, 206, 225, 234, 264
Belarus 18, 53
Belgium 23, 230
Belohradsky, Václav 233
Beneš decrees 5, 9, 38–39, 44, 63, 97, 237–238, 258, 262
Bibo, Istvan 25
Bielasiak, Jack 70
Blocher, Christoph 38
Bohemia 2, 4, 18, 204, 205, 224, 225, 254, 256, 258
border regimes 5, 41
Börzel, Tanja 260
Bosnia 33
Bossi, Umberto 38
Brandt, Willy 236
Brubaker, Rogers 141, 149
Brzezinski, Zbigniew 33
Bugár, Béla 40, 67
Bulgaria 101
Buzková, Petra 79, 83

Canada 22, 23, 149, 154
Čarnogurský, Jan 17, 21–22, 23, 27, 173
Catholicism 20, 24, 205
Chernomyrdin, Viktor 34
China 207
Christian Democratic Movement (KDH) 22, 52, 57, 67, 71, 166, 173, 177
Christian Democratic Party (KDS) 73
Christian Democratic Union (CDU) 38, 230, 237, 238
Christian Democratic Union (KDU-ČSL) 70–3 *passim*, 76, 77, 80, 84, 166, 168, 174, 177, 204–209 *passim*, 215
Christian Social Union (CSU) 38, 230, 231, 237, 238, 260
Christianity 204
citizenship theories 140–146
  see also under Czech Republic, Slovakia
Civic Campaign (OK) '98 57–58
Civic Democratic Alliance (ODA) 70–76 *passim*, 177, 205, 209, 211, 215
Civic Democratic Party (ODS) 17, 31, 32, 44, 70–76 *passim*, 81, 94, 166, 167, 173, 174, 177, 182, 203–215 *passim*, 234, 239
  Euroscepticism 167–168
  see also Klaus
Civic Forum 69, 71, 89
Civic Movement (OH) 71, 72, 74
Coexistence (Slovak party) 52, 71
Communism 191
Communist Party of the Bohemia and Moravia (KSČM) 74, 78, 166, 169, 174, 175, 177, 207, 209, 210, 213–215, 239
conditionality 7, 99–100
  see also under Slovakia
Copenhagen criteria *see under* European Union
Council for Mutual Economic Assistance (CMEA) 124, 126, 170, 181
Council of Europe 101, 103, 107, 150, 184, 188
Croatia 18, 23–24, 53, 119
cross-border co-operation 250–253, 261–262
  see also under Czech Republic: relations with Germany
Cyprus 95, 101, 139
Czech Republic
  banking 119–122
  citizenship 11, 29, 150
  civil service reform 92

civil society 88, 91
co-operation with Visegrád countries 41, 45
corruption 92–93
ČSSD–ODS coalition 42, 77, 82–84, 93–94, 182
economic conditions 36, 70, 75, 83, 87, 94, 115–116, 117, 129–132
electoral system 80, 82
EU accession process 87, 93–97
EU Agenda 2000 Opinion 93, 140, 146
EU referendum 191, 214
EU Regular Reports 83, 115, 118, 190
Europe Agreement 87, 184
European identity 25–28, 203–211, 229–230, 240–242
Euroscepticism 6, 12, 29–31, 167–170, 174–179
'exceptionalism' 4, 10, 16, 35–36, 167, 181–182
foreign direct investment 126–129
media 82–83, 95
national identity 148–150, 188, 227
NATO accession 32–33, 87, 208–221, 212, 216, 221, 242
parliamentary elections 70–82
party development 69–84
comparison to Hungary 73, 74, 77, 78, 79, 80
comparison to Poland 73, 74, 77, 78, 79
party public opinion 76
privatisation 36, 70, 83, 89–91, 118–119
public opinion on EU 38, 42–43, 45, 166, 199–217, 260–261
'red-scare' tactics 76, 78
relations with Austria 38–39, 96–97
relations with Germany 8–9, 12–13, 37–40, 97, 220–243, 253–266
border affairs 225–226
cross-border co-operation 253–266
economic exchange 222–223
Euroregions within 226–228, 255–257
popular opinion on 38, 234, 262–263
reconciliation 257–258
Slovaks living 24, 146
state-building 3–4, 35–36
Sudeten Germans 6, 9, 18, 38, 97, 148, 149, 221, 224, 230–231, 232–233, 238–239, 242, 253, 260, 262, 264
trade with EU 124–127
Czechoslovak Communist Party 53, 60, 71
Czechoslovak Social Democratic Party 71–72
Czechoslovakia 18–19, 23, 25, 88, 89, 100, 181, 183, 240
elections 22, 71–73
Czech–Slovak relations 3–4, 10, 17–25
Czurka, Istvan 75

Dahrendorf, Ralf 154
Delpérée, Francis 23
democracy 142–144
see also under Slovakia
Democratic Party (DS) 52, 57, 71, 166
Democratic Round Table 58, 106
Democratic Union (DU) 52, 57, 166, 177
Denmark 230
Deutsch, Karl 11, 250–252, 255, 261–262
Diamond, Larry 18, 59
Dienstbier, Jiří 32, 181, 228
Dlouhý, Vladimír 75, 229
Duleba, Alexander 170
Ďurica, Milan 151
Dzurinda, Mikuláš 7, 31, 32, 34, 40–42, 44, 57, 66, 116, 129, 139
government of 10, 60–61, 63, 107–109, 147, 191

Economic and Monetary Union (EMU) 11, 31, 114, 129, 190, 202, 212
Eichengreen, Barry 127
England 142–143
Estonia 20, 95, 101, 138
European Bank for Reconstruction and Development (EBRD) 99, 124
European Charter of Regional Languages 153
European Defence Identity 33
European Free Trade Association (EFTA) 125
European Single Act 212
European Union
Agenda 2000 28, 36, 93, 101, 103, 115, 122, 129
see also under Czech Republic; Slovakia
Central Bank 131
Commission 39, 87, 88, 110, 115, 187, 191, 260
Common Agricultural Policy (CAP) 175
Common Foreign and Security Policy (CFSP) 33
Copenhagen criteria 28, 101, 113–115, 123, 171
Council 110
Copenhagen summit 101, 182
Essen summit 101
Helsinki summit 100, 102, 108

Luxembourg summit 93, 100, 101–102, 103, 106
Madrid summit 182
Court of Justice 233
enlargement 99–103
Parliament 30, 104–105, 108, 109, 186, 187, 231, 237
PHARE programme 101, 152, 226, 256, 259, 260
political criteria 100–101
Regular Reports 87, 88
Treaty of Amsterdam 100, 181, 202
Treaty of European Union 140, 145, 169, 170, 175, 181, 186, 189, 190, 202, 212, 233
White Paper 182
Euroregions 221, 222, 226–228, 254–257

federalism 21
Fico, Robert 42, 44, 65, 66, 139
see also Smer
Finland 29
Fischer, Joschka 31
France 24, 145, 204, 209, 223, 241, 258
free movement of labour 39, 239
Freedom Union (US) 75, 76, 77, 80, 84, 93, 166, 168, 174, 177
Friedman, Milton 27

Gabcikovo Nagymaros dam 40
Garton Ash, Timothy 236
Gauleider, Frantisek 108
Genghis Khan 205
Geremek, Bronislaw 43
German Democratic Republic 125
Germany 80, 129, 142, 189, 201, 206, 209, 211, 213, 220–243, 250–266
support for EU enlargement 39, 224, 238
Gershman, Carl 59
globalisation 207
Greece 101, 201, 213
Gregr, Miroslav 84
Gross, Stanislav 79, 83

Haider, Jörg 31, 38, 39, 175, 238
Hamžik, Pavol 109
Handl, Vladimír 181, 259
Havel, Václav 12, 22, 25, 26, 34, 35, 69, 73, 88, 89, 151, 154, 220, 228, 257, 262
Eurooptimism 183–187, 191–192
Heater, Derek 143
Hitler, Adolf 24, 205
Hlinka, Andrej 19
Holland (Netherlands) 186, 230
Horn, Gyula 40
Houzvicka, Václav 264
Hrib, Stefan 37
Hungarian Christian Democratic Movement (MKDH) 52, 71
Hungarian Civic Party (MOS) 52
Hungary 18, 25, 28, 52, 54, 70, 95, 100, 101, 119, 124, 125, 126, 167, 181, 240
Huntington, Samuel 78
Hus, Jan 27
Húska, Marián 138

India 207
Institute for Public Affairs 60
integration theories 250–253
International Helsinki Federation 149
International Institute for Management Development 123
International Monetary Fund 99, 116
INTERREG 8, 260
Iraq 34
Islam 204, 205, 209

Jacobson, David 141, 142

Katzenstein, Peter 13
Kavan, Jan 32, 41
Klaus, Václav 10, 12, 22, 26, 27, 35, 37, 41, 71, 81, 89, 113, 120, 129, 215, 217, 227, 239
attitude toward EU 36
economic liberalism 36, 129
end of political era 17, 35, 45
Euroscepticism 2, 30–31, 36, 77, 167, 175, 181–183, 187–192, 200, 203, 233–234
years in power 70–77 *passim*
Kohl, Helmut 230, 238, 257
Kohl, Richard 127
Kosovo 32, 33, 187
Kováč, Michal 55, 56, 106
Krajči, Gustáv 56
Kramar, Václav 27
Kraus, Michael 22
Kryl, Karel 62
Kumermann, Daniel 78
Kundera, Milan 26, 229
Kusy, Miroslav 19

Lamers, Karl 237, 240
Latvia 20, 101, 102, 138

Laughland, John 26
Le Pen, Jean-Marie 172
Left Bloc 72, 73
Lenin, Vladimír 83
Liberal Social Union (LSU) 72, 73, 74
Libya 34
Lickova, Jana 149
Liechtenstein 36
Lijphart, Arend 80–81
Lithuania 20, 101, 102, 138, 185
Lukashenko, Aleksandr 53
Luptak, Jan 171
Luptak, Lubomir 27
Lux, Josef 76
Luxembourg 36, 230

Maastricht criteria 115, 129–130
Maastricht Treaty *see* European Union: Treaty of European Union
Major, John 188
Malta 95, 100
Mansfeldová, Zdenka 216
Marks, Gary 252
Marshall, T. H. 141, 142–143
Masaryk, Tomas Garrigue 18, 19, 25, 35, 88, 148, 151, 187, 191
Mečiar, Vladimír 7, 10, 16, 17, 19, 22–24, 28–37 *passim*, 40–5 *passim*, 51–67 *passim*, 70, 73, 98, 104–107 *passim*, 116, 122, 124, 140, 151, 154, 155, 170, 172
  downfall of 17, 35, 60–61
  on EU 17, 27–28, 30, 104, 106, 138, 165, 175–176
  on Hungarians 30, 40
  on NATO 33
  non-democratic rule 2, 18, 28, 52–53, 55–56, 138–139
  political opposition to 42, 52–53, 56–58, 105–106
  on Roma 29
  see also Movement for a Democratic Slovakia; Slovakia: non-democratic rule
Meehan, Elizabeth 142, 143
Mendelson, Sarah 253
Merlik, Vladimír 121
Migaš, Jozef 61, 174
Miklos, Ivan 42
Milosevic, Slobodan 24, 30, 53
minority rights 29, 251
  see also under Slovakia
Mochovce *see* nuclear power controversies
Mock, Alois 238
Moravčík, Jozef 165
Moravia 204, 224
Movement for a Democratic Slovakia (HZDS) 17, 33, 42, 52, 65–67, 70, 98, 104, 108, 152, 166, 170–172, 174, 176, 177
  see also Mečiar
Movement for Self-government Democracy–Society for Moravia and Silesia (HSD–SMS) 71, 72, 73
Munich agreement of 1938 18, 30, 208, 209

nationhood 141–142, 144
  see also under Czech Republic; Slovakia
Nazism 191, 231, 257
Necas, Petr 31
North Atlantic Treaty Organization (NATO) 32, 187, 208, 232, 240
  see also under Czech Republic, Slovakia
Northern League 20, 38
nuclear power controversies 9, 38–39, 96–97

Oostlander, Arie 138, 155
Orbán, Viktor 44, 63–64
Organization for Economic Cooperation and Development (OECD) 64, 127, 130, 132
Organization for Security and Cooperation in Europe (OSCE; also CSCE) 32, 101, 107, 149, 150
Ostpolitik 236–237, 242

Pakistan 59
Palacky, Frantisek 37, 148, 151
Palko, Vladimír 173
Party of Civic Understanding (SOP) 52, 107, 108, 172–173
Party of Greens in Slovakia (SZS) 52, 57, 71
Party of the Democratic Left (SDL') 52, 107, 166, 173–174
Party of the Hungarian Coalition (SMK) 52, 107, 147, 172–173
Patocka, Jan 25
Peasant Party 72, 73
Pensioners Party 77, 81
People's Party 69, 72
Perron, Catherine 261
Philippines 59
Pick, Otto 33
Pilip, Ivan 75
Pithart, Petr 228

Poland 25, 28, 36, 41, 43, 52, 54, 70, 95, 100, 101, 119, 124, 125, 167, 181, 221, 240, 241, 254, 259
Pope John Paul II 27
Portugal 101
Poselt, Berd 38
Prague Spring of 1968 18, 21, 24, 27, 30, 88, 208
Prokeš, Jozef 172
Public Against Violence (VPN) 52, 69, 71
Puchala, Don 262

Reich, Simon 236
Republicans (SPR-RSČ) 72, 74, 77–78, 81, 82, 150, 166, 170, 174, 177
Risse, Thomas 13, 260
Robertson, George 67
Roma 4, 29, 65, 92, 147, 149–150, 154, 204–205
Romania 101
Ruml, Jan 75, 76
Rusko, Pavol 44, 65
Rusnok, Jiri 118
Russia 24, 185, 205–210 *passim*, 221, 240
  see also under Slovakia

Saxony 254, 258, 259
Schamp, Eike 251
Schäuble, Wolfgang 232, 237, 240
Schengen agreement 5, 41, 43, 95
Schimmelfenning, Frank 253
Schmögnerova, Brigita 66
Schröder, Gerhard 39, 239, 258
Schüssel, Wolfgang 38, 238, 239
Schuster, Rudolf 108
Schwarz, Hans-Peter 235
Seidel, Jutta 259
Serbia 53
Seselj, Vojislav 172
Sierra Leone 59
Skalnik Leff, Carol 19
Slovak Christian and Democratic Union (SDKU) 66, 67, 166, 173
Slovak Democratic Coalition (SDK) 52, 57, 105–106, 107, 172–173
  see also Dzurinda
Slovak National Council 22
Slovak National Party (SNS) 22, 34, 52, 71, 104, 108, 151, 152, 166, 171–172, 174, 177
Slovakia
  banking 123
  Central Referendum Committee 105
  citizenship 152–155
  civil society 43
  conditionality in EU accession 11, 98–99, 110–111
  Constitutional Court 104, 105, 106
  constitutional reform 64–65
  democratisation 28, 36–37, 53–55
  economic conditions 65, 116–117, 130–132
  electoral law 57, 64
  electoral participation 53, 58
  EU accession process 41–42, 64, 108–109, 172
  EU Agenda 2000 Opinion 28, 101, 103, 115, 122, 140, 147
  EU Regular Reports 41, 64, 103, 108, 109, 115, 118, 122
  EU warnings to Slovakia 104–105, 107, 138
  Europe Agreement with EU 100, 102, 105
  European identity 25–28
  Euroscepticism 6, 12, 170–179
  failure to make 1st wave of EU enlargement 28, 37, 55, 101–102, 106, 171
  financial scandal over EU funds 119
  foreign direct investment 126–129
  foreign policy orientation 16–17, 33–34
  Hungarian minority 4, 18, 29–30, 40, 42, 60, 61, 64, 106, 147, 149, 151, 152
  Jews 152
  Joint Parliamentary Committee with EU 105, 108
  media 57, 64, 108
  minority rights 4, 28, 64, 104, 108
  modernisation 20–21
  national identity 19, 20, 61–62, 151–153
  nationalism 22, 54, 61–63
    comparison to Croatia 23–24, 30, 53
    comparison to Serbia 30, 53
  NATO accession 33–34, 41–42, 171, 173
  non-democratic rule 18, 28, 30, 52–53, 55–56, 59–60, 104–107
  non-governmental organizations (NGOs) 57
  parliamentary elections 42–43, 51–52, 65–67, 107, 154, 175
  public opinion on EU 42, 45, 60, 64, 166
  public opinion on NATO 60
  presidential elections 64, 108
  privatisation 122–123, 129, 154
  referendums 34, 56–57, 105, 106–107, 154
  relations with Hungary 37, 40
  relations with Russian Federation 6, 34, 106, 170, 205

state-building 3–4
trade with EU 124–127
'velvet revolution' 53–54
Slovenia 20, 101
Smer 42, 65
Social Democratic Party (ČSSD) 32, 35, 74–84 *passim*, 93, 166, 168–169, 174, 177, 182, 209, 215
see also Zeman
Social Democratic Party of Slovakia (SDSS) 52, 57
Socialist Party 69, 72
Soysal, Yasemin 141
Spain 101, 211
Špidla, Vladimír 79, 84
Stoiber, Edmund 38, 231, 238
Stroehlein, Andrew 82
subsidiarity 202, 252
Sudetendeutsche Landsmannschaft 38, 224, 230–232, 257, 264
Sweden 79, 80
Switzerland 38
Syria 34
Szomolányi, Soňa 43, 62

Taggart, Paul 166, 177
Temelin *see* nuclear power controversies
Thatcher, Margaret 25, 30
Tilly, Charles 141, 143, 144, 155
Tošovský, Josef 75, 93, 182
Tudjman, Franjo 24, 30, 53
Turkey 100, 138

United Kingdom 24, 29, 79, 145, 154, 209, 210, 223, 240
United Nations High Commissioner for Refugees (UNHCR) 104, 150
United States 187, 206–211 *passim*, 233, 258

Vaculik, Vudvik 26
Van den Broek, Hans 36, 105, 167
'velvet divorce' 16–25, 70, 73, 81, 87, 89, 164–166, 183
'velvet revolution' 53–54, 69, 87, 90, 180, 228
Verheugen, Günter 9, 39, 190
Visegrád group 8, 41, 43–44, 63–64, 167, 181, 241
see also Czech Republic: co-operation with Visegrád countries, 'exceptionalism'
Vlachová, Klára 74
Vlams Blok 20, 22

Wallace, Helen 13
Warsaw Pact 181
Weimar triangle 241
Weiss, Peter 174
Wendt, Alexander 13
Williams, Kieran 74
Worker's Party (ZRS) 34, 52, 104, 166, 171–172, 175
World Bank 99
World Economic Forum 36, 167

xenophobia 29, 149, 154, 172
see also Republicans

Yoder, J. A. 254
Yugoslavia 23, 24, 25, 31, 185, 186, 216

Zahradil, Jan 31
Zajac, Peter 62
Zakaria, Fareed 18, 59
Zaoralek, Lubomir 32
Zeman, Milos 10, 31, 42, 76–79 *passim*, 93, 182
Žiak, Miloš 165
Zich, František 263
Zielenec, Josef 33, 75, 181, 229, 230, 232